Young Adult Literature In the Seventies

A Selection of Readings

edited by

JANA VARLEJS

The Scarecrow Press, Inc.
Metuchen, N.J. & London
1978

Library of Congress Cataloging in Publication Data
Main entry under title:

Young adult literature in the seventies.

Bibliography: p.
Includes index.
1. Books and reading for youth. I. Varlejs, Jana.
Z1037.A1Y68 809'.89283 78-6562
ISBN 0-8108-1134-0

Manufactured in the United States of America

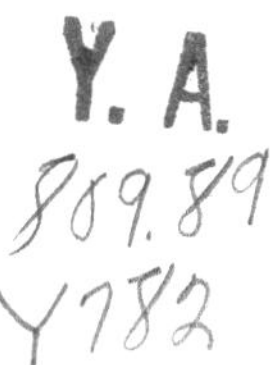

CONTENTS

INTRODUCTION

Everyone agrees that there is a literacy crisis in America today. The fact that so many high school graduates can barely read and write is blamed by some on television and by others on poor teaching. Whatever the combination of causes, it is clear that the failure to develop the habit of reading for pleasure and for information is a contributory factor. Daniel Fader, among others, has pointed out that one of the problems is that kids do not see adults reading very much. Another obstacle is that too many parents, teachers, and librarians abrogate the responsibility to guide and encourage the young reader somewhere around the junior high age, just when distractions and choices multiply. Only the most avid and mature readers will continue the reading-for-pleasure habit during adolescence; most need motivation and some guidance.

Unfortunately, few adults know enough about adolescent reading interests or are familiar with those books which are most likely to be meaningful to young adults. Very few public libraries fail to provide special collections and services for children, but a great many see no need for equal attention to the needs of young adults. Junior high and high school librarians generally have barely enough time and resources to provide materials and services in support of the curriculum, and seldom can indulge in the luxury of reader guidance. Teachers, too, are often caught in a lock-step curriculum, or associate "adolescent literature" with the mediocre formula novels dominating the field not too long ago.

The purpose of this collection is to serve as an introduction to the field of young adult reading for professionals and parents interested in getting kids "hooked on books." Included are articles on reading interests, on the state of the art of writing especially for teens, on trends and controversies. The selections are uneven in quality, and not all the writers espouse views with which I agree. My main concern was to provide an overview, to identify some of the issues, and to offer some guideposts for future exploration.

For the uninitiated, some explanation of semantics may be helpful. A number of contributors to this collection speak of "adolescent literature." What *is* adolescent literature? It is not necessarily adolescent, nor--with some rare exceptions--is it literature in the strictest sense. Definitions vary from the narrow one of "junior novel" to the inclusive one of "anything kids read." Most authors of the articles collected in this volume lean toward the broader definition, and often include books originally written for adults in their lists of "junior novels" (written specifically for teens). Catcher in the Rye, I Never Promised You a Rose Garden, A Separate Peace, Mr. and Mrs. Bo Jo Jones, Red Sky at Morning, Manchild in the Promised Land are examples of adult books which we now associate almost exclusively with young adult readers, and which continue to remain in print largely due to this readership.

While the majority of selections deal primarily with books written expressly for young adults, the reader should not be misled into focusing on these books to the exclusion of adult material. The junior novel is a stepping-stone, the first rung on the ladder from children's books to adult books with teenage appeal, to the great works of literature (at least, that has been the traditional tenet of young adult librarians). One reason that this collection is weighted in the direction of the junior novel is that this is the genre least familiar to adults who can influence the reading of adolescents. As Donelson and Haley point out in the first article, the best remedy for that is to start reading the books.

Another reason for the emphasis on the junior novel in this collection is that a veritable revolution in the genre took place in the late sixties, setting off a chain reaction of controversy and new interest on the part of educators, librarians and writers. Some of these arguments are still in process, but the consensus is that the shift toward greater realism and more sophisticated literary form has been salutory. "Adolescent literature" has been dignified by the formation of the Assembly on Literature for Adolescents within the National Council of Teachers of English, and ratified by the publication of many junior novels in mass market paperback format, and merits more attention today than it once deserved.

In conjunction with the materials listed in the bibliography, this collection should help the professional or parent to acquire a basis for helping young adults toward enjoyable reading experiences. However, no amount of theoretical background or perusal of reviews can substitute for the knowledge and enthusiasm of the person who reads widely, enjoys it, and can communicate that pleasure to a young person. What Margaret Edwards has said about librarians and libraries applies to teachers and schools as well:

> ... if every other ingredient in young adult work is present, it will fail if the librarian does not read, not just for himself, but as a professional, for others. He must read constantly and widely enough to meet any reader, deprived or accelerated, on his own ground and over a period of time, develop the young person to his full potential as a reader.... Though we have computers, teletype, microfilm, Xerox, A.V., our imprint on society is still minimal in comparison with what it might be if we read widely and got enough books into the hands of the people --especially young people. [Margaret Edwards, "No Barefeet," prepared for ETN Series: Continuing Education for Public Librarians, 1971. Available as part of SURVIVAL KIT from the American Library Association, Young Adult Services Division.]

ACKNOWLEDGMENTS

I wish to thank Marian Scott, who taught me more about young adult librarianship at Rutgers than I realized at the time; Caroline Coughlin, who offered friendly criticism; the Mid-Manhattan Branch of the New York Public Library, which had almost everything I needed (except good copying machines); and Eric Moon, whose patience has been Job-like.

Thanks especially to all the authors, editors, and publishers who have generously given permission to reprint the material in this collection.

PART I

ADOLESCENCE AND LITERATURE: TOWARDS A CRITIQUE

(a tree grows ...)

EDITOR'S NOTE

The increasing respectability of what is called adolescent literature is largely due to the better writing found in recent junior novels. As Dorothy Matthews suggests, "there are certainly enough works of quality to deserve a thorough-going study. The junior novel merits more than the once-over-lightly kind of treatment it has received to date" (see page 36). While she urges more serious criticism of the books as literary works, Scharf and Yoder are more concerned with how literature affects or reflects the adolescent experience.

Carlsen, the best-known exponent of the relationship of reading stages to the development process, concurs with Donelson and Haley: "first let's just share our student's involvement with a book. Later we can help him see connections between what he is reading and his own life, and still later help him to see how the story's patterns and designs harmonize with and carry the content of the idea" (see page 14).

ADOLESCENT LITERATURE:
You Mean That Garbage Written for Kids Who Can't Read?*

By Kenneth L. Donelson and Beverly A. Haley

Literature written for adolescents, that amorphous body of material read by kids from about the 4th grade on through 10th or 11th grade, has been around for better than 70 years. During that time, it has picked up a heritage, a wide number of readers, and many vociferous critics. At the beginning of any adolescent literature course, the professor can anticipate objections from some students who are convinced that reading adolescent literature is inherently a waste of time for both English teachers and students. Usually, the loudest objections come from students who have never experienced adolescent literature, good or bad, and who base their comments on that highest form of objectivity, total ignorance. Our experience suggests that lumping all adolescent literature together for judgment is a simplistic kind of criticism.

And professional literature has many critics of adolescent literature, some of them widely known and lovingly quoted by English teachers.

> Ever since the writing of "juveniles" has become a commonplace practice among the writing fraternity, there has been a tendency to accept the product with only the most superficial of criticism. It will hardly be news to anyone who has managed to keep up with the general output that much of it is really third-rate....[1]

> At present, many junior writers are busily grinding out thinly fictionalized tracts on such subjects as brotherhood and the evils of teenage alcoholism. Tendentious, sentimental, stereotyped, and often wretchedly written, most junior fiction is literature only in the broadest sense of the term. Its chief raison d'être is that it offers reading to the young which their elders approve.[2]

Both writers, however, temper their remarks by suggesting or implying that adolescent literature might infrequently produce material

---

*Reprinted by permission of the authors and publisher from <u>The Clearing House</u>, 47:7 (March 1973), 440-443.

not wholly bad, a qualification lacking in many critical articles.[3] Without much question, the most frequently cited criticism of adolescent literature appeared in Freedom and Discipline in English, a fairly recent but now nearly forgotten work on the English curriculum.

> Claims are frequently advanced for the use of the so-called 'junior books,' a 'literature of adolescence,' on the ground that they ease the young reader into a frame of mind in which he will be ready to tackle something stronger, harder, more adult. The Commission has serious doubts that it does anything of the sort. For classes in remedial reading a resort to such books may be necessary, but to make them a considerable part of the curriculum for most students is to subvert the purposes for which literature is included in the first place. In the high school years, the aim should be not to find the students' level so much as to raise it, and such books rarely elevate.[4]

Teachers critical of adolescent literature might be intrigued by older articles bearing titles like "Blowing Out the Boy's Brains," or "Dietary Laws of Children's Books" and suggesting a heritage of criticism.[5]

And in faculty lounges, school classrooms, or wherever teachers gather, English teacher attacks on adolescent literature are hardly rare.

> 'Why are you [a high school boy] wasting your time with trash like that? You're supposed to be preparing yourself for college. Please use the approved book list I gave you for your outside reading.'
>
> 'You mean I'm supposed to read junk that those kids like? What kind of English teacher do you think I am?' (Overheard at a faculty party, a conversation between teacher and counselor.)
>
> 'For Pete's sake, Bob, another sports story! That's absolutely the last one. You've got to broaden your reading horizons.'
>
> 'For the last time, do not report on any more books like The Outsiders. It's about time you began to read adult books, things your parents want you to read. You're in high school now, not grade school.'
>
> 'Adolescent literature? What's that? Oh! You mean that garbage written for kids who can't read?'
> 'Have you ever read any of it?'
> 'No, and I'm not going to, either. Why should I spend the few available hours I have for reading on--on--(strug-

> gling for a ladylike but derogatory word) on--you know--*that*? I have little free time at best, and I want to read *only* the very best. I'd say the very same thing to my students.' (And she would, too.)
>
> (Dialogue between one of the authors and a teacher.)

Okay. Why should any English teacher spend precious time reading material which is admittedly not adult literature and which has produced no great or necessarily enduring works? Indeed, why should any adult feel a professional responsibility for reading something read almost entirely by young people?

We believe there are five good reasons why teachers need to know adolescent literature from firsthand acquaintance.

First, respectable criticism of any field begins with actual contact with that field. If teachers insist on criticizing or damning adolescent literature, they ought to do so from having read it, not from assuming its inherent badness. Henry Gregor Felsen's *Hot Rod* may indeed be a dreadful book, as one of the authors was told several years ago by a teacher, but that criticism must be predicated upon having read the book. Attacks on books as varied as Zindel's *The Pigman*, Hinton's *The Outsiders*, Heinlein's *Have Space Suit, Will Travel*, or Emery's *Sorority Girl* have been made while the critics had no reading knowledge of the books in question. English teachers should demand of themselves what they rightfully demand of their students--a careful reading before offering value judgments. A critic without close knowledge of the field in question is not merely an unreliable source; he is an intellectual fraud.

Second, adolescent literature has produced some well written books, and these books have the right to be judged on an equal basis with children's literature and adult literature. If much adolescent literature is literary "garbage," much of any year's production of adult books is likewise "garbage." (Besides, who is to determine what is "garbage" and why?) Adolescent literature has produced its share of hack writers writing unimaginative books about current social problems, but the adult literary world has its stable of hack writers writing books to order, books calculated to appeal to this year's sensation or next year's social ill. But adolescent literature has produced books as good as Zindel's *The Pigman*, Wersba's *The Dream Watcher*, Neufeld's *Lisa, Bright and Dark*, Speare's *The Witch of Blackbird Pond*, Wojciechowska's *A Single Light*, and Stolz's *Pray Love, Remember*, all worth reading for interest and literary merit by teacher and student alike.

How can English teachers discover whether these (and many more) books are really worth their time? There's only one way--read them. That won't solve the problems of the teachers' time, but it might solve an even greater problem, whether they are worth the students' time, and for good teachers that's a much more significant problem.

Third, adolescent literature is worth knowing because kids often know it already and they read it for good reason. If English teachers know the books their students are reading, it must follow that they may find out something about their students' needs and interests. Adolescence is a time of questioning, of doubting, of fearing, of wondering, and of setting lifelong attitudes. Finding answers, or at least what choices there might be, is of paramount importance at this stage of a young person's development. Aesthetic appreciation can be cultivated, too, but it is not the prime importance for most students at this age.

Adolescent literature may frequently offer superficial answers, just as it may offer sensible answers or tentative life styles, but whether superficial or sensible, English teachers ought to know what kids are reading if they really mean to take that old educational cliché, "find where they are and start from there," seriously. Teachers don't need to approve of where their students are, but they need to assess that point if they're ever going to find the key to taking students any further. And where most students are is often adolescent literature.

Teachers ought to know books like Eyerley's Radigan Cares (politics and social responsibilities), Zindel's My Darling, My Hamburger (sex and pregnancy), Hentoff's I'm Really Dragged but Nothing Gets Me Down (the draft and Vietnam), Hinton's That Was Then, This Is Now (drugs), Donovan's I'll Get There. It Better Be Worth the Trip (alienation and loneliness), Bonham's Durango Street and Viva Chicano (racial problems), Wersba's Run Softly, Go Fast (father-son estrangement), or Ney's Ox: The Story of a Kid at the Top (mixed-up children).

And teachers should know them for at least two pedagogical reasons: to understand what students like so teachers can recommend other books, and to know which adolescent books are worth recommending to kids having trouble reading anything--a primary responsibility of the English teacher who cares. And how do English teachers know them? There's only one way--read them.

Fourth, adolescent literature is useful and usable in the classroom. It serves as one way of getting kids started on a lifetime reading pattern. It can be used comparatively with adult literature. As a theme or archetype is introduced, examples from adult literature and adolescent literature can be discussed, not to prove the superiority of the former but rather to illustrate different approaches to common ideas. Students then have a basis for comparison and can learn to make judgments.

If they don't read some "garbage," how will they learn to recognize "good" literature or learn to judge individual books on the strengths and weaknesses inherent in each? For example, the problem of alienation is treated in Zindel's The Pigman and Hinton's The Outsiders in adolescent literature and Salinger's Catcher in the Rye and Camus' The Stranger in adult literature; the problem of cultural clash is handled in adolescent literature like Hentoff's Jazz Country and Marshall's Walkabout and in adult works like Ellison's Invisible Man and Paton's Cry, the Beloved Country. Adolescent literature can be used in free reading, thematic units, electives, indeed in almost anything English teachers do.

Last, adolescent literature is worth the time and attention of English teachers because it's fun and fast reading. If teachers and students alike read for many different reasons at many different times, the main reason for voluntary reading is enjoyment. Why is it that so many English teachers teach as if they had forgotten why they entered English teaching in the first place, because they enjoyed reading? Yet, in too many classrooms, enjoyment of reading seems to be the least important reason for reading. Students are told that they should read significant works to learn about the heritage of the western world, to deal with ideas, to keep abreast of social ills, to know great writers, in short everything except the main reason we all read--because we enjoy what we read.

The primary purpose of literature, after all, is to entertain. If it also edifies, so much the better, but first in importance is enjoyment. And adolescent literature is enjoyable to many young people and it can be enjoyable to most adults willing to take works on their own merits, not on some predetermined set of literary criteria. Works as dissimilar as Dizenzo's Phoebe (pregnancy), Merrill's The Pushcart War (satire on man's foibles), Lipsyte's The Contender (boxing and Black problems), L'Engle's A Wrinkle in Time (science fiction), Hunt's No Promises in the Wind (the depression), Alexander's The High King (fantasy), Tunis' Go, Team, Go (basketball), and Stolz's A Love, or A Season (sex) are genuinely enjoyable reading.

Perhaps, just perhaps, if English teachers read adolescent literature trying to find what students liked about it, they also might find their students. They might possibly discover that adolescent literature was enjoyable reading. It might be an eye-opener to some teachers. That those teachers cared enough to try to find why students read what they did might also be an eye-opener to some students.

In a survey conducted by the White House Conference on Youth in cooperation with the Future Teachers of America, students who responded felt that the "single most important factor in their education is the teacher."[6] To these students the qualifications necessary for being a good teacher include "open-mindedness, adequate knowledge of subject matter, an understanding of the problems of teen-agers, and genuine interest in schools, and in youth."[7] In many schools meetings were held to discuss the survey questions and one of the dominant points emphasized is that if "the student believes that there is genuine interest in him, he is more apt to respond with interest and diligence."[8]

Are these comments not proof enough of the importance of

the English teacher's firsthand knowledge of adolescent literature? Is that too much to ask? Think of all they have to gain from reading adolescent literature. Maybe more important, think of all they have to lose if they don't.

Notes

1. Frank G. Jennings. "Literature for Adolescents--Pap or Protein?" English Journal, 45 (December 1956), 528.

2. Harvey R. Granite. "The Uses and Abuses of Junior Literature," The Clearing House, 42 (February 1968), 337.

3. Alice Krahn. "Case Against the Junior Novel: The Public Librarian's View," Top of the News, 18 (May 1961), 19-22, and Esther Millet. "We Don't Even Call Those Books!" Top of the News, 20 (October 1963), 45-47.

4. The Commission on English. Freedom and Discipline in English, (New York: College Entrance Examination Board, 1965), 49.

5. Franklin K. Mathiews. "Blowing Out the Boy's Brains," Outlook, 108 (November 18, 1914), 652-654, and Montrose J. Moses. "Dietary Laws of Children's Books," Bookman, 51 (July 1920), 587-591. But see also another highly critical article: Wilson Follett. "Junior Model," Bookman, 70 (September 1929), 11-14.

6. Carolyn Boiarsky and Nelda Pedersen. "Youth Speaks Out About Teachers," Today's Education, Vol. 60, No. 8 (November 1971), 45.

7. Ibid.

8. Ibid.

LITERATURE IS*

By G. Robert Carlsen

When George Mallory was asked why he wanted to climb Mount Everest, he responded with the now famous words, "Because it's there." And when someone asks why we read literature, the best answer I can find is "because it's there."

Every once in a while groups of self-appointed intellectuals get themselves uptight about the status of literature and the status of reading in a culture. They feel that something must be done to defend a fragile flower against the trampling of barbaric boots. Really this seems nonsense to me. Literature is not so delicate that it needs any special protection ... nor is reading. If it were so, then no outside defense would do much to nourish it back to health.

Man is basically a *maker* (the literal meaning of the word poet). After satisfying the basic physical needs of living and sometimes even in the process of satisfying them, he creates. From the depths of his nature comes the need to decorate, to rearrange materials into patterns, and to imitate and represent the world as he perceives it. He creates with the pigments of the earth, with his own motions and sounds, and sooner or later, with his language.

Man, we are told, is a tool-making animal. I suggest that equally we are story-making animals. A certain number of people in any culture have a linguistic disease akin to alcoholism: Something impels them to the activity of playing with words, arranging and rearranging them to see what they will do. Anyone who really writes or who has lived with a writer knows what I mean. There is no happiness for such a person unless the process is underway. *When* it is underway, there is little importance in life outside the growing design. Neither war, social revolution, depression, persecution, imprisonment, nor a materialistic culture seems to deter these people.

---

*Reprinted by permission of the author and publisher from *English Journal*, 63:2 (February 1974), 23-27.

> We are literature-creating and literature-consuming animals. In the long course of human history, literature seems to transcend military victories, political institutions, and economic accomplishments.

And something deep within us impels us to cherish the product of the writer. I have watched it happen over and over. Given a modicum of reading skill, some free time, and accessibility to literary materials, people read ... not every person, but most. People read in cramped bunks under the arctic ice. They read 40,000 feet above the earth. They read as they have their hair cut or dried, and while they wait for the dentist. People read in bed, in the bath tub and occasionally sitting upright in a chair.

We are literature-creating and literature-consuming animals.

Throughout human history, we have instinctively placed a value on literature somewhat above the value that we place on other things. Literature is usually more valued than games of chance, more valued than landscape gardening, more valued than interior decoration--it has even been more valued, I think, than urban planning. In the long course of human history, literature seems to transcend military victories, political institutions, and economic accomplishments.

Readers find in literature a variety of rewards, none perhaps of greater merit than another. I should like to consider some of these satisfactions in a bit of detail.

1) The reader finds himself unconsciously absorbed in the imaginary world and action on the page. He momentarily escapes, slipping the surly bonds of real life, to live in a world more splendid, certainly more exciting, and perhaps more beautiful than his own. The world out there disappears. When the reading is finished, he is disappointed--let down. Sometimes it takes an hour or a day to return to reality.

A reader who experiences this involvement finds it good--something to be sought again and again. It is like heroin. It hooks him. We have a series of clichês to express this feeling: "It was the kind of book that I couldn't put down." "I just hated to finish it. I wanted it to go on and on." "Do you have another book as good as this one?"

This is a valued experience, one that often occurs for the first time with juvenile series books. Until a reader has had such an interaction with a book, I am convinced that nothing else in literature will ever mean very much to him.

2) Learning about people, times, and places is another satisfaction that comes from literature. The avid reader is filled with rags and tags of information. A colleague on a bus trip discoursed

for an hour on diving. Finally I asked, "Are you a diver?" "Hell no," he replied, "but I've read everything Ellsberg ever wrote." The reader delights in finding out about life in China and Africa, in the Middle Ages and in Victorian England. He roams the inner-city and mingles with the jet set. He discovers bell ringers and public relations executives. He knows about fire ants and the smell of camels, about life in communes and the practice of witchcraft. He has seen crass power politics in operation and has puzzled over the tragic devotion of a good woman to a cad. It is a melange of knowledge, this that comes from literature. It might be learned more directly from factual material, but probably not so indelibly. Beginning a book, the reader never knows what bits and pieces of information he will gain, what "breaks" in his experience he will fill, but this is part of the fun of reading. It's like assembling an infinitely huge jigsaw puzzle whose pieces gradually begin to fit together.

> Reading literature is suddenly meeting ourselves, encountering situations similar to our own, rediscovering our own emotions and relationships.

---

3) Reading literature is suddenly meeting ourselves, encountering situations similar to our own, rediscovering our own emotions and relationships. We never know quite when this is going to happen. A girl read, "When in disgrace with fortune in men's eyes," and suddenly she was face to face with her feelings about being dismissed as a summer camp counselor after an all night bender with a young man. Veterans in Fitzsimmons Hospital after World War II read the Odyssey because it was the only thing they could find that echoed their own experience of returning from war. A boy relived his feelings of guilt with Roskalnikov. He had discovered a fire hose attached to a hydrant outside the city hall of his home town. What more fun than to put the end in the basement window and turn on the water. But no one discovered the prank for hours. The town's records were destroyed and the foundations of the basement undermined.

I plague people from time to time by asking them to describe a book they would like to have an author write just for them. If it is a work of fiction, would the major character be male or female? How old? Would the book take place in the present, past, or future? What would be the geographic setting? And finally, what would happen? The single most prevalent pattern with mid-teens, and a rather common pattern with adults, is a book that projects their own life patterns. Here is a response from a sixteen-year-old boy, I.Q. about 120, but doing C, D, and F work in school:

> It would be about a guy about ready to leave home but not quite. He doesn't have anything to say to his old

> buddies anymore. They haven't had a fight or anything, but when he meets them on the street they just don't have anything to say to one another. The only person he can talk to is his girl. She lives twenty miles away in a neighboring city. Whenever he goes to see her, he stays up too late and he gets it from his folks when he gets home. His only other interest is in his car. He works on it too late at night and then he gets it from his folks and his teachers some more. I would like to see the book written in such a way that he gets out of school, gets a job, gets married and settles down.

Why it should be so significant to a reader to meet and re-experience even unpleasant aspects of his own life has always mystified me just a bit. Maybe it is related to what Sylvia Plath said about The Bell Jar: First one has to write autobiographically in order to free oneself to write a real novel. Perhaps a reader has to read autobiographically for a period in order to overcome his own provincialism and read on a human scale. It is interesting how many of the most widely read teen-age books tend to be first person accounts with the ring of psychological case studies on the experience of adolescents.

> Readers have always testified to the special satisfaction of reading and appreciating a well-made work of literature. But no one has been able to spell out exactly what it is.

Though we glorify our individuality and our uniqueness, we find comfort in discovering that we are not alone, that others live and feel as we do, that someone, an author, has understood us.

4) But the satisfaction most often gained from reading involves the projection of the mystery of our experience of life itself. Literature projects for us the unsolved dilemmas of human life ... those things that trouble us deeply and have seemingly troubled men from the dawning of human consciousness. Literature seldom solves these dilemmas or offers explanations. Rather it presents a living situation that throws us back on ourselves. There is the conflict between the will of the state and one's own inner light. There is the conflict between our vision of and desire for the good, the pure, the righteous, and our equally strong instincts toward the cruel, the sadistic, the vulgar. There is the constant uncertainty about reality and its true nature. (Does it reside in us or outside of us?) We have never really understood the degrees of freedom we possess; nor have we ever grasped the meaning of birth and love and death. But we come to see, each in his own way, that the stories of other people and what they have experienced record something significant about what it means to be a human being on

this planet. For most readers, literature is as close to philosophy as they ever get.

5) But shot through all of these is another kind of pleasure which we designate as aesthetic. Perhaps the aesthetic quality of literature is the warp upon which the other things are woven. At any rate, there is a satisfaction that comes from the contemplation of a well-made object. There is satisfaction when one sees the harmony of the total pattern. We are left, at least momentarily, with a sense of inner harmony in our own lives. Readers have always testified to the existence of this kind of satisfaction. And most have said that it is the deepest and most important reward of all. But no one has really been able to spell out exactly what it is, or how it operates. Like the noun, we know that it exists, but we cannot define it.

I have suggested five different but overlapping satisfactions which derive from literature. I am not sure that one is more valuable than another. Each is worthwhile to the individual experiencing it at the time he experiences it.

I do want to hypothesize that in the customary pattern of growing up there are periods of the reader's life when one of these is more important to him than the others. Nevertheless, I do not want to imply that at any one period, he is entirely devoid of interest in the others. Suppose we think of a flow chart, like the one I have sketched (see below).[1] Late childhood and early adolescence is the period when the reader generally demands complete absorption in what he reads. This is the period of unconscious delight. This does not mean that "seeing oneself" or "aesthetic experience" are completely absent, but they are not as important as uncritical with-

Flow Chart of Developing Concerns in Literature

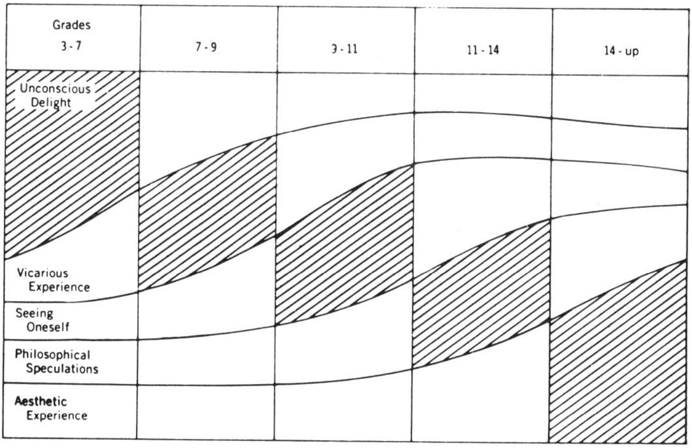

drawal into the fabric of the story. Next, in early junior high school, the reader is somewhat reality bound and seeks vicarious experience in reading. He collects information the way he collects match box covers or stamps. By middle adolescence, he becomes ego absorbed and wants books that are about himself. These may be realistic or they may be symbolic. As he matures, in his late teens and beyond, he finds literature the avenue for philosophical-religious-psychological speculation. And perhaps it is the sated reader who turns at last to the only satisfaction that is left--the aesthetic--which takes on an importance now that it did not have earlier.

> Teachers should just share their students' involvement with books. Later they can help young people see connections between their reading and their lives, and still later, to see how the story's designs harmonize with the content of the idea.

As teachers, we present literature or we read literature with young people because it is there and because people of all ages have found it satisfying and valuable. Although what we emphasize will change as the individual matures, first let's just share our student's involvement with a book. Later we can help him see connections between what he is reading and his own life, and still later help him to see how the story's patterns and designs harmonize with and carry the content of the idea.

I suppose we come closest to doing it right in the elementary schools and in colleges. Perhaps we are too tense at the high school level, too eager to hurry students' maturation. We may be inclined to select materials that are too difficult, hoping they will gain satisfactions for which they are not yet psychologically ready.

Let me conclude by presenting a passage from a new novel by Theodore Wessner called *The Car Thief*. Alex, from a lower class, motherless home, is a compulsive auto thief. He is eventually sent to a detention home where he leads a bleak existence with an assorted group of delinquents. One day a box of battered books is brought to the dormitory and the boys are allowed to paw through them.

> Alex started to read a book called *Gunner Asch*, starting it mainly because he knew how to read, although he was intimidated by the mass of words. He had never read anything but the lessons in schoolbooks--assignments in history or science.... But the novel was simply written and fairly easy to understand, and he soon became interested enough in what was happening to stop reminding himself page after page that he was reading a book, to

turn the pages to see what was going to happen next.

He sat on the floor reading until he grew sleepy. When his eyelids began to slide down and his head began to cloud, he lay over on his side on the floor to sleep awhile.... When he woke he got up and carried the book with him to the bathroom....

He became so involved in the story that his legs fell asleep. He kept reading, intending to get up at the end of this page, then at the end of this page, if only because he would feel more comfortable with his pants up and buttoned, but he read on. He rose finally at the end of a chapter, although he read a little into the next chapter before he made himself stop.... Then he checked the thickness of pages he had read between his fingers, and experienced something he had never experienced before. Some of it was pride--he was reading a book--and some of it was a preciousness the book had assumed. Feeling relaxed, unthreatened, he wanted to keep the book in his hands, for what it offered. He did not want to turn the pages, for then they would be gone and spent; nor did he want to do anything but turn the pages.

He stepped over legs again and sat down to read, as far from anyone as he could get, some fifteen feet, to be alone with the book. He read on. Something was happening to him, something as pleasantly strange as the feeling he had had for Irene Sheaffer. By now, if he knew a way, he would prolong the book the distance his mind could see, and he rose again, quietly, to sustain the pleasant sensation, the escape he seemed already to have made from the scarred and unlighted corridor. Within this shadowed space there were now other things--war and food and a worry over cigarettes and rations, leaving and returning, dying and escaping. The corridor itself, and his own life, were less present....

His heart rose to the bottom of his throat occasionally, and he stopped reading occasionally, to let his feelings settle and enjoy an afterglow, and if he looked up, if he looked at the window, his eyes did not accurately focus on anything but took pleasure only from those things which moved within. It may have been war, which made large things small and small things large for those in the book, and for himself as well, and for the melding of the two. Mr. Kelly could not have known, nor did Alex have any idea himself, how ripe he had been to be taken by a book. Confinement and quiet. It was so pleasant that he feared he would be caught for doing something wrong, as if it were not only the life in the pages of the book which had taken breath in the reading, but his own, as if this were a violation.[2]

Notes

1. For another discussion of this topic see Margaret Early. "Stages of Growth in Literary Appreciation," English Journal, 49 (March 1960), pp. 161-167.

2. The Car Thief, by Theodore Wessner (Random House, 1972), page 99.

MORAL DEVELOPMENT AND LITERATURE FOR ADOLESCENTS*

By Peter Scharf

Until recently, there has been little investigation of the precise role played by literature in adolescent development.[1] This paper offers that a clue to the relationship of literature to adolescent development may lie in an understanding of the adolescent's evolving moral conscience. We will suggest that as the adolescent matures in terms of moral thinking, the meaning of particular literary experiences may shift dramatically. By understanding changes in adolescent moral thinking we may be able to better understand how literature affects the adolescent at different developmental stages.

Kohlberg's Theory of Moral Judgment

Our approach requires an explanation of Kohlberg's theory of moral judgment. The theory was developed at Harvard University by Kohlberg and his associates.[2] It argues that there is an invariant sequence in moral judgment. Longitudinal studies indicate that individuals in a number of different societies move sequentially through each of six moral stages. Moral development occurs through age twenty-five; however, individuals progress at different rates, and some people become fixated at primitive stages of moral thought.

The six stages are divided into three levels: the preconventional (stages one and two), the conventional (stages three and four), and the post-conventional or principled (stages five and six), as shown in Table 1.

The preconventional mode of moral problem-solving is typically associated with preadolescent children (ages ten to twelve) and morally fixated adults. At stage one there is an orientation toward punishment and obedience, toward superior power. The physical consequences of human action determine right and wrong regardless of their human meaning. Stage two assumes that right action becomes that which satisfies one's own needs. Human relation-

*Reprinted by permission of the author and the American Library Association from Top of the News (Winter 1977), 131-136.

TABLE 1

Classification of Moral Judgment into Levels and Stages of Development

Levels		Stages of Development	
Level I.	Preconventional	Stage 1:	Obedience and punishment orientation
		Stage 2:	Naively egoistic orientation
Level II.	Conventional	Stage 3:	Good-boy orientation
		Stage 4:	Authority and social-order maintaining orientation
Level III.	Postconventional	Stage 5:	Contractual legalistic orientation
		Stage 6:	Conscience or principle orientation

Source: adapted from Lawrence Kohlberg, "Stage and Sequence," in Goslin, ed., Handbook of Socialization (New York: Russell Sage, 1967).

ships are viewed in terms of the market place: "You scratch my back and I'll scratch yours."

The conventional level becomes dominant in late preadolescence (ages twelve through sixteen). At stage three we have what we call the good boy/good girl orientation. Good behavior is what helps others and is approved by them. One gains approval by being "nice" or exhibiting behavior which will be approved by others. At stage four there is a shift toward fixed definitions of social duty and concern with firm social rules and a respect for formal authority.

The postconventional (or principled) level first appears in late adolescence (late high school or early college years). Stage five is a legalistic contract orientation, generally with utilitarian overtones. Laws which are not constitutional, that violate human rights or are not in the general interest, are judged to be invalid at stage five.

The transition from stage four to five is often stormy. Before moving to stage five, the adolescent often rejects the conventional moral categories of teachers and parents while declaring that all values are relative and meaningless.

At stage six, Kohlberg postulates there is a basis for rational agreement to moral principles. There are universal principles of justice, of ideal reciprocity, the equality of human rights, and the respect for the dignity of human beings as individual persons.

Moral Maturity and Literature

At each stage of development, particular literary issues are especially salient. While, clearly, great literature has an impact upon almost any age or developmental level (for example, Dostoevski's Crime and Punishment[3] can be read at age thirteen as a mystery story and at age twenty as a complex study of human morals), it may still be argued that the moral focus of particular literary works may be especially psychologically significant at specific stages of development.

For example, certain novels of style and manners are of great appeal to conventionally reasoning early adolescents. Ivanhoe by Scott, concerned with courtly attitudes and romantic love, is of continuing appeal to early adolescents seeking to discover the rules and mores of social interchange in their own society. In contrast, Ibsen's Enemy of the People[4] only makes sense much later when the adolescent is able to differentiate his or her own moral principles from community norms. Similarly, complex novels of social responsibility such as Camus' The Plague[5] and Melville's Moby Dick only become psychologically meaningful when the late adolescent has acquired the ability to clearly weigh in his or her own mind the rights of the community with the legitimate moral claims of the individual.

These differences in moral concerns of literature may be described in terms of three distinct "types" of literature:

- The literature of social expectations: significant in attaining conventional moral orientations, that is, stages three and four.
- The literature of social revolt: significant in the rejection of conventional moral thought.
- The literature of affirmation: significant in the acceptance of post-conventional moral principles.

The Literature of Social Expectations

One of the key developmental tasks of early adolescence involves the adolescent's anticipating and accepting the legitimate expectations of his social world. This is the core of Kohlberg's third and fourth stages (the conventional level). In any historical era, the content of conventional moral thinking may differ. The Amish adolescent may be socialized into a highly prescriptive, regulated set of norms and role expectations. For the suburban youth, the norms will be more humanistic and open-ended. Still, in each milieu, the adolescent grapples with a key developmental question: What does this society expect of me?

When the literature of social expectations is critical of society it poses an alternative set of conventional norms to those which are attacked. For example, one fourteen-year-old black student suggested after reading Claude Brown's Manchild in the Promised Land[6] that the book "showed how if a black man tried hard he could be accepted, even if the whites were prejudiced and didn't want you." A young Jewish girl in the same class suggested upon reading Herman Wouk's Marjorie Morningstar[7] "that the book showed how people are not nice to Jewish girls and make them feel bad, no matter what they do to convince people they are really trying to belong."

This literature of social expectations stimulates a sense of moral conventionality by praising "appropriate" social attitudes. Often protagonists will represent heroic values which are reflected and emulated by young readers. Villains are often portrayed as "unfeeling" or "cruel" in often one-dimensional, somewhat stereotyped ways. Good literature of this type presents a coherent moral universe in which good and evil are polarized and defined. This provides a platform of social conventions upon which the early adolescent can differentiate his group's social ideology from other philosophies. While this type of literature may seem "corny" or "sentimental" to adults, it is a necessary stage toward the learning of more complex personal moral philosophies.

Much of the literature popular in early adolescence deals with the social expectations theme. Biographies are especially rich in information on the appropriate social expectations of society. One youngster may be drawn to a biography about Martin Luther King; for another, it will be the narrative of Joe Namath's career; for another, a novel about Susan B. Anthony might be significant. Usually, novels popular through age thirteen deal with themes which are moralistic in the sense that characters are defined as either good, bad, heroic, or cowardly in a given society. Historically based fiction has a similar impact in its detail about a tradition and its expectations.

The Literature of Social Revolt

Typically in middle adolescence, many adolescents come to increasingly question the moral order of their society. In any historical era this may take a unique form. Youth will become Freedom Riders, Skinheads, LSD "freaks," or Klansmen. They will join S.N.C.C. (Student Nonviolent Coordinating Committee), Y.A.F. (Young Americans for Freedom), the Hare Krishna, or the Communist Party. They will follow people as diverse as Martin Luther King, Ghandi, the "fifteen-year-old perfect master." The key to any such commitment is the youth's critique of society as it stands. The youth rejects the conventional moral order and seeks to find his own.

Needless to say, this questioning is disturbing to many adults, including librarians. They fail to see that such a rejection of conventional societal truth is a critical step in the adolescent's defining for himself an autonomous value base. Of course, some youth will become fixated in one rigid ideology or another (Hitler and Abbie Hoffman may be good examples of permanent nihilistic fixation).

For most, however, the beginning of social doubt and questioning is a necessary developmental step toward finding a set of autonomously chosen, universal moral principles.

The surfacing of doubt requires a new literature. A key to this type of literature is the rejection of social conventions. Salinger's The Catcher in the Rye[8] is a good example of such a critique. As the protagonist, Holden Caulfield sees his world as hypocritical and shameful. Adults lie to adolescents and to each other. Nobody really believes in any of society's expectations and roles. Success is mere conformity. Love is a bourgeois excuse to become respectably "settled."

The adolescent reading The Catcher in the Rye strongly identifies with Holden Caulfield's rebellion. Most adolescents by age sixteen have begun to have strong doubts about the perceived moral propriety of their parents and teachers. Their initial questioning is no doubt stimulated by the vivid images in The Catcher in the Rye and through similar picaresque novels. For example, one suburban high school student noted:

> The character in the novel Catcher in the Rye showed me how screwed-up things are in society. It shows that the morality of people is really old-fashioned and out of date. It really gets you thinking about what SOCIETY is like....

Similarly, in one discussion about Heller's Catch-22[9] with some bright high school seniors, a seventeen-year-old boy offered that the book showed how "in an upside-down world, you gotta be upside-down to see things right-side-up." The popularity of Castaneda's books on Don Juan among adolescents may be understood in terms of contemporary adolescent questioning of Western notions of rationality, science, and progress. Such works clearly stimulate a process of moral doubt which has roots in both the polarization of the youth and adult cultures and the pluralism of American values. While such doubt is threatening to some adults, it should be seen as a necessary (but not final) step toward attaining truly principled values. Unless the adolescent rejects what is arbitrary in conventional social norms he cannot seek to move toward values which are truly internal and universal.

The Literature of Affirmation

In The Rebel[10], Albert Camus writes:

> Who is the Rebel? A man who says no, but by saying no does not imply renunciation.... To say yes, by saying no.... (p. 6)

As in Camus' statement of moral rebellion, Kohlberg argues that beyond a rejection of social morality comes an affirmation of principles. Much literature involves a quest for universal moral and metaphysical meaning. This literature becomes increasingly important in early adulthood.

Much of the world's great literature deals with these ultimate human values. In the realm of ethics, Buber, Camus, Orwell, Dostoevski, Melville, and others all attempt to pose ethical principles which provide moral limits to human conduct. Such writers as Hesse, Nietzsche, Castaneda, and De Chardin powerfully explore the question of the metaphysical meanings underlying daily experience. Much great poetry moves toward finding an ultimate standard of beauty and truth.

In these works of affirmation there is some kind of ultimate human meaning or value. The works move toward some moral, metaphysical, or aesthetic truth which is seen as nonrelativistic and ultimate. They offer that there are some values which are worth affirming, something positive to live for.

The literature of affirmation, though critical for later development, is probably the least accessible to most adolescents. On reading Hesse's Siddartha,[11] one high school senior offers in a paper: "I didn't understand it but I think it made me think that there was some purpose in experiencing life as it comes." Another student commented on Camus' Plague, "that it raised the question of when it is right to let people die, and what one might die for."

The final stage is psychologically quite distinct from both an early adolescent conformity as it is from the relativism and nihilism of middle adolescence. The search for transcendent values through literature offers a bridge to a full adulthood where, in Erik Erikson's terms, the young adult seeks to make meaningful and self-determined choices in the realms of love, work, and meaning.

This movement toward a mature adulthood has special meaning in a world of cultural change and conflicting value systems. Only adults who have reflected upon and developed a clear set of inner values can hope to cope with the flux of the last quarter of the twentieth century. In this search for values, books and libraries have a unique task. If libraries can encourage meaningful personal searches among young people, they can play a vital role in the process of moral development. To do this, they must create a climate of openness toward the exploring youth and gear their offerings to the developmental concerns and interests of the emerging adolescent.

References

1. Lawrence Kohlberg. "Moral Judgment, Tragedy and Pathos" (unpublished Harvard manuscript).

2. Lawrence Kohlberg. "Stage and Sequence," in Goslin, ed., Handbook of Socialization (New York: Russell Sage, 1967).

3. Fedor Dostoevski. Crime and Punishment (New York: Dutton, 1966).

4. Henrik Ibsen. Enemy of the People (New York: Bantam, 1960).

5. Albert Camus. The Plague (New York: Random House, 1948).

6. Claude Brown. Manchild in the Promised Land (New York: New American Library, 1965).

7. Herman Wouk. Marjorie Morningstar (New York: Pocketbooks, 1955).

8. J. D. Salinger. The Catcher in the Rye (New York: Bantam, 1956).

9. Joseph Heller. Catch-22 (New York: Dell, 1964).

10. Albert Camus. The Rebel (New York: London, 1950).

11. Herman Hesse. Siddhartha (New York: New Directions, 1961).

THE RITES OF PASSAGE:
A Study of the Adolescent Girl*

By Jan Miller Yoder

> "Trying to find myself in a hide-and-seek between worlds..."[1]

General Characteristics

One of the primary concerns of adolescents is their transition period into adulthood. Although adults later refer to this time as "the good old days," for the adolescent it is a time characterized by isolation, explosion, and rebellion. It is a time punctuated by doubts, experiments, and reflexive thinking. One of the modes of exploration often sought by the adolescent is literature. It offers a means by which they can examine themselves within their environment while events and solutions are manipulated and evaluated.

The adolescent's rites of passage is a transition from the dependence of childhood to the social, psychological, and physical maturity of adulthood. The age is marked by an intense drive to get away from the previous attachments, along with an equally intense desire to go back to old relations. The transition period begins approximately at the age of twelve and continues to the ages of twenty-one or twenty-two. Agee[2] has characterized the initiation period according to three phases: the separation from childhood; the transition; and the incorporation into the adult community.

James W. Johnson[3] identified several characteristics of adolescents which are often observed in novels dealing with adolescent initiation:

1) a sense of loss from the past and an anxiety of the future;
2) an awareness of a change in the body;
3) a sexual confusion, generally emphasized for the female protagonist;
4) a feeling of isolation and loneliness;
5) an emphasis on escape or flight brought on by the feeling of isolation; and

*Reprinted by permission of the author and the publisher from News from ALAN (Fall 1976), [3]-[5].

6) a growing or unresolved conflict with the family.

Until recently, the female adolescent has been excluded from in-depth study. In the best novels about adolescents from 1920-1960, ninety per cent of the protagonists were males. Not until the late 1950's were female adolescents treated with the same frankness as male protagonists. Often the books which did frankly portray the female were not considered as the best literature about adolescents.

Initiation Rites

The initiation process which involves the separation--transition--incorporation phases is similar for both males and females, but the environment in which it takes place is generally altered. The establishment of a heterosexual relationship appears more frequently in novels when the protagonist is a female, and sexual intensity is more pronounced. Girls are involved in fewer gang or crowd affiliations than are male protagonists. The female protagonist is less concerned with future identity roles in occupations and her adventures are often psychological rather than physical.

Phase I - Separation

Literal separation of the novice from the community was sometimes practiced in primitive cultures.

In the novel, Julie of the Wolves, Julie, an Eskimo, had married at the age of twelve, left her husband the next year and wandered about on the North Slope of Alaska. Near the end of her journey she was visited by a hunter and his wife. The wife, questioning Julie's isolation, remarked:

> 'I thought perhaps this was the beginning of your periods, and that your family had sent you to a hut to be alone. The old grandmother who raised me did that, and I was miserable and so unhappy, because no one does that anymore.'
>
> Miyax (Julie) shook her head. 'I am not yet a woman.' (160)

Today, although there is no formalized ritual, there is usually a specific time when the girl begins to feel the separation. It may be a physiological awakening, a specific incident which separates the child from the parent or the past, or a feeling of ambivalence which creates isolation.

In Are You There God, It's Me Margaret, Margaret, 12, and her friends anxiously awaited the onset of puberty after having spent a year imitating the older girls. When her first period began, she joyfully proclaimed: "Now I am almost a woman!" (148)

Jeannie in A Long Way Home from Troy noted the ending of childhood:

> Like one day you're out riding bikes with your friends and the next day ZAP, a whole new world is unloaded onto your innocent shoulders--a fun-filled world of teenform bras, naughty dreams, romantic traumas, and heart-to-heart talks with Mother. (71)

Sometimes there is a particular incident that cuts off childhood. Frankie, 12, in A Member of the Wedding, always slept with her father.

> One night in April, when she and her father were going to bed, he looked at her and said, all of a sudden: 'Who is this great big long-legged twelve-year-old blunderbuss who still wants to sleep with her old Papa.' And she was too big to sleep with her father any more. She had to sleep in her upstairs room alone. She began to have a grudge against her father and they looked at each other in a slant-eyed way. She did not like to stay at home. (20)

Frankie continued to lament the fact that she was too old to sleep with her father, but too young to donate blood; too young to join the neighborhood teen gang, but too old to play like a child. She cried now about things that had never bothered her before, and because she was isolated from her former friends (they were thirteen) she spent much time alone just thinking. Sometimes she took walks in the evenings:

> She was afraid of these things that made her suddenly wonder who she was, and what she was going to be in the world, and why she was standing at that minute, seeing a light, or listening, or staring up into the sky: alone. She was afraid, and there was a queer tightness in her chest. (20)

Anne Frank: The Diary of a Young Girl illustrates the growing tension between her parents and herself, particularly with her mother. She lamented: "I can't really love Mummy in a dependent childlike way--I just don't have that feeling." (258) Earlier in the book she expressed her feelings of separation from those around her:

> If I talk, everyone thinks I'm showing off; when I'm silent, they think I'm ridiculous; rude if I answer back, sly if I get a good idea, lazy if I'm tired, selfish if I eat a mouthful more than I should, stupid, cowardly, crafty, etc...." (57)

Phase II - Transition

"Once the separation is complete, the novice remains withdrawn as he undergoes the intense instruction which prepares (him) for adult life."[4] The transition period takes the protagonist on an unknown journey--where he is tested. It is during this process that he evaluates himself and the new world, acquiring the knowledge concerning the "privileges and responsibilities (or burdens) of adulthood."

Sometimes the journeys are literal ones; sometimes they are simply the journey of isolation to affiliation. But always they consist of the psychological searching of oneself. Often sexuality is introduced during this period because it has partly created the separateness from childhood; it is a new experience, and it can be a means to self-identity. Peer groups are especially important because they provide a common bond for adolescents where they can experience mutual comradeship and enjoy the affiliation of a group.

The symbol of the journey is depicted in various ways in the novels. In A Nice Fire and Some Moonpennies, Maizie, 16, hitchhikes alone to a large city in order to experience the use of drugs. Along the way she is introduced to a new side of life: new forms of sex; an evaluation of her relationship with Jasper, her boyfriend; her responsibility to her mother; and the world of drugs. She is eager to return home, uncertain as to whether she should tell her mother about her experiences, but certainly convinced that she will be able to cope with the standards of her community.

Julie in Julie and the Wolves took a literal journey in order to escape her marriage, but on the journey she had to decide who she was going to be. She visualized going to the United States, but while she was alone, she reverted to the old Eskimo way of life. At one point, she entertained the idea of completely forsaking the modern world and she replaced her worldly possessions with symbols of her ancestral past. At the end of the journey, as she entered civilization again, she was forced to consider the impracticability of her remaining a traditionalist. She was forced to make an adult decision.

Egocentrism and emancipation are also marks of this period. Honor Arundel's two books, The Terrible Temptation and The Blanket World, provide a framework for the examination of an adolescent completing the transition stage to the incorporation stage of adulthood. Jan Meredith, 18, leaves for college with a determined idea of who she is and what she will become.

> All my childhood it seemed that I had been longing for some exquisite moment when I would be grown-up and free of obligations. (Terrible Temptation, 21)

At Edinburgh she soon met the charming, devoted, and irresistible Thomas. She admitted that she loved him, but she refused to discuss marriage or her moving in with him.

> In my opinion there is no real difference between being married and living together.... you still, if you want to end the affair, have rows and recriminations and tears....

> Thomas was trying to pin me down into a precise pattern when I wanted to enjoy each moment, each hour, each day, for itself alone. (93)

And then amid her well-ordered, clearly directed life came the news that her mother was dying.

> Then there was anger. I was angry that I hadn't known, angry that my peaceful student life had been disturbed, angry that she should be dying so painfully and pointlessly; and, more selfishly, angry at myself that I'd agreed to come home when there was nothing I could do, angry at the pull of family ties which I thought I had learnt to ignore; angry at my brother's assumption that I would immediately stop whatever I was doing and come home to the death bed scene. (The Blanket World, 2)

While she was at home, Jan displayed childish tantrums and David, her brother, chided her: "It's time you grew up and took some responsibility." (61)

Finally on her twentieth birthday, at the home of her rich girlfriend's parents who were having a birthday party in her honor, she received the news that David's wife was ill and he needed her. "So I was back in a train again, faced with the longest journey of my life." (133)

Another protagonist reaches her self-identity and maturity through a sexual experience. Jeannie, 17, in A Long Way Home from Troy, journeyed away from the acceptable social patterns of her class as the title suggests. She fell in love with a school hood, Truck Hardy, and this relationship separated her from her parents and her old friends. She experienced a satisfactory sexual experience, but in the process she began to realize that Truck was not suitable as a lifelong partner. He had been her means of breaking from her parents' control, the moral code, and the social system. She declares that to love him for purely physical reasons was "immoral" and concluded that "doing it on the back seat of a car didn't make a woman out of a girl, you had to give a lot more than that." (210) With the help of her brother, she stopped seeing Truck, applied for the college of her choice (not her mother's) and accepted her role within her social structure again.

Keil[5] notes that there are some notable differences between the adult and the child which are partly resolved during the transition state: (1) greater intellectual powers in the adult; (2) higher degree of integration in the adult; (3) higher form of fantasy life, more closely related to reality; and (4) specific changes in the individual's relationship with others. The transitory stage becomes a period of learning--a period of testing ideas, clarifying values, and of formulating and establishing a lifelong value system.

Phase III - Incorporation

> The culminating ceremony of the initiation ritual is the incorporation of the novice into the adult community. This phase is very important, for without incorporation all previous ceremonies have been useless. The transition rites are endured in seclusion or in an unfamiliar environment, but incorporation rites in primitive initiation are generally witnessed by the entire community, signifying to all that the novice is now "a new one," a member.[6]

In several novels the protagonists change their names as they are accepted into new roles. In A Member of the Wedding, Frankie was a childhood name; F. Jasmine was used while she was separated; and Frances was used when she returned home. Julie in Julie and the Wolves reverted to her Eskimo name during her journey--Miyax--and used Julie when she decided on her role in the modern world. In The Summer Before, Alex was used before her journey and Alexandra was used after she had returned to her new role.

At least one adult supports and greets the protagonists as they enter their new roles. Jeannie, A Long Way Home from Troy, is welcomed back "to the club" by her brother, who had also struggled earlier with drugs as his escape. Her parents are also very supportive. Each of the other protagonists, Jan, Julie, Frankie, Alexandra, and Maizie had their families waiting for their return from their journey, whether it was literal or psychological. And in each case, the knowledge that the girls had gained during the transition period made their relationships much stronger and easier to endure.

The process of maturity is generally "a painful one and success is usually achieved with some residual emotional scar tissue."[7] Even in the most successful initiations, much pain, uncertainty, and personal loss is experienced. Physical pain and emotional stress often accompanied primitive cultural rites, and today fraternities and sororities often initiate pledges with forms of fear, pain, and embarrassment.

The ultimate success or failure of the protagonists' incorporation rests primarily upon their emergence of self in conjunction with their views of the world. They must have the ability to evaluate and learn from everyday experiences. They must be able to perceive and put into "proper perspective the code of conduct expected of them by the society in which they live."

Keil summarizes the qualities of the adolescent who has reached or is in the process of reaching psychological maturity.

> An individual often seems like a different person after adolescence than he was ever before. (He) grows to accept and respect his own uniqueness and that of others; to develop the capacity to tolerate frustration and disappoint-

ments; to find pleasure and satisfaction in living and working and in their association with other people; these are earmarks in maturity. Upon these qualities will depend the individual's choice of profession, success of marriage, excellence as a parent, contribution as a citizen, general efficiency, and emotional and physical health.[8]

Notes

1. Patricia Winsor. The Summer Before. New York: Harper & Row, p. 237.

2. Hugh Agee. "Adolescent Initiation: A Thematic Study in the Secondary Schools," Richard Meade and Robert Small, editors, Literature for Adolescents. Columbus, Ohio: Charles E. Merrill, 1973, p. 134.

3. Agee, p. 135.

4. Agee, p. 134.

5. Norman Keil. The Universal Experience of Adolescence, New York: International University Press, 1964, p. 854.

6. Agee, p. 134.

7. Keil, Universal. p. 852.

8. Norman Keil. The Adolescent through Fiction. New York: International University Press, 1959, p. 289.

Bibliography of Literary Sources

Arundel, Honor. The Blanket World, New York: Thomas Nelson, Inc., 1973.

________. The Terrible Temptation, New York: Thomas Nelson, Inc., 1971.

Blume, Judy. Are You There God? It's Me, Margaret, New York: Dell Publishing, 1970.

Frank, Anne. Anne Frank: The Diary of a Young Girl, New York: Pocket Books, 1971. (Published 1947.)

George, Jean. Julie of the Wolves, New York: Harper & Row, 1972.

Heffron, Doris. A Nice Fire and Some Moonpennies, New York: Atheneum, 1972.

McCullers, Carson. A Member of the Wedding, Boston: Riverside Press, 1946.

Mills, Donia. Long Way Home from Troy, New York: The Viking Press, 1971.

Windsor, Patricia. The Summer Before, New York: Harper & Row, 1973.

WRITING ABOUT ADOLESCENT LITERATURE: Current Approaches and Future Directions*

By Dorothy Matthews

There has recently been an upsurge of academic interest in literature for children and adolescents. With the Modern Language Association now recognizing the importance of this branch of study, more attention is being called to the need for a body of criticism to insure academic respectability for work in this area. Although specialists writing about books for young people come from diversified discipline--education, library science and English--they are united in a common desire to be taken seriously.

But adolescent literature, a relative newcomer to the publishing scene, presents special problems to would-be critics. How, for instance, should one approach the discussion of junior novel? What concerns should be uppermost? What kinds of articles are most useful and important? A look at the output of professional journals over the past five years gives some idea of the writing presently being done and points up the need for some new directions.

Although categorizing is admittedly artificial and arbitrary, it might be useful, for the purposes of this article, to see recent writing about adolescent literature as falling into three general types:

(1) Articles that stress reader response. Ever since the emergence of the first junior novel, books for adolescents have been discussed in context with observations about teen-agers themselves--their interests, tastes and needs. This is natural and proper. Reading surveys, lists of popular titles, and reviews of new books in the light of student concerns are all extremely useful. There will continue to be a need for articles like M. Jerry Weiss' "The Adolescent in Literature--Feeling It!" (*Arizona English Bulletin*, April 1972) which calls attention to new books which evoke an emotional response or Geraldine LaRoques's "A Bright and Promising Future for Adolescent Literature" (*Arizona English Bulletin*, April 1972) which ties in recent novels with current topics of interest. Since most articles of this kind are primarily concerned with affective responses, the approach tends to be descriptive and prescriptive rather than critical.

---

*Reprinted by permission of the author and publisher from the *Arizona English Bulletin* (April 1976), 216-219.

(2) Articles that are functional. Much current writing about adolescent literature is focused on the practical. Special issues of periodicals like English Journal and Arizona English Bulletin offer a wealth of ideas for integrating junior novels into the activities of the classroom. Accounts of successful teaching units, descriptions of outside reading programs, and specialized lists of books arranged by subject and theme are a godsend to teachers too busy to be able to keep up with the floods of new materials. Although many of the longer articles of this kind include brief commentary about the literary qualities of the novels, here again the writer's primary intention is obviously to be informative rather than analytical.

(3) Articles that center on the books themselves. One of the most striking generalizations that can be made about recent articles devoted primarily to the books for their own sake is that not many writers concentrate upon a single work and deal with it exclusively in terms of a literary exegesis. Most tend to generalize about the field or discuss several junior novels within the same essay. Although few of these articles represent a purely critical point of view, they do illustrate types of approaches which offer possibilities and methodology for more in-depth criticism. Let me identify six kinds of central concerns expressed in articles in this category and comment briefly upon the literary or quasi-literary approach taken.

CONCERNS IN ARTICLES ABOUT THE BOOKS AS LITERATURE

1. Adolescent Literature as a Genre

Since the fifties, much of the writing about adolescent literature has been a kind of apologia, usually accompanied by attempts to define the junior novel as a form. The most interesting recent articles about teen-age books as a genre have come from the authors themselves. For instance, Isabelle Holland in "The Walls of Childhood" (Horn Book, April 1974) speaks of the confusing and misleading distinctions commonly made between adult and juvenile books, referring as a case in point to her own novel Cecily, which was written for adults but reviewed by Young Adult reviewers. Sylvia Engdahl, a noted writer of science fiction, also sees teen-age fiction as being in a kind of limbo, a state which makes the going hard for authors and critics like ("Do Teenage Novels Fill a Need?" English Journal, February 1975). The Horn Book is probably the best source for finding such author commentary. It is important to heed the opinions of the practitioners in the field since their ideas frequently give insight into the special problems of finding a technique and style appropriate for teen-age audiences.

Since discussions of adolescent literature as a genre usually concentrate upon formal distinctions, articles of this kind are useful in providing a sound basis for criticism. There can certainly be no question of the academic respectability of genre criticism since this approach goes back to Aristotle, who, in differentiating between such forms as the lyric and the epic or comedy and tragedy, established a lasting school of critical methodology.

2. Patterns in Junior Novels

There have been a few recent articles in which groups of junior books have been examined in a search for recurrent elements. An informative example of this kind of approach can be seen in Barbara Martinec's "Popular-But Not Just a Part of the Crowd: Implications of Formula Fiction for Teenagers" (English Journal, March 1971). Through a survey of the works of six novelists, she was able to identify a formulaic pattern underlying the plots and character schemes of selected popular books.

Such documentation of valid generalizations about sub-categories is a valuable first step in arriving at an understanding of characteristic narrative structures in junior novels.

3. Themes and Underlying Issues

Approaching a work of literature through an examination of themes is part of a long tradition. Sociological criticism, for instance, has flourished since the nineteenth century when critics came to see literature as a vehicle which portrays information about society and has, therefore, the potential for effecting social change. Examples of discussions of junior novels within a thematic framework can be seen in Gayle Nelson's "The Double Standard in Adolescent Novels" (English Journal, February 1975) and Jean McClure Kelty's "The Cult of the Kill in Adolescent Literature" (English Journal, February 1975). Both articles deal with the social realities as broken homes, delinquency, and racial discrimination are dealt with frequently and frankly in much recent literature. There is a need for more criticism that treats these issues within a literary context.

4. Sources and Influence

The study of literary history has traditionally been as central an academic pursuit as literary criticism, and, indeed, historical scholarship provides an invaluable context for informed analysis and interpretation of individual works. The tracing of subliterary of "pop" currents which influence the mainstream has gained prestige of late and is especially useful for a study of fiction for children and young adults. Alan S. Dikty's "Thrills and Adventures for Only Fifty Cents" (Arizona English Bulletin, April 1972) is a welcome example of this kind of scholarship. By dealing with relatively inaccessible information about the reading fare of yesterday's juveniles, this kind of article can make a genuine contribution toward providing a lineage for much adolescent literature. More studies of the little-known best sellers of the past would fill gaps in our knowledge of sources and analogues for today's books.

5. Relationship Between Author and Work

There is unquestioned value in analyzing a work in the light of an author's total output. This is an especially sound approach for students of adolescent literature. By its very nature, the average junior novel is too slight of substance to necessitate, or even be able to support, much probing analysis or interpretation. After all, authors writing for an audience of young readers intentionally avoid complexity--either in content or technique. However, the study of several novels by the same writer can bring an awareness of elements of style indiscernible in a single work seen in isolation. Examples of attempts at this kind of criticism can be found in the Spring 1972 Arizona English Bulletin, which includes articles about such writers as Nat Hentoff, Mary Stolz and Jeannette Eyerly. This kind of approach can also be fruitfully aligned with the biographical.

6. The Individual Book

A very encouraging sign for those anxious for a more critical approach to adolescent literature is the fact that articles are finally beginning to appear that give exclusive and full attention to a single junior novel. Loretta Clarke's "His Enemy, His Friend: A Novel of Global Conscience" (English Journal, May 1973) and "The Pigman: A Novel of Adolescence" (English Journal, November 1972) can serve as examples of a largely "new critical" approach. It is unfortunate that there are so few writers who give detailed consideration to such matters as character interaction, voice, and the relationship of structure to meaning.

The above description of six currently used approaches to adolescent literature is meant to be suggestive. Although the bulk of the articles now appearing in journals cannot be considered "pure criticism,"--the majority are casual and relatively thin--they do represent the beginnings of a treatment of teen-age fiction from a literary perspective.

There are, of course, other valuable critical approaches that are not represented. For instance, a concern for archetypes should also inform future criticism of adolescent literature. Although there are many varieties of archetypal critics, they all concern themselves with the inherent forms that recur or are reflected in literature of universal appeal. Central to this school of criticism are the works of C. G. Jung, Swiss pioneer in depth psychology, Northrop Frye, whose theory combines genre criticism with archetypal criticism, and Joseph Campbell, who, in his well known mythic studies, has applied and popularized many of Jung's ideas.

Since adolescents frequently face psychological stresses related to their own maturation, they should be provided with books that offer "another way of knowing." Only specialists knowledgeable about the close relationship of the psyche, universal patterns of ritual, and creative expression are capable of writing the kind of criticism that can be useful in answering this particular need.

Probably the critical approach which would be most useful now is that identified with such New Critics as Cleanth Brooks and Allen Tate, who emphasize the importance of a close analysis of a literary work without recourse to anything outside the book itself--i.e. to biographical, historical or sociological information. Even the best of present studies of junior novels tend to concentrate upon only the most obvious elements of style. There is a real need for serious treatment of adolescent fiction similar to that given established works. Paul Heins, who edits the Horn Book, has stated:

> ... A child's book deserves to be probed as much as an adult book for general questions of diction, structure, significance of detail, literary integrity. Not for the purpose of what is often called "dry" analysis, but for the joy of discovering the skill of the author.

Although teen-age fiction cannot boast of such masterpieces as Alice's Adventures in Wonderland or Wind in the Willows, it is possible to point to a marked improvement in the quality and stature of recent books. There are certainly enough works of quality to deserve a thorough-going study. The junior novel merits more than the once-over-lightly kind of treatment it has received to date.

I am not suggesting that all articles about adolescent literature should be literary or critical in orientation. Books for young people should continue to be discussed in terms of their educational, moral, therapeutic, and entertainment values. There is a continuing need for non-critical approaches which describe and prescribe. But the fact that high school students cannot discern beyond the plot-character-theme kind of analysis should not preclude mature criticism. Certainly contemporary authors suffer when their artistic efforts do not attract the right kind of critical attention. When their books are described exclusively in functional and affective terms, they are cheated of the lively and informed intellectual climate required for a nurturing of their talents.

Specialists teaching and studying in the area owe it to themselves and their profession to encourage more responsible efforts toward the building of a corpus of serious literary criticism. Lillian Smith said, as long ago as 1933, that "children's books do not exist in a vacuum, unrelated to literature as a whole. They are a portion of universal literature and must be subjected to the same standards of criticism as any other form of literature." All kinds of experts are needed to do justice to the worthwhile books currently appearing for teen-agers. It is time that those whose expertise is literary contribute their share by writing about adolescent literature.

PART II

SOME HISTORICAL PERSPECTIVES

(that was then ...)

EDITOR'S NOTE

Those who care about kids and about books and want to bring them together sometimes wallow in the muds of sententiousness and selfrighteousness. I know of no better antidote than Ken Donelson's occasional time-machine trips, of which "What of the Teaching of Literature in School? ..." is a fine example.

The rest of the articles in this section are also useful reminders of the fallibility of adults who presume to guide the reading of the young. Hutchinson's survey is especially useful as an overview of the development of the field, and also defines the major issues as they emerge. Many are still with us--questions of selection criteria, the worth of the junior novel, censorship.

FIFTY YEARS OF YOUNG ADULT READING, 1921-1971*

By Margaret Hutchinson

The purpose of this paper is to survey the field of young adult reading for the last fifty years by examining articles indexed in Library Literature from its inception in 1921 to the present. The articles selected were under the headings Young People's Reading, Youth's Literature, Youth's Reading, Young Adult's Reading, or Young Adult Literature. Material on the techniques of working with young people, devices for motivating reading, how to give book talks, and so on, have purposely been omitted.

In an article published in 1968, Katherine P. Jeffery,[1] a young adult librarian, precedes a survey of book selection policies with a little history. According to Jeffery, "The earliest systematized attempts at specialized service to adolescents were directed to the out-of-school youth, in particular, to those fourteen-to-sixteen-year-olds who left school for economic reasons and went to work in factories, stores and offices.... The book selection for these young people of forty to forty-five years ago emphasized further education, vocational training, the classics as part of an educated person's reading, how-to-do-it books, and popular fiction."

Most of the articles of that period, however, are concerned, not with the out-of-school youth, but those young people who were increasingly remaining in school through high school.[2] Teachers faced with an expanding and increasingly diverse clientele were forced to abandon the notion that every young person should read the same books. But with the era of individualized reading, the need for reading guidance became apparent. In an early article on this subject, Hannah Logasa,[3] then librarian of the University High School, Chicago, concluded that, "The aim of reading guidance should be to inspire pupils with an intellectual interest so strong that it is a driving force. Technique for this type of guidance is yet in its infancy." She listed the psychological and social considerations that enter into the reading guidance of high school pupils. In 1927, Martha Pritchard[4] classified readers into five types, and made suggestions for dealing with each type. Her typology is not without interest nearly half a century later:

---

*Reprinted by permission of the author and publisher from Top of the News (November 1973), 24-53.

Type A. The young person who absorbs everything available in print.

Type B. Boy or girl who reads only fiction.

Type C. The youth who spurns reading as a "high brow" occupation which his manly mind (or her womanly activities) has no time for unless the reading is a school assignment, hated and done as slightingly as possible.

Type D. The practical minded person who reads for information or study but lacks appreciation of the imaginative in literature.

Type E. The type wanting magazines, short stories or newspapers. Lacking sustained interest in a whole book.

The interest in classifying readers into groups, in order to be able to help them select books they will like, extended to groups that would nowadays be called "exceptional children." Margaret Drew Archibald[5] described attempts to make readers of girls with low IQs, many of them poor. This is an unusual work for the time, because it simply describes the girls and their tastes as they are. Perhaps the author knew there was no hope of ever leading these girls to the classics. But this seems to have been the secret hope of most who wrote about reading guidance in the 1920s, and there was a good deal of discussion about developing "taste." Mary S. Wilkerson,[6] a children's librarian, for example, decried the low level of taste among older boys and girls:

> It seems unfortunately to be true that much of the fiction read by older boys and girls belongs to this group of unsuitable or mediocre books. The reason for it is twofold: first, their taste is not sufficiently trained to discriminate between the good and the cheap; and second their craving for "lots of excitement" leads them chiefly to second-rate authors whose breathless activity satisfies even the restless adolescent. The western and the mystery story are for this reason the prime favorites.

Such books, the author argued, stunt mental growth, and misrepresent life. But the young people, then as now, seem to have been sturdily resistant to the suggestions of their elders.[7]

Secondary enrollments rose from 4,800,000 in 1929-1930 to 7,100,000 in 1939-1940,[8] and the experiment with "extensive reading" continued. Adherents of the classics did not yield to the new methods without a struggle, however, for the literature of the period includes a number of bitter attacks upon those who taught them.

> ... books that are apparently discovered for oneself, not stiffened and chilled by having been long set aside in the educational refrigerator for required consumption, possess almost always a lure of individual adventure for the young mind that makes

> their influence deeper and more lasting and gives a richer savor to their quality. Required formalized reading of the classics has forever deprived much great and beautiful literature of the influence it should have had in the later intellectual life of intelligent men and women.[9]

> I was and am convinced that the demise of those classics, so far as the average boy or girl en route to college was concerned, is traceable directly to the college entrance examination boards.[10]

> Well-meaning English teachers once dissected them for us, poked around for the intangible in them, tried to unscrew the inscrutable for us, and fixed us, for the most part, so we shall never open those books again.[11]

> Schools have so often been stupid in this respect. In what is often well-meaning zeal to educate taste--the admirable and real goal--they press too hard. Instead of tactfully shaping their students' taste by a gradual process, they too often force certain established books and accepted standards upon them. What very often results is that students become trained seals doing tricks nicely.[12]

As a minority report, there is an amusing piece in the New Statesman and Nation of January 1, 1938, which defends the classics, and suggests, tongue-in-cheek, that the popular modern literature be made unpopular by using the same methods that had previously caused the young to be bored with the classics: "Give the children lumps of it [The Scarlet Pimpernel] to translate into French and make them write out their favourite passage fifty times as an imposition."[13]

Nevertheless, the suspicion of "extensive reading," and of the library, must have remained quite strong, for in 1932 we find Azile Wofford[14] saying that "so far as we can determine there is no direct connection between the use of the library and school failures."

While some workers were busy discussing what young people should choose to read, others were busy finding out what they actually did choose. These studies took three forms. The first grew out of the study of adolescent psychology and individual differences. W. T. B. Mitchell,[15] a medical doctor and student of mental hygiene at McGill University, for example, suggested that "Many adolescents read voraciously. There is a tremendous urge in the face of this new-found concept of self to broaden their experiences through reading," and Helen L. Bell,[16] after psychological study, suggested adolescents be given "(1) stories of adventure, (2) biographies of persons of significant achievements; (3) plays; (4) poems; (5) books of science, nature, hobbies, sports; (6) certain books labeled classics whose appeal is universal."

A second approach was more direct: some librarians and editors began to make surveys among the young people. In 1931 May Lamberton Becker,[17] who had been associated with the *Saturday Review of Literature*, *St. Nicholas*, and *The Scholastic*, summarized the contents of 774 letters from young people telling about their favorite books. "From these letters I found, of course, that romance and adventure topped the list. It is impossible to separate these two terms because so many of their favorite romances are also adventures and so many of their adventure stories were romantic." *Lorna Doone*, *Ramona*, and *Ben Hur* were favorites. Becker also noted: "There is an extraordinary continuance in popularity of such tepid, sentimental, and old-fashioned romances as *Janice Meredith*, *When Knighthood Was in Flower*, and *Little Shepherd of Kingdom Come*. Their popularity is much greater in the smaller, outlying districts, and the reasons for this probably are that the libraries are not so good as in the cities--." The young people wanted lots of action in their books, and they disliked introspective discussion. Another demand of the age group was for "stories about its own particular kind of life--stories about the young people of today, family stories, and school stories. There are very few good ones, because a *good* book for boys and girls must be written because the writer *can't* help writing it."

Not all librarians who made surveys had as large a sample as Becker, nor as much insight into the results. P. G. Chancellor,[18] librarian at a preparatory school, noted a high proportion of modern publications among the books the boys polled enjoyed. Their favorite authors (1938) were Kenneth Roberts, Nordhoff and Hall, Sinclair Lewis, Edgar Allan Poe, Somerset Maugham, Rafael Sabatini, R. L. Stevenson, Conrad, Steinbeck, O. Henry, and Charles Dickens. L. Toomey,[19] of the St. Louis Public Library, analyzing book reports, noted a dislike for slow-moving books and long descriptions. Louise E. Hill,[20] surveying a group of 1,500 junior high school students in California, found a tendency to read author series. "As was expected, the greater part of the books named were fiction. Animal stories, of course, took top honors, with mysteries a close second...." Howard Pease was the favorite author, and *Silver Chief* the favorite book.

Yet a third approach to understanding what young people like to read was made by experienced librarians contemplating their own libraries. Irene Smith,[21] describing a library in a predominantly Jewish slum, commented, "They want books that seem to the librarian years in advance of their age [*Of Human Bondage*, *Lady Chatterly's Lover*]--We have a sophisticated public. These boys and girls have grown up under post-war conditions, nurtured by the tabloid and the movie. They ask in perfectly casual manner for all the modern fiction that public libraries usually restrict or charge to gray-haired patrons with misgivings." Ethelwyn Wickson,[22] of the Toronto Public Library, noted, "When I look at our intermediate fiction shelves I feel that we have too much 'petty stuff'--What we need are more books that are realistic, grim even, and yet not cynical--books which will give the average boy or girl the satisfaction of that contact with actual living which they seem to want most of all."

It was apparent by the mid-thirties that the selection of reading material for young adults was a key factor in what was coming to be known as the "reading problem." As one student put it, someone had to "pick out the ones [books] I picked out for myself."[23] Jean C. Roos,[24] of the Cleveland Public Library, pointed out that the responsibilities of those who select books for adolescents are particularly heavy, because the "standards, tastes, and judgments" of the young people are in process of change, and because they accept books as true pictures of life. She suggested that the most important problem was to select books with values, "values in the creation of real characters set in the midst of real issues." Mabel Williams,[25] of the New York Public Library, thought certain adult books should be added to the young adult collection: "some so-called mediocre adult books because they have the simplicity of style, language and plot that these boys and girls still require." These, she felt, could be used to bridge the gap between children's and adult's fiction. Alice Cowles Morris,[26] a high school librarian, suggested that the library must provide the kind of book which will prove popular, but, because of the high school obligation to improve taste, only the best of each type.

But, given access to well-selected books, would young people read? Librarians were apparently not sure that they would, for the decade of the thirties witnessed a proliferation of devices for motivating reading and advertising books that it is not within the scope of this paper to discuss. These devices went under the name of reading guidance, but the only real advance in the technique of advising young people about their reading, which Hannah Logasa and others had begun to explore so hopefully in the previous decade, came with the invention of "reading ladders." Ruby Ethel Cundiff,[27] of the library school at Peabody College, strongly recommended using such lists: "These are not just subject lists, but lists of books which try to meet the interest which makes the reader like the original book. Following that interest, the next book broadens it...."

In spite of everything, many young people were reclutant to read, and in the 1930s there developed a gradually increasing awareness of the reasons for this reluctance. Margaret Scoggin,[28] of the New York Public Library, suggested in 1936 that "By reluctant we too often mean reluctant to read what we think they should read." She thought young people might be discouraged by required reading, defeated by the adult collection, limited in reading ability, or put off by library regulations. Homer P. Rainey[29] pointed out that many young people had never mastered the mechanics of reading.

One author spoke of the value of books with no reading matter but a few captions.[30] But it was Amelia Munson[31] of the New York Public Library who, in 1939, tabulated all the types of nonreaders.

- There are a few for whom the mechanics of reading set up almost insurmountable obstacles.
- Then there is the original thinker who distrusts books.
- One reason why some folks won't read is that they have not learned to find their way among books. Put beside them another group that, far from not having been trained to read, has been overtrained. Not only have ways been studied out and cleared for them through the jungle of reading, but jungles have been made to grow where none existed, solely for the discipline and mastery attained in hacking one's way out. I refer, of course, to the old-time presentation of literature in the schools.
- Non-readers who want entertainment from books.
- The manual-minded.
- A small group who deliberately turn their backs upon reading as unessential in their scheme of things--They have tried it and found it wanting.

Munson offered hope for each group but the last. These find their aesthetic satisfactions elsewhere than in books, and Munson was content that they should do so. Meanwhile, Dora V. Smith[32] was asking that librarians "see the reading program whole," with its facets of reading skill, reading guidance, appreciation and taste, recreational reading, individualization, and sharing books.

At the same time, in the late 1930s, a reevaluation of the reasons for reading was taking place. If a knowledge of certain classics was no longer to be considered the mark of an educated man, why read at all? The idea began to evolve that the reason for reading was to broaden the reader's horizons. As the author, Rachel Field,[33] who abhorred book lists put it, "No life is long enough, or full enough, to hold all that we could wish of experience or accomplishment, and so since we were all born with a hunger for experience we must reach out to supplement our own through the experience and thought of others. There is not time enough for all we would see and hear and know." Reading should not be over-classified and over-regulated; young people should read about everything--even love.[34] The hope was that teenagers would be so enthusiastic about books that widened their experience of life, that this type of fiction would seem "as valid and imminent as any other reality,"[35] and that the taste for hair-raising adventure stories and love stories far from the truth would disappear.[36] Walter Prichard Eaton,[37] professor of drama at Yale University, urged the need for realistic fiction with familiar settings: "Their budding imaginations must be exercised on problems of their own lives, on the problems which they see in the lives around them.... As the power to recognize familiar problems and experiences in the stories of life close at hand develops, this same power of the imagination will broaden and deepen so that the boy will find in the really great stories of other days and other times those common elements that belong to human nature and human relationships and that make every story of the sort we call 'classic' essentially modern...."

It is evident from what was being written in the 1930s about young people and their reading, that a number of able people were concerned with the matter and that a great deal of intelligent speculation was taking place. Mitchell's idea of the self-concept as a motivating factor in reading; Becker's insight that young people need stories about themselves, and the reason why there were so few good ones; Smith's observation of the maturity of the reading done by the teenagers; Wickson's feeling that there was too much "pretty stuff" on her library shelves; the realization of the importance of selection of books with values; the glimmering that reading is not for everyone; the reexamination of the "why?" of reading: all have a modern ring. It is possible to add other examples. In 1934 Douglas Waples[38] lamented the lack of basic research. In 1935 Dorothy Hopkins[39] began to explore the social significance of reading. In 1936 Cam[40] spoke of providing library services in a neighborhood where "There are few scholars. Life is certainly not cloistered. It is lived principally on the street." In 1937 Constance Rourke[41] noted that the barriers between reading for adults and reading for children were breaking down. And by 1939 Waples[42] was suggesting that the development of a discerning taste might be only for a lonely few. It must have been a lively and interesting time to be involved with young adult literature. One gets the feeling that anything might happen.

The War and Post-War Years

What happened was the second world war. Energies which might have been devoted to a new literature for the young adult were expended elsewhere, and things went on much the same as before. "Extensive reading" was a success, at least according to some writers:

> The general conclusions drawn from such investigations shows that under such programs, if properly guided, young people grow in their power of discrimination in choice of books and develop familiarity with various forms of literature.[43]

And the same author states: "Strange as it may seem, some young people today are reading the 'classics' even when not required to do so." The crux of the matter remained individual guidance, and a few articles continued to appear discussing problems and techniques in this area.[44]

There was some interest in the effect of the war upon young people's reading. A survey by Ethel L. Cornell[45] in 1941 (before Pearl Harbor) contains little new except that, of the fiction titles read, 55 percent were from the adult lists, and that adult fiction was the most popular reading category, followed by biography, young adult fiction, and drama, in that order. By 1943 Marie Nelson Taylor,[46] a public librarian, was saying that young people could not be sheltered from "the realities of the present conflict" and was publishing a list of war-related books. Margaret C. Scoggin[47] claimed in the same year that the reading interests of young people had not been materially changed by the war:

> Inevitably the war has had its effect upon young people's reading. Since their courses, vocational guidance and training in jobs are all geared to "total conflict," some of their reading reflects wartime uses and needs. The comforting fact is that, despite social wartime applications, the reading interests of young people show amazing continuity.

Technical books and aviation books were, of course, popular, but then they always had been.

> Of wide general interest to all boys and many girls are the accounts of the men in the thick of the fighting. Here are hero tales; interest in them is as old as the history of mankind.

War had influenced the girls' reading more subtly:

> One gets the conviction that girls feel much less at ease in the world than boys, and are concerned mainly with carrying on until the war is over and the men come back.

But the basic lines of reading remained unchanged, and this, Scoggin felt, was a hopeful sign.

Other writers disagreed, and felt that the war had caused a change in reading patterns. For one thing, the amount of reading done had declined sharply while young people were reading war books, often "beyond their grade level."[48] Journalist accounts and novels were the most popular types:[49]

> The adventure story, once western in flavor, is now military. The vocational account must deal with WAACS and WAVES, servicemen and spies.[50]

By the end of the war in 1945, Kathryn A. Haebich,[51] a librarian and girls' counsellor, found teen-agers "somewhat bewildered by the world situation and what it is doing to their normal dream of home and family life." They wanted books "which help them achieve their major tasks of adolescent development. They want to learn to get along with age-mates of both sexes, to achieve independence of adults, to accept social responsibility, and to develop a philosophy of life adapted to the world in which they live." Girls wanted love stories. Boys wanted books about adventure, sports, the sea, and war, "probably because the primary aim of every teen-age boy is to achieve mastery of body and adopt a masculine sex role."

This emphasis upon "developmental tasks" was not a new idea; it was a part of the discipline of psychology as it had evolved up to that time. In 1943 Gladys B. Johnson[52] had published a booklist for each of the five developmental tasks of adolescence as defined by the psychologist, Havighurst: adjustment to age mates (Huckleberry Finn), independence of family (Forsyte Saga), occupational orientation (Microbe Hunters), social participation (Barren Ground), and development of the self (Of Human Bondage). In the same year, Lucile Vickers,[53] a high school librarian, had published a list of nonfiction books on "problems of living." Books were also thought of as tools for teaching tolerance,[54] and good citizenship.[55] As early as 1940 Willard A. Heaps[56] was claiming that "books do aid in adjustment," although he admitted that "many adolescents resent any intrusion upon their privacy. If they feel that a book is being chosen in order to make a contribution to their welfare, they are bitterly indignant.... The individual appeal must be more subtle and ingenious."

Clearly, by the end of the second world war many people were thinking of books as a means to an end (adjustment), not as an introduction to the adult world, given to youth made intellectually and emotionally mature by the world crisis and by exposure to the media of radio, newspaper, and motion pictures.[57]

> The years of World War II marked a change in the status of the thirteen-to-nineteen-year-old person, both within the family and within the community. Because his labor was needed as older men and women went off to war and his financial status made him one of a commercially exploitable group, he had, as never before, money to spend on himself--money not needed, as during the depression years, for general family support. Intellectually, his increasing participation in affairs outside the home made him ripe for the development of the whole teen-age sub culture. Indications of this change appeared in the number of separate departments for teens, young adults, young people, and young moderns which developed in public libraries in the mid-forties and early fifties.... This is the period that marked the rise of the teen-age or junior novel, with its emphasis on middle-class life, on the high school student, on popularity, on boy-girl relationships, on high school sports, and of the career story which was more story than career.[58]

It is obvious that the genre that came to be known as the teen-age novel met the needs of the time. Not only did the adolescent subculture develop following the second world war, but it was a time of affluence, and money was available for such luxury items as books for young people of a narrow age range. Authors and publishers obliged with a spate of books designed to please the young people: short, entertaining, easy to read, and about themselves.[59] At the same time, they were designed to please parents and teachers by dealing with teenage problems--always successfully resolved --and thus hopefully giving the young people assistance with "life adjustment." It is neither surprising that books of this type developed nor surprising that there were few good ones, for most people seemed to have forgotten what May Lamberton Becker[60] had said in 1931: "a good book for boys and girls must be written because the writer can't help writing it."

Criticism was a long time coming. It was not until 1955 that Richard S. Alm,[61] a professor of English and education, analyzed the group of junior novels. Many of them he called "sugar puff" stories, lacking in insight and writing ability. "Their stories," he said, "are superficial, often distorted, sometimes completely false representations of adolescence." He also castigated them for stock characters, too-easy solutions to problems, model heroes, saccharin sentiment, oversimplification, single motivation, the notion that nothing is impossible, the attainment of maturity without development, and inconsistencies in characterization. In spite of this list of sins, Alm did find some "better" junior novels, including the extremely popular Seventeenth Summer (Daly), and others by Cavanna, Felsen, and Stolz. Four he categorized as "outstanding": The Yearling (Rawlings), Johnny Tremain (Forbes), Goodbye My Lady (Street), and Swiftwater (Annixter). Whatever their defects, it was recognized that these books were useful, for by "directing their novels dead-center to adolescent interests and concerns, these writers encourage younger adolescents to read."[62] Furthermore, they were popular (and profitable).[63] They were not seriously attacked until the 1960s.[64]

Young adults of the period were not confined in their reading to the junior novel. A publisher of the time presented evidence that "the high school librarian thinks, buys, and recommends primarily in terms of junior books, while the attention of the young people's librarian in the public library is two-thirds devoted to adult books."[65] The selection of adult books for young adults had become a matter of concern as early as 1948.[66] On May 15, 1948, Booklist published a "retrospective list of recent adult books for the more mature young people of high school age," because there was a "general demand" for such books.[67] While some books were excluded from this list because their "appeal was judged to be outside the range of even the most mature young person's interest," books were not excluded because of a certain frankness that might be offensive to some. The Booklist committee recommended "re-examination of standards in relation to the adult books for use with young people," and put forward their own:

> Our questions were: Will it appeal to young people? Will it increase their insight into human motives and behavior, or does it distort and confuse?

These committee members were obviously aware of the problems of selection which were to come to a head a year or so later with the publication of J. D. Salinger's Catcher in the Rye. The history of this controversial book was summarized by Katherine Jeffery[68] in 1968:

> first adopted by the then current crop of college students, then by their younger brothers and sisters, [it] is perhaps the archtypical problem book in the setting of standards of book selection for the young adult. Creating controversy by its use of vulgar language and its depiction of a young person in need of psychiatric help, it had violent partisans among young adult librarians and teachers, as well as equally violent vocal opponents. Meanwhile young people read the book and accepted or rejected it as it answered their needs. It finally arrived on the road to neglect by being accepted for class study. In retrospect and in the light of present day permissiveness the book seems a small coal to have generated so much heat.

Perhaps the furor over the Catcher in the Rye acted as a warning. In any case, it seems that, with a few courageous exceptions such as Margaret Scoggin, who in 1952 was pleading with young adult librarians to accept the responsibility for "knowing and discussing with young people themselves everything that they read,"[69] most young adult librarians preferred to be conservative in what they chose from the adult lists for the teenagers to read.[70]

The years following the second world war also produced an astonishing number of surveys of young people's reading.[71] They tend to be repetitive, and may be briefly summarized: Although the amount of reading done tended to decline in high school, about two out of three young people queried were reading some sort of book outside of school assignments. The percentage of young people who really liked reading apparently remained fairly constant. There was a wide range of reading ability. Most young people read a mixture of teen-age novels and adult works. They showed a preference for recent works and best sellers. Several studies noted the influence of movies and other media on book choices. Sex was an important factor in reading interests. Boys preferred novels of adventure, girls those of romance. Some claimed to notice "trends" towards sports (both fiction and nonfiction), biography, science and science fiction, vocationally oriented works, and personality development. There were "shortages" in some areas, for example, hunting and psychology. One author noted that "cowboys only create a stir when their horses sell them to the readers" (Vroman). Another noted that attempts to keep certain books from the young usually failed: "No use not adding or banning Gentleman's Agreement, Deep Are the Roots, Citizen Tom Paine. They will read them; you can be sure of that" (De Angelo).

In addition to the surveys, there were a few commentaries on the reading of young adults. Lloyd W. Babb,[72] a high school librarian, expressed dissatisfaction with the criteria which average high school students used in choosing books for leisure reading, and attempted to classify their reasons for reading. Virginia Tozier[73] commented upon the effect of the peer group: "The majority of pupils in a secondary school are enslaved by the collective opinion of the group which powerfully affects all personal activities including voluntary reading." In 1955 Publisher's Weekly offered a pair of articles on the reading motivations of young people. Lewis Perry,[74] speaking of boys, stressed their desire for independent selection, which was, however, balanced by a fear of being "different." Esther Millett,[75] speaking of girls, stressed their reliance upon fashion, even in reading, along with their tendency to be in a hurry and to be lazy. This made the need for easy access to books with "a minimum of irrelevant description, honesty of purpose, simplicity and clarity of style and construction" a necessity. Ruth Hill Viguers[76] also spoke about reading motivation, suggesting that young adults read in part because they are afraid: "they want to learn how to talk and act acceptably today by the practice they have while identifying themselves with the characters in their stories."

Moving into the Sixties: Content, Quality, Values

In contrast to these other writers, whose chief concern seems to have been with groups of readers, G. Robert Carlsen[77] wrote about individuals:

> Each person must discover that reading is an absorbing and fascinating activity. For most individuals this discovery comes late in childhood or early adolescence. It comes when the individual has developed enough competence in reading skills so that these do not interfere with his interaction with the reading material. It usually comes when the individual has gained some maturity in his own living so that his interests have some stability. He finds a focal point for reading that meets a need he has.

This focal point may be the works of an author; a type of book (e.g., animal stories); a historical period; a geographical area; "a particular tonality or quality"; or a topic on which the young person seeks information. Carlsen suggested that librarians know the reading interests of young adults, for "Interests have remained fairly constant over the fifty-year period that they have been studied and they show singularly few geographical variations." But the real challenge was to find a good fit between a youngster and a book, and to build bridges between one reading interest and another. He was less concerned with the quality of reading than with keeping the young person interested in some book, although he conceded that "when a child is in the middle of an all-consuming reading interest, we do try to build ladders within it by suggesting to him books of increasing subtlety within the area."

Carlsen, a professor of English and education, continued his research into the reading of young adults. (He seems to have been the first to do any such sustained research.) By 1966 he was beginning to publish his findings: by studying the reading records of many young people, he had been able to discover patterns in their reading.[78] Briefly, between twelve and fourteen "amost inevitably the child finds that he likes a book of adventure in which an individual is cast adrift somewhere and makes his way back to security," or a mystery, "the kind of stories that involve mistaken identity, a lost will or stolen papers." The preferences of boys and girls differ, within this framework, in predictable ways. By fifteen or sixteen, girls like gothic romances and historical novels, boys like stories of physical courage and real-life adventure, while both like "stories of people like themselves, living lives not far different from their own." They may begin to read adult books. By seventeen, both sexes ask for books in which the reader can continue his search for personal values, books dealing with deprived or persecuted peoples or social injustice, "books that skirt the psychological fringes of the human soul," and, most appealing of all, books that show others maturing into early adult life. Dr. Carlsen summarized by saying:

> the adolescent reader is generally in the process of discovering the really unconscious delight that reading can offer him in terms of escape to a world of intensified action and emotion. He is often in search of a world that will assure him of his own importance and gratify his ego, a world in which the adolescent is idyllically free of adult supervision.... At about fourteen or fifteen a youngster finds the book a safe way of seeking out some of the answers to his own inner problems and fears. It will not invade his privacy as a counselor would. Finally, in late adolescence the reader begins to discover that literature has much to say about the basic dilemmas of mankind. The aesthetic delight in perfection of form and literary technique comes late in the reading scale.

Carlsen[79] suggested that many adolescents fail to develop in their reading because their teachers concern themselves with books of the right type or difficulty, rather than with books of the right content: "the evidence is reasonably good that they like or dislike a book or a poem or a biography or a play, pretty much on the basis of its subject matter. Surprisingly, the so-called difficult books are not difficult if the subject matter is appealing and books that are called easy books are not easy for the adolescent if the subject matter does not fall within these established boundaries." Nevertheless, he concluded that reading patterns could also be determined by types of books, from the juvenile series book, through the junior novel, to the popular adult book, to the modern classic, and, at college age, the great classic.[80]

It was time that someone put the classic in some kind of perspective, for the educational panic following the Russian launching of Sputnik in 1957, combined with the pressure of the war babies upon the colleges, had revived the debate about their place in education. This debate had not been a popular one since before the second world war, although a Canadian, M. Fraser,[81] had wondered as early as 1951 "if we are doing as much as we might for the very brightest." By 1959 Sister M. Camillus,[82] a college librarian, was classifying readers into three types: "going steady" readers, who read to find answers to their social problems; "Peyton Place" readers, who read to impress their peers with their sophistication; and "Moby Dick" readers, who read for layers of meaning. She added: "I think we, as librarians, must make every effort to lift our readers step by step through the 'going steady' reading, over the 'Peyton Place' reading and into the Moby Dick reading as pleasantly as possible." In the meantime the classic, or at least books that the whole class read together, had returned to the classroom, in the wake of the "New English" curriculum and the ready availability of the paperback.[83] In 1963 Florence Hascall[84] made a strong plea that young people be made to read the classics and be offered no special rewards for doing so: "Let us stop shielding, babying, coddling their unformed minds in the matter of books. Let us be realistic and expose them to as wide and great a collection of writers as we can."

Clearly, the spirit of the times in the early 1960s pushed young adult librarians into opening their shelves to a wide variety of authors, old and new, writing on a wide variety of subjects. As early as 1958 Ruth Hill Viguers[85] had pointed out that "teen age books are not enough. The young people who became creative readers in the children's room will not be satisfied with a steady diet of mediocre books; and the good books, the books that will open new vistas to them, should be available always." Even the high school libraries became less conservative. As one writer put it, "I believe that high school librarians must take the responsibility for having the best literature on the shelves, both classic and modern."[86] And Margaret Edwards,[87] of Baltimore's Enoch Pratt Library, pushed vigorously for books that would broaden adolescents' experience, both "the classics they can understand" and "the best of modern writing."

Books for the young adult were to be selected not only for literary excellence and maturity of content, but for the values they contained. In 1957, the year of Sputnik, one librarian was claiming: "I have tried to untangle their childish thinking by handing them the kind of books that will help them formulate a basic philosophy."[88] The theme is repeated by a number of authors in the next few years. Anne Emery[89] spoke of the need for values in books for the young adult, because youth is the time that standards and ethical convictions form. Madeline Irrig,[90] a college librarian, spoke of developing character through reading. Dorothy M. Broderick,[91] a professor of library science, offered a bibliography of works treating such questions as:

> To what extent do books for children and youth reflect the values and ideals of our society? To what extent do they reflect national and world changes? Most important,

> to what extent and in what ways are children using books to form their values and to meet the social, psychological, and even economic problems that they face? How do books meet children's needs?

And somewhat later, Margaret Edwards[92] expressed her opinion that "the present crisis in reference work with school assignments is acute and must be faced but we must do more than help the young barbarian pass his courses in school. The awakening of his mind, the enlargement of his spirit, the quickening of his understanding through books are still the greatest contribution the library can make to him and his city and his country."

The Sixties: Relevance, Realism, and Intellectual Freedom

There was bound to be controversy. In 1958 Marie Blanche MacDonald[93] published an article, "Shake Hands with Mrs. Grundy," in which she pointed out that adolescents live under many restrictions and that their reading should be restricted, too. She felt that, "The average adolescent will understand when we shall tell them that they are not quite ready for the stories of adult experiences presented in serious fiction and will be content to wait." Margaret Edwards[94] disagreed. In "Mrs. Grundy Go Home," published two months later, she expressed the opinion that young people will not be content to wait, but will find the books they want to read someplace. She quoted Clifton Fadiman: "if a young person cannot understand what he reads, it will not harm him, while if he can understand, he is ready to read of life situations truly presented. It is a disservice to the young, who mature at different rates, to recall them to 'peurile interests and simplified writing' when there is a desperate need for the young to expand their experience of the world."

These were the opening guns of a battle over censorship which raged in the first half of the 1960s. It centered largely on sex, rough language, and sometimes the religious or political content of a book.[95] Were these books damaging to youth? Could youth be denied access to them in a democracy?

There seems to have been pretty general agreement that the activity of any group which tries to impose private standards upon the general public is vicious, and that one cannot "deny certain books to adults because they might possibly be read by the young also."[96] The question of which books to select for the young was more problematical--and it came to be recognized that selection is a form of censorship.[97] As has been pointed out, standards of selection for the young were being revised at this time in the direction of admitting books that might formerly have been excluded, if their intent was not to corrupt,[98] and of judging a book as "a literary product, not a moral preachment."[99] The crux of the problem was whether youth should be permitted to read <u>anything</u>, or whether certain material should be denied on the grounds that it would be damaging at a period in the life of an adolescent when character and values were being formed.

Some writers favored completely free access, on the grounds that salacious books were readily available anyway, and that "Even sincere efforts at censorship raise uncomfortable questions: why do we want to censor? what areas of human experience have we closed to discussion? ... Who is to censor and on what grounds?"[100] The important thing was not access to books, but discussion of them with adults. As some of the advocates of free access pointed out, some of the "classics" should make the censors' hair stand on end.[101] This group won a victory when, in 1967, an ALA preconference on intellectual freedom and the teenager took the position that adolescents should have free access to adult literature.[102]

But not everyone was convinced. Max Rafferty,[103] then superintendent of public instruction for the California public schools, undertook to present "the other side." He asked for careful censorship of books the young read, in the sense of selection by teachers and librarians. Questionable modern books, such as the Catcher in the Rye, should be assigned only to those who had read the classics, and thus had a background for evaluating them properly. Some books should be banned altogether: "No one in a responsible position wants to barge in and start censoring books intended for adults only. But faced with the torrent of printed filth currently being poured into our society like sewage into a stream, if librarians or anyone else think the American public is going to sit passively while this kind of corruption is made available to children at the taxpayers' expense, they have another think coming." Books, Mr. Rafferty believed influence behavior: "Logic, it appears, would compel librarians to concede that, if bad books don't do any harm, then good books certainly don't do anybody any good."

Mr. Rafferty was an angry man, and his speech was in places lacking in good taste, as apparently were some other speeches at the time. His "Other Side" speech called forth a number of letters, both praising and attacking him,[104] but after that the controversy seems to have quieted. Perhaps both sides were too embarrassed to continue. It is also possible that it closed prematurely, for a number of interesting points had been raised in its course. The fact is that no one knows the effect of reading upon the young adult.[105] It had been suggested that youth did a good deal of censoring on their own,[106] and that they did not really understand the censorship issue.[107] It was even suggested the pertinent question was not intellectual freedom but the role of the emotions in reading and understanding.[108]

Meanwhile, the emphasis on challenging reading had brought teenage novels under attack,[109] not because they were badly written (for, as Frank Jennings pointed out, "Most current teen-age fiction, whatever its other many shortcomings, has a familiarity, an easy control over the mechanics, at least, of our language that was hard to come by a generation ago."[110]) but because they were written to a pattern. Speaking of girls' books, Vivian J. MacQuown[111] said:

> A teen-age romance is a book written to fairly rigid specifications for girls between the ages of twelve and eighteen. The heroine should be a person of the upper middle class and she must have a problem to solve. The problem must be solved in approximately 200 attractively bound pages, in reasonably good English, with virtue triumphant.
>
> One of the serious failings of writing to such a pattern is that the characters are cardboard and the plots contrived. Stereotyped characters and unconvincing plots may emerge as the result of unskilled writing but I suspect that, in the case of the teenage novel, they arise from the strict and narrow form.... In fact, I submit that it is almost impossible to write a true work of art under the ground rules of this genre.

Worse, these books were attacked as lacking thought-provoking content. Kenneth R. Shaffer,[112] of the school of library science at Simmons College, attacked not only the teen-age books but the whole movement which isolated the young adult in special rooms in the library, with a special literature advertised by all manner of devices. "In the end," he said, "we produced of course, a vacuum. Publishers eagerly and profitably obliged by commissioning ... a literature ... with a maximum intellectual impact of pablum.... The teen-age novel, Shaffer[113] claimed, gives a false picture of life, even of teen-age life. Furthermore, the genre was found on examination to be didactic. Arthur Daigon,[114] an editor, investigated the themes and values in books selected by sixty girls and sixty boys in junior high school, with a range of reading ability. He found that:

> In Freudian terms, these are "super-ego" novels. They work on the assumption that males are aggressive and potentially dangerous to society, while females are passive, tending to jeopardize their individuality. These novels are society's means of redressing the imbalances, of curbing excessive groupiness in girls, and excessive individualism and aggressiveness in boys.

Such attacks did not go unquestioned, although it is noticeable that the defense of the teenage novel took the form of mentioning its usefulness with "less sophisticated or less precocious young persons"[115] or with slow readers.[116] Publishers, in any case, were ready to respond with more realistic and more thought-provoking books. Dorothy Broderick called 1965 "a banner year for thought-provoking books, and those who would bury juvenile publishing had better take another look at the corpse."[117]

Before examining these newer junior novels, it might be well to take a look at the young readers of the 1960s. Some surveys of the period[118] seem to indicate that little had changed since the previous decade. Others show some change in reading interests toward books more mature and more oriented toward special problems. A report in 1960 lists Animal Farm, Crime and Punishment, and The Ugly American among the favorites.[119] Young adult librarians the following year reported that All Quiet on the Western Front, Diary of a Young Girl, The Night They Burned the Mountain, and To Kill a Mockingbird were popular in their libraries,[120] while young people were nominating War and Peace and Of Human Bondage as "good books."[121] In 1963 Esther Millett[122] reported a group of ninth and tenth graders who were slow readers being enthusiastic about such books as To Kill a Mockingbird, A Separate Peace, Hawaii, and The King Must Die. And so the story goes through 1965 (Black Like Me, 1984, Brave New World),[123] and 1966 (Lord of the Flies, Up the Down Staircase)[124] and 1967 (Jazz Country, North to Freedom).[125]

The young adult of the 1960s seemed to be primarily concerned with three areas:

> 1. The individual--his growth, personality, and philosophy....
>
> 2. ... social problems and social responsibility, whether it be the great national concern of Civil Rights or the problem of the mentally retarded, the alcoholic, or the juvenile delinquent.
>
> 3. He is concerned for the world he lives in on both the national and the international levels....[126]

These concerns were also noted by experienced librarians, authors and other lay people.

The concern with the self was noticed first: as early as 1952 Elizabeth Ritts Goebel[127] was saying that all teens are much alike in their awareness of themselves, their unsureness, their hero worship, their clannishness, and their feeling of invincibility. In 1954 Dora V. Smith[128] noted that adolescents ask for a sense of reality in their stories. Increasingly, writers spoke of young people being confused, left-out, frustrated, in conflict with society.[129] Some writers bemoaned the organization child, his lack of family life, and the deadening of his curiosity by "how to" education.[130] By 1965 Jane Manthorne,[131] a public librarian, noted that young people were interested in people but not in heroes. And they wanted to do something about their world. Something was apparently happening to young people. The population explosion, urbanization, changing values, and, perhaps most important, the influence of the media, especially television, were changing them.[132] While the general development and major problems of adolescents had not changed drastically with the years,[133] their environment had made them a new breed.[134]

What this new breed was looking for in books was, according to various observers, first, people: "Unable to find them in our civilization of machines and statistics, they turn to books. For in the end books are but the voices of people...."[135] Second, they wanted the voices of these people to be honest, to give them a clear picture of the real world with all its shadings of good and evil.[136] As Kenneth Shaffer[137] put it in 1965, "The image of adolescence as happy-go-lucky, baton-twirling, automobile-driving, money-in-the-pocket, twisting, coke-drinking, boy-and-girl-hand-in-hand Elysium" had begun to look pretty thin. Third, they were looking for books about their real problems in the present-day world, books "reflecting the cool and cruel climb for status, the risks of daredevil dragging, the bewilderment of the young facing the mixed-up adult world, and youthful violence, presented without sensationalism."[138] They were looking for relevance.

The search by the young for books of relevance took them to school and public libraries and to paperback bookstores. Young adults were demanding the right to read anything, so that there came to be "no such thing as a young adult book."[139] At the same time, publishers were attempting to meet the demand in new books which they designated as for young adults in their lists.

Among the earliest were books about Negroes, a publishing venture which had grown to prominence with the Civil Rights movement combined with the availability of federal funds to buy books for schools in disadvantaged areas. It was hoped that, if young Negroes could find a picture of themselves and of their way of life in books, it would help them to overcome their reading difficulties and bolster their self-image. The fact that many of these children did have reading problems had been recognized for many years,[140] but special reading materials for them did not exist in any quantity.[141] There was a gradual increase in the number of biographies, poetry books, and books of fiction between 1941 and 1959, and at the same time stereotyping diminished gradually.[142] Then, in the 1960s, came an outpouring of books, many of them second-rate.[143] Such books presented certain difficulties in addition to the normal problems of authorship. In 1965 Gloria Johnson,[144] a school librarian, made a plea for editing that "encourages the presentation of well-rounded characters, not 'angels' or caricatures; ... encourages the use of regional vernacular where suitable, not overdrawn and inconsistent dialect, and ... discourages the use of derogatory names and epithets except when needed for historical accuracy or forceful action." She also asked that authors present Negro characters in all walks of life. A number of the books of this period, however, dealt with life in the ghetto, and their authors made an attempt to "tell it like it is."[145] Such books served the double purpose of stimulating "understanding and empathy toward the problems of the underprivileged on the part of the relatively privileged majority of youngsters," and of giving youngsters living in inner cities books that would interest them.[146] The experiment was sufficiently successful to stimulate the production of books about minorities other than the Negro.[147]

Books about minority youth with problems were the forerunners of books about all sorts of youth with problems. Publishers queried in 1968 felt that teenage fiction was becoming more sophisticated because of changing tastes among young people and because editors were allowing writers to break many old taboos.[148] Novels depicting teenage pregnancy (Sherburne's Too Bad About the Haines Girl) and imperfect parents (Neville's It's Like This, Cat) began to appear,[149] and in 1969 one writer noted that:

> During 1968 and 1969, an unusual number of juvenile novels aimed at an audience of young teens and attempting realism have allowed pot to be puffed and sex to rear a timid head.[150]

A number of people felt that more intensified efforts along the same lines were needed. Nat Hentoff,[151] for instance, admitted that his Jazz Country was "deliberately diluted." Among school kids, he said, "criticisms were sharp and frequent, both of me and of other writers of books for 12+. There were many more hang-ups in being young, I was told repeatedly, than were even intimated in most of the books they'd seen." Nevertheless, he felt that a writer could make contact with these "children of McLuhan"

> because their primary concerns are only partially explored in the messages they get from their music and are diverted rather than probed on television. If a book is relevant to these concerns, not didactically, but in creating textures of experience which teen-agers can recognize as germane to their own, it can merit their attention.

Among other things, violence was to be admitted to books for the young, at least under certain conditions.[152] And sex was coming to be thought of as something that should play its part naturally in the juvenile novel.[153] In short, young people were thought to be "better able to dig sex, drugs, out-of-wedlock pregnancies, and bumbling parents" than their "escapist parents."[154] Faced with these demands for more and more relevance and realism on the part of writers and young people, however, editors and librarians have been accused of timidity.[155]

Questions for the Seventies

At the present time, the issue of censorship seems to be rising once more, but without the sound and fury that characterized it a few years ago. In 1968 Eli M. Oboler[156] broached the subject, suggesting that perhaps librarians are not "truly interested in complete freedom for the young." A rebuttal was shortly forthcoming, stating the position that librarians can make their greatest contribution to the young by guiding their search for values.[157] But the fact is, as Oboler[158] pointed out, "At this point, we really don't *know* for sure what the actual cause-and-effect relationship is between reading and behavior," although one or two tentative studies have been made.[159] In fact, we know very little about young people and their reading, and there is need for a great deal more research.[160] Meanwhile,

> an assumption seems to be made almost universally by the adult society that certain types of reading can have undesirable effects upon mind and character, and therefore necessarily upon conduct. Therefore, the argument follows, that it is the duty of society to place restrictions upon the availability of such reading matter....
>
> The library profession itself, which owes its existence in a sense to the (unproven) premise that books can have beneficial effects upon behavior, tacitly accepts the complementary premise that some books can have adverse effects upon the behavior of some people.[161]

The question is a complex one, especially in the case of schools, because of the "apparent incompatibility of two ideas: (1) adolescents must gradually be led to the appreciation of mature, adult literature, and to the development of their critical faculties by exposure to controversy and (2) the school's curriculum and the reading provided under the school's auspices must reflect in some way the values of the adult society."[162] Certainly some critics have found the new, "relevant" junior novels to be didactic, moralizing, and not entirely free from the traditions of wholesomeness and the pontifications of wise adults.[163]

The settings of some of these novels are realistic, even grim, but none of the scenes depicted belong to an exclusively adult world; young people have long since entered a realistic and grim world through the medium of television and/or through the reality of their personal experiences. "The programs our children watch are largely the ones planned for adults and packed with violence. In adult newspapers and photo magazines children follow the pictures as eagerly as their parents."[164] Children nowadays know just about everything their elders know.[165] In view of this it is necessary to look at books from a different perspective, and it is not surprising to find The Diary of Anne Frank and Death Be Not Proud are favorites in the sixth and seventh grades,[166] or to find an 11-year-old commenting favorably on The Good Earth.[167] These are simple books, given a knowledge of birth and death and the inhumanity of man. But it may be that we need to examine books and young people more carefully, and that if we do we shall discover criteria by which to identify books for children, books that make a transition between childhood and adult, young adult books, and books for more mature adults. Only a small start has been made in this direction. Both Virginia Heffernan and Dorothy M. Broderick agree that there is a difference between the level of factual material a young person can read, and the level of fiction he can digest. But level in fiction is a matter of emotional rather than intellectual maturity, and is to be judged by the ability to see behind the facts of a story, rather than by the content of the story itself.[168] (The demand for "relevance," for the here and now, may turn out to be a sign of immaturity in reading, not of sophistication.)

Another matter that deserves more careful study than it has been given hitherto is the matter of access to books. Becker[169] noted differences in the reading of young people in centers with large libraries and of those in outlying districts forty years ago, and there is evidence that such differences are still with us. Linda F. Lapides[170] recently published the results of two surveys made at Baltimore's Enoch Pratt Library in 1960 and in 1970. This article documents a shift in the interests of young people to such books as Joy in the Morning and Mr. and Mrs. Bo Jo Jones, and to books about the experiences and conditions of black people today. Their reading was revealed to be neither "light, recreational, or diversional." While some of the titles in the Pratt survey can undoubtedly be accounted for by the large number of Negroes in the population of Baltimore, the list as a whole presents a startling contrast to another recent list of favorites in a small, midwestern high school, where senior boys included Incredible Journey and Red Car among their favorites.[171] The only book on both lists was Black Like Me. Without raising the question of which list is "better," it does seem pertinent to inquire into the effects of access to good books in all its ramifications.

But what is a good book? There seems to be a trend in recent years to judge books on their own merits instead of whether they are good for some purpose. Authors are being asked to forget that they are writing for teen-agers,[172] and the literary quality of a work is to be considered first in its assessment.[173] This means both the quality of the writing, and the author's honesty in speaking of the world as he sees it. As Newbery winner Emily Neville put it, "The real world with its shadings of light and dark is so much more beautiful than a rigid world of good and bad. It is also more confusing. I think the teenage reader is ready for both."[174] It is hoped that if authors are free to write as they think and feel, certain stereotypes that are still with us will tend to disappear.[175] Some controversial materials which have literary merit and honesty appear on the library shelves for, as John Igo pointed out, most of the world's greatest literature is controversial or, as he puts it, are "immoral books, morally written."[176] Contact with such books may do less harm than contact with second-rate books, for "second-rate books come from second-rate minds, and it is better to leave people to make their own spontaneous approach to life than clutter their thinking with cliché responses."[177] On the other hand, contact with a variety of original, first-rate minds might make a "bastion against pressures toward conformity which in large part are overwhelming motion pictures, radio, television, and the press."[178]

While there is a new emphasis on book selection, there are also stirrings of interest in a new approach to reading guidance. Authors must be allowed to speak for themselves:

> ... we must remember to step aside and not intrude ourselves between the author and the reader by sermonizing and pointing out lessons. We must let the author tell the reader. Our function is to interest the young person in taking the book and, after he has read it, enjoying it with him.[179]

The important thing is to bring individuals to books which will provide them with "moments of being," or at least the impending sense of one.[180] It is also coming to be recognized that such "moments of being" are available in other media, and that "... much energy and time would be conserved if we conceded that to many young people, reading is a drag, and concentrated our efforts on the audio-visual epiphanies (moments of being) that might be triggered." This emphasis on the individual, if it is carried out with honesty and with the support of intelligent investigation, is what gives promise that media (including books), can be made the agents for building autonomous personality in many of our young people.[181] They might even lead us back to a sense of humor, "rooted and grounded in perspective on human experience, in a sense of proportion, of the relative value of things."[182]

References and Bibliography

1. Katherine P. Jeffery. "Selecting Books for the Young Adult Collection in the Public Library," Library Trends 17:166-75 (Oct. 1968).
2. "American education grew phenomenally during the quarter century following World War One: each year more students studied in larger schools for longer periods of time...." Lawrence Cremin, The Transformation of the School (Vintage Books, 1961), p. 274.
3. Hannah Logasa. "Elements in Reading Guidance," Public Libraries 27:147-51 (1922).
4. Martha Pritchard. "Reading Guidance for High School Pupils," New York Libraries 10:206-8 (May 1927).
5. Margaret Drew Archibald. "Teen Age Girls as Book Lovers," Library Journal 52:856-57 (1927).
6. Mary S. Wilkerson. "Fiction Reading for Older Boys and Girls," ALA Bulletin 16:266-67 (1922).
7. H. B. Preston. "Capitalizing the Pupils' Judgment of Books," Library Journal 50:210 (1925).
8. Cremin. The Transformation of the School, p. 274.
9. Helen E. Haines. "Adventures in Reading for Young People," ALA Bulletin 24:513-15 (1930).
10. Oscar H. McPherson. "Reading Hobbies," Library Journal 56:733-38 (1931).
11. Lloyd Shaw. "Touching the Intangible," Wilson Library Bulletin 10:110-13 (Oct. 1935).
12. P. G. Chancellor. "What School Boys Read," Publishers' Weekly 134:2212-15 (31 Dec. 1938).
13. "Boring the Young," New Statesman and Nation 15:8-9 (1 Jan. 1938).
14. Azile M. Wofford. "Bridging the Gap," Library Journal 57:813 (1932).
15. W. T. B. Mitchell. "Adolescent Interests and Their Reading," ALA Bulletin 28:732-35 (Sept. 1934).
16. Helen L. Bell. "Reading Guidance and the Adolescent," Wilson Library Bulletin 9:235-38 (Jan. 1935).

17. May Lamberton Becker. "The Tastes of the Teens," ALA Bulletin 25:634-35 (1931).
18. Chancellor. "What School Boys Read."
19. L. Toomey. "Reading Interests of the Teenage," Wilson Library Bulletin 13:188-89 (Nov. 1938).
20. Louise E. Hill. "High School Students Like Fiction," Publishers' Weekly 135:1585-87 (29 April 1939).
21. Irene Smith. "Adolescent Reading," Library Journal 57:837-41 (1932).
22. Ethelwyn Wickson. "Reading Interests of Average Intermediates," Wilson Library Bulletin 9:25-26 (Sept. 1934).
23. Shaw. "Touching the Intangible."
24. Jean C. Roos. "Book Selection and the 'Good' Reader," ALA Bulletin 28:735-38 (Sept. 1934).
25. Mabel Williams. "'Seventeen' and the Public Library," Library Journal 59:821-23 (1 Nov. 1934).
26. Alice Cowles Morris. "Book Selection as a Trust," Library Journal 64:887-89 (15 Nov. 1939).
27. Ruby Ethel Cundiff. "Will It Hold My Interest?" Peabody Journal of Education 14:83-85 (Sept. 1936).
28. Margaret C. Scoggin. "Do Young People Want Books?" Wilson Library Bulletin 11:17-20 (Sept. 1936).
29. Homer P. Rainey. "How Can Libraries Help to Meet the Needs of Youth?" ALA Bulletin 31:406-14 (July 1937).
30. Rose McGlennon. "Aid to the Ailing: The Active School Library," Wilson Library Bulletin 12:367-70 (Feb. 1938).
31. Amelia H. Munson. "Some Folks Won't Read," Educational Method 19:142-47 (Dec. 1939).
32. Dora V. Smith. "Reading--a Moot Question," ALA Bulletin 32:1031-40 (Dec. 1938).
33. Rachel Field. "Reading and Writing," ALA Bulletin 33:677-80 (1 Oct. 1939).
34. Eva Schars. "What! No Love Stories?" Nation's Schools 19:31-32 (Jan. 1937).
35. Emma Gelders Stone. "A Parent's View of Young People's Reading," Library Journal 62:827-29 (1 Nov. 1937).
36. Schars. "What! No Love Stories?"
37. Walter Prichard Eaton. "Imagination Needs Exercise," Library Journal 63:667-68 (15 Sept. 1938).
38. Douglas Waples. "A Look Ahead at Adolescent Reading," ALA Bulletin 28:397-400 (July 1934).
39. Dorothy Hopkins. "Young Peoples Reading and the Changing Times," Wilson Library Bulletin 9:291-96 (Feb. 1935).
40. Hester H. Cam. "A Social Approach to Adolescence," Wilson Library Bulletin 10:379-81 (Feb. 1936).
41. Constance Rourke. "American Traditions for Young People," ALA Bulletin 31:934-38 (Dec. 1937).
42. Douglas Waples. "On Developing Taste in Reading," Harvard Educational Review 9:413-23 (Oct. 1939).
43. Frieda M. Heller. "New Designs in Teen-age Reading," ALA Bulletin 34:192-93 (Aug. 1940).
44. See Mabel Zimmerman. "The Library Goes to the English Class," Wilson Library Bulletin 15:38-9+ (Sept. 1940);

Virginia Teitge. "Follow the Romany Pattern," English Journal 29:206-11 (March 1940); Ethel L. Cornell. "Can Librarians Help Unusual Readers?" ALA Bulletin 35:160-65 (March 1941).

45. Ethel L. Cornell. "The Voluntary Reading of High School Pupils," ALA Bulletin 35:295-300 (May 1941).
46. Marie Nelson Taylor. "Facing the War with Our Young People," Wilson Library Bulletin 17:656-58 (Apr. 1943).
47. Margaret C. Scoggin. "Young People's Reading Interests Not Materially Changed in Wartime," Library Journal 68:703-6 (15 Sept. 1943).
48. Helen L. Butler. "Motivating Reading in Wartime," Library Journal 68:460-63 (1 June 1943).
49. C. R. P. Sievens. "Survey of Wartime Reading of Students at Brookline, Massachusetts," Library Journal 69:752-53 (15 Sept. 1944).
50. Butler. "Motivating Reading."
51. Kathryn A. Haebich. "What Are Adolescents Reading?" Wilson Library Bulletin 20:289+ (Dec. 1945).
52. Gladys B. Johnson. "Books and the Five Adolescent Tasks," Library Journal 68:350-52 (1 May 1943). The books mentioned are merely examples.
53. Lucile Vickers. "Education for Living," Wilson Library Bulletin 17:654-5+ (April 1943).
54. Margaret Kessler Walraven. "Reading: The Librarian's View," English Journal 32:198-203 (April 1943).
55. Lillian M. Enlow. "Teaching Good Citizenship," Wilson Library Bulletin 15:392-93 (Jan. 1941).
56. Willard A. Heaps. "Bibliotherapy and the School Librarian," Library Journal 65:957-59 (15 Nov. 1940).
57. Louise Dinwiddie. "Best Sellers and Modern Youth," Library Journal 65:957-59 (15 Nov. 1940).
58. Jeffery. "Selecting Books."
59. Alice Cowles Morris. "A Good Short Book, Please," Wilson Library Bulletin 17:712-13 (May 1943).
60. Becker. "The Tastes of the Teens."
61. Richard S. Alm. "The Glitter and the Gold," English Journal 44:315-22+ (Sept. 1955).
62. Stephen Dunning. "The Most Popular Junior Novels," Library Journal 84:3885-87 (15 Dec. 1959).
63. Virginia Westphal. "The Teenage Novel, A Defense," Library Journal 89:1832-33+ (15 April 1964).
64. One cannot leave a discussion of the junior novel in the late 1940s and 1950s without mentioning the concurrent rise of "science fiction." For an analysis of this genre, see Robert A. Heinlein, "Ray Guns and Rocket Ships," Library Journal 78:1188-91 (July 1953).
65. Vernon Ives. "Teen-age Reading," ALA Bulletin 47:400-4 (Oct. 1953).
66. A. C. Kennedy. "Serving the Young and Their Reading Interests," Library Journal 73:1794-95 (15 Dec. 1948).
67. D. Winifred Jackson. "Selecting Adult Books for Young People," Top of the News 5:5-6+ (Dec. 1948).

68. Jeffrey. "Selecting Books."
69. Margaret C. Scoggin. "Fables They Shall Not Read," ALA Bulletin 46:323+ (Nov. 1952).
70. In 1957, for instance, the "Interesting Adult Books of 1957 for Young People," chosen by the ALA, included seven nonfiction books; three biographies, one of them fictionalized; five books of memoirs, or "true stories"; and five works of fiction, two of them war stories. Selections for 1958, 1959 and 1960 are similar. I have read a number of these books, and find them, for the most part, wordy and dull.
71. Martha Huddleston. "Teen Age Reading Habits," Wilson Library Bulletin 22:53+ (Sept. 1947); "Teen Agers Do Read," Wilson Library Bulletin 23:178-79 (Oct. 1948); Laura E. Vroman. "Trends in Reading in Junior High School," Wilson Library Bulletin 23:678-80 (May 1949); Rachel W. DeAngelo. "Trends in Reading in Senior High School," Wilson Library Bulletin 23:675-78 (May 1949); Florence Powell. "Students Choice," Library Journal 76:488-91 (15 March 1951); Virginia Tozier. "What Motivates Secondary School Voluntary Reading?" Wilson Library Bulletin 30:166-69 (Oct. 1955); Aimee K. Kulp. "Teen-agers Won't Read!" Wilson Library Bulletin 29:614-15 (April 1955); Dorothy Pierman. "But Johnny Is Reading!" Wilson Library Bulletin 30:623 (April 1956); and others for the 1950s quoted in the sections "Ages Twelve to Fifteen" and "Ages Twelve to Nineteen" of Jean Spealman Kujoth. Reading Interests of Children and Young Adults (Scarecrow, 1970).
72. Lloyd W. Babb. "Guidance in Recreational Reading," English Journal 41:201-4 (April 1952).
73. Virginia Tozier. "What Motivates."
74. Lewis Perry. "What Makes Sammy Read?" Publishers' Weekly 167:1024-26 (12 Feb. 1955).
75. Esther Millett. "What Makes Sally Read?" Publishers' Weekly 167:1022-24 (12 Feb. 1955).
76. Ruth Hill Viguers. "Invitation to the Feast," Horn Book 34: 449-58 (Dec. 1958).
77. G. Robert Carlsen. "The Magic of Bringing Young Adults to Books," Wilson Library Bulletin 33:134-37+ (Oct. 1958).
78. "Patterns in Reading," Publishers' Weekly 190:29-39 (8 Aug. 1966). Report of a speech by Carlsen to YASD of ALA at their 85th convention.
79. G. Robert Carlsen. "The Right Size," Top of the News 23: 55-62 (Nov. 1966).
80. These findings formed the basis of Carlsen's Books and the Teen Age Reader (Rev. ed. Harper, 1972) which remains a significant contribution.
81. M. Fraser. "Youth and the Classics," Canadian Library Association Bulletin 7:175-78 (March 1951).
82. "Adult Books for the Young Adults," Top of the News 16:12-20+ (Dec. 1959).
83. Francis X. Cleary. "Why Johnnie Is Reading," Education 82: 305-8 (Jan. 1962).
84. Florence Hascall. "No Lollipops," Horn Book 39:86-91 (Feb. 1963).

85. Viguers. "Invitation."
86. Lois Blau. "The Novel in the High School Library," *Wisconsin Library Journal* 60:178-81 (May 1964). Reprinted in Dennis Thomison. *Reading About Adolescent Literature* (Scarecrow, 1970).
87. Margaret A. Edwards. "A Time When Its Best to Read and Let Read," *Wilson Library Bulletin* 35:43-45 (Sept. 1960).
88. Frances Lombard. "Rid the 100's of Deadwood," *Library Journal* 82:1339-40 (15 May 1957).
89. Ann Emery. "Values in Adolescent Fiction," *Library Journal* 83:1565-57 (15 May 1958).
90. Madeline Irrig. "Developing Character Through Reading," *Wilson Library Bulletin* 33:571-73 (April 1959).
91. Dorothy M. Broderick. "The Opportunities That Books Offer," *Library Journal* 84:3891-3901 (15 Dec. 1959).
92. Margaret Edwards. "Taming the Young Barbarian," *Library Journal* 89:1819-21 (15 April 1964).
93. Marie Blanche MacDonald. "Shake Hands with Mrs. Grundy," *Wilson Library Bulletin* 33:148-49 (Oct. 1958).
94. Margaret A. Edwards. "Mrs. Grundy Go Home," *Wilson Library Bulletin* 33:304-5 (Dec. 1958).
95. John A. Myers. "The Realistic Novel and the Gold Ring," *Catholic Library World* 38:167-71 (Nov. 1966).
96. Frederic R. Hartz. "Obscenity, Censorship and Youth," *Clearing House* 36:99-101 (Oct. 1961).
97. Hoke Norris. "Two Kinds of Censorship," *PTA Magazine* 59:11-12 (March 1965).
98. "What Books for the Young Adult?" *Library Journal* 89:4103-6 (15 Oct. 1964).
99. Norris. "Two Kinds."
100. James R. Squire and Robert F. Hogan. "Where is the Danger?" *PTA Magazine* 59:12 (March 1965).
101. John A. Myers. "The Realistic Novel."
102. E. Geller. "Two Cheers for Liberty," *Library Journal* 92:3109-13 (15 Sept. 1967).
103. Max Rafferty. "The Other Side: Hardest of All Things to Come By," *Wilson Library Bulletin* 42:181-86 (Oct. 1967).
104. See *Wilson Library Bulletin*, 42:368-69 (Dec. 1967). Also Jean Smith, "A Public Library Trustee Looks at the 'Other Side,'" *ALA Bulletin* 62:111-12 (Feb. 1968).
105. David K. Berninghausen. "An Exploratory Study of Juvenile Delinquency and the Reading of Sensational Books," *Journal of Experimental Education* 33:161-68 is an example of research on the subject.
106. Helen Gothberg. "Young Adult Censorship; Adult or Adolescent Problem?" *Top of the News* 22:275-78 (April 1966).
107. Audrey Sabadosh. "Teenagers View Censorship," *Top of the News* 22:278-80 (April 1966).
108. Esther Helfand. "Love and Humanity--Not Intellectual Freedom," *Top of the News* 24:47-54 (Nov. 1967).
109. Jean E. Crabtree. "The Challenge of Quality Reading for Young Adults," *ALA Bulletin* 55:419-20 (May 1961).
110. Frank G. Jennings. "Literature for Adolescents--Pap or

Protein?" English Journal 45:526-31 (Dec. 1956).

111. Vivian J. MacQuown. "The Teenage Novel: A Critique," Library Journal 89:1832-35 (15 April 1964). See also Catherine Robertson. "Young People and Spoon-Fed Reading," Ontario Library Review 44:248-49 (Nov. 1960).

112. Kenneth R. Shaffer. "What Makes Sammy Read?" Top of the News 19:9-12 (March 1963).

113. _______. "Teenage Elysium: Our Own Delusion," Library Journal 89:4976-78 (15 Dec. 1964).

114. Arthur Daigan. "Novel of Adolescent Romance," Library Journal 91:2152-56 (15 April 1966).

115. Sarah L. Siebert. "Taking Shaffer to Task," Top of the News 20:67-69 (Oct. 1963).

116. MacQuown. "The Teenage Novel."

117. Dorothy M. Broderick. "Carping Critics, Instant Experts," Library Journal 90:3690-92 (15 Sept. 1965).

118. For example, see Ruth G. Rausen. "The Junior High Reader," Top of the News (Nov. 1966); Anthony J. Soares. "Salient Elements of Recreational Reading of Junior High School Students," Elementary English 40:843-45 (Dec. 1963); Ruth Strang. "Teen-age Readers," PTA Magazine 55:10-12 (June 1961); and articles by Charles E. Johnson, Beryl I. Vaughan, Jo M. Stanchfield, Paul Witty, and J. Harlan Shores reprinted in Kujoth, Reading Interests of Children and Young Adults.

119. Margaret W. Dudley. "What Young Americans Are Reading," Library Journal 85:3170-71 (15 Sept. 1960).

120. "What Young Americans Are Reading," Library Journal 86:1955 (15 May 1961).

121. Nick Aaron Ford. "What High School Students Say about Good Books," English Journal 50:539-40+ (Nov. 1961).

122. Esther Millett. "We Don't Even Call Them Books!" Top of the News 20:45-47 (Oct. 1963).

123. Helen Wilmott. "YASD Asks the Young Adult," Top of the News 21:143-47 (Jan. 1965).

124. "Young Adults Disclose Favorite Reading, Library Uses, in Westchester Survey," Library Journal 91:2184 (15 April 1966).

125. "Publishers Hear Young Adult Panel Talk about Reading Tastes," Library Journal 92:284-85 (15 Jan. 1967).

126. Wilmott. "YASD Asks."

127. Elizabeth Ritts Goebel. "Teen-age Reading," Library Journal 77:941-43 (1 June 1952).

128. Dora V. Smith. "Books--A Source of Strength for Youth in a Free Land," Top of the News 11:9-17 (Oct. 1954).

129. Jerome Cushman. "Today's Bewildered Youth," Library Journal 84:611-14 (15 Feb. 1959).

130. Harriette Arnow. "Reading without a Purpose," ALA Bulletin 53:837-39 (Nov. 1959).

131. Jane Manthorne. "The Age of the Acronym," Wilson Library Bulletin 40:84-86 (Sept. 1965).

132. H. B. Maloney. "Humanities Today," Clearing House 38:380 (Feb. 1964). See also Cushman, "Today's Bewildered."

133. Compare, for example, two analyses of the adolescent by child-study experts: Marynia F. Farnham. "Who Is the Young Adult?" Top of the News 14:46-50 (Oct. 1957) and Armin Grams. "Understanding the Adolescent Reader," Library Trends 17:121-31 (Oct. 1968).
134. Marjorie Sullivan. "Reading for Relevance," Library Journal 93:4693-95 (15 Dec. 1968).
135. Harriette Arnow. "Reading Without."
136. Ursula Nordstrom. "Honesty in Teenage Novels," Top of the News 21:35-38 (Nov. 1964).
137. Kenneth R. Shaffer. "Teenage Elysium," Library Journal.
138. Susan Hinton, quoted in Sullivan, "Reading for Relevance."
139. Mary Mace Spradling. "There Is No Such Book," Top of the News 21:346-48 (June 1965).
140. Benjamin F. Smith. "The School Librarian and the Reading Process," Journal of Negro Education 17:114-19 (April 1948).
141. Dorothy Sterling. "Soul of Learning," English Journal 57: 167-80 (Feb. 1968).
142. Charlemae Rollins. "Books about Negroes for Children," ALA Bulletin 53:306-8 (April 1959).
143. Ann Durrell. "Goodies and Baddies," Wilson Library Bulletin 44:456-57 (Dec. 1969).
144. Gloria Johnson. "The Fifth Freedom: Presenting the Negro in Books," Top of the News 22:62-63 (Nov. 1965).
145. Sterling. "Soul of Learning."
146. Frank Bonham. "Return to Durango Street," Library Journal 91:4188-99 (15 Sept. 1966).
147. Frank Bonham and James Duggings. "Are We for Real with Kids?" Top of the News 23:245-52 (April 1967).
148. "Change in the Teens and in the Publishers," Publishers' Weekly 193:91-92 (26 Feb. 1968).
149. Phyllis Zucker. "The Junior Novel Revisited," Top of the News 25:388-91 (June 1969).
150. Diane Gersoni Stavn. "Watching Fiction for Today's Teens," Library Journal 94:4305-6 (15 Nov. 1969). But it is worth noting that novels of this type were not a completely new invention. Several earlier efforts are mentioned in Margaret Walraven. "Trends in Children's Books: Young People," Texas Library Journal 26:112-15 (Sept. 1950).
151. Nat Hentoff. "Fiction for Teen-agers," Wilson Library Bulletin 43:261-65 (Nov. 1968).
152. James C. Giblin. "Violence: Factors Considered by a Children's Book Editor," Elementary English 49:64-67 (Jan. 1972).
153. John Neufeld. "The Thought, Not Necessarily the Deed," Wilson Library Bulletin 46:147-52 (Oct. 1971).
154. Joan Bodger Mercer. "Innocence Is a Cop-out," Wilson Library Bulletin 46:144-46 (Oct. 1971).
155. Lyle Wilson Warrick. "Where Hentoff Left Off," Wilson Library Bulletin 43:266-68 (Nov. 1968); Mary Kingsbury. "Ostriches and Adolescents," Journal of Education for Librarianship 11:325-31 (Spring 1971); and Linda Lapides.

"Question of Relevance," Top of the News 24:55-61 (Nov. 1967).

156. Eli M. Oboler. "The Grand Illusion," Library Journal 93: 1277-79 (15 March 1968).
157. Vincent M. Inghilterra. "A Note of Dissent," Library Journal 93:3183 (15 Sept. 1968).
158. Oboler. "The Grand Illusion"; also Beverly Sigler Edwards. "The Therapeutic Value of Reading," Elementary English 49:213-17 (Feb. 1972).
159. Shirley Fehl. "The Influence of Reading on Adolescents," Wilson Library Bulletin 43:256-60 (Nov. 1968); also Sister Mary Corde Lorang. Burning Ice: The Moral and Emotional Effects of Reading (Scribner's, 1968).
160. Alexander Beinlich. "On the Literary Development of Children and Adolescents," Bookbird v. 6, no. 1 (1968), p. 17-22.
161. John J. Farley. "The Reading of Young People," Library Trends 19:81-88 (July 1970).
162. Farley. "The Reading of Young People."
163. John S. Simmons. "Lipsyte's Contender: Another Look at the Junior Novel," Elementary English 49:116-19 (Jan. 1972). Also Natalie Babbitt. "Between Innocence and Maturity," Horn Book 48:33-37 (Feb. 1972).
164. Nancy Larrick. "Baby Dolls Are Gone," Library Journal 92: 3815-17 (15 Oct. 1967).
165. Margaret Mead, the anthropologist, speaks to this point in a number of her writings. The situation is, of course, a return to an older order of things rather than something new. See Philippe Ariès. Centuries of Childhood (Vintage, 1965).
166. Larrick. "Baby Dolls."
167. American Girl (April 1972), p. 17.
168. Virginia Heffernan. "The Blurred Boundary," Top of the News (Nov. 1964) and Dorothy M. Broderick. "The Twelve-Year-Old Adult Reader," Library Journal 90:2321-27 (15 May 1965).
169. Becker. "The Tastes of the Teens."
170. Linda F. Lapides. "A Decade of Teen-age Reading in Baltimore," Top of the News (April 1971).
171. Mary DesJardins. "Reading and Viewing," School Libraries v. 21, no. 3 (Spring 1972).
172. Natalie Babbitt. "Between Innocence."
173. John Rowe Townsend. "Standards of Criticism for Children's Literature," Top of the News 27:4 (Spring 1971).
174. Quoted in Ursula Nordstrom. "Honesty."
175. See, for example, recent discussions of women in books for the young: Diane Gersoni Stavn. "The Skirts in Fiction about Boys: A Maxi Mess," Library Journal 96:282-86 (15 Jan. 1971); Mary Ritchie Key. "The Role of Male and Female in Children's Books--Dispelling All Doubt," Wilson Library Bulletin 46:167-76 (Oct. 1971); Diane Gersoni Stavn. "Reducing the 'Miss Muffett' Syndrome," Library Journal 97:256-59 (15 Jan. 1972).

176. John Igo. "Books for the New Breed," *Library Journal* 92: 1704-5 (15 April 1967).
177. Peggy Heeks. "Books for Adolescents," *School Librarian* 14: 133-39 (July 1966).
178. David Morris. "TV Selects Public Library Books," *ALA Bulletin* 62:460 (May 1968); also Marjorie Sullivan. "Books, Readers, and Individuals," *Top of the News* 27:292-98 (April 1971).
179. Margaret Edwards. "A Book Is to Read," *Southeastern Librarian* 19:198-203 (Winter 1969).
180. Laura M. Jones. "Epiphanies or Plastic Bags?" *Canadian Library Journal* 28:373-77 (Sept. 1971).
181. Sullivan. "Books, Readers."
182. Dora V. Smith. "Books--A Source."

FORTY YEARS WITH BOOKS AND TEEN-AGE READERS*

By G. Robert Carlsen

In the fall of 1939, I decided, rather reluctantly, that I needed a teacher's certificate and signed into the classes of that remarkable woman, Dr. Dora V. Smith, at the University of Minnesota. One class was entitled "Adolescent Literature." Although I did not know it at the time, Dora V. was probably the first to offer such a class in an American university, in which she separated the reading of teen-agers from children's literature on the one hand and from adult reading on the other. Even today this kind of differentiation has not been clearly acknowledged. Librarians will still argue that young adults really read anything that adults read and teachers of children's literature glory in discussing books about homosexuality, unwed mothers, and psychotic disorders.

But Dora V. recognized that there is a body of literature that is unique to teenagers. This consisted of books written consciously or unconsciously with the teen-age reader in mind and a body of adult literature that ultimately is taken over and kept alive by successive generations of teens: books like _Gone with the Wind_, _A Lantern in Her Hand_, or more recently, _Catcher in the Rye_ and _A Separate Peace_.

In the thirties, and for years afterward, _Silas Marner_, _Julius Caesar_, _A Tale of Two Cities_, _Ivanhoe_, _The Lady of the Lake_, _The Idylls of the King_, _Snowbound_ were the standard teaching vehicles in the schools. The average running time allotted to each work was six weeks. Discussion about the teaching of literature centered on how to make these texts appealing to students. Dora V. turned the discussion around by asking what literature has something to say to boys and girls. Long before the word _relevant_ became educationese, she said that we must look for books which are about the teen-ager's interests and concerns.

The books we talked most about were the early Tunis books: _The Iron Duke_ and _The Duke Decides_, stories about how a big athlete in a small town must come to terms with being a small athlete when he goes to Harvard. She was enthusiastic about _Young Fu on the Upper Yangtze_ as the experience of a teen-ager in another culture

---

*Reprinted by permission of the author and publisher from _Arizona English Bulletin_ (April 1976), 1-5.

who experiences emotions and confusions identical with those of American youth. Call It Courage by Armstrong Sperry was held up as a tremendous picture of the teen-ager having to overcome his fears. Then there were the vocational books of Helen Boylston and Stephen Meader. Boylston took the Horatio Alger pattern of "success through hard work," set it against an accurate background of nurses' training of the time, and gave us the Sue Barton books. When I started teaching I used to say that the reason so many junior high girls wanted to become nurses was that they had all read and loved Sue Barton. Stephen Meader brought out T. Model Tommy about a high school student's starting a trucking business. So many facts are given that the book is almost a manual for beginning an operation. The book was printed in classroom editions and was often used in place of Silas in boys' classes in vocational schools. It is a book of rugged individualism: Tommy and his widowed mother shun things like WPA.

Then there were the adventure stories of Howard Pease (The Jinx Ship and The Tattooed Man) in which a teen-ager tests himself against the rigors of the sea as a sailor. Some of the best of the animal stories had already been written: Lassie Come Home, The Yearling, The Voice of Bugle Ann, and National Velvet.

There were many beautiful stories with a historical background. Their characters, often teen-agers, were strong and good. Titles included Spice and the Devil's Cave, Messer Marco Polo, Lance of Kanana, and the wonderful stories of Polish legend: The Trumpeter of Krakow, and the Prisoner of Vilno. These books were almost like simplified epic poems. Kate Seredy won the Newbery Prize for her White Stag in which she tried to evoke the history of the Hungars in their migration from Asia into Europe.

Just as the war was beginning came a book that seemed head and shoulders above everything so far published. In fact I still think of it as marking the coming of age of teen-age literature. The book, Seventeenth Summer, was written by a young woman still in college. It details a seventeenth summer in Fond de Lac, Wisconsin, and the first real romance that is broken at the end of summer when the heroine goes off to college. Here was a coherent novel, told in the first person, that captured adolescence from the inside as the adolescent sees it. Most of what had been written before has an element of adults looking back at adolescence. The real difference can be seen if one compares Seventeenth Summer with Booth Tarkington's Seventeen, in which the adolescent is a comic butt. In the forties, Seventeenth Summer was read by almost all teen-age girls. And in spite of supercilious comments about how much more sophisticated the young are today and how naive Seventeenth Summer seems, it is read by numbers of girls in the 1970s.

World War II produced a flood of books. Most of them written by young men hardly out of their teens, they had an immediacy that adolescents loved. Students read The Raft, an account of Rickenbacker's survival on a raft on the open sea. See Here, Private

Hargrove was one of the first accounts of what it was like to be drafted. A great favorite was The Snow Goose, which climaxed in the evaculation of Dunkirk. Tunis wrote about the European underground in books like Silence Over Dunkirk. Thirty Seconds Over Tokyo, They Were Expendable, and P. T. 109 dealt with the war in the Pacific. Johnny Got His Gun (recently popular) seemed too horrible at the time it was written for boys faced with immediate induction into the army. War, to the surprise of everyone, remained popular after the war, up to Vietnam, when suddenly there seemed to be a revulsion among adolescent readers against this kind of experience.

During the late '40s, through the '50s, and into the early '60s a whole group of writers were steadily turning out highly popular books specifically for teen-age readers. Notable among these was John Tunis with his sports stories which moved from baseball and football to basketball and soccer. Stephen Meader alternated between a historical adventure story and a vocational story. Howard Pease dealt with the contrast between a young man's romantic dream of the sea and the harsh reality. James Kjelgaard turned out a whole kennel of dog stories. James Summer tried to use teen slang to hit at teen-age problems. Florence Means wrote beautifully crafted and tender stories of America's minorities: the Indian, the Black, the Spanish speaking, the Nisei. Betty Cavanna, Rosemary du Jardin, Anne Emory, and Mary Stolz regularly wrote of girls, usually of the upper middle class, and their problems of going steady, problems with their families, their feelings of inadequacy, etc.

In 1951, almost ten years after Seventeenth Summer, came another great milestone, The Catcher in the Rye, this time a book which got at the teen-age male's psyche the way no previous book had. It was condemned by great numbers of adults for two reasons: It dared to use teen-age language as frankly as almost every teen-age male used it, and it dealt frankly with the sexual confusions of a boy in growing up. Almost every male reader, teen-ager and adult alike, found it a tremendously moving book because he recognized himself as Holden. The initial response of females was divided between outright shock and great amusement. A year later came Anne Frank's The Diary of a Young Girl, which does almost exactly for females what Catcher does for males. Anne had a different impact because it was produced in play form, in which the war background of the book dominated the psychological picture of maturation, whereas the actual diary had the opposite balance. But Catcher became the germinal book that has continued to influence the whole group of "tell it like it is" books of the '60s and '70s.

A couple of types of stories seemed to peak during the 1950s and then disappear. One such was the car story. Boys at the time seemed to have the same kind of love affair with a car as girls still have with horses. By all odds the most widely read car book was Henry Felsen's Hot Rod. There were also stories of sports car and rallies, of professional racing cars, of classic antique cars and their reconstruction, and the races. There were enough such stories that it was possible to list car stories as a category on a teen-age reading list. Today bikes seem to have supplanted cars in boys' affections and no one to date seems to have written a bike story with the guts of Hot Rod. Reading about cars still is a prime interest of teens but in the 1970s it has shifted to the magazines like Hot Rod and Motor Trends.

The vocational story, the descendant of Sue Barton, was another type of book that peaked about 1950. These were written to a set formula. A young person just out of high school or college enters a vocation. The story follows what happens through the first year. All information about salary, the working conditions, the activities in the vocation are documented. The intent was to give vocational information painlessly. But as in most stories written for ulterior purposes, characterization and plot patterns tended to be highly stereotyped. For example, there is almost always an experienced person who tries to do the hero in. But after many discouragements and setbacks the hero is always successful. There usually is romance on the side. Teens loved them because the vocation was always portrayed as aggressively humanitarian and the hero was always successful after a short period of time. So the books were highly wish-fulfilling. I made out countless lists of vocational stories and prided myself on the fact that I could, in fact, cover almost all vocational fields. A standard reference tool was Haebich's Vocations in Fact and Fiction.

Yet another book that peaked during the fifties and sixties and has since declined is the fictional sports story. There were perhaps eight or ten authors who regularly wrote sports stories. The dean of these was John Tunis. Others were Phil Harkins, Gene Olson, William Cox, C. H. Frick, Dick Friendlich, William Gault, William Heuman, Joe Archibald. Sports stories of the earlier periods had been almost completely about baseball or football. By the '60s one could do a pretty good roll call on most major sports: baseball, tennis, hockey, surfing, skiing, track, swimming, golf, fold-boating, gliding, boxing. Like hot rod stories these have given way to nonfictional biographies of sports figures. There were few accounts of girls in sports, and a female author, C. H. Frick, used only her initials and never had a picture on a dust jacket.

Nineteen-sixty brought another landmark book: A Separate Peace by John Knowles. It is interesting to note the ten-year intervals between the landmark books, Seventeenth Summer, Catcher in the Rye, and A Separate Peace, that all three books are told in the first person, and all were written by relatively young authors. Gene, in A Separate Peace, is an adult revisiting his prep school where he once again tries to understand his adolescent love-hate relations with Finney in their school years which saw the adult world erupt into World War II. Though the narrator is an adult, the book is singularly free of adult characters. Holden, in Catcher in the Rye, fought against adults. In A Separate Peace, the world is one almost exclusively of teen-agers. Both of these kinds of worlds are found in the flood of books in the late sixties and the seventies.

The late sixties brought drugs, alienation, student activism, flower children, communes, and the sexual revolution. At least these were the common generalizations about teens that the media impressed upon us, even though the majority on campuses never joined a peace march, or burned a draft card, or joined a commune. But the books for teens pictured the commonly believed stereotype. Popular books were Go Ask Alice, which was a diary of a girl who went the drug route; and The Outsider, which showed the alienation of three teen-age brothers. The Peter Pan Bag dealt with a life in a Boston commune. Drop Out presented the plight of the teen-ager who leaves school. My Darling, My Hamburger shows the sexual tensions brought to bear on youth. Run Softly, Go Fast deals with a Jewish boy's progressive alienation from his parents. Usually told in the first person, and usually having echoes of Catcher in the Rye or A Separate Peace in them, these books seem like fictionalized case studies. In fact a frequently used technique was the character's writing a journal to gain insight about himself, sometimes even as a narrative for a lawyer, a probation officer, or a doctor.

Along with these later books there has been a progressive breaking of all the old taboos. One of these has been that of tabooed words. Catcher caused a furor because it used a small handful of forbidden words. As late as 1961, C. H. Frick decided to quit writing for adolescents because of the controversy over a very mild epithet in Comeback Guy. Today there seems no language that isn't found in teen-age books. Look for instance at the first page of Dan McCall's Jack the Bear.

Along with language it is interesting to trace the history of sex in teen-age books over the past thirty or so years. A graduate student recently compared Seventeenth Summer, a romance laid in the early 1940s, with The Cheerleader, laid in the 1950s, and A Long Way Home from Troy, in the late 1960s. In the first, the characters are only dimly aware of sexual urges. "Sex is for adults." In the second, sex is a game with fixed rules. "How far do you go on which date?" You alway report your score to your friends afterwards. In the last book, sex is a normal part of the relationship between a dating couple and does not really have anything to do with the permanence of their relationship.

Some writers used sexual incidents and themes, but these were "dangerous books" that publishers printed with calculated risks. In general, they died, probably from a dearth of sales. Madeleine L'Engle wrote The Small Rain in the '40s. I still think it her finest book. It has been revised and published in part under the title Prelude. In the original story, an American girl in a girls' school in Switzerland is accused of lesbianism by other girls and she actually sleeps with her piano teacher and gets away without becoming pregnant. This latter fact was the most condemning thing of all about the book at the time it was published. Henry Felsen published Two and the Town in 1951, in which after a single sexual encounter a teen-age girl does become pregnant and the families force the couple to marry. The year it appeared, a Kansas librarian said, "Well, it may cost me my job, but I am going to order it." James Summers wrote The Limits of Love on the theme that adult society shouldn't be surprised if sex takes place with young people when it gives them absolute freedom when they are at the height of their sexuality.

But it wasn't until the late '60s that it became commonplace for girls to become pregnant and go through the turmoil of what to do (Too Bad about the Haines Girl, Phoebe, Mia Alone). Abortion is a viable answer in My Darling, My Hamburger or in Bonnie Jo Go Home. The Girls of Huntington House is about a home for unwed mothers. In Love Child, though adult, the unmarried mother decides to keep her child instead of placing it for adoption. In Judy Blume's new book, a high school girl with advice from her grandmother goes to the Goldman clinic for contraceptive devices in anticipation of her developing relationship. In most new books, the characters menstruate, have erections, and masturbate.

In the seventies there have been gentle nudgings into the homosexual relation between males (Sticks and Stones, The Man without a Face, Cages, and Trying Hard to Hear You). It is interesting that this last book appears on everyone's current reading list of best books ... even on the prestigious YASD list, Still Alive: The Best of the Best, 1960-1974. Its only possible claim to fame is that it deals with a previously taboo subject in an otherwise very mediocre book. Interestingly, lesbians have not made their appearance in a specifically teen-age book. Oral sex is probably just around the corner since it has become so prominent in adult love stories.

Another development in teen-age literature has been the slow emergence of the ghetto book. Until recently most of the characters have been upper middle class whites living in single family homes in comfortable neighborhoods of mid-sized towns. There were a few books about the poor. An example was the adult book, A Tree Grows in Brooklyn, which was read by millions of teens during the late forties. Laid in a cold-water flat, the economic problems faced by the family were dreadful, but there was nothing physically frightening about the community. And basically upper middle class values prevailed in the family structure. There was faith in the power of education to get one out of one's present condition and at the end of the book, the mother marries a man who has a substantial income and the family can look back on the struggles they have been through with a certain amount of tender sentiment. Florence Means and Jesse Jackson wrote a series of ethnic books, but these present clean, well-ordered lives. Deprivation is undergone with full acknowledgment that life will be better later on. Mary Stolz presented a New York public housing project and Phyllis Whitney, before turning to Gothic romances, wrote about migrant workers and the fight in a suburb to keep out a low-income housing project. But still the poverty striken characters remain middle class and strive for middle class values.

One of the first attempts at an inner city story was The Twenty-Third Street Crusaders by John Carson in 1958, and the first really compelling book was Frank Bonham's Durango Street in 1965.

In the mid-1970s some of the finest of the new books are increasingly symbolic. They are stories that have layers of possible meaning, often have archetypal dimensions. A few critics saw Catcher in the Rye as a Christ story, but most readers reacted to Holden simply as a living adolescent. Perhaps a few more realized the symbolic patterns of A Separate Peace. But recent books like Cages, The Chocolate War, Slake's Limbo, The House of Stairs, A Little Demonstration of Affection, even Rumble Fish, tug at the reader because of the "something below the surface" that seems to be happening.

There are many trends during this almost fifty year period that I have not discussed: bibliotherapy, the animal story, the concern with female status, etc.

The adolescent novel struggles between often conflicting demands made of it. It must first of all be a book that teen-agers will read. To be such it must have fast-moving action, fairly stereotyped characters a couple of years older than the reader, who do things he secretly wishes he could do, and arrive at a happy ending. At the same time it must be something like a work of literature. It must magically balance elements of content and language to form a deeply satisfying pattern that gives esthetic value. Also it must teach social and personal values. It should demonstrate to the young how to move out of his confusions toward socially acceptable goals. For example, most of the books on homosexuality may be sympathetic and understanding, but in the long run they show the gay as an unhappy if not tragic individual. And seemingly, many writers want to use this genre to analyze the teen-ager and his society. Thus, they write the fictionalized case study. So the teenage book is subject to greater pressures than is the children's book or the adult novel. The balance among these four pressures seems to have swung from time to time during the twentieth century. I remember the books of the thirties as being literary, concerned with story as story and told with beauty of language. During the late sixties, books tended toward the case study of the teen-ager and the society he inhabits. The best books (Catcher in the Rye, Anne Frank, A Separate Peace, Swiftwater) have succeeded in meeting all four demands.

WHAT OF THE TEACHING OF LITERATURE IN SCHOOL? WHAT OF BOOKS FOR YOUNG PEOPLE? Some Old Questions and Some New Answers*

By Ken Donelson

How Should an English Teacher Present Literature?

"The first duty of the teacher of literature is, therefore, to see that his pupils have abundant opportunities to read good books. Reading must begin early and must never cease. There is no central theory or doctrine of literature that may be mastered in a year or a term of a school course. The essential thing to aim at is the acquisition of a store of memorable reading. The teacher must know what the good books are, and must perpetually watch to assure himself that the books he recommends are really taking vital hold on minds. The danger to be dreaded is that reading grow perfunctory, a task done to please the teacher, not spontaneous, not impelled by inner motive."

(Samuel Thurber, "How to Make the Study of Literature Interesting," School Review, September 1898, p. 491)

"Present-day teachers are 'exposing' boys to books rather than forcing them to read those which adults think are good for them. Instead of condemning a book the boy reads, they say very little and see to it that a book of a higher type with a similar theme is put within his reach. Teachers strive to find the interests of the individual boy, and then make available for him the books related to such interests. The skilled teacher knows books herself, has read widely of juvenile literature, and is able to direct reading interests. She prefers that the boys read 'something' rather than 'nothing' for although a youth may have the 'dime dreadful' habit, she has something on which to build. Her duty resolves itself into one of substitution.

Familiarity with the books boys recommend to each other often gives the teacher ability in directing the individual who has not formed the reading habit. The habit is the thing to strive for, and the interests may be widened by skilful directing on the part of the teacher or parent."

(Berenice B. Beggs, "Present-Day Books Eclipse Alger Thrillers," English Journal, November 1932, p. 728)

*Reprinted by permission of the author and publisher from Arizona English Bulletin (April 1972), 116-121.

"Curricula and courses in English will not alone produce desirable results. Much effort that is lost might be turned to good account if all teachers were more sympathetic in their methods of directing pupils' reading. To tell a pupil to read a certain book often inhibits the desire to read even a very desirable book. A necessary prerequisite for intelligent and sympathetic direction in the matter of reading is a discriminating knowledge of books and a thorough acquaintance with the psychology of childhood and adolescence. And teachers who would assume this important and difficult task must be fitted by nature and training for this very special duty.

In concluding I will suggest three lines along which the school should endeavor to improve voluntary reading. These are:

(1) That some definite plan of co-operation between teachers and pupils be organized whereby teachers may become acquainted with the reading habits of individual pupils and be able more efficiently to minister to their needs.

(2) That the school be more vitally related to the public library by cooperating with the librarian to aid pupils in selecting books. A plan similar to this is already in vogue in some places.

(3) That types of mental character and attitude as revealed in the quality of voluntary reading, should be carefully studied and the results correlated with the quality of school work accomplished, in order to aid both teacher and pupil to adjust the work of the school to the needs of the latter."

(Franklin Orion Smith, "Pupils' Voluntary Reading," *Pedagogical Seminary*, June 1907, pp. 221-222)

What Do We Know about the Reading Interests of Boys?

(The following conclusions were derived from a committee survey of reading interests studies in the early part of the Twentieth Century. The committee noted that there had been a high degree of correlation between the conclusion of most of the investigators of reading interests, and the following were what the committee felt to be the most valuable conclusions about the reading interests of boys.)

"1. That up to eight or nine years age there is very little difference in the reading interests of boys and girls. Up to this time, both are primarily interested in juvenile fiction, fanciful, imaginative literature and that's-why stories as means of satisfying the cravings for experience.

2. The greatest divergence of reading interests of boys and girls comes between ten and thirteen years of age, reaching the highest point between twelve and thirteen. The chief causes of this divergence lies in the fact that the fighting and rivalry instincts are stronger in boys while the material instinct is developing in girls of this age.

3. Boys have little or no interest in strictly juvenile fiction after twelve.

...

5. The maximum amount of reading in every instance is done between the sixth and eighth grades, the average being in the

seventh grade at about fourteen years of age. At this period ninety-five percent of the boys prefer adventure while seventy-five percent of the girls prefer love stories, stories about great women, about clothes. For boys adventure, war, travel and exploration, stories about great men, hold interest in the order named. Interest in biography and history is confined to those authors who can write in the form of an exciting story.

. . . .

7. The sex instinct is the directive force in the choice of literature through the 'teens.' Imagination is largely guided by the books read at this period. Wholesome romance, love stories, adventure, stories of construction, and poetry selected from the standpoint of adolescent need, should be provided.

8. Adult fiction, science and adventure rank highest with the 'teen' age boys, while the girls are interested in adult fiction and stories of home life."

(Danylu Belser, Chairman, "The Reading Interests of Boys: A Committee Report," Elementary English Review, November 1926, pp. 292-293)

What Kinds of Books Should Girls and Boys Read?

"... The modern schoolgirl is not reading a vicious literature; her taste is healthy, and for that let us be thankful in an age that produces much that is corrupt and unedifying. Nevertheless it were folly to disguise the fact that the reading of inferior novels, this filling the mind with scraps and tags of information, is harmful in the highest degree. If she does not read the great novels in her youth, she is never likely to do so: partly because, later on, she will naturally want to keep abreast of contemporary literature, and partly because she will have no desire to read them. If till the age of eighteen or nineteen her taste for good literature has not been cultivated--or, to put it more truly, if till this age she has cultivated a taste for inferior books and really appreciates them--it is unnatural to expect that after twenty her taste will alter to any considerable degree. Why is it that rubbishy novels have such an enormous circulation to-day, and that these same novels are published in their hundreds and thousands? Is it not largely due to the fact that the middle class who form the bulk of novel-readers have no standard of taste? Having never read a good novel, they do not recognise a bad one when they see it.

. . .

The school, therefore, and parent can do much to prevent that deterioration in taste that is so apparent on all sides, and this without anything in the nature of a revolution. Parents should sternly forbid the reading of more than one magazine a month, for the indiscriminate reading of magazines is perhaps more harmful than anything else; it creates a distaste for reading anything but 'snippets' and the lightest of literature, and gives the reader an air of superficial knowledge that is far worse than downright ignorance. The spaces in the mind may be filled; it is difficult to clear away rubbish. Magazine-reading is to the mind what constant 'whiskies and sodas' are to the body; it prevents the digestion of anything solid, and the taste for it grows with what it feeds upon."

(Florence B. Low, "The Reading of the Modern Girl," The Nineteenth Century, February 1906, pp. 282 and 286-287)

"When I was a boy, I remember reading in school certain literary masterpieces. When I was in the sixth grade I read Enoch Arden, A Dog of Flanders, and The Nurnberg Stove--beautiful things written for adults. Enoch Arden I could not understand at all. The other two were very slow-moving and not altogether within my grasp, but I liked them better than Grammar. In the seventh grade I read Evangeline and The Courtship of Miles Standish, both also beautiful things written for grown-ups....

My class went from seventh grade into high school and plunged at once into the study of the Roger De Coverley Papers, Sesame and Lilies, and Silas Marner. I wrote some beautifully (or dutifully) appreciative themes on these. I next slept through Macaulay's essay on Somebody, and Addison's essay on Somebody Else. I think Addison proved the more soporific. My last recollection was using the butcher knife and scalpel on Julius Caesar and Burke's Speech on Conciliation with America. Ah, how we sliced and cut and pried! We did a masterly bit of dissection, and thereby I got into Harvard.

Throughout this study of literature I was aware of a growing distaste for the books and authors studied. Since then I have found this distaste fixed. A volume of Shakespeare's complete works--a prize for scholarship while in high school--lies always before me on my desk. Daily I look at it and wonder why I can not find any joy in it. Trusted friends tell me that I don't know what I am missing. I feel ashamed. But Shakespeare is a closed book to me still.

Shortly after leaving college I began to teach English. And from the first I vowed that I would murder no masterpieces either by presenting them to boys before they were old enough or by dissecting them in the classroom, bit by bit, hunting down allusion after allusion to its lair. I vowed that books should be read only by boys who were old enough to enjoy them, and that they should be read for enjoyment as complete units. Automatically thereby I limited my activities to younger boys, for you can't get anybody into college by this method. But the delight of helping small boys into Bookland has far exceeded any satisfaction I might have had in getting big boys into college."

(Hubert V. Coryell, "Getting the Boy to Read," Good Housekeeping, October 1923, pp. 210-211)

What Should the English Teacher Do When Her Tastes Conflict with Parental Tastes?

"A story I recently read in regard to the subject of reading will illustrate my point. A schoolgirl, in some paper sent up to her teacher, had spoken most enthusiastically of a certain lurid and sensational story by a popular authoress, and her teacher recognizing the evils of that style of literature, wrote upon the margin of her paper, on returning it, 'Not suitable'; to which the girl's father wrote in reply, 'Why on earth not?'

Since such is the situation, it remains the high privilege of the teacher to perform this duty of creating a taste for wholesome reading in youth, and to lead them to the various sources where they can make discoveries of their own. In this way their powers of reflection will be exercised properly. The great danger in the use of general reading lies in its selection. Here again, before a teacher can successfully and intelligently select for her adolescent pupils kinds of literature best suited for them, she should have intimate knowledge of their physical, mental and social characteristics. Adolescents do not have to be coaxed to read. They are only too eager, as they thirst for the quick glow, touch, and sentiment of life so well delineated in good literature."

(Harriet V. Barakian, "Adolescent Literature," Education, February 1923, pp. 375-376)

Is There a Body of Literature Every Student Should Read?

"There is a peculiarly persistent Victorian affectation that there are some books that 'every child should know.' This notion has its roots in the Renaissance; but it needs to have its branches pruned. Every child should know the world in which he lives as thoroughly as it lies in him to know it. This world includes traditional lore and characters, 'classic' tales and long-enduring, if not eternal, verities. It is well to assimilate a great deal of this intellectual background. But it is more urgent to learn the present world and the world in which he is going to live. Some children are inclined to organize their ideas on a basis of historical retrospect--they ask, What came before that, and before that? Others, however, no less intelligent and no less valuable as social assets, seem to be quite indifferent to what went before; they are the pragmatists who ask, What of it?--and look to see what can be done here and now. Moreover, while the classics should be accessible to all, it is worse than useless to cultivate an affectation of appreciation for 'the best'--and it is desirable to cultivate the realization that classics are always and everywhere in the process of making."

(Sidonie Metzner Gruenberg, "Reading for Children," The Dial, December 6, 1917, p. 576)

Is Literature for Young People a Recent Phenomenon?

"The period of fifty years last past has witnessed an increasing volume of this literature [literature for the young], and also the growth of a sentiment in favor of it. The disposition to separate the reading of the young from the reading of the mature is of very modern development, and it has resulted in the creation of a distinct order of books, magazines, and papers. Not only has there been great industry in authorship, but great industry also in editorial work.

The classics of literature have been drawn upon not so much through selection as through adaptation.... In a general way, this great hoarde of young readers in America has created a large number of special writers for the young, and both readers and writers have been governed by the American life which they lead."

(Horace E. Scudder, "Literature in the Public Schools," Atlantic Monthly, August 1888, pp. 226-227)

Is Adolescent Literature Defensible as Literature?

"... I have one pet literary quarrel. It is both perpetual and perennial. I am out of all patience with those superior persons--often writing folk--who seem to think that boys' books are a sort of literary poor relation to be sent around to the back door. True, the book of fiction for the adolescent lacks the tradition that surrounds the novel. Nevertheless, it has its own dignity, fine and stalwart, and need not lower its head in the best of literary company. Give it time. The man who writes a real book for a boy has written a book that has no age limitation. He has fashioned a piece of art. No writing man can do more than that--very few have achieved that much."

(William Heyliger in The Junior Book of Authors, eds. Stanley J. Kunitz and Howard Haycraft. N.Y.: H. W. Wilson, 1935, p. 186)

"(1) The number of incredibly silly books for boys is rapidly multiplying.

(2) The number of boys who read them has also multiplied, partly because there are so many more convenient libraries, partly because the books circumvent the old-fashioned parental hostility to fiction by being innocuous and moralistic *ad nauseam*.

(3) The general slovenliness with which this mass of reading matter is written and printed increases even faster than the appalling rate of production; and nine-tenths of it is saturated with diction and grammar of exactly the sort that drives college teachers distracted by its obstinate persistence in undergraduate writing.

(4) It is impossible to resist the conclusion that such woefully written stuff, distributed by hundreds of thousands of copies a year to boys young enough to accept it as good, has had a great deal to do, and will have more, with our national insensitiveness to the decencies of language, our frequent confusion of mere cheapness with humor, and our adult hospitality to printed matter equally defiant of all civilized standards.

As a nation of responsible parents we could not manage much worse if we were systematically trying to cultivate in our offspring a firm foundation for poor taste and inability to read anything of consequence."

(Wilson Follett, "Junior Model," The Bookman, September 1929, p. 12)

"The average writer for boys had made the deadly mistake of writing down to his audience. If he only knew it, he ought to write up to it. Within the past month an editor of a famous American magazine said that boys wanted stories of action, action, action, and that they had no sympathy for shades of feeling; in other words; that everything with them was black and white. This is the mistake that has kept juvenile literature down in the rut....

The boy of to-day is interested in the life of to-day. In a lesser sense, to-day's problems are his own problems. He reads the newspapers. In school he discusses topical events.... He's interested in all phases of modern life because in a few years he'll be in the thick of things. But always the story must be interpreted to him through the feelings and actions, experience and reactions, of someone close to his own age and a part of his own world. Bearing this in mind, there is no reason why the boys' novel is not possible."

(Quoting William Heyliger in "The New Boy and the Old Book," The Literary Digest, December 25, 1920, p. 31)

Should We Use Modern Literature?

"The teaching of literature is sterile unless an understanding of modern as well as the older literature is taught. Current literature is a large part of the reading of educated men and women. It will be all the reading of most high-school and many college graduates. To teach only books of by-gone years because they have stood the test of time is to pretend that today does not exist, that only what is old is good. Modern people won't believe that, and if they are not taught to read current literature intelligently, they will read it unintelligently. Most college graduates preparing for teaching have not received instructions in modern literature as a part of their liberal arts course. Such instruction should be required of every prospective teacher of English...."

(Ernest R. Caverly, "The Professional Training of High-School Teachers of English," Educational Administration and Supervision, January 1940, p. 38)

Do Librarians Encourage Realistic Books for Young People?

"Why worry about censorship, so long as we have librarians? True, these worthy arbiters of our literary pabulum cannot hale an author into court for offenses against their esthetic preferences, but they can--and do--exercise a most rigid censorship over what the dear public shall--and shall not--read....

A recent number of the Wilson Bulletin contains a list of books which are under the ban, not because any of them are what we euphemistically call 'sophisticated,' but solely because the librarians do not care for that type of literature.

The maker of this Index Expurgatorius does not suggest, more or less timidly, that there may be better books for boys and girls than those on the restricted list. We might all agree with such a statement, but when we see our favorite juvenile authors classed with those who are barred from the mails--NOT TO BE

CIRCULATED--we feel that a mild protest may not be amiss."

(Ernest F. Ayres, "Not to be Circulated?" Wilson Library Bulletin, March 1929, p. 528)

"A young man has to sneak out behind the barn to read Huck Finn these days. But the A. L. A. [the American Library Association] keeps anything real, honest, or good in the Locked Closet behind the librarian's desk. Let's go to the Bang-Bang-Shoot-'em-up-Ben movies for their 'realism,' says the A. L. A.--they shall not read anything which won't do the little baskets just worlds of good.

...

Aside from Tarzan and the lousy scientification the kids can sneak into the shops and buy and hide behind a baseball mitt, there are not four new kid's books on the market which a thinking child will read without a bribe.

...

But let a spot of blood, let a good round 'damn' appear in a kid's book and the A. L. A.'s suede-clad thumb goes down on it. Little American children shall not know that life is real except from things printed on the sidewalks, and what Pop says when he comes home."

(Robb White, letter to the editor of the Saturday Review of Literature, August 12, 1939, p. 9)

Do Good Books Ever Become Old and Dated?

(During the last few years of the Nineteenth Century, yearly meetings were held by the Conference on Uniform Entrance Requirements in English to make recommendations on books to be used for college entrance examinations and books to be used for voluntary home reading by young people, books that would help kids get into college or help them stay there once they were admitted. The entire list of recommended books for 1899 is not given below, only a very few of the recommended books, but some of those few might give English teachers pause if they truly believe that a great book is one that is never forgotten and if they believe that colleges have a papal infallibility to cite what are the great books, of one year or of any time.)

"On motion, the report of the committee appointed at a previous meeting to prepare a list of books for voluntary reading was adopted with certain modifications, and is here presented in its amended form.

The following list is offered by the Conference in the hope that it may prove of service to teachers in guiding the reading of boys and girls at home."

Addison and Steele: Selections (especially Sir Roger de Coverley).
Blackmore: Lorna Doone
Bulfinch: Age of Fables
Burroughs: Selected essays
Cowper: Letters
Curtis: Prue and I: The Duty of Educated Men
DeQuincey: Opium Eater

Foster: Life of Goldsmith
Froissart: Chronicles
Gaskell: Cranford
Green: Short History of the English People
Holmes: Autocrat of the Breakfast Table
Johnson: Rasselas
Kingsley: Hypatia; Water Babies; Westward Ho
Landor: Selections from the Imaginary Conversations
Lockhart: Life of Scott
Bayard Taylor: Views Afoot
Tyndall: Hours of Exercise in the Alps

("A Summary of the Proceedings of the Meetings of the Conference on Uniform Entrance Requirements in English, 1894-1899," pp. 13-16)

CHOOSING WITH COURAGE: THE YOUNG ADULT BEST BOOKS, 1965-1969*

By Linda F. Lapides

The "Best Books" list is one reflection of the state of young adult librarianship in this country. Judging from the selection of best books in the mid-sixties, that state gave cause for concern. It seemed either that young adult librarians were sidestepping the issues and the point of the list, not always clearly stated at the time, or that book selectors at Enoch Pratt marched to a different drummer. I must confess the latter alternative was one I barely contemplated, though I'm certain that it was in my subconscious. In any case, once placed in print, these ideas turned out not to be parochial. Others had similar feelings and took issue.

What characterized the "Best Books" lists of this demi-decade? I would say that it was a time marked by a subtle shift in approach, a change in attitude and awareness that changed the content of the list. It was also a period of confusion due to an allegiance to a double standard of selection. Although the list is touted as being one of proven or potential interest to young adults, one that is selected on the basis of young adult appeal, this was not always the case nor was it always the basis for selection. In the words of one chairman within the time span, "In making the final selections the committee members continually asked each other, 'are these the adult books which have been published in the twelve month period which we think are best for young adults?' We were not choosing the most popular, nor the 'come-what-may young adults should read,' but rather those books which were, in our professional judgment, the best."

Now there is some discrepancy between choosing the best books in a librarian's professional judgment and choosing interesting books on the basis of young adult appeal. Those most appealing to youth are not necessarily the best, and the best books are not necessarily those with the most appeal for youth. "Best" Noah Webster defines as "having good qualities in the highest degree." Is this what we are really looking for, books possessing "good qualities in the highest degree"? What books could we select that

---

*Reprinted by permission of the author and publisher from Top of the News (June 1976), 359-364.

would really be "good" for teenagers? None, according to Philip Roth.

"Reading," he contends, "isn't good for you" anyway. "Brushing your teeth is good for you; eating raw vegetables is good for you; keeping your feet dry is good for you, et cetera, et cetera. What is normally considered good for teenagers is what keeps [their] temperature normal, [their] behavior normal, and, above all, [their] attitudes normal, safe and unexplosive.... The reading of novels ... is undoubtedly bad for you. Novels do not pussyfoot around. They can leave you sulky, angry, fearful and desperate. They can leave you dissatisfied with the life you are living. Sometimes, upon finishing a book, you can't help but dislike yourself--for being smug or narrow or callous or unambitious, for sharing in any of the hundreds of ways in which we are all of us without feeling or without understanding. Novels can make you skeptical and doubting--of your friends, of your family, of your religion, of your country; they can reveal to you that the kind of person you happen to be or think you want to be isn't really worth being."[1]

Another novelist, John Braine, suggests that "at the age of 18 one can get pleasure and profit from the most meretriciously bad books, just as one can enjoy and be nourished by the most appalling gastronomic combinations."[2] Perhaps we can compromise, keep the alliteration, minimize the confusion, attract the reader, and call the list "Bad Books for Young Adults." In short, while I have no quarrel with the criteria, "Best Books" is a deceptive title. The books we consider and select do not necessarily possess "good qualities in the highest degree." Nor is that really what we are seeking. We want books that speak to youth, are meaningful to them, stimulate them, entertain them, make them think, and, above all, books that they will enjoy reading. Robert Frost, as a teacher, pointed out, "I want the boys in their classes to enjoy their books because of what's in them. Criticism is the province of age, not youth. They'll get that soon enough. Let them build up a friendship with the writing world first."[3] Once I asked a teenager why he didn't like books. He said simply, "I never read a book I liked." Whose fault was it? He obviously made attempts. His comment always haunted me. One may not like a television program or a movie, yet still see another; but books don't get many additional chances. It's important to be tuned into the teenage world so you can succeed early in the game, as it is only after youth like to read that one can lead them into "the best."

It is impossible for every title on a national list like "Best Books" to suit every librarian or every library. Nor is it humanly possible for the committee to compile unerringly a list guaranteed to be the perfect reading and buying guide for all school and public libraries across the country and for adolescents of all shapes, sizes, colors, religions, all levels of maturity and intelligence. The list might not evoke agreement but it should command attention and respect. Most of all, it should be credible. Librarians who discover year after year that popular and important titles are omitted while those titles on the list quickly become candidates for discard begin to lose the faith as well as their young adult readers.

During the period 1965-69 the list did move forward to meet more realistically the needs of those for whom it was intended; it became more credible. My judgment and objectivity might suffer from the fact that I was a committee member in 1968 and 1969. What was the period like? It was clearly not the best of times, but could they get any worse? It was the time of deep and controversial involvement in Vietnam, of racial violence, of increased drug addiction, tragic assassinations, student rebellions, and the Kerner Commission report with its indictment of white racism. It was also the time of Twiggy, the mini-skirt, the generation gap, flower power, and the Beatles, whose international record sales overtook those of Bing Crosby, the long-time "crooner" king. And it was the time when man walked in space and on the moon. Clearly man had succeeded better on the moon than he had on earth.

Of all this history, the two events with the most impact on youth were the war in Vietnam and the racial unrest. Ironically, you couldn't pay people to check out books on Vietnam, but the excitement generated by books by and about black people was incredible. They barely grazed the shelves before swift fingers removed them. Nor was the mixture of terrific pride and indignation experienced by youth being exposed to the black heritage, experience, and literature for the first time limited to blacks. A young adult librarian from an upper-middle class family told me her teenage brother wished he were black. Contrast this with the comment of an elderly black woman standing on a street corner and addressing no one in particular, "Don't know why I was born a nigger, ain't got nothing to be proud of." The year was 1966 and I had just come from a preview of the film The Weapons of Gordon Parks. How I would have liked to have waved a wand and make her young again to grow up in a more hopeful time.

If the "Best Books" list failed at all during this period, it was in the omission of such titles as My Sweet Charlie (1965), Five Smooth Stones (1966), Hog Butcher (1966), and two titles, already classics of the black experience, Manchild in the Promised Land (1965) and The Autobiography of Malcolm X (1965). Sammy Davis, Jr.'s Yes, I Can did appear, and interestingly enough is the only title on the 1965 list of "Best Books" still to survive in Pratt collections. Fourteen titles out of twenty-five were added. It is doubtful that the inclusions of A Choice of Weapons and Jubilee to the 1966 list sparked the debate that the addition of Cleaver's Soul on Ice did in 1968. Durango Street, which has had steady circulation since its publication in 1965, was never eligible for the list, as teenage novels were not added at the time.

All of these titles are still going strong and evoke strong reactions from youth. Of My Sweet Charlie a young teenage reviewer for "You're the Critic" wrote, "Even though the book is fiction its characters seem to come alive. I have never read such an intensely exciting, deeply compassionate novel as this one." About Five Smooth Stones came the comment, "I must admit that, for the first time, I have been emotionally jolted by a novel, a mere story.... Miss Fairbairn must truly be a most remarkable authoress because she has the power to take a fictional character and make him appear real enough to involve her readers completely." Manchild in the Promised Land evoked the following: "I don't care what race you are, when you probe the pages of Claude Brown's autobiography, Manchild in the Promised Land, you become a young Negro boy set loose in the ignorant streets of Harlem." And isn't this what we want? What better way for youth to understand the turmoil festering in this nation than to be able to step into someone else's shoes and experience it from their point of view. I could not agree more with Joan Aiken, who says, "I'm sure that wherever there is real trouble in the world, the basic cause of it is lack of imagination, simply failure to project, treating other people as if they were things."[4]

Why weren't Manchild and Malcolm X added? They were frank and controversial and they scared librarians at the time. Nor did Pratt add Manchild immediately. But it seems to me that the "Best Books" list should lead the way and be an example to which librarians can turn for support. As for My Sweet Charlie, which saw a resurgence after the TV show and is back in print in paperback, it appeared with little promotion and quickly went out of print. I will never forget the reply of a Doubleday gentleman when asked why the book was no longer available, "Our representatives in the South didn't like it much."

The sexual revolution was heralded by the Young Adult Services Division with the admission of two unwed pregnant ladies, one of whom quickly, to its 1967 "Best Books" list: Jean Thompson in The House of Tomorrow and July Greer in Mr. and Mrs. Bo Jo Jones. Sex was out in the open and no longer the dirty word it was in the previous decade. However, both ladies suffer--Jean gives her baby up for adoption and July's infant is born dead. One of the most controversial books of the period from the committee's point of view was Kirkwood's Good Times, Bad Times (1968), dealing with homosexuality. There was heated debate and a close vote but it never made the list. Nevertheless, it is still popular. Teenagers were consumed with curiosity about drugs. It didn't necessarily mean they wanted to turn on themselves, but they wanted to know what it was like and what desperation, tedium, or emptiness made people turn to heroin. Dick Schaap's Turned On, also on the 1967 list, was one of the first true stories of personal tragedy due to involvement with drugs and not just a clinical survey of which drug does what, and is still in demand, though out of print in hardback and paperback. In 1968, for the first time, a book of cartoons appeared on the list, though not without dissension. But in the end, Charlie Brown and his friends emerged victorious to cheer a rather humorless generation. Humor is indeed a scarce commodity. All of us need to learn to laugh at ourselves and at life's absurd moments. If anyone is a perceptive master of the human and canine situation from its most ridiculous to its most poignant, it is Charles Schultz. His strips, said a newspaper editorial writer, often "make a keener, more important point than any that is expounded by the wordsmiths."[5] During these years the lists contained more nonfiction (2/3 nonfiction to 1/3 fiction), the usual smattering of sports, science, suspense, and topical books such as Belfrage's Freedom Summer (1965), MacLean's When Eight Bells Toll (1966), Kunen's The Strawberry Statement (1968), and Alice Lynd's We Won't Go (1968), which serve their purpose but in due time are replaced with something newer or more current.

Out of curiosity I riffled through our local reviews and discovered that titles on the "Best Books" list with a brief or nonexistent YA lifespan at Pratt are those of which reviewers said: "special" (Levitt's An African Season, 1967); "a fairly good recent book on the subject of migrant workers, should you find a reader for it" (Moore's The Slaves We Rent, 1965); and "possibly of limited appeal but it should be purchased" (Manry's Tinkerbelle, 1966). While those that live for many years on the YA shelves are described as: "moving, always readable" (Park's A Choice of Weapons, 1965); "will stimulate talk, thought and tears" (Thompson's House of Tomorrow, 1967); "a beautiful book" (Potok's The Chosen, 1967); "teenagers will beat down the doors of the library for this one" (Head's Mr. and Mrs. Bo Jo Jones, 1967); and "a fast moving intensely human account" (Roth's I'm Done Crying, 1969). Would there were more titles to which all those positive adverbs and adjectives could apply.

It was the 1967 list, the one that heralded a change in the tone of the lists and got down to the nitty-gritty, that sparked the following words from Bronxville, New York: "Dear Library Association: I read this list aloud to my husband and he asked if it has been printed by Ralph Ginsberg! No wonder the young people have problems if the literature that is recommended has such low ideals and morals." This message was scrawled across the cover of the 1967 list of "Best Books for Young Adults" and signed "Mother of six who hopes you omit booklists altogether if there is nothing better."

I do not think there was ever a time when such criticism was not directed toward books. Samuel Goodrich, alias Peter Parley, attributed "much of the vice and crime in the world ... to those atrocious books put in the hands of children"[6] such as Jack the Giant Killer, which he considered a bloody tale, and Puss-in-Boots, which had as its central character a feline who was not only a liar but a cheat. Indeed young adult librarians have a responsibility. In addition to encouraging teen-agers to read, they have to educate parents that simply reading about unwed pregnant youth, drug addicts, or violent individuals will not make their teenagers mothers or junkies or murderers. This point was well made by the gentleman who wrote to the editor of a Baltimore paper upon learning that the Maryland Board of Motion Picture Censors had deleted the scene in Walt Disney's The Vanishing Prairie showing the birth of a baby buffalo. "I do not think," he wrote, "that seeing the birth of a buffalo will encourage any children to give birth to baby buffaloes."

Early in my career at the Pratt Library a portion of a young adult meeting was devoted to a book selection problem, whether Dan Jacobson's Evidence of Love, a tale of miscegenation in South Africa with a frank love story, should be added to the young adult collection. We decided in its favor. Afterward, Mr. Edwin Castagna, the then new director, who was in attendance, stood up and admitted he was pleased. He had not participated in the discussion because he did not wish to influence the outcome, but said that whenever a difficult decision was to be made, he hoped the library would stand on the side of courage. I have never forgotten that statement and I hope none of us will, whether in selecting titles for the "Best Books" list or in adding titles to our individual young adult collections.

References

1. Philip Roth. "They Won't Make You Normal," in In My Opinion: The Seventeen Book of Very Important Persons (New York: Macmillan, 1966), p. 65-66.

2. John Braine. "A Novelist Should Stick to His Last," New York Times Book Review, Jan. 10, 1965, p. 1.

3. Jean Gould. Robert Frost: The Aim Was Song (New York: Dodd, 1964), p. 239-40.

4. Joan Aiken. "Between Family and Fantasy: An Author's Perspectives on Children's Books," Quarterly Journal of the Library of Congress, Oct. 1972, p. 318.

5. "2 Different Kettles" [Editorial], Evening Sun, May 15, 1975, p. A16.

6. Samuel Goodrich. Recollections of a Lifetime (New York: Miller and Orton, 1857), Vol. 1, p. 169.

PART III

THE NEW REALISM AND OTHER TRENDS

(this is now . . .)

EDITOR'S NOTE

In 1972, Nancy Larrick recognized and applauded the revolution which had occurred in the late sixties in writing for young people.[1] She tells of an eighth grader for whom the books which "tell it like it is" and use the "language of the streets ... are the books that say what I'd like to say." Larrick then presents the problem that has been with us ever since: how do you reconcile adults' instinct to protect youth from harsh reality with young people's need to relate their reading experience to the world as they know it?

The ensuing argument has taken ugly censorial turns at times, mindlessly silly ones at others. Occasionally it has produced some rational and useful criticism, such as Richard Peck's: "in pursuit of relevance, too many current offerings fall too neatly into categories: sexual problems ... drugs ... death ... ethnic and racial groups ... the characters become case studies."[2] He reminds us that not much has changed, after all--the ingredients, perhaps, but not the recipe.

John Neufeld points out that one of the most "relevant" adolescent concerns--sex--continues to be sidestepped by writers for young adults.[3] In "The Maturation of the Junior Novel: From Gestation to the Pill,"[4] Lou Willett Stanek echoes Neufeld's conclusion that the whole truth about sexuality continues to be a taboo. While the new realism has produced more titles about premarital pregnancy, a close look at the books reveals them to contain "old ideas against a new backdrop."

By 1977, Robert Unsworth has identified less than a handful of books which treat male adolescent sexuality in a realistic manner. He complains that "leaving sex out of a novel that purports to examine male maturation and growth is like writing a cookbook without mentioning food."[5]

Speaking of other aspects of realism in young adult books, Stanek notes that kids cannot accept the idea of evil teenagers in _The Chocolate War_ and do not want the rabbits in _Watership Down_ to die: "Perhaps the formula shouldn't change, perhaps young adult literature should remain escape literature, a way station, a super way to fantasize, dream, play a game, and be reassured."[6]

Nevertheless, the new realistic books are being read by

young adults, and therefore are presumably meeting a need. In an article noting the paradoxical trend toward realism in children's books and toward fantasy in adult books, Patrick Merla suggests that:

> Young and old alike are suddenly finding the strangest books meaningful. Why? Because they ask, in some fashion or other, What is REAL?... we are living in a moment of history when people are consciously seeking answers to problems of existence ... the current literary trends may be indicative of that search, and the paradox of "reality" for children versus "fantasy" for adults may be double-edged--children looking for facts to help them cope with an abrasive environment while adults probe a deeper, archetypal reality that can transform society altogether.[7]

I think he has failed to note how many teenagers, as well as adults, are reading adult fantasy, but his definition of the appeal of this genre applies also to teens.

What we need to remember is that teenagers are no more monolithic in their tastes than are adults, and that the junior novel constitutes only a small portion of the reading matter consumed during adolescence.

Notes

1. Nancy Larrick. "Divorce, Drugs, Desertion, the Draft: Facing up to the Realities in Children's Literature," Publishers' Weekly, February 21, 1972, 90-91.

2. See page 101-103.

3. "The Thought, Not Necessarily the Deed: Sex in Some of Today's Juvenile Novels," Wilson Library Bulletin, October 1971, 147-152.

4. Lou Willett Stanek. "The Maturation of the Junior Novel: From Gestation to the Pill," School Library Journal, December 1972, 34-39.

5. See page 122.

6. See page 167.

7. Patrick Merla. "'What Is REAL?' Asked the Rabbit One Day," Saturday Review, November 4, 1972, 49.

TWO OF THE BEST CONTEMPORARY WRITERS FOR ADOLESCENTS*

By Ken Donelson

Two of the best contemporary writers for adolescents, Nat Hentoff (author of Jazz Country and I'm Really Dragged But Nothing Gets Me Down) and Susan Hinton (author of The Outsiders and That Was Then, This Is Now) wrote articles in the New York Times Book Review during 1967 which are still valid criticisms of adolescent literature. Hentoff's "Tell It as It Is" (May 7, 1967, pp. 3, 51) contains these lines. "... I don't believe that printed fiction is an entirely anachronistic medium for those of the young who, so far, have not felt drawn to it. There are questions and ambivalencies endemic to adolescence that songs and even films have not begun to explore in ways that are compellingly meaningful to the young. Perhaps fiction still can ... My point is that the reality of being young--the tensions, the sensual yearnings and sometimes satisfactions, the resentments against the educational lock step that makes children fit the schools, the confusing recognition of their parents' hypocrisies and failures--all this is absent from most books for young readers.... Where is the book that copes with the change in sexual values--if not yet sexual behavior on a large scale--among adolescents? Where is the book that even mentions an erection? And what of marijuana and LSD and Banana-highs? What is there about society that is leading more and more of the young to drop out of it, if only momentarily and experimentally? ... To read most of what is written for young readers is to enter a world that has hardly anything to do with what the young talk about, dream about, worry about, feel pain about. It is indeed a factitious world, and that kind of writing for teen-agers is not worth doing, because it is not worth their reading.... And so, I expect, I'm going to try again. Not writing at them, but about them and about myself, about possibility, about the good, kind, decent grown-ups who once were young and now allow napalm to fall on children. About what one person, one naked human being, can do to stay as whole as he can in a time of the banality of evil. But if I preach, I fail. However, if I can find in fiction the truth that only fiction can tell, I may be able to continue that dialogue. Even--to be utopian--with one or two of my own children."

---

*Reprinted by permission of the author and publisher from "Shoptalk," Arizona English Bulletin (April 1972), 135.

Hinton's "Teen-Agers Are for Real" (August 27, 1967, pp. 26-29) is even more remarkable for it is the testimony of a 19 year-old girl. "Teen-agers today want to read about teen-agers today. The world is changing, yet the authors of books for teen-agers are still 15 years behind the times.... Nowhere is the drive-in social jungle mentioned, the behind-the scenes politicking that goes on in big schools, the cruel social system in which, if you can afford to snub every fourth person you meet, you're popular. In short, where is reality? ... The teen-age years are a bad time. You're idealistic. You can see what should be. Unfortunately, you can see what is, too. You're disillusioned, but only a few take it as a personal attack.... Most kids nowadays date for status. There are cliques and classes and you date so you can say you had a date with so-and-so.... But violence too is a part of teen-agers' lives. If it's not on television or in the movies, it's a beating-up at a local drive-in. Things like this are going to take place as long as there are kids. Only when violence is for a sensational effect should it be objected to in books for teen-agers. Such books should not be blood and gore, but not a fairyland of proms and double-dates, either. Sometimes I wonder which extreme does the most harm.... Teen-agers know a lot today. Not just things out of textbooks, but about living. They know their parents aren't superhuman, they know that justice doesn't always win out, and that sometimes the bad guy wins.... Writers needn't be afraid that they will shock their teen-age audience. But give them something to hang onto. Show that some people don't sell out, and that everyone can't be bought. Do it realistically. Earn respect by giving it."

IN THE COUNTRY OF TEENAGE FICTION*

By Richard Peck

People say the damnedest things to the writers of teenage fiction. The other day at a book conference in New Orleans a librarian said to me, "What my young readers need is a novel about a black adolescent unwed father on a Honda."

Days later I was still puzzling over a possible plot line for that protagonist when an editor in New York asked me, "When are you going to write a *real* novel?"

"A *real* novel?" I asked menacingly.

"Well, you know, a novel for adults."

I simmered silently, sparing him the lecture I'm about to deliver now. It seems to me that trying to write a valid novel for a young reader--let's say a thirteen-year-old who is at a sensitive and troubled point in life--is at least as important and far more challenging than writing a "real, adult novel."

It's a harder job because of the pitfalls. No one who has passed through adolescence can re-enter it with vision unblurred by personal nostalgia and the kind of publicity the current youth scene receives. It's a great temptation to preach, to patronize, to pander, to placate, and especially to propagandize. And, of course, most writers of juvenile fiction will never see ... let us say, twenty-five again.

An exception to be mentioned at once is S. E. Hinton, whose best-selling *The Outsiders* (Viking) was written when she was a teenager. It is a novel full of unheeded hints for elder writers of young fiction. *The Outsiders* portrays the warmth of belonging to a group that all young people need. Instead of the hard-edged realism of contemporary causes and faddish problems, it tells an exciting tale in unabashedly melodramatic terms. The world of newspapers and parents and school and foreign wars lies beyond the perimeters of a story about belonging.

We Americans live in the world's most self-conscious, identity-seeking society. We're not sure who we are, and many of us would like books to tell us and to tell our young people. Those of us who have lived and traveled abroad know the futility of trying to generalize about anything American. Two-hundred million inhabitants of a pluralist, youth-oriented, upwardly mobile, mildly literate society are not readily catered to or categorized. Most writers who set forth to capture the essence of the American Experience are doomed to frustration, both at the typewriter and by the publisher. Yet we still hanker after perfection--the right combination of words.

In probing literary history our self-conscious quest for the Great American Novel still haunts us a bit. And the youthful hero recurs from *Huckleberry Finn* through Thomas Wolfe to *Catcher in the Rye*, augmented by Fitzgerald and Hemingway--those creators of eternal children trapped in adult bodies. At the same time, particularly if we're librarians, we know that the novels that have captured American readers in the largest numbers include *Uncle Tom's Cabin*, *Ben Hur*, *Gone with the Wind*, *Peyton Place*, and *Love Story*. This year we're trying to figure out whether *Jonathan Livingston Seagull* is a novel, a sermon, or a hymn to life and death. All we really know is that it's an overwhelming success with all ages. What does this tell us about the impact of our reading upon ourselves and our offspring?

Nothing very coherent. But we do know that books span the generation gap. *Winnie-the-Pooh* (American by adoption if not by birth) isn't the exclusive province of childhood. *Catch-22* is no more limited to a readership of World War II vets than *Deliverance* is directed to middle-aged hunters. And *The Member of the Wedding*, *Catcher in the Rye*, *A Separate Peace*--are these teenage fiction? They are about adolescents and adolescence. They were written presumably for adults. I suspect that all three were written as intensely personal documents with no sense that they would become required school readings.

A survey of what teenagers read during their summer vacations was recently conducted by J. A. Christensen. He reported in *Media & Methods* magazine that the three most widely read authors were Ray Bradbury, Hermann Hesse, and F. Scott Fitzgerald, in that order. Farther down the list came a staggering range. Jacqueline Susann rubbed shoulders with Ayn Rand and Daphne Du Maurier. Truman Capote, Mario Puzo, and Charles Dickens found themselves gathered in close proximity.

This bracing catholicity of youthful reading tastes will come as no surprise to librarians. If young people read what everyone else reads, however, the writer of novels specifically directed to them may well feel threatened. He doesn't, of course, because the juvenile market is booming. In a youth-oriented society books are being tailored to young tastes as surely as clothing, though they are not as well marketed. Still, adolescent fiction is increasing in visibility. And someone is reading these novels apart from the reviewers.

Most of the estimated 2,500 books for young readers published annually are never ordered by bookstores. The commercial counters are stocked instead with the solid sellers and the series books that already have a faithful following.

Schools have begun to buy youth novels in paperback--often for reluctant readers who can't be persuaded to read through the conventional curriculum. If a representative range of current titles is to be found anywhere, it will be in the library.

Youth novelists and librarians therefore have a common cause. We want the attention of the newest generation. After the initial trauma of television, we find that many youngsters raised in front of the screen do find time to stop watching and start reading. And we want to win more of them over. When novels of the historic past and the adult future fail to capture them, we want to be ready with new incentives to a reading habit that will last.

Not everyone is on our side. Some critics maintain that a separate adolescent fiction is superfluous. Speaking at the Children's Book Council, Natalie Babbitt said, "Teenagers do not need a fiction of their own. They are quite ready to move into the world of adult fiction."

Those who are ready _do_ move on. Many young people today are just like young people have always been--anxious to be as adult as possible. But many are not. Many are patients in the remedial reading clinic. Some of them appear to be terminal cases. The permissive home and the watered-down school curriculum have betrayed them. The basic skills were not imposed, and attention spans were not stretched. There are college freshmen abroad in the land who aren't ready for a seventh-grade textbook.

The legacy of the decade just past is another matter. Nat Hentoff has written a youth novel entitled _In the Country of Ourselves_ (Simon & Schuster). The title is symptomatic of a well-publicized, poorly evaluated phenomenon--the consuming self-centering of the young in a youth-oriented society. Some time during the 1960s the young were allowed to become a country of themselves. This sense of near nationality came to a full flowering, and nothing has happened since to diminish the idea. The voting, credit-card-carrying, liberated young flow more freely through our society than we elders can hope to do. And in their free-flowing way they make society their own.

It's logical that many young people, regardless of reading skills, want to read about their fictional contemporaries. They are liable to choose books as they choose friends, more as mirrors than windows. The experiences of adolescence are increasingly valid to those who see few advantages in being adults.

Still, the best youth novels portray adolescence as a maturing process. Though the focus may be upon being young, there is a sense of the future--a sense of becoming, as well as being. The worst portray youth in a vacuum; its protagonists are hopelessly young forever, dominated by a wicked adult establishment.

In his Three Roads to Awareness (Glencoe) Don Fabun wrote,

> Perhaps all stories should begin with the word "and." Perhaps they should end with the word "and" too. It would remind us that no experience ever begins; there was always something that preceded it. What really began, for us, was our awareness of something going on. At the end, the word "and ..." would remind us that no story ever really ends--something more will happen after.

This sense is particularly important for a novel aimed at the early teens. It is dishonest to conclude a story about fifteen-year-olds with "... and they lived happily ever after." No one does. The best and worst usually lie ahead. Yet, the other extreme is a fashionable pessimism in which maturity means corruption.

Returning to that black adolescent unwed father on his Honda and getting down to cases, we've passed the time for asking if teenage fiction is necessary. It's an established, economic fact. Next season's publishing lists promise an even greater flow. The publishers assure us that teenage fiction is increasing in quality as well as volume. With no sense of irony, they point out that adolescent fiction is coming of age.

The present trend may well have begun in the antediluvian year of 1950 with the publication of Hot Rod (Dutton) by Henry Gregor Felsen. Dedicated to the Des Moines Safety Council, Hot Rod was the strong story of a boy's love affair with his custom-built Plymouth:

> Bud Crayne rounded a curve at fifth and faced into the setting sun. For the next ten miles the highway ran straight and level across open farm land. Ninety-nine out of a hundred drivers rounded that curve and coming on the flat immediately increased their speed. Bud held at fifty. He had his reasons for staying at fifty. Bud always had a reason for driving at a particular speed.

Good old middle-American Bud, with his James Dean cool and his ducktail haircut. He wasn't academically gifted, of course, but far from dropping pills, he didn't even know what they were. Bud's pushing forty now and probably peering anxiously over his adolescent child's shoulder, wondering what's in that book called Dinky Hocker Shoots Smack! or The Rotten Years.

The teenager of the seventies lives in a more complex world than Bud Crayne's flat plains. Between then and now we've lived through the assassination of a president whom adolescents cannot remember, the Age of Aquarius, busing, occasionally legalized abortion, the decline of the WASP, televised moonshots, the radicalizing of the schoolhouse, and a generation of war, among other events that have efficiently effaced the past.

There's a wide expanse of troubled ground to cover. In pursuit of revelance, too many current offerings fall too neatly into categories:

Sexual Problems

Paul Zindel's My Darling, My Hamburger (Harper & Row)
John Donovan's I'll Get There, It Better Be Worth the Trip (Harper & Row)
Jeanette Eyerly's The Phaedra Complex (Lippincott)
Isabelle Holland's The Man Without a Face (Lippincott)

Drugs

(anonymous) Go Ask Alice (Prentice-Hall)
S. E. Hinton's That Was Then, This Is Now (Viking)
Lee Kingman's The Peter Pan Bag (Houghton Mifflin)
Mary Calhoun's It's Getting Beautiful Now (Harper & Row)

War and Antiwar

Ester Hautzig's The Endless Steppe (Thomas Y. Crowell)
Mary Stolz's By the Highway Home (Harper & Row)
Joe W. Haldeman's War Year (Holt, Rinehart & Winston)
Jill Paton Walsh's Fireweed (Farrar, Straus)

Death

John Donovan's Wild in the World (Harper & Row)
Gunnel Beckman's Admission to the Feast (Holt, Rinehart & Winston)
Paul Zindel's The Pigman (Harper & Row)
Eric Rhodin's The Good Greenwood (Westminster)

Ethnic and Racial Groups

Frank Bonham's The Nitty Gritty (Dutton)
Virginia Hamilton's The Planet of Junior Brown (Macmillan)
June Jordan's His Own Where (Thomas Y. Crowell)
Ernest J. Gaines's A Long Day in November (Dial)
Florence E. Randall's The Almost Year (Atheneum)
Marian T. Place's Retreat to the Bear Paw (Four Winds Press)
Nathaniel Benchley's Only Earth and Sky Last Forever (Harper & Row)
Audree Distad's Dakota Sons (Harper & Row)

Following Kent State, there was a publishing spate of "political juveniles" at the time when collegiate crises were filtering down toward the junior high. Writing in the New York Times (November 7, 1971) Benjamin DeMott said,

> ... the defects that mar most problem political juveniles are of two kinds--excessive detachment (inability to feel the exciting, promising newness of politics to youth) and excessive righteousness (lack of responsiveness to the humanity, however ignorant, of the benighted opposition.)

DeMott was reviewing three novels: Hentoff's In the Country of Ourselves, Maia Wojciechowska's The Rotten Years (Doubleday), and John Neufeld's Sleep Two, Three, Four (Harper & Row). In The Rotten Years a teacher, Mrs. Jones, spurs her history class students to community activism, ultimately causing a crazed parent to burn her to death. DeMott says of the teacher,

> Now and then she invites her students to work their way through to knowledge of why elders think and feel as they do. But the martyrdom of Mrs. Jones, together with the paucity of concrete attempts to reach for understanding of other men's fears and anxieties, becomes at the end a powerful incitement to youthful self-pity.

In a more recent novel, Mary Stolz's Leap Before You Look, (Harper & Row), a tolerant pair of parents and their far-out son debate the values of their different worlds in a way that begins to give the reader a choice of allegiances:

> Mr. Ferris glanced in the rearview mirror at his son, whose hair stood up in a great dingy halo, and who met his glance with an expression of guileless happiness. 'You know, Father, you and Mother should make more of an effort to catch up with the times. She tells me it's so long since you've been to a movie that you've never even seen a naked body on the screen.'
>
> 'We didn't like movies when there weren't any naked bodies on it,' Mr. Ferris muttered. 'No reason to go now, just because there are.'
>
> 'No, but that's one of the things I mean. Our movies show what we *are*, to a great extent. Open and honest--about nakedness in part, of course, but not just nakedness of the body. We're trying to strip the human mind of its pretentious coverings, too.'
>
> 'Who's we?'
>
> 'Me. People my age. The kids' age, here, too. People your students' age. You'd have a better insight into the people you're teaching if you listened to our music and saw the kind of shows we like.'
>
> 'I don't have to listen to all that caterwauling or turn voyeur in order to lecture on the Congress of Vienna. And were young people always so pompously possessive? *Our* movies, *our* music--'
>
> 'Yes,' said his wife. 'We were.'

The most simplistic, and propagandistic, novels revolve around single issues: Robert Coles's The Grass Pipe (Atlantic

Monthly Press) about drugs, Jeannette Eyerly's Bonnie Jo, Go Home (Lippincott) about abortion. Perhaps the single largest trend within the trend is the more multifaceted problem of ethnic identity.

In the past, young Puerto Ricans, Chicanos, blacks, and Indians had little or nothing to read that related directly to their lives. Today, there is no lack of minority protagonists and situations. But it would seem that most authors miss the mark, imposing vicarious and adult attitudes on books about ethnicity instead of personality. The characters become case studies.

There's no denying that too many American families, regardless of ethnic group, live in the surroundings described in Frank Bonham's Viva Chicano (Dutton):

> Below him, the buildings of the Project were neatly fitted together in the forms of T's, E's, and H's, each building three stories high and flatroofed. The boxy structures, dozens of them, were laid out like a puzzle to test the intelligence of rats. Even a stupid rat, Keeny thought gloomily, would have sense enough to stay out of them.

In the name of political, racial, or sociological realism, too many novels leave their characters where they find them, seething in a static landscape. But America is still an upwardly mobile society. Young people still respond with the freshness DeMott mentioned. And especially our youngest readers like a story that will take them out of themselves. Kaye Webb, of England's Penguin books, puts it simply, "The pressured thirteen-year-old wants yarns." The pressured American thirteen-year-old too often gets problems he didn't know he had. These include a few he never would have were they not in vogue.

Propaganda, dead earnestness, and that old American search-for-the-self dominate the field in American titles. We have to turn to Britain for a significant body of juvenile novels that don't force issues. Linda Davis of Collins Publishers in London says that Collins "is not interested in the problem novel." Nor is England so haunted as we are by adolescence as a separate entity. Margaret Clark of the Bodley Head says, "We don't believe in books for any level. Our teenagers are resentful of being singled out."

A modest list of recent overseas offerings includes, Night Fall by Joan Aiken (Holt, Rinehart & Winston); Jean in the Morning by Janet Sandison (St. Martin's); Operation Neptune by Christopher Nicole (Holt, Rinehart & Winston); The Runaways by Victor Canning (Morrow); Josh by Ivan Southall (Macmillan); Thursday by Catherine Storr (Harper & Row); The Year of the Stanger by Allan Campbell McClean (Walck); The Seal-Singing by Rosemary Harris (Macmillan); The Owl Service by Alan Garner (Walck); and two books, The Longhorn Trail (Prentice-Hall, and London: William Collins Sons) and North Against the Sioux (London: William Collins Sons) by Kenneth Ulyatt who writes about the American West as if he's been there.

"Good yarns" aren't limited to imports, of course. Nor is all contemporary, relevant realism necessarily harsh. Anyone who has ever taught school knows that young people are more caught up in personal concerns than abstract causes. It's the television news camera that is fixated upon sit-ins, protests, and riots.

Most youngsters, particularly the readers among them, are seeking shelter, or at least a place to catch their breath. In an age of sagging adult authority, they increasingly seek shelter from the tyranny of their peers. Too few books are reflecting their need to grow independently, without marching behind other people's causes and without looking back at their parents in anger. Too few books are fulfilling their need for solace and even friendship. There is sex-violence-social problems on the one hand, Tolkien fantasy on the other. And not enough middle ground.

At the Dartmouth Conference in 1966 Frank Whitehead said, "Until well on into adolescence these reactions [to reading] are intuitive, impermanent, and intensely personal."

The most successful youth novels, like The Outsiders, follow this lead, exploring the very personal problems of the young, with the wider world of adults, causes, and conditions as a backdrop. The real challenge for the writer, it seems to me, is to state some of the external problems in a contemporary language. Occasionally someone manages it. Here, the young protagonist of George A. Woods's Vibrations (Harper & Row) thinks,

> Maybe I'm a gangly ape or some kind of a creep. Maybe girls don't like me because I've got pimples and my shoes aren't shined. There's something wrong because I'm walking along this road with no one and I'm tired and I wish I were dead.

Even when they deal on the most personal level, though, many novels deal in distortion. Too many young characters suffer greatly exaggerated personal problems. Mental illness is a major theme, almost always traced to parental neglect or insensitivity. There's a whole battalion of the young walking wounded, emotional and physical cripples. If these disabilities are meant to dramatize the insecurity that most adolescents feel about their minds and bodies, the technique is usually far too heavy-handed. In Mildred Lee's The Skating Rink (Seabury) a boy decides to quit school where he has been shamed for his stuttering:

> It wouldn't be like the other times he'd quit--letters from the truant officer, tears from his stepmother, beatings from his father. He was too big for a licking now--a good two inches taller than his father--and he thought the old man might be glad not to have to buy shoes for him so often. Walking the two miles from the Faraday farm to the big new high school in Wesley was hard on shoes, especially cheap ones. It wore them out in a hurry.

> 'How come you've got to walk it when I pay taxes for a bus to carry you?' Myron Faraday had said in the beginning, anger gathering like a cloud in his face that shrank in upon its bones a little more with each year's petty failures. 'Looks like you just can't stand it to act like ever'body else. Got to be different--like you was tetched.'

Whatever the problem, inevitably it only requires two paragraphs to return it to the source--the unsympathetic adult. Being the works of adults, most novels overemphasize the adult impact. The stuttering boy in *The Skating Rink* is scorned by his classmates. Yet it is his father who must play the heavy.

The best juvenile novels, like all novels, are the rarities. The renegades that allow a little liberating laughter. The ones that raise human questions without providing pat solutions and stock scapegoats. Those that recognize and salute youth as a part of the continuum of life. Such examples as, M. E. Kerr's *Dinky Hocker Shoots Smack* (Harper & Row); J. M. Couper's *Lottery in Lives* (Houghton Mifflin); Mary Stolz's *Leap Before You Look* (Harper & Row); Adrienne Richard's *Pistol* (Atlantic Monthly Press); Hope Campbell's *No More Trains to Tottenville* (Saturday Review Press).

In another place and age, Beatrix Potter, the creator of Peter Rabbit, wrote, "My books were made small to fit children's hands, not to impress grown-ups." Striking the right chord in that tentative time between childhood and adulthood is another matter. One which most authors haven't mastered.

For a final answer to that editor who refers glibly to real, adult novels, I turn to Isaac Singer, perhaps the master storyteller of the age:

> In our epoch, when storytelling has become a forgotten art and has been replaced by amateurish sociology and hackneyed psychology, the child is still the independent reader who relies on nothing but his own taste. Names and authorities mean nothing to him. Long after literature for adults will have gone to pieces, books for children will constitute the last vestige of storytelling, logic, faith in the family, in God and in real humanism.

THIRTY POPULAR ADOLESCENT NOVELS*

By Al Muller

Armstrong, William H. Sounder. New York: Scholastic Book Services, 1969.

Bonham, Frank. Durango Street. New York: E. P. Dutton, 1965.

_______. The Nitty Gritty. New York: E. P. Dutton, 1968.

Cavanna, Betty. The Boy Next Door. New York: William Morrow, 1956.

Craig, Margaret. It Could Happen to Anyone. New York: Thomas Y. Crowell, 1961.

Dizenzo, Patricia. Phoebe. New York: Bantam, 1970.

duJardin, Rosamond. Practically Seventeen. New York: Scholastic Book Services, 1949.

Eyerly, Jeannette. Drop-Out. New York: Berkley Publishing Corporation, 1963.

_______. A Girl Like Me. New York: Berkley Publishing Corporation, 1966.

_______. Escape from Nowhere. New York: J. B. Lippincott Company, 1969.

Freedman, Benedict and Nancy. Mrs. Mike. New York: Coward-McCann Publishing Company, 1947.

Head, Ann. Mr. and Mrs. Bo Jo Jones. New York: The New American Library, 1967.

Hentoff, Nat. Jazz Country. New York: Harper and Row, 1965.

_______. I'm Really Dragged But Nothing Gets Me Down. New York: Simon and Schuster, 1968.

Hinton, S. E. The Outsiders. New York: Dell Publishing Co., 1967.

_______. That Was Then, This Is Now. New York: Dell Publishing Co., 1971.

Hunter, Kristin. The Soul Brothers and Sister Lou. New York: Charles Scribner's Sons, 1968.

Kingman, Lee. The Peter Pan Bag. New York: Dell Publishing Co., 1970.

Laing, Frederick. Ask Me If I Love You Now. New York: Scholastic Book Services, 1968.

Maxwell, Edith. Just Dial a Number. New York: Simon & Schuster, 1971.

---

*Reprinted by permission of the author and publisher from English Journal (September 1974), 97-99.

Neufeld, John. Lisa, Bright and Dark. New York: New American Library, 1969.
Neville, Emily. It's Like This, Cat. New York: Harper and Row, 1963.
Sherburne, Zoa. Too Bad About the Haines Girl. Middletown, Conn.: American Education Publications, 1967.
Speare, Elizabeth George. The Witch of Blackbird Pond. New York: Dell Publishing Co., 1958.
Stirling, Nora. You Would If You Loved Me. New York: Avon Books, 1969.
Swarthout, Glendon. Bless the Beasts and Children. New York: Pocket Books, 1970.
Wojciechowska, Maia. Tuned Out. New York: Dell Publishing Co., 1968.
Zindel, Paul. The Pigman. New York: Dell Publishing Co., 1968.
_______. My Darling, My Hamburger. New York: Bantam Books, 1969.
_______. I Never Loved Your Mind. New York: Bantam Books, 1972.

It is no secret that the content of the adolescent or junior novel has been changing, breaking away from many of the characteristics which once defined the genre. In order to gain specific information about the changing nature of the genre, I recently examined thirty adolescent novels. The purpose of this article is to compare my findings with those presented in 1967 by James E. Davis in his article, "Recent Trends in Fiction for Adolescents" (English Journal, May, 1967, pp. 720-724).

Davis noted that the twenty-three novels which he examined treated the general subject of growing up and featured adolescent characters trying to achieve "satisfactory heterosexual adjustment" and independence while trying to cope with such problems as dropping out of school, early marriage, and "the bomb" (pp. 724-725). Many of his conclusions hold true for the thirty novels examined in my study. For instance, growing up is a common topic. But the problems dealt with in the thirty novels are somewhat different than the ones identified by Davis. The characters in these books face problems that are frequently controversial, including premarital pregnancy, the violence of street life, alcoholic parents, drug abuse, mental illness, and death.

Traditionally the problems facing adolescent characters appearing in adolescent novels were always solved, often through the blatant use of coincidence. Characteristically, the adolescent novel ended "happily" with the reader promised that the teenaged characters faced only bright and trouble-free futures. However, Davis noted a trend away from unrealistically easy solutions to problems (p. 721), and there are indications that the trend away from the contrived happy ending is continuing.

In fact, it is impossible to find a single characteristic ending which fits all thirty novels. Instead, three types of conclusions emerge: happy, optimistic, and pessimistic. Twelve of the thirty novels examined in the present study end in the traditional manner. Fourteen end optimistically, meaning that the endings are not conclusions but beginnings. In such novels, the adolescent characters solve specific problems or gain insights into life, but there are no promises that their futures will be story book perfect. For example, Cathy in Just Dial a Number discovers the need to acknowledge publicly her unintentional role in the accidental deaths of her friend's parents, but the novel does not deal with how Cathy must learn to live with her guilt feelings.

Four of the novels end in a decidedly pessimistic manner. In My Darling, My Hamburger, two of the four central adolescent characters must live with the tragic effects of an illegal abortion. By the end of That Was Then, This Is Now, Bryon is a bitter and depressed youth not unlike an existential hero in a novel by Jean-Paul Sartre. Finally, the reader of either Phoebe or Too Bad About the Haines Girl knows that the two pregnant, unmarried teenagers will not have desirable futures.

Davis also noted that most of the novels he examined attempted to treat life truthfully (p. 721), but later he indicated that traditional societal taboos were honored in the novels. He wrote that he seldom encountered "any allusions to sexual activity other than kisses" and that some profanity could be found only after a "hard look" (p. 722). Apparently, the occasional taboo violations which Davis found were the beginnings of a trend toward a more candid treatment of life in a genre which was once dedicated to protecting young readers from the real world. In the thirty novels examined in my study, people die, are divorced, drink, fight, use drugs and participate in other activities formerly only described in books for adults. However, this is probably of less concern to the classroom teacher of English than the appearance of profanity and the treatment of sex in the novels, for these two matters seem to be basic concerns of all committees concerned with "wholesome education."

"A hard look" is not required to find profanity in most of these novels. In fact, characters swear in sixteen of the thirty novels, though they typically swear only under extreme provocation and rarely just for the fun of it.

When acknowledging that sexual interests and related activities and problems are treated candidly in many adolescent novels, it is important that "candid" not be confused with "sensational." In many of these novels, sexual activities are not only alluded to but directly reported. However, there are no sex scenes which equal those appearing on television, just as there are no sex scenes on television equal to those appearing in neighborhood movie theaters. Furthermore, if scenes in which the teenage characters "make out" appear, the narration is typically more concerned with reporting a character's moral confusion than with reporting the physical details of the scenes. Also, sexual desires are usually fulfilled only in those novels which go on to explore the dilemmas of pregnant, unmarried teenagers, and in the best tradition of the Victorian Theater, the curtain is always dropped long before the characters become seriously involved.

Davis found that adolescent novels characteristically endorse traditional values and standards (p. 722). This characteristic appears to have remained constant, despite the fact that many formerly taboo subjects are treated. For example, the traditional respect for getting an education is endorsed highly in most of the novels and is always endorsed in those novels featuring adolescent characters who are economically unfortunate--Drop-Out, Durango Street, The Nitty Gritty, The Outsiders, and Sounder. The traditional family unit is overtly endorsed in novels such as The Peter Pan Bag, Practically Seventeen, and The Witch of Blackbird Pond. Alcohol is condemned in three novels--The Nitty Gritty, The Pigman, and Drop-Out.

However, little is to be gained by mentioning all of the traditional values endorsed in current adolescent novels. Rather, the greatest benefit may be derived from an examination of the endorsements of values which relate to the more controversial topics treated in the novels, topics such as sexual interests, abortion, drug usage, and violence.

Premarital chastity is endorsed in all but one of the novels which acknowledge teenage sexual interests (Paul Zindel's I Never Loved Your Mind). In such novels as It Could Happen to Anyone and You Would If You Loved Me, adolescent characters resist sexual temptation for all of the traditional reasons, and they are rewarded. In those novels in which teenagers fail to resist temptation, they typically are "punished" by becoming pregnant after their first and only "mistake." (Phoebe in the novel by the same name is an exception; it took her all summer to get pregnant.) In such novels, the miseries which these teenagers endure are cataloged, and the reader is told that such miseries will continue throughout the characters' lives.

The horrors these pregnant teenagers are made to endure inevitably cause the characters to consider having abortions, but abortions are not endorsed in adolescent novels. Consequently, abortions are rejected out-right by a few characters who carefully explicate the reasons behind their decisions. Other characters actually visit an illegal abortionist (There is no such thing as a legal abortion in these thirty novels), but they retreat in horror and moral revulsion upon the first appearance of the abortionist who, centuries ago, might have been mistaken for Grendel's mother. Only one central adolescent character actually has an abortion, Liz in My Darling, My Hamburger; she nearly dies, and wishes she had.

Drug abuse is condemned in all of the novels which either treat it extensively or just barely mention the subject. The degree of condemnation which drug use receives depends upon the amount of consideration the subject is given. For example, in Just Dial a Number, a few teenagers smoke marijuana at a party, and another character maintains that smoking marijuana is just a silly fad. However, in a novel like Escape From Nowhere or Tuned Out, novels in which drug abuse is the central topic, drugs are shown to lead to tragedy or near tragedy.

Violence is condemned in the novels in which it appears. The theme of Durango Street is that violence breeds violence. In novels such as The Outsiders and That Was Then, This Is Now violence results in tragedy. Violent police tactics are condemned in The Soul Brothers and Sister Lou, as are the violent tactics of a Black militant group. In none of these novels is violence glorified or depicted in graphic detail.

Traditionally, the adolescent novel has been characterized as being didactic when endorsing conventional values and mores. Davis found that his novels were didactic, but were "less directly so than" their earlier counterparts (p. 723). This trend away from "hard core" didacticism seems to be continuing, though the novels are obviously concerned with "teaching." Very few of the thirty novels have narrators or characters who preach, and only three of the novels get carried away while delivering messages to the reader. The Nitty Gritty determinedly preaches the work ethic. Drop-Out is a blatantly contrived morality play warning teenagers against dropping out of school, and It Could Happen to Anyone includes a major sermon on the topic that going steady is the root of all problems.

Davis noted that parents in adolescent novels, usually the father (p. 722), are responsible for helping their children arrive at an understanding about life. This is rarely the case in these thirty novels. For the most part, the adolescent characters themselves figure out what is happening or what has happened to them. This apparent trend away from the image of parent-as-oracle indicates an additional characteristic of these novels: frequently, the parents are not capable of helping their children. Some parents are well-meaning but ineffectual, as is Bryon's mother in That Was Then, This Is Now. Other parents are so caught up in their own concerns that they are unaware of their children's needs. This is the case in Lisa, Bright and Dark and in Tuned Out. Furthermore, many parents are the source of the problems facing their children; such parents appear in Escape From Nowhere, The Pigman, Bless the Beasts and Children, and Ask Me If I Love You Now.

Davis noted that adolescent characters are generally from "socially and economically, fortunate families" (p. 722), but he noted a trend away from novels populated exclusively with teenagers from the upper classes. Excluding the historical novel The Witch of Blackbird Pond and the recently rereleased Mrs. Mike, seven of the thirty novels feature adolescent characters who are from less than economically fortunate families, and very few of the characters are from wealthy families. Typically the characters in these novels are from the lower middle class and the middle class, and this observation indicates that the trend which Davis noted is continuing.

Just as the family status of the characters is no longer fixed, the adolescent novels are no longer exclusively set in small towns or rural areas. In fact only four of the thirty novels are set in small, tranquil towns. The majority of the novels are set in suburban and urban areas, and significantly four of the settings are inner-city ghettos.

It is difficult to write conclusions for a paper which is essentially a series of conclusions, but a few general observations may be appropriate. The first is that the conclusions arrived at in this paper are by no means definitive. New adolescent novels are being published regularly, and consequently, there is a need for continuing investigations of the genre's changing nature. A second observation is that the increasingly candid nature of the subject matter treated in the genre calls for English departments to re-examine their book selection policy, or perhaps prepare an original book selection policy, so that they will be prepared to defend the use of the increasingly popular adolescent novel in the classroom.

QUO VADIS ADOLESCENT FICTION?*

By Joan Talmage Weiss

In the last ten years the adolescent novel has changed radically. Almost gleefully many writers of fiction have established the "grim trend" or "new realism" in which all the previously taboo subjects were torn open for the examination and sometimes titilation of the teenage reader.

We know that our young people are growing up faster. We know that they are "reading up" at such a high rate of speed that books written for the teenager are now found in the fifth and sixth grades. We know that through television social and political issues have taken over the old Children's Hour. With all of this increased knowledge and sophistication a young person is catapulted into life and its strains and tensions at a much younger age. As Margaret Mead has said: "This is the first generation in which parents learn from their children."

As teachers of English we must be wary of the publishing market place where sales appeal rules over intrinsic merit. Some but not all adolescent novels ride the bandwagon of themes that are currently "in," alienation, loneliness and senility--*The Pigman* by Paul Zindel; drugs--*Go Ask Alice*, Anon.; the generation gap and homosexuality--*I'll Get There; It Better Be Worth the Trip* by John Donovan; racial and social hostility--*The Outsiders* by S. E. Hinton; and mental illness--*Lisa, Bright and Dark* by John Neufeld. Death, unwed pregnancy, divorce, the fractured family, the alcoholic mother, junky brother and father on welfare have been prodded, probed and petrified.

Most of the above examples have proved to be worthy novels and I assign several in my classes. Yet what we must ask ourselves is this: Are we looking for essential qualities, qualities like honesty, timelessness of content, believable characters who mature and change? If so, drugs and sex and death should be presented as only one integral part of the warp and woof of human experience. We can no longer shield young people from explicit language; this is the *lingua* of their peers if not of their families. We must deal with taboo subjects but I agree with Josette Frank in that "we must

---

*Reprinted by permission of the author and publisher from *Arizona English Bulletin*, April 1976.

offer books with integrity of purpose, authenticity, moral and social validity, and more important, the sound resolutions they offer." We can and must walk the fine line between didacticism and shock-for-shock's sake. I rebel against any novel which presents violence for the sake of violence; yet ours is a violent world. When a young adult meets violence in the pages of a well-written book like Slaughterhouse Five by Kurt Vonnegut, Jr. or Clockwork Orange by Anthony Burgess, he or she will be more prepared to meet and recognize the gradations of violence in the real world. Similarly, life is not all grimness and horror. If young people don't find hope in their reading as they can in Maya Angelou's I Know Why the Caged Bird Sings and Maia Wojciechowska's A Single Light, they may lack the strength to survive everyday corrosive life. If this sounds a bit strong let us remember that ultimately optimistic books can be supportive instead of depressing.

Let us then examine three adolescent novels published in 1975 as examples of fiction which transcend the topicality of the day, which come to terms with universal themes and which meet critical standards of literary worth. Fortunately these three books form positive models of literate reading for teenagers in Junior and Senior High School.

Is That You, Miss Blue? by M. E. Kerr (Harper, 1975) forms a study of tolerance for Flanders a high schooler sent off to a girls' boarding school. Religious tolerance comes into action when the zany teacher Miss Blue, who hangs a picture of Jesus in the W.C. and talks to Him directly, turns out to be a sympathetic and misunderstood human being. Flanders' intolerant impatience and irritation change to true closeness with her roommate Agnes who is handicapped by a hearing/speech loss. Moral tolerance comes when Flanders remeets her mother who had "run away" with a younger man and had alienated her sensitive daughter. Flanders finds her mother living alone and working in New York.

> You're still my little girl, she said, but you're very much your own girl now too, aren't you?

Flanders is stunned by her mother's perception. Valid philosophy comes from the least expected source when her mother says:

> You're going to meet a very old person one day. And when you do, you're going to have only her to answer to, and only her to be responsible to, and only her to look back with and decide what it was all about ... and that old person is yourself. I hope you'll be prepared for her.
> That's hairy, I said. Hairy and heavy.
> But it's true, mother said.

Business ethics are examined through Flanders' father whose fad-following business, Attitudes, Inc., has run the gamut from psychosomatic medicine and handwriting analysis to encounter therapy.

When Flanders watches him interviewed and "destroyed" by a TV personality, either the veracity of the media, her father or both are ripped open to question.

Of course the poignant ending is reminiscent of other nostalgic closings like in Where the Wild Fern Grows by Wilson Rawls and The Slave Dancer by Paula Fox.

> I still have a daydream that sometime I might come upon Miss Blue. She was only around forty and she wouldn't be that much older now.... She suddenly appears. I see the light blue eyes look up--remembering the time I would see them trying to connect with someone else's. Our eyes meet. I smile. Does she recognize me, or remember me at all?
>
> Miss Blue, I say. It's me. Is it really you?

Kerr uses this nostalgic device to dramatize the typical girl teenager's ambivalence toward an older, wiser woman.

A totally different novel is Z for Zachariah by Robert C. O'Brien (Atheneum, 1975). It falls into the survival formula set in the not-so-distant future when there are only two people left on earth: Ann Burden (double meaning?), sixteen, and John R. Loomis, a chemist who has suffered radiation poisoning. Again told in a first person diary form to increase immediacy, Ann lives in perpetual fear with only a dog named Faro for trusted companionship. Loomis wanders about believing he is alone.

Ann's first moral dilemma is whether she should have warned Mr. Loomis against swimming in the "dead" or radioactive stream. He helps her run a tractor while suffering a fever of 104. Communication between them builds until Ann fantasizes that they will be married in a year or two and she will have children, just like her mother did, but within a religious ceremony. The title comes from the Biblical alphabet book where "A is for Adam ... C for Christian ... and Z is for Zachariah." This "last man" foreshadowing immediately gives the reader a feeling of foreboding.

This disturbing novel builds tension when Loomis approaches Ann's bed at night and she panics and runs. Although nursed back to health by her, Loomis slowly becomes her enemy, using the dog to track her scent, even shooting to maim her. When he burns her few possessions in her cave, she steals his "safe suit"--over which he's previously murdered a co-worker--and walks toward a place where birds are flying, unable to live or compromise with him. She is full of hope, fantasizing about finding a room full of children she can teach.

Told in simple style yet showing the full turnings of Ann's mind, this novel presents both the bright and dark side of human nature. It is grim. It is reality set in the future. It is even frightening. But it is not shock for shock's sake. Ann never gives up trying to survive. Her tenacity and undaunted hope illustrate one new trend in novels for young people.

Still another novel worth reflection is Isabelle Holland's Of Love and Death and Other Journeys (Lippincott, 1975). Set in contemporary northern Italy, Meg, sixteen, has followed her expatriate mother and her second husband throughout Europe. Meg adores her mother and follows her lead of conducting art tours in Perugia and Assissi for traveling Americans. They feel ambivalent about their tour groups; i.e., they hate their blind herdism but love their naiveté. They both thrive on art history, literary allusions and a running understated repartee.

In discussing marriage, Meg's free-spirit mother says:

> It's only been with Peter that I've been both free and loved, and that's why I love him so much. Everybody sees him as a sort of overweight clown, fiddling about with his Latin documents and his unsuccessful porn. But he knows how to love more than anybody I've ever known. And I'm not talking about sex, although he's good at that too. But I don't think even in his mind he's ever tried to make anybody do anything. Probably that's why he's so unsuccessful ... except in loving people.

This straight-arrow tone is alternated with sophisticated bantering amongst "the pride"--composed of Meg, Meg's mother, Peter and Cotton, an artist of sorts with whom Meg is madly in love.

> Mother, I burst out. Do you think when I'm all grown up he'll be in love with me?
>
> My darling child ... how can I possibly tell? You mustn't ask questions like that. That's like me ... like trying to lock up the future, make it happen the way you wrote it. It doesn't work that way. You have to live a day at a time.

More ambivalence pours into the novel when Meg's mother, facing surgery for cancer, reveals that Meg's father is alive and coming to Italy. Meg finds herself engulfed by grief and fear for her mother as well as fear and curiosity about her real father. As she learns chunks of their past so does the reader. Meg's father is an Episcopal minister, is married to a lady doctor and they have suffered the death of a young son. The father-daughter conversations are sensitively handled and the reader feels great sympathy for both.

Interestingly enough the mother and father do not have an obligatory scene together; yet each is conscious of the other, marvelously tolerant, even respectful. The mother is terminally ill yet, with gay bravado, insists on hikes and picnics with "the pride."

When she dies Meg is sent to live with her father much

against her will. She finds herself a worldly American with no identification with the States. She wanders around in a daze, unable to attend school. The second wife is supporting but understated. Then Cotton's painting arrives, a painting of Meg's mother in a floppy hat with her hazel green eyes sparkling with mischief and laughter and love.

> I was crying and my chest was hurting but I said, It's good. It's very good. It's the best work he's done. He's got that special thing Mother had ... I never knew what to call it.
>
> It was joy, father said. She was filled with it, more than anyone I've ever known.
>
> And I knew he was right. But something terrible was happening inside me. That horrible body I had last seen that had stayed in the front of my mind hiding everything else was gone, and what was left was knowing that Mother was dead, and I would never see her again, and the pain was beyond anything I could have imagined.
>
> I was crying and so was Father, who was holding me.
>
> What's happening? I gasped. What is it? The tears felt like a scalding river pouring out of me.
>
> It's grief, Father said. I was afriad you'd never really grieve. It's good. Go on and grieve.
>
> So I cried and cried for what felt like a long time. Father, what should I do? I finally asked.
>
> Why, do what your Mother would have you do--live your life with as much joy as you can.

This forms a multi-leveled, disturbing novel, expertly written and deeply thought provoking. It demonstrates that an adolescent novel can deal with taboo subjects without shocking. Death from cancer is a grim subject; so is an uprooted teenage girl. Yet these questions are explored as only one level. The other side of the coin are basic human qualities like compassion, emotional maturity and experiencing aesthetics.

Considering these three novels, all published in 1975, we can see that they hold honesty, timelessness of content, believable characters who change and mature and sound resolutions to universal human problems. Hopefully they form a microcosm to answer the Quo Vadis of Adolescent Fiction. Reading valid, literate novels reinforces what Margaret A. Edwards wrote in _The Fair Garden and the Swarm of Beasts_ (Hawthorn Books, 1969).

> What can books do for these young people? Their most important contribution is to supplement experience, to intensify their lives. However long these young people may live, most of them will know few months or years that are filled with meaning. They will experience few passionate love affairs, few victories, few overwhelming griefs, few moments of insight and inspiration. Without books they can live and die naively innocent of so much

experience. But the young person who reads can live a thousand years and a thousand lives. In a few hours, at any time, he can add to his meager experience another whole lifetime condensed to its meaningful moments, with all the dull, uneventful days left out.

THE GOVERNOR AND ADOLESCENT LITERATURE*

By Kenneth Donelson

Sometime in December 1972 or January 1973, a reporter from the ASU STATE PRESS called me to see if she could get a story about changes in adolescent literature over the last few years. I agreed, she did the interview, she wrote the story, and it appeared in several local newspapers. I was quoted (accurately) as saying that adolescent literature had taken some steps towards more mature topics and better writing and specifically cited *Lisa Bright and Dark*, *Edgar Allen*, *The Girl Inside*, *Sleep Two Three Four*, *Sticks and Stones*, *Run Softly Go Fast*, *In the Country of Ourselves*, *Twink*, *A Girl Like Me*, *Radigan Cares*, and *The High King* as some sort of evidence. While a couple of people objected to this or that, I'm sure the whole business would have soon died had not former Governor Jack Williams devoted one of his morning radio talks to my remarks (though I was never mentioned). Here's the text of Mr. Williams' "Yours Sincerely" radio talk of February 27, 1973.

"Thank you and hello again. For those who are seeking real knowledge, try Aesop's *Fables* or the *Book of Proverbs*, or any of the old folk stories that are handed down from generation to generation.

Bright, modern, chrome-plated wisdom seldom lasts very long. I recall a story about a mother leaving her children with the admonition, 'Now, be good and don't put beans up your nose.' Do you recall it? When she returned, of course, the children all had gone to the cupboard, found the bean bag, and were all screaming and crying with beans up their noses.

My reason for recalling this was inspired by an article that stated, adolescent books have changed drastically since *The Rover Boys*, *The Youth's Companion*, *Mark Tidd*, a character created by Clarence Buddington Kelland--and the adolescent books I read. I am told that books for teens in grades 7 to 11 are now dealing with drugs, homosexuality, teen-age pregnancy, generation gaps, protests, draft dodgers, alcohol and divorce. If there is any truth in the old story about not putting beans up their nose, there may be a mistake in encouraging literature which describes homosexuality, divorce,

---

*Reprinted by permission of the author and publisher from *Arizona English Bulletin*, April 1976.

draft dodgers, etc. The old heroes of adolescent books couldn't drink, smoke or swear. Now, virtually all taboos are more and more ignored.

Somehow I think that I received a better understanding of the rules of life from the moralistic books I read, than had I been exposed at an early age to all the aberrations of sex and morals. As a reporter, as one active in the community, as a school board member and a councilman, as a mayor and as a governor, I probably have seen in my adult life more aberrations of behavior than the majority of people. Yet, I've had no inclination to go in that direction, perhaps because the habits and standards that I somehow acquired--even without a father, but with a strong, magnificent mother--provided a framework to protect me.

I ran across a list of books recommended for adolescent readers. We were advised, very fortuitously, that the books are all in paperback.

Here they are: *Run Softly, Go Fast*, tells the story of the alienation of father and son; *Sticks and Stones*, concerning the problems of a sensitive boy who was thought to be a homosexual; *In the Country of Ourselves*, the protest movement in high school; *Sleep Two, Three, Four*, a political thriller with a 1983 setting; and *Too Near the Sun*, the disintegration of an 1800 commune.

Others included *Lisa, Bright and Dark*, the horrors of a girl who discovered she is insane; *Edgar Allen*, the problems when a white couple adopts a black child; *Twink*, a handicapped child; *The Girl Inside*, the mental breakdown of a girl; *A Girl Like Me*, the pregnancy of a teen-age girl; *Radigan Cares*, the subject being politics; and *The High King*, life in an imaginary kingdom.

The last one sounds more along the line of what I used to read. But what has become of *Alice in Wonderland*, *Gulliver's Travels*, *Treasure Island*, *Robinson Crusoe*, and the magnificent Zane Grey stories of the West?

Are they available at all? Wouldn't it be interesting if people in authority recommended one or two of them, despite the fact that the publishers are pushing the new books? I am sure that part of all we'll ever be is found in what we read.

In the formative years, how frightening to think that our teenagers are reading about the mental breakdowns of a girl, the pregnancy of a teen-age girl, the horrors of a girl who discovered she is going insane, the alienation of father and son, the problems of a sensitive boy who is thought to be a homosexual.

Surely, that can come later, can't it?

Thank you so much for listening, and so long you all."

HOLDEN CAULFIELD, WHERE ARE YOU?*

By Robert Unsworth

Holden Caulfield is over 40 now. The hero of J. D. Salinger's The Catcher in the Rye (Little, 1951), the novel that spawned a generation of realistic, earthy fiction for young adults, is, if he's in any way like the rest of his contemporaries, struggling through a change of life. Dave Mitchell, who in Emily Neville's It's Like This, Cat (Harper, 1963) bought a cat because his father told him that dogs were educational, is now pushing 30. Still, at least two things about young adult novels remain unchanged: a shortage of good, contemporary, personal fiction that features the problems and joys of the coming-of-age years for boys and an almost complete absence of novels that give an honest, effective picture of the impact of sexual awareness on the male teenager.

Authors and publishers have mined the rich fields of female puberty since Maureen Daly's Seventeenth Summer (Dodd, 1942); while equally abundant ore in the masculine vein has, for the most part, gone unnoticed. This is not to say that there are no good young adult novels of boyhood, simply too few, and to plead for more.

Traditionally, two molds have been used to produce YA fiction with male protagonists: adventure stories--with heavy emphasis on historical adventure--and sports. But both have lost ground to nonfiction over the past several years, The Christophers, Gaults, and Butterworths do not "move" as they once did. John R. Tunis is gone in more ways than one.

Boys, librarians are told, do not read as they once did, and it may well be because there is so little being written that speaks to them, that probes the sensitive subject of male adolescence. Publishers, forever market-conscious, encourage their authors to produce novels with female leads. Yet there is no strong reason for publishers to hold back novels about boys, because there *is* good evidence that girls will read them. Judy Blume did well with Then Again, Maybe I Won't (Bradbury, 1971), the story of Tony Miglione's struggle with a new neighborhood and growing sexual awareness.

---

*Reprinted by permission of the author and publisher from School Library Journal (January 1977), 40-41.

John Donovan's I'll Get There; It Better Be Worth the Trip (1969) and Remove Protective Coating a Little at a Time (1973, both Harper) are never labeled as "boys'" books. T. Ernesto Bethancourt's New York City, Too Far from Tampa Blues (Holiday, 1975) can safely be recommended to both sexes. It makes no difference that a boy is the protagonist in M. E. Kerr's humorous If I Love You, Am I Trapped Forever? (Harper, 1973) or that it is an 18-year-old boy who dies in Paige Dixon's tender May I Cross Your Golden River? (Atheneum, 1975). The point here is that the market can probably well bear more fiction about the male experience, and boys will have fewer excuses for not reading fiction.

Unfortunately, the tendency is for good male writers to write mainly about females. Richard Peck is an example. Aside from his excellent Dreamland Lake (Holt, 1973), his only book about boys is The Ghost Belonged to Me (Viking, 1975), which is set in 1913 and is more a picaresque novel than a story dealing in any meaningful way with boys' adolescent problems. Only Nat Hentoff, Harry Mazer, and John Donovan come to mind as writers with more than a novel or two published who have restricted themselves to writing realistic fiction about boys.

Thus, most fiction about males is written by females, albeit quite capably at times. The male experience as portrayed in novels by women, while valid for the most part, is often incomplete. It will take more male authors examining the subtleties that make the father-son bond different from the mother-daughter or mother-son relationship to fill the gap. And it will take more John Donovans, more Don Mosers (A Heart to the Hawks, Atheneum, 1975), and more daring publishers as well to treat in great quantity and depth the vital area of male sexuality in the teenage years.

Fathers in fiction (they are almost as uncommon as television fathers) are often no more than another seat at the dinner table, slipping in and out to work, often consumed by their jobs, rarely communicating with their sons. Frequently, if present, the father is an unappealing lout who, if he communicates at all with his son, does so in bellows. A typical example is Tink Rowlandson's father in Fritzhand's Life Is a Lonely Place (Evans, 1975), who is unable, despite clear evidence, to believe that his son's friendship with a 27-year-old male professor is not a homosexual relationship. In Nat Hentoff's disappointing This School Is Driving Me Crazy (Delacorte, 1976), Sam Davidson's father is a man totally insensitive to his son as well as to the students in the private school he heads. Jason Hurd's father in Susan Terris's The Drowning Boy (Doubleday, 1972) loves guns, weightlifting, and his daughter but hates his son because the boy can't swim and writes left-handed.

In addition to an absence of novels dealing meaningfully with father-son relationships, it also remains for more YA authors and publishers to admit that sexual awareness plays an overwhelming part in the lives of young men. Indeed, aside from sports and perhaps a hobby, sex is probably the young man's consuming preoccupation.

But even in those novels with heavy male-female story lines, male sexual urgings often receive no more attention than they do in the comic strips. Alan Bennett of M. E. Kerr's If I Love You, Am I Trapped Forever? actually seems to be speaking for publishers' concerns rather than defending his own sense of privacy when he says early on in the book, "I'm not going to describe in detail the very personal things that take place between me and Leah. I'm not writing this book for a bunch of voyeurs." It is fear of censorship, not voyeurism, which plagues too many young adult novels to a degree where the image of the male in the junior novel is woefully incomplete. Leaving sex out of a novel that purports to examine male maturation and growth is like writing a cookbook without mentioning food.

We do not need explicit sex in teenage fiction any more than we need the head-in-the-sand approach to sexuality that seems to be the current norm. There is a middle ground. Castigated by some for her realism (she has been called the Grace Metalious of teenage fiction), Judy Blume handles noctural emissions and concern with sex tastefully in her Then Again, Maybe I Won't. Thirteen-year-old Tony worries about wet sheets, ill-timed erections, and his interest in the 16-year-old girl next door who undresses with open blinds. Not at all uncommon concerns at 13.

Or consider this passage from Robert Cormier's The Chocolate War (Pantheon, 1974), written for older teenagers. High school student Jerry Renault is sneaking a look at the magazines in the local drugstore:

> Why did he always feel so guilty when he looked at Playboy and other magazines? ... He had once bought a girlie magazine, paying for it with trembling fingers--a dollar and a quarter, his finances shot down in flames until his next allowance. And he didn't know what to do with the damn thing once it was in his possession. Sneaking it home on the bus, hiding it in the bottom drawer of his room, he was terrified of discovery ... Finally ... Jerry had sneaked it out of the house and dropped it into a catchbasin.... A longing filled him. Would a girl ever love him? The one devastating sorrow he carried within him was the fear that he would die before holding a girl's breast in his hand.

Mildred Lee's Fog (Seabury, 1972) treats family life, friendship, retardation and death, and the growing sexual awareness of her 17-year-old protagonist, Luke Sawyer, as well as any young adult novel. Luke is a lad with a happy family life, decent if unsuccessful father, good friends, and the very normal beginnings of romance. Early in the novel Lee has this moving description of Luke's first sexual stirrings:

> Before he had ever dreamed she could be his girl Luke had more than once caught himself staring at the

> spot on Milo's chest where the chain ended, his mind guiltily picturing the heavy gold ring and the frail, gold cross lying side by side between the twin hillocks of her breasts (Luke did not know where he got that from but it had a fine Biblical sound).
>
> Whenever this happened, something great and a little frightening took place inside Luke Sawyer.... His heart galloped, his breathing became so rapid it threatened to choke him. All in the space of seconds.
>
> He was always terrified these changes would show on the outside....

Mention of Luke's sexual awakening in the story is infrequent but effective, and certainly there can be no objection to this ingredient, so essential to the story.

Don Moser's A Heart to the Hawks is unusual in several respects, and the author handles sex well if in a non-serious manner. It is the story of two highly intelligent boys, Mike Harrington and his close friend Corcoran, in post-World War II Ohio. It is also about Mike's trained hawk, his dreamer-inventor father, a save-the-environment theme, and Angeline Karman's budding body. It's alternately serious, funny, sad, and charming with Angeline's "conical breasts" and "sculpted legs" playing no less an important part in the success of the story than any of its other elements.

On the other hand, Marcus Rosenbloom, the fat, sensitive boy who searches for his father in Harry Mazer's The Dollar Man (Delacorte, 1974), is understandable but incomplete. Thirteen years old, Marcus is concerned with wet dreams but nothing else as far as sex is concerned, though he falls in with a fast crowd that introduces him to marijuana and liquor. Mazer seems to acknowledge the problem early in the novel but then drops it, as if sex to a youngster was something that cropped up only occasionally, like a stomach-ache. There is sex in Barbara Berson's What's Going to Happen to Me? (Scribners, 1976)--another tale of a fatherless boy--but it's cold sex, without emotion and heartless--the nonerotic type of sex that Barbara Wersba spoke of in "Sexuality in Books for Children" (SLJ, February 1973, p. 44).

I doubt that we will get full, sensitive portrayals of male adolescent sexuality in any numbers as long as publishers and authors (and reviewers) ignore its significance and until more male authors address themselves to the task. We live in an era that claims that boys can cry and can show emotion without fear of reaction on the part of their peers. Hopefully, this also means that they can enjoy the "romantic" out in the open, that their reading need not be restricted to books with "macho" themes. Like girls, boys have need for rites-of-passage fiction that relates to and possibly relieves their anxieties, notably sex, and that convinces them that they do not agonize alone.

NEW READING MATERIAL: THE JUNIOR NOVEL*

By Al Muller

A popular topic of discussion is the changing nature of the junior or transitional novel. Typically, such discussions center on the increased sophistication of the subject matter treated in recently published novels, such as premarital sex, death, drugs, street life, and so on. The changing nature of the genre raises several questions related to the effective use of the genre as a means of helping young readers make the transition from reading children's books to reading more artistically complex adult works. Specifically, there is a need to determine if the increased sophistication of the subject matter treated in the novels is reflected in an increased sophistication of the genre as a literary form, and if the genre has gained increased literary sophistication, there is a need to examine the increased artistry as a possible liability to the established role of transitional literature.

Traditionally, the junior novel has been characterized as being easy to read. In consequence, it was safe to assume that the novel would present few, if any, reading difficulties to the student who possessed the basic decoding skills. This assumption was solidly based upon certain established characteristics of the genre--characteristics which assured ease of reading. Typically, a junior novel was a novel of incident rather than a novel of character, in that the concern of the novel was with the depiction of physical action rather than with the exploration of a character's emotional or moral confusion. The novel, therefore, presented the student with no difficulty in following the story line, as the majority of children's stories, and certainly comic books, are plot oriented.

In the development of plot, the story progressed in strict chronological order, eliminating the need for the student to struggle to unravel the intricacies of time shifts. Also, only rarely was the story line encumbered with a potentially distracting subplot. As an additional aid to the reader, the junior novel was traditionally narrated from the omniscient point of view which allowed the narrator to guide the reader toward the discovery of the novel's thematic in-

*Reprinted by permission of the author and publisher from Journal of Reading 18:7 (April 1975), 531-534.

tent, if not simply telling the reader the novel's theme. As an additional aid to easy reading, the junior novel was written in a strictly formal and unadorned style, void of such literary devices as allusions, irony and extended metaphors.

In order to determine if these characteristics continue to exist despite the changing nature of the genre, I recently examined thirty-one junior novels popular with contemporary adolescents. The novels were selected with the help of forty-eight middle school and high school librarians from fifteen states throughout the continental United States. (See novel listing at end of article.)

To begin, my study demonstrated that the increased sophistication of subject matter dealt with in the junior novel is, in fact, reflected in an increased literary sophistication of the genre. This conclusion is demonstrated in the fact that twenty-six of the thirty-one novels are novels of character, not novels of incident. This change in emphasis demands that the reader not only follow the story line but must be capable of interpreting the physical action to understand the origins of a character's feelings and dilemmas. Perhaps the most extreme example of this new interest in character study is Wojciechowska's Don't Play Dead Before You Have To. This novel is an extended dramatic monologue, similar in form to The Fall by Albert Camus. Furthermore, this interest in character study has resulted in the recent and unprecedented use of the interior monologue in the junior novel. This sophisticated literary device is used in eleven of the thirty-one novels, demanding that the reader have the ability to recognize and deal with sudden shifts from internal to external action and back again.

The increased artistic sophistication of the junior novel genre is demonstrated further in the abandonment of the strict, chronological progression of action. In thirteen of the novels, the time flow is altered through the use of flashbacks, and in two novels, Phoebe and Too Bad About the Haines Girl, the use of flashbacks is the rule, not the exception. Significantly, the progression of action is radically altered through the use of in media res in three novels, Bless the Beasts and Children, The Longest Weekend, and Run Softly, Go Fast. The time shifts appearing in recent junior novels clearly demand that the reader, in order to follow the story, must be capable of constructing on his own an accurate chronological sequence of events.

Structure, Style Change

In addition to the altering of time sequences, the reader of the new junior novel must deal with another obstacle in following the story. The use of subplots is increasing in the junior novel. Nine of these novels include fully developed subplots. These subplots do not exist independently as "little stories" but are fully integrated into the central story lines. The reader must be able to recognize and follow the subplots if the stories are to be enjoyed, but the subplots must also be interpreted and used to complement the stories if the novels are to be understood.

Another change in the characteristics of the junior novel genre is that the novels are no longer narrated exclusively from the omniscient point of view. No longer is an all-knowing narrator present to guide the reader, and the situation is further complicated for the young reader by some experimentation with the first-person point of view in such novels as *The Pigman* and *Dave's Song*. In these novels, there are two narrators who narrate alternating chapters. This pattern of narration demands that the reader successfully identify the changing interpretations of events.

Traditionally, the junior novel was written in a formal and unadorned style. However, the styles of these novels are far more sophisticated than in the past, and therefore might present reading obstacles to the young student. For example, all of these novels are written in an informal style which includes the use of slang and jargon with which a young reader might not be familiar. In such novels as *Durango Street* and *The Outsiders*, there are slang expressions which might be common to members of street gangs but not to a suburban, middle class student. The novels dealing with mental illness include some limited medical jargon, and novels dealing with the drug problem obviously include the jargon of the drug culture. Other novels such as *Phoebe* and *My Darling, My Hamburger* include the use of verbal irony which is difficult to recognize.

The style of these novels is further adorned through the use of literary allusions for the purpose of developing a novel's theme. For example, in *Red Sky at Morning*, the novel's theme is developed through allusions to Homer's *Odyssey* and to Ernest Hemingway's "Hemingway Hero," and it seems unlikely that a young reader would be familiar with these works. In other novels such as *The Peter Pan Bag*, the obvious allusion to James Barrie's play is developed into an extended metaphor used to describe the illusionary freedom of communal living. *The Contender* is another example of the increasing artistic sophistication of the junior novel genre; in the book a complex pattern of light and dark imagery is developed to present the novel's thematic concern for participation in, rather than escape from, life.

The literary sophistication of the junior novel has increased, and it can no longer be assumed that the novel will present no reading obstacles to a younger student. In consequence, the classroom teacher and the reading teacher may no longer assume that a student will be capable of easily reading, enjoying, and understanding a junior novel found on the shelf.

This conclusion is by no means an indictment; in fact, it is welcomed. Perhaps now more than ever, the junior novel possesses the characteristics and sophistication for being a viable tool for introducing students to and preparing them for reading serious, adult literature. However, the increased sophistication demands that the teacher know about the novels he or she suggests and that the teacher be prepared with readiness activities to help the student deal with the sophisticated literary devices and techniques which will be encountered in a particular novel.

Novel List

Armstrong, William. Sounder. Scholastic Book Services, 1969.
Arundel, Honor. The Longest Weekend. Grosset & Dunlap, Inc., 1973.
Balducci, Carolyn. Is There a Life After Graduation, Henry Birnbaum? Houghton Mifflin Company, 1971.
Bonham, Frank. Durango Street. E. P. Dutton & Company, Inc., 1965.
Bonham, Frank. The Nitty Gritty. E. P. Dutton & Company, Inc., 1968.
Bradford, Richard. Red Sky at Morning. J. B. Lippincott Company, 1968.
Dizenzo, Patricia. Phoebe. McGraw-Hill, Inc., 1970.
Eyerly, Jeannette. Escape From Nowhere. J. B. Lippincott Company, 1969.
Head, Ann. Mr. & Mrs. Bo Jo Jones. G. P. Putnam's Sons, 1967.
Hentoff, Nat. I'm Really Dragged, But Nothing Gets Me Down. Harper and Row, Publishers, 1968.
Hentoff, Nat. In the Country of Ourselves. Harper & Row, Publishers, 1971.
Hentoff, Nat. Jazz Country. Harper and Row, Publishers, 1965.
Hinton, S. E. The Outsiders. The Viking Press, Inc., 1967.
Hinton, S. E. That Was Then, This Is Now. The Viking Press, Inc., 1971.
Hitze, Naomi. You'll Like My Mother. G. P. Putnam's Sons, 1968.
Hunter, Kristin. The Soul Brothers and Sister Lou. Charles Scribner's Sons, 1968.
Kingman, Lee. The Peter Pan Bag. Houghton Mifflin Company, 1970.
Laing, Frederick. Ask Me If I Love You Now. Scholastic Book Services, 1968.
Lipsyte, Robert. The Contender. Harper and Row, Publishers, 1967.
Maxwell, Edith. Just Dial a Number. Dodd, Mead, & Company, 1971.
McKay, Robert. Dave's Song. Hawthorn Books, Inc., 1970.
Neufeld, John. Lisa, Bright and Dark. S. G. Phillips, Inc., 1969.
Sherburne, Zoa. Too Bad About the Haines Girl. William Morrow & Company, Inc., 1967.
Stirling, Nora. You Would If You Loved Me. M. Evans & Company, Inc., 1969.
Swarthout, Glendon. Bless the Beasts and Children. Doubleday & Company, Inc., 1970.
Wersba, Barbara. Run Softly, Go Fast. Atheneum Publishers, 1970.

Wojciechowska, Maia. Don't Play Dead Before You Have To. Harper and Row, Publishers, 1970.

Wojciechowska, Maia. Tuned Out. Harper and Row, Publishers, 1968.

Zindel, Paul. I Never Loved Your Mind. Harper and Row, Publishers, 1970.

Zindel, Paul. My Darling, My Hamburger. Harper and Row, Publishers, 1969.

Zindel, Paul. The Pigman. Harper and Row, Publishers, 1968.

PART IV

ON WRITING FOR TEENAGERS

(i'm really dragged ...)

EDITOR'S NOTE

The argument about the new realism is in part an extension of the older one on the need for a genre such as the junior novel. Many agree with Natalie Babbitt, who believes that "teenagers do not need a fiction of their own: they are quite ready to move into the world of adult fiction." Sylvia Engdahl is one of those who disagree. Her article in this section presents the case for the opposition, but also draws attention to the frequently unrecognized fact that a book for young adults is a book _marketed_ as a young adult book.

June Jordan's concern is broader, but also more specific in terms of the responsibility she feels as a writer for youth. She decries the "pointless, self-indulgent, status-quo-protecting, and irresponsible garbage" that goes under the name of realism, and feels that the young, especially, need some good news, alternatives to "feed and nourish the spirit."

Nat Hentoff also is aware of the writer's responsibility, sometimes painfully so, because his readers let him know how seriously a book can affect a teenager. This evidence of potential impact is perhaps the most conclusive argument in favor of the junior novel.

Ultimately, the better writers simply write as they feel they must, and theirs are the books most likely to be meaningful to young adults.

DO TEENAGE NOVELS FILL A NEED?*

By Sylvia Engdahl

An author of novels for adolescents faces a problem not shared by other writers. I am sometimes confronted with the opinion that my profession fills no need--that the writing of fiction for today's teenagers is unessential, or even unwise. Those with some knowledge of the field are most prone to feel that it is a waste of time and talent. By the ignorant, the writer may be viewed with the perennial suspicion that a serious novelist, if good, would soon "graduate" to writing for adults--an assertion requiring no reply. A view less easily dismissed is that of experts on literature for youth who believe that an author who does not choose to write adult fiction should direct his or her books toward preadolescents. According to this view, there is no literate audience in between. Because it is a prevalent view, teenage fiction resides in a sort of limbo.

The question of whether teenage fiction is needed has received a good deal of attention during the past few years, primarily in journals read by librarians. Yet it seems to me that the controversy has been centered on side issues: issues that often obscure an information gap of which many teachers and librarians are unaware. Discussion about what is wrong with contemporary teenage fiction--and what is right with it--cannot be meaningful apart from clear understanding of _what_ it is; and I find that people unfamiliar with publishing procedures have no such understanding. In debating the value of fiction for teens, most fail to define the category to which they are referring.

Just what is a teenage novel? The simplistic answer is obvious: a teenage novel is one intended for adolescent readers. To many people, however, the very words of this statement have connotations that exclude the better teenage novels of today. No truly adequate definition can be given except in terms of factors distinguishing teenage novels from adult ones. And when considering these, it is important to recognize that only one factor has bearing on the designation "teenage" (or "junior" or "young adult") as ap-

---

*Reprinted by permission of the author and publisher from _English Journal_ (February 1975), 48-52.

plied to a novel by the book trade and review media. That designation is determined solely by the structure of the publishing business. A novel suitable for adolescents is "teenage" if it is issued by the children's book department of a publishing house, and "adult" if it is issued by the adult department. From an organizational standpoint, these departments are wholly separate; and although many criteria may affect the initial decision as to which will handle a given novel, once that decision is made the book is permanently categorized. The book's maturity, as judged by readers after publication, has nothing whatsoever to do with its classification, which is based mainly on marketing considerations.

This separation at the publishing level is more significant than it may seem, for it has far-reaching effects--some good, some bad--on the nature of novels made available to adolescents. Moreover, it is highly pertinent to the debate concerning whether or not a "teenage" category is worthwhile. The raison d'être of that category is not literary, but commercial. No one doubts that there is a need for books appropriate for teenagers to read. The real, underlying question is whether we need books to be read only by teenagers. And surely we do not. I cannot imagine writing a novel that I felt was of interest only to people within some particular age range; my books are enjoyed by ten- to twelve-year-olds of advanced reading ability, and also by quite a few grownups. But I direct them most specifically to readers of high school age, since they have characteristics which, in the climate of today's publishing field, mean that if they were not issued by children's book departments they would not be published at all.

I cannot deny that I say this with a tinge of regret, not because I see anything preferable about being an "adult" novelist, but because the outlook of modern teenagers seems to me in many respects healthier than that of their elders. Authors often find the children's book field less restrictive than the adult market in that it is less subject to the dictates of current fashion. As C. S. Lewis said, "They label their books 'For Children' because children are the only market now recognized for the books they, anyway, want to write."[1] The statement is perhaps even more applicable to teenagers; teenagers, having little regard for what is fashionable among adults, do not care that an optimistic view of the universe is not now in vogue. Their conception of "realism" is uncolored by the pronouncements of cynical critics--an issue that I have discussed in greater detail elsewhere.[2]

However, whether or not one shares my personal reasons for favoring a youthful audience (and many writers do not), it is indisputably true that adolescent readers need novels of a kind not presently being produced by publishers' adult departments. Natalie Babbitt writes, "Teenagers do not need a fiction of their own: They are quite ready to move into the world of adult fiction."[3] This might well be the case if contemporary adult fiction were more representative of the range of literate tastes than it has become; but the fact is that it does not even meet the needs of all older adult readers, let alone the youngest. Though worthwhile novels of past decades retain their value, suitable new ones are rare. Ms. Babbitt, wondering "if there is such a category as a teenage audience,"[4] cites partial reading lists for her sons' high school English classes consisting entirely of adult books--not one of which, I notice, was published within the last ten years.

Publishing trends have undergone drastic upheavals during that period. The present adult market demands fiction of a kind that adolescents lack the experience and emotional maturity to cope with. Critically-acclaimed novels frequently treat themes in which adolescents are not even interested. But the nature of junior books has also been radically altered, a situation of which not all high school teachers are yet aware. Times have changed since publishers labeled insipid mysteries and school romances "ages 13 up"; both the old triviality and the old taboos are disappearing. Some of the books being issued by children's departments would have been published as adult a decade or two ago.

By no means do all such books qualify as literature. As Ms. Babbitt points out, they frequently suffer from deficiencies that would prevent their being considered true literature no matter what audience they were meant for. But hasn't it always been necessary to evaluate novels individually? The lowering of their age designation carries no implication that one should lower one's standards of judgment; nor, despite contentions of people who rate value in terms of "relevance," does increased maturity of adolescent fiction's subject matter necessarily imply sufficient maturity of presentation. Many teenage books that have appeared in the wave of enthusiasm for the "new realism" have been justly criticized for superficiality. One cannot argue with the reviewer who wrote, "You can't turn a bad novel into a good one by filling it with pregnancy, pot and the pill."[5]

Yet neither can one say that the existence of bad teenage novels tells against the need for good ones. In recognizing that shallow and superficial books are to be found among the newest fiction for adolescents, one must remember that shallow and superficial adult fiction also appears rather frequently. One might remember, too, C. S. Lewis's well-known statement: "No book is really worth reading at the age of ten which is not equally (and often far more) worth reading at the age of fifty.... The only imaginative works we ought to grow out of are those which it would have been better not to have read at all."[6]

Though Lewis was referring to books for pre-adolescents, the same principle applies to those directed toward adolescents. And it should be noted, before attempting to define adolescent fiction more fully, that there is no way to determine a particular novel's intended audience except through evaluation of the book itself or its reviews. Seekers of teenage fiction must bear in mind that for their purposes, any age or grade levels stated in the publisher's announcements, on the dust jacket, or at the heads of reviews are meaningless. These estimates apply only at the elementary school level, and even then they are inconsistent, since every publishing house has its own policy and the policies change from year to year according to sales experience. Thus one book's "10 to 14" designation may be the equivalent of another's "12 up," and the former may sometimes be given to a more difficult book by the same author.

This is a reflection of the uncertain status of teenage fiction at present. There was a time when most publishers set age level designations unrealistically high. Unfortunately, some over-corrected at the same time they were introducing books of increased maturity, and the result has been general confusion. Children's librarians are becoming wary of books marked "16 up," which may indeed be filled with pregnancy, pot and the pill; while high school librarians who stopped buying--and reading--the output of children's departments before mature books began to appear retain the no longer reliable habit of automatically subtracting two or three years from the figures given. It is an ironic fact that some of the best new books for adolescents reach their intended audience mainly in public libraries large enough to have internal reviewing systems through which recommendations can be made to buyers for the adult collection; the more mature teens rarely visit children's rooms.

These novels are unheard of outside the specialized field of children's literature (though the new paperback trend may help the situation if current distribution problems can be solved). The hardcover editions of modern books for young people are sold almost exclusively to libraries. No attempt is made to market them to the general public, and few bookstores stock any but major award winners and the work of local authors. This, in fact, is the basis of the strict separation between fields in the publishing world, and its impact is great. It means that young people's books are advertised and reviewed primarily in publications read by librarians. It affects timing: Books are not published intermittently throughout the year, but are grouped into spring and fall lists for compatibility with school and public library ordering practices; children's editorial departments are organized around this schedule. Moreover, there is no expectation of producing instant best-sellers--the review procedures employed by libraries cause long delays between publications and shelving of teenage novels, which, unlike most adult ones, are kept in print for many years.

In most respects, this library orientation is a good thing for children's literature; it tends to preclude publication of books that will not remain valuable long past the current season. Furthermore, librarians are more discriminating buyers than the public at large, and they need not purchase young people's books merely to meet public demand, since the public does not even hear the titles of such books prior to seeing them--although this consideration is at times overridden by demand for novels of current topical interest. (Too often, these days, mere <u>topical interest</u> is confused with <u>contemporary theme</u>, as in the case where an author was advised by a librarian that young readers needed a novel about "a black adolescent unwed father on a Honda."[7]) On the whole, because the market is composed of professionals, editorial standards are apt to be higher in children's departments than in the adult departments where the prime aim is large, quick sales.

This is increasingly true now that funding problems are causing libraries to become more and more selective. And the more selective they are from the literary standpoint, the better off young readers will be--we do not need any more mediocre books. However, there is some danger that selectivity based upon insufficient funds will eliminate not only books of comparatively low quality, but also those of comparatively low readership. No one can afford to purchase--or to publish--novels that will not be widely read. Under present conditions, the best teenage novels will be the first to disappear, since they are not as widely read as those that can be appreciated by children of lesser maturity. Publishers have made an effort to bring out books appropriate for high school age readers of today, yet it is through the large public libraries, not the high schools, that they are being circulated. Though high school librarians often know of them, their funds are limited, too; they must give first priority to books requested by teachers.

It should therefore be asked whether teenage novels are worth teachers' attention, and if so, why. In defining what they have to offer, I can best begin by stating what they do <u>not</u> offer, for there are a number of prevalent misconceptions concerning their purpose.

First, few if any of the good ones are easier reading than the average adult novel considered suitable for younger high school students. Writers for teenagers do not limit vocabulary, nor do they use a less complex style than they would in fiction for adults (except in the case of stories specifically produced for "slow readers," which are not really "novels" in the literary sense). Some teenage novels are relatively short, but others--most of my own, for instance--exceed many adult novels in length. A serious novel for adolescents is distinguished from adult material by its conceptual and emotional levels, not by its reading level.

Second, novels of quality for teenagers do not preach. A writer who approaches young people in a condescending way receives short shrift from today's editors and reviewers. One can use a story to reflect one's views, just as an author of adult fiction can--but they must be views about life, not about how young people, as distinguished from other people, ought to look at it.

Third, teenage novels, if good, are not devoid of concepts worth pondering and worth discussing. Although fiction for the young ordinarily stays within the bounds of good taste, its themes are confined neither to traditional ideas nor to fashionable new ones. Thus it can hardly be called uncontroversial. An author cannot present honest opinions without evoking disagreement from some proportion of readers, and teenagers scorn books that are not honest.

A fourth thing novels for adolescents do not offer is shelter from the world as it is. Because of their honesty, such books cannot ignore the grimmer aspects of life any more than they can ignore aspects some adults consider shocking. The young do not want shelter. They know that people rarely live happily ever after; it is worse than useless for fiction to pretend otherwise. At the same time, however--and again for the sake of honesty--teenage books with true depth do not foster the notion that reality is uniformly grim. Even readers who have found it so are entitled to know that a bright side does exist.

Finally, contemporary teenage novels are not mere vehicles to provide reluctant readers with a fictional reflection of their own lifestyle and their own specific problems. It is true that many deal with settings and incidents familiar to the present teen generation; as Richard Peck says, young people "are liable to choose books as they choose friends, more as mirrors than as windows."[8] But he goes on to say: "Still, the best youth novels portray adolescence as a maturing process. Though the focus may be upon being young, there is a sense of the future--a sense of becoming, as well as being."[9] Relevance--real relevance--lies in this, not in a mirror image.

What, then, does distinguish teenage fiction from adult fiction, if not shallowness of a sort properly considered obsolete? It is largely a matter of two things, I think: complexity and viewpoint. These, at any rate, are the only allowances I make in my own writing for the youth of my intended audience.

Obviously, adolescents cannot absorb ideas of as great complexity as more experienced readers. They cannot follow as many interwoven threads, or perceive such involved interrelationships; nor do they possess the knowledge to make sense of allusions. This is not because they are "too young" for adult material; it is because they have had *too little time* to develop background. If a book is to be meaningful to them, it must be clearly focused. When it is based on complex ideas--as mine, which are set in hypothetical future worlds, usually are--the discussion of those ideas must be to some extent oversimplified. Lack of complexity, however, should not be confused with lack of profundity. In the words of one noted editor, "A book with good unity can have limitless depth. Only the circumference need be limited."[10] A teenage novel can and should have more than one level, and the deeper ones will be noticed by the most mature readers alone.

The other crucial factor that determines whether a book is meaningful to adolescents is viewpoint. This is more than a question of the age of the protagonist, though normally, the principal viewpoint character should be young. The real issue is the book's outlook. As everyone knows, teenagers neither share nor understand the outlook of adults with whom they are in actual contact; they cannot be expected to fathom the view of those for whom most contemporary adult novelists write. It is not merely that there is much in modern adult fiction the young do not comprehend--the reverse is also true. Fiction for teenagers is more than a watered-down version of adult literature with excess complexity screened out. I do not mean that it portrays the "youth subculture," although some of it may. In essence, outlook is independent of culture. Adolescents, not knowing this, tend to like adult books that reject our culture and dislike those that accept it. They need novels with a fresh outlook on all cultures: ours, theirs, others of this planet, and those of hypothetical worlds. Viewpoint concerns perspective on the universe and on the future, which is what I believe today's young people are seeking.[11] Too many adults have given up the search.

There are, of course, some fine adult novels with viewpoint and level of complexity suitable for today's high school students, novels that English teachers know well. These will be read for many years to come, and their worth will not diminish. But each year they become further removed from our time, and the supply of new material to supplement them is not growing noticeably larger--at least it does not appear to be if one discounts the publishing trend toward issuing books of substance as teenage books. As a result, adolescents are sometimes urged to attempt books beyond their understanding; from a real-life world that is complex and confusing enough, they are plunged hopelessly out of their depth into a fictional world of mature concepts and emotions. This not a "realistic" world to the young--it is simply an incomprehensible one. It is unlike theirs, and asking them to enter it serves only to increase their alienation.

Lest teachers who agree immediately rush to the library with hope of finding a whole new body of literature appropriate for reading lists, it must again be emphasized that outstanding novels are the exception rather than the rule in the teenage field, just as they are in the adult field. Moreover, books of high quality for young adolescents are more plentiful than comparable ones for older adolescents. There is a good reason for this. Since the major market of children's book departments consists of children's librarians, publishers are understandably reluctant to bring out books that are too mature for sixth and seventh graders. Authors are therefore under pressure to oversimplify somewhat more than would be necessary if there were a large acknowledged high school market. Although many preadolescents have adult reading skills, their viewpoint and the level of complexity that meets their needs, cannot also meet the needs of high school juniors and seniors. Until the status of teenage fiction is established, there must be a certain amount of compromise.

In the case of my own novels, this has not been as serious a problem as with some, since their interplanetary setting interests children who might otherwise find them difficult; furthermore, they can be read on several levels. They have been widely circulated among preadolescents, and I am very happy that this is so. Yet I would like them to reach the readers for whom they were intended, too. The most recent, <u>Beyond the Tomorrow Mountains</u>,[12] is centered upon problems of deep concern to introspective older adolescents, but beyond the comprehension of most twelve-year-olds. It thus strikes some people as a bit heavy. Reviewers whose aim is to evaluate usefulness in the upper elementary grades often either ignore aspects of a book perceptible only to more mature readers, or feel that they slow its pace--which for younger boys and girls is indeed true. Where fast action is sought, this is legitimately considered a defect; still it is my belief that today's teenagers want and need fiction that emphasizes the inner events of its characters' lives more than the outward ones.

Increasingly, the adolescents of our time are interested in questions: questions about life and its meaning, about the future of civilization, about man's place in the universe. No author can give them answers. But I feel that books directed toward the young can encourage them to go on looking for answers--which, surely, is one of the major goals of education. And if they can, teenage novels do fill a need.

Notes

1. C. S. Lewis. "On Juvenile Tastes," in *Of Other Worlds* (New York: Harcourt, Brace & World, 1966), p. 41.
2. Sylvia Louise Engdahl. "Why Write for Today's Teenagers?" *The Horn Book Magazine*, XLVIII (June, 1972), pp. 249-254.
3. Natalie Babbitt. "Between Innocence and Maturity," *The Horn Book Magazine*, XLVIII (February, 1972), p. 36.
4. *Ibid.*
5. John Rowe Townsend. "It Takes More Than Pot and the Pill," *New York Times Book Review*, LXXIV (November 9, 1969, Part II), p. 2.
6. C. S. Lewis. "On Stories," in *Of Other Worlds* (New York: Harcourt, Brace & World, 1966), p. 15.
7. Richard Peck. "In the Country of Teenage Fiction," *American Libraries*, 4 (April, 1973), p. 204.
8. *Ibid.*, p. 205.
9. *Ibid.*
10. Jean Karl. *From Childhood to Childhood: Children's Books and Their Creators* (New York: John Day Company, 1970), p. 67.
11. See my article, "Perspective on the Future: The Quest of Space Age Young People," *School Media*, 1 (Fall, 1972), pp. 27-35.

12. New York: Atheneum, 1973. A sequel to *This Star Shall Abide* (New York: Atheneum, 1972).

BETWEEN INNOCENCE AND MATURITY*

By Natalie Babbitt

In this country we have an idea that teenagers are a terrible problem. The category _teenager_ itself is a new one, of course. It made its first appearance during the Second World War and was created partly by parents, partly by manufacturers, and partly by Frank Sinatra. No one seems quite sure what to do about teenagers or with teenagers. Young children do not especially distress us, but once a child leaves grammar school for the murky halls of the junior high, we are apt to stand back and scratch our heads in perplexity. It would seem that teenagers are not at all a link between innocence and maturity, the way they ought to be, but a curious group that exists independent of both, like an island under a bridge.

Society has attempted to tie teenagers into the scheme of things in a number of ways--most of them abortive--and has fallen into a number of interesting assumptions about them. The most prevalent of these assumptions is that a teenager's mind is tabula rasa. Psychiatrists would have it that our personalities, and to a large extent our characters, are formed in the first four years of life, but most of us reject that theory. It is too terrifyingly final --too soon. Therefore, when our children come into their teens, we have a kind of last-chance-for-gas-before-the-thruway feeling that now is the moment to drum away, because obviously their personalities are not formed and they are desperately in need of moral instruction. Nowhere is this attitude more apparent than in the recent so-called teenage fiction.

Moral instruction in young people's stories is hardly new. Lewis Carroll was probably the first to pinpoint it when he told us that Alice "had read several nice little stories about children who had got burnt, and eaten up by wild beasts, and other unpleasant things, all because they _would_ not remember the simple rules their friends had taught them." And, of course, it would be useless to try to ban instruction from children's books altogether. Such a ban would put too great a strain on human nature. We adults will never be able to resist the joys of giving advice, though it seems questionable whether the kinds of advice we have to offer these days will be of much use in the world our children will inhabit. Nevertheless,

---

*Reprinted by permission of the author from _The Horn Book Magazine_ (February 1972), 33-37.

there is a difference between gentle instruction of the kind that underlies much of children's fiction and the hellfire-and-brimstone that dominates the new novels for our non-children, the teenagers.

One of the routes society has hit upon as a useful link to the teenage island is something called the Zeitgeist. Supposedly, by this we mean subjects directly pertaining to the real world of real experiences that are going on right now. The Zeitgeist has been around for a long time, of course, but until now it has functioned in fiction for young people mostly at a secondary level. I remember it first as Want and Ignorance, the two children hidden under the robes of the Ghost of Christmas Present, and I met it again in The Water-Babies, Hans Brinker, and stories of that ilk. Certainly it has always provided the background of poverty, inequality, and outright cruelty in fairy tales, in the face of which the heroes and heroines act out their marvels of conquest. But recently it has been elevated to a starring role in stories that are directed exclusively towards teenagers. Hope, joy, beauty, and most of all, humor, have been relegated to the wings of this new fiction, and the Zeitgeist, becomingly costumed as Relevance, is attempting to carry the full weight of the performance. Zeitgeist by itself, it seems to me, makes a pretty thin show.

One of the differences between good stories and stories that are not-so-good, whether for children or for adults, is this: In not-so-good stories, the author's motivation is apt to stick out like the proverbial sore thumb. If you read all the novels of Sinclair Lewis, for example, you find that although Lewis was deeply and sincerely concerned with social problems, his writing was effective only in the novels where his concern took the form of a natural milieu for a compelling central character. We remember Babbitt because George Babbitt rings true as a real person distressed by a particular kind of problem, not as a puppet for the demonstration of the problem. Nobody reads Ann Vickers any more, for Ann is not the central character. The true hero of Ann Vickers is the unsavory conditions of American prisons.

In the new teenage fiction, the motivation is very obvious indeed. It is as if authors had said, "Here is a brand new group of people. They have nothing to read except Nancy Drew mysteries. Let us write something just for them." You can imagine a dialogue developing:

"Yes, we should write for them, but they're a difficult bunch. How can we catch their attention?"

"We must be relevant."

"Yes, but what's relevant to teenagers?"

"Well, for instance, social problems."

"What kind of social problems?"

"All the new horrors--homosexuality, drugs, alienation, premarital sex."

"That seems sound. These are genuine problems. And we can toll the warning bell at the same time."

"Yes--it is our duty to warn them of the pitfalls of modern life."

And so the stories are written, some with beauty and many with sincerity, but somehow they fall short of classification as literature.

There are at least two reasons for this failure. One is that the Zeitgeist screams for attention from beginning to end; and as I said before, it makes a very poor central character. There never has been a good play in which the stage set overpowered the actors. A second reason for the failure of these tales is that in a curious way they do not go far enough. It is as if the authors felt that teenagers should be exposed to desperation, but only up to a certain point. We seem to be saying that they are, after all, not adults, so we must temper things. Let the readers be heated but never scalded. We do not want to discourage them utterly, after all.

But a true and honest story is not made whole by this kind of withdrawal from logical extremes, nor even by the extremes themselves. Actually, these new novels often miss their mark not only through timidity, but also through narrowness of vision. Even in the blackest hours, there are other things in life besides desperation. And a story which deals only in desperation becomes not drama but melodrama, a one-legged stool which cannot support its own weight.

Two of those other things in life, two things which fine literature is never without entirely, are the threads of hope and humor. Hope and humor are not panaceas stoically to be eschewed, but genuine aspects of life--the very aspects which make it possible for us human beings to toil forward through the direst of situations. Fiction does not become more honest if it omits hope and humor. It becomes, in fact, dishonest in the sense that one dimension does not define a cube.

It seems to me foolish to say that the problems of modern life are inappropriate subjects for young people's fiction. It would take superhuman skill at overprotection these days to shield any child from the dismal and dismaying flaws in our society. But it is just as foolish to assume that teenagers, so recently graduated from such books as Charlotte's Web (Harper) or The Hobbit (Houghton), are going to be enthralled by a new kind of story--presumably their very own--which tells them that life is one long tunnel of despair. And consider those unfortunate youngsters who were given only the pretty books to read as young children. They are going to become even more distrustful of adult motives when they are switched on their thirteenth birthdays from stories that are rosy-pink to those that are suddenly and inexplicably bruise-green. If we want to help them find their way, we need to accept the fact that they will do better with a more honest and balanced mixture than the new teenage fiction is offering them.

Let us be quite clear about something. Obviously somebody is buying these new novels, but it does not seem, to me at least, that anyone is reading them. Here is a partial reading list for my fifteen-year-old son's high school English class: *Mutiny on the Bounty*, *Travels with Charley*, *Ethan Frome*, *Uncle Tom's Cabin*, *The Grapes of Wrath*, *Babbitt*. And here are some of the stories my thirteen-year-old is reading: *The Yearling*, *Man Without a Country*, *The Legend of Sleepy Hollow*, *Lilies of the Field*. It rather makes one wonder if there is such a category as a teenage audience. I honestly believe we are producing books for people who are not there to read them. Teenagers do not need a fiction of their own: They are quite ready to move into the world of adult fiction.

There is one more thing to be said on this subject. My husband and I are both deeply involved with college-age students, he as a college president and professor, and I as a humble workshop instructor. We have both become aware of the growing interest of this age group in children's books--that is, books supposedly written for preadolescents. These college students want to read children's books, to write them, to illustrate them, to plumb the depths of their philosophies. I am not exactly sure why this is so, and neither are they. I have, in fact, two nineteen-year-old students who are spending the entire semester rereading the books they loved as children, and writing major papers on why these books are still meaningful and useful and attractive to them. The books they are rereading are not teenage novels. (As young teenagers, these two read many of the same books that my teenagers are reading, and they learned more about human suffering from these than can be learned from a roomful of the new, more tepid teenage novels.) No, the reading list for the paper they are planning to write includes such children's authors as Milne, Carroll, Baum, E. B. White, and C. S. Lewis. Can it be that we are at last to be gifted with a generation of adults who recognize that there is, in addition to children's books, a genuine category called literature for children--with everything that the term implies? We have been waiting for a long time for the distinction to be made--ever since Alice Liddell hit puberty.

I would like to suggest that authors who wish to write for teenagers accept the fact that they are in reality writing for adults --very young adults, no doubt, but intelligent, critical, skeptical, and quick to spot a phony. They are living, every day, through the things we older adults are pompous enough to attempt to describe to them. It is a little like standing fully dressed on the shore and yelling to a swimmer that the water is wet. It is time we stopped yelling at teenagers about the wetness of the water, and started trying to share with them the continual process of discovery of all the elements of life, a process through which we are endlessly passing, all of us together--regardless of age.

YOUNG PEOPLE: VICTIMS OF REALISM IN BOOKS AND LIFE*

By June Jordan

Hard to say what's real anymore.

I mean, is Watergate real?

More than 667,000 square miles of Atlantic Ocean classify as squalid--ocean mileage spoiled by plastic rubbish and randomly collected filth. How are 667,000 square miles real to anyone in any way? It's hard to say.

Used to be that folks would argue long about "The Truth" of things. And, somehow, that made more sense; debate about the truth used to seem reasonable and even constructive because the truth was taken as the meaning, or as the most satisfying interpretation of experience.

But we have abandoned the truth, per se. In fact, as a subject of our passionate interest, the truth has been lost to our despair and justified distrust resulting from the unprecedented perversion of words, and the unprecedented, powerful mockery of communication itself. Now we have fallen to a more confounding, a more dangerous level of dispute.

Annihilation and the Loss of Rational Cool

On this relatively new level, the terms are nothing less than terms of very existence--terms acknowledged as real, as possible, or terms judged inadmissible, or else unimportant, or else "unrealistic." So the consequences of such argument can be annihilating, as a matter of fact; if you will not allow that either my difficulty or my happiness is real, then either or both of these exist in jeopardy. And so do I; it is the jeopardy of possible extinction resulting from your disbelief or ignorance or indifference or hostility. Any one of those will serve to construct my absolute peril.

---

*Reprinted by permission of the author and publisher from Wilson Library Bulletin (October 1973), 142-145.

Then given the serious nature of disagreement about what's real, or realistic, it is perfectly frightening to look around and consider the popular, current uses of those concepts Reality and Realism. When you hear that the President has determined the urban centers of America to be free from crisis and into an okay condition of well-being, you can lose your rational cool trying to extrapolate his sense of what's real.

When we hear about the increasing prosperity we enjoy as the consequence of record-breaking crop production and corporate expansion of the profit margin; when you listen to pronouncements on historic peace that has been waged and won, by America, around the world; when you consider the weak and faraway deadlines set for the termination of waste, and irresponsible industrial behavior--an exploitative pattern directly affecting our most precious resource: our capacity to survive--you may well wonder about the reality contact of the powerful.

On the other hand, famine is real. In Africa today there is the awesome and immediate spectre of ten million human beings dead from hunger unless the rest of us will become aroused and respond to this incontrovertible reality. Ten million human beings will die unless we acknowledge they are real. Their hunger is real. And our responsibility to help them, is that "real," is that "realistic"?

Meanwhile, here at home, malnutrition, illness, crime, inequity, avarice, egotism, hatred, deceitfulness, predatory habits of misconduct in human affairs, violence of every sort, and multiplying signs of anomie, abound; they are real factors of our common, shared reality. No question. But, they are factors, not the total thing.

Honest-to-God "Live" People

Balancing out the picture there are honest-to-God live people, real folks, out there, among us, working overtime to teach somebody how to read; working overtime to organize fund-raising functions on behalf of the African peoples otherwise facing starvation; working overtime to make their shaky marriage less shaky, make it an elastic, truly supportive, intersecting form for both of them; working overtime to expose and eliminate crimes of negligence or crimes of contempt for others, working overtime to learn how to love and be loved.

In other words, just as there is evidence of our aggressive tendencies, there is equal evidence of our non-aggressive inclinations. Or, there is the success of China, when the issue is the feeding of families, as well as the tragedy of India. Or, for all the American communes that have failed according to report, there remain the Israeli Kibbutzim which have not failed, and which provide convincing models of a good idea.

I mean to suggest that reality is a pretty mixed, big bag. And, in fact, there is room, there is need, for argument among us as to what it is; what we will search for as real, what we will take into a sensitive, compelling focus as reality.

But I must testify, as a writer, as someone committed to radical, positive change, that the argument over what's real/what's realistic is not widely accepted as legitimate nor is any argument permitted whenever it can be squelched by dint of power, for instance the power of a negative consensus, the power of a demoralizing, routine perspective, the power of those mighty interests riveted to the proposition that the status quo represents the best of all possible worlds because it represents *them* and, therefore, necessarily, excludes other people, other values.

But despite the obvious complexity of what's real, what's going down, and what's coming up in our heads, the dreams, the increasing capability of folks to know, understand and then transform--despite all of this, when somebody tells you: "Be realistic," it's a bet that he or she means *Stay Where You Are*, *Hang On*, *Be Cynical*, *Adjust*, *Be Tough*, *Be Cool*, *Be Contemptuous of All Glad Tidings* but take the bad news for granted *and* to heart.

Now this "be realistic" conspiracy is an insidious and, sometimes, a calculated distortion of reality. Its most benign effect obliterates fully half our facts, half our potentiality for new and effective political and social undertaking. In the name of realism, the cop-out, the surrender to the unbearable, the frequently horrifying, the commonly, plain *wrong*, pigheaded, and the painful--the cop-out becomes a virtue of ostensibly sophisticated wisdom. I don't know anything about sophisticated wisdom but I do believe a cop-out is a cop-out, *period*, no matter if it is a fashionable ducking out the door, and no matter how concerted are the efforts to enforce it: a cop-out is a cop-out.

Applauding Sick Books

In the name of realism, book reviewers applaud books crammed with relentless, so-called documentation of pathology flowering from a pivotal, perverted faith in a pathogenic, miserable and hopeless condition of being which is, allegedly, our realistic condition. In the name of realism, the writer finds himself or herself encouraged or forcibly spurred to invent problems, to build conflicts, to design characters of incredible fallibility and self-centered inconsequence.

In the name of realism, the equally creative work of inventing solutions or of inhibiting the development of conflicts by designing characters of their environment so that conflict would seem actually contrived, or of research obdurately directed toward uncovering of little known genuine heroes, heroines, and verifiable happy and peaceful ways of living--this equally creative work, more often than not, is unmistakably discouraged and ridiculed, even at the proposed stage when the publisher and the other media get hold of a creative writer and thinker.

I happen to feel, very strongly, that what goes down under the name of realism is, 95 per cent of the time, pointless, self-indulgent, status quo-protecting, and irresponsible garbage. Writing differs, intrinsically, from all the other mass communications media, but I have yet to see clear signals that the publishing industry wishes to capitalize upon this difference in a fundamental life-affirming manner. Specifically, I have yet to see clear signals that the publishing industry intends to exploit its potential as a fundamentally alternative source of information: a source of information fundamentally different from the information carried by the newspapers, television, and film. I am talking about information about human beings, human nature, human society.

Folks Desperate for a Love Story

For a while, I have been thinking about Love Story and its runaway career. Look like folks was pretty desperate for a story of love between a man and a woman; and, apart from its merits or demerits as literature, even this story did not escape that particular realism of the doomed Romeo and Juliet tradition.

Or, look at Jonathan Livingston Seagull. My fifteen-year-old son Christopher, when he read Jonathan Seagull, he said, "People are improving, maybe. What do you think?" I was staggered. After he explained his reaction at length I was still staggered, but this is what Christopher made me understand, at last: that, since Jonathan was not a pornographic/sado-masochistic/smear composite of a character or plot, and since the book was selling so terrifically well, he thought that maybe people were improving, maybe people could be interested in and influenced by works that do not simply exacerbate the howling of our angry, fearful, starved-out spirits. What he said staggered me, as well, because Jonathan is, after all, a seagull. He is a seagull idea of a possible human being. This seagull phenomenon relates, in my head, to the successful phenomenon of the Don Juan-Castaneda books which developed into huge underground bestsellers. And, as most of you know, the Don Juan-Castaneda books bring news of an entirely other reality, a reality far out for most of us most of the time. For me, these three: Love Story, Jonathan Livingston Seagull and the Don Juan trilogy, point to an absurdly neglected appetite and to a legitimate need strangely neglected or denied by publishers and writers alike.

As a former student remarked to me after reading a recent book about African Americans, "It's stale. The problems have been described and analyzed, already, to death. Where are his ideas, what is his program, so we can get over, get past the problem into something else?" As far as I know--as a reader and as a writer, the answer is that books deliberately setting out to provide tame or believable or practicable good news or alternative, experimental possibilities of conduct--books, including fiction books, of course, deliberately setting out to solve problems, and to depict new ways of living without perpetuating loneliness and fratricide and colossal insanity--such books are rare, and becoming more rare. Love Story was a freak, and, in any case, it is a short story of short love. Seagull is a "seagull" story. Castaneda writes about a reality where food stamps do not, cannot, figure as significant in any way. This leaves us, and young people, especially, in a victimized position; we find ourselves passive victims of our parents, of our government, of the destruction of our planet as a place to live and grow and thrive and know and teach love. That is our position as victims every day.

And the special positive reality interference promised by every book we pick up has mostly proven not to be special enough, not to resist our daily realism with the equal realism of devoted, revolutionary, exceptional, plausible, necessary, urgently overdue, alternative stories, models, facts--alternative information that can feed and nourish the spirit otherwise overwhelmed by destructive, loathsome, painful images of ourselves. I am opposed to the apparent, overwhelmingly negative reality that consigns us to frustration, shame, and impotence. I am opposed to this status quo with all of my being.

My Manifesto

And so I have resolved that I will attempt, in all of my written work, to devise reasonable alternatives to this reality, and to offer these alternatives particularly to young readers. They are the ones who have known Southeast Asia and Center City degradation since birth; they are the ones we have failed, in these so many ways, and we are the ones who owe our children something else, right now--some good news, a chance, a story of love gracing an entire family or an entire community for thirty to forty years, a manual for the assertion of human rights versus private property rights, more reference sources clearly listing the groups and the individuals who are busy doing what kinds of urgently required, humane work, on behalf of other lives just because it is right and feels good to undertake and pursue such work.

I think it is our most serious business to insist upon the support, invention, discovery, or development of good news as real news about reality. The good news will report and instigate activity: swift, dense, widespread, immediate, far-reaching activity in the name of a new realism where victims will have become actors enabled to struggle, intelligently, for radical, life-saving change.

Let us be realistic and know that the status quo reality must be transformed, and realism must be redefined to include an end to atrocity and the beginning of a new, worldwide situation in which the African famine of today would be impossible because enough of us would have acted, three years ago, when the drought began, to galvanize reserve programs commensurate to this emergency.

As a writer, I have chosen this commitment to a new realism, consciously, during the past year: I will not write anything unless I can learn how to craft it into usable, good news, or usable information to interdict and humanely supersede the reality of some particular bad news. I wish you would take these criteria into consideration when you recommend books, when you order them--I wish we would passionately seek and find alternatives to Watergate and famine unrelieved and cruelty and selfishness, as usual.

I wish publishers would cease and desist their perpetuation of the status quo under the misleading mantle of "realism."

I wish many other poets and writers would try on these alternative criteria for their own creative work.

So, unless we do really manage to come through with usable, believable, practicable, desirable alternatives to our present realism, in books and in our lives, what do you suppose we can expect, and what do you suppose we will deserve, and what do you know will happen to the future of our children?

BACK TO YOU, NAT: HEARING FROM THE TEEN-AGE READER*

By Nat Hentoff

A distinct difference, I find, between writing books for young readers and for adults is that the former are much more likely to write back.

Jazz Country, for example, has been out there since 1965, but assessments keep arriving:

"How come that father is so *good*, so understanding? He's not real."

"You're right," I answer. "That was the first fiction of any kind I ever wrote, and the father was one of my mistakes. He really doesn't exist at all."

"Are the jazz musicians in the book based on real people," I am asked every other month or so, "or did you make them up? If you did, how do you make up people?"

The musicians began to be imagined, I tell them, out of fragments of memories of real people, and then I let go and tried to make up someone quite new. The dominant musician in *Jazz Country*, Moses Godfrey (about whom readers ask most), has a touch of Charles Mingus and Dizzy Gillespie and Thelonious Monk; but, I assure my correspondents, he's very much different from any of them.

In 1968, I sent forth *I'm Really Dragged But Nothing Gets Me Down*. Written for somewhat older youngsters than *Jazz Country* was, *Really Dragged* has returned more and longer letters.

A fifteen-year-old girl tells me she's "madly in love" with Jeremy, "the draft-resister," in the book. (But are you sure he resisted the draft? Read the last chapter again, I suggest.) She asks if she can send me some of *her* work, and ends:

---

*Reprinted by permission of the author and publisher from *Wilson Library Bulletin* (September 1972), 38-41. Copyright © 1972 by The H. W. Wilson Company.

"P.S.: Where I found the courage and insanity to write this will be forever unknown to me."

I sometimes wonder where I, forty-six, find the nerve to write novels for fifteen-year-old girls. Or for a sixteen-year-old who writes back:

> I want to learn how to follow the course of migratory birds in flight south; how to check how many American houses are painted red; how to understand someone speaking an unknown language. Where do people go if they're crazy to learn things and too crazy to stay on the old Board of Ed. leash? Enclosed is a stamped envelope.

My God, I only wrote a story. I'm not Ivan Illich.

Well, I didn't *only* write a story. The fiction I write for young people--for any people--is intended to get them to ask questions. I write fiction, after all, to ask questions of myself.

"Your book doesn't have an end," a reader of *Really Dragged* writes. "What does Jeremy do about the draft?"

What do *you* think he does? What do you think he should do?

I am delighted to hear from teachers and librarians who understand that the book is not supposed to come to the same conclusion for every reader. A teacher in Galesburg, Illinois makes plays out of some of the chapters in *Really Dragged*. The plays allow a lot of room for her students to improvise, to take different roles in the book, to try to make some of the loose ends in the characters' lives come together. That is, come together on that particular day.

Another teen-age reader of the book writes:

> I'm against war, but now you've got me thinking about the Second World War and whether I'd have been against that too. But it's different now, isn't it, with the H-bomb?

Yes, I write back, I think it is; and that's why some people who are not absolute pacifists call themselves nuclear pacifists.

The messages from out there--questioning, arguing, suggesting themes for the next book--are buoying to get. It's reassuring to hear from time to time that the books are still alive and still capable of generating intense debates among some of their readers. ("We've been hassling," a reader of *Jazz Country* writes from class, "about whether you really meant that *no* white person can *ever* play real jazz." No, that isn't what I meant. But there are *particular* kinds of dues white people have to pay in the learning process, I tell him.)

It was also good to get another kind of message--my most encouraging literary award--from a librarian in Brooklyn several years ago. "More copies of Jazz Country," he told me, "were stolen this winter than of any other book in the children's section."

Recently, another novel for the young, In the Country of Ourselves, started its way. That book leaves a lot more questions unanswered than the first two. Or, as John Holt observed in a letter to me, "You leave the reader in a good deal of doubt about which side he's supposed to be on."

I sure do. This one's about radicals and revolutionaries--or so they think of themselves--in a high school. It's also about what school is supposed to be for. (Not the same for everyone.) And as I was writing the book, a tough sardonic, complicated principal took over a lot more of the action than he was originally supposed to. He much intrigues me, being considerably more unpredictable than I had at first imagined; and so he--and some of the kids--are going to be part of a fourth novel because I have more questions to ask of them and of myself.

Meanwhile, the first two novels have been sectioned off into lesson plans in some schools. I feel rather ambivalent about that, remembering how novels were taught to me in certain morgue-like English classrooms during my years at Boston Latin School. As each chapter ended, there were numbered questions to answer before we could move on, but they were seldom my questions.

On the other hand, I am decidedly curious as to how teachers and librarians these days might handle the kinds of suggestions I saw in one manual that had to do with Really Dragged. In that book, Jeremy, trying to measure himself as a potential draft-resister, often clashes with his father (who, unlike the father in Jazz Country is not, I think, too good to be true).

At one point the father tells his son: "You've got two choices. You go into a monastery or you become part of the world. You become part of the world, you become part of it all--the good, the bad, the lying, the cheating, the exposing, the covering up again. Once you make that choice, the rest is a matter of degree."

Using that statement "as a springboard," the manual suggests, "the teacher will want to direct his students in investigating whether this is a truth. If becoming a part of society is to become a part of the evil, then to what extent should we accept and/or compromise with it?"

Yeah, how about that, teacher? For that matter, how about that, author?

The manual also focuses on another character in the novel, Mike, a total pacifist: "It is important to have the students react to Mike's philosophy that to register for the draft is to give the government power over you. A discussion should consider to what extent, if any, a government has the right to exert power over the individual...."

I don't mind that lesson plan at all--provided the teacher doesn't have a neatly universal answer prepared, no matter what happens in the discussion.

There's much current rhetoric about teachers and librarians learning with and from young people, as well as sharing some of their own earned experience with students. But it can and does happen if there's some trust involved on both sides, and getting to that point is not often easy. Once it does begin to happen, however, the mutual confronting of difficult questions--with no set answers in the back of any book--can lead to real probing of the uncertainty and ambiguity of what it is to be in the world for which the school is purportedly "preparing" the youngster.

The moral minefields in that world outside the school are very much in my mind when I write for young readers. As is my recognition that nearly all of them have watched a great amount of television and thereby know, or think they know, much more about nearly everything than youngsters of my generation thought we did. These kids do not have to be "protected" from worldly knowledge and its attendant dilemmas. What they are in need of is encouragement to sort out some kind of meaning, some kind of purposeful pattern for themselves out of all that "information" they're getting from everywhere. The images, the sounds, the skewed polyrhythms of actual and vicarious experiences.

Although my intention is to help stimulate just that kind of seeking, I must also say that I am occasionally jolted when a young reader writes to say that something I've written actually has affected his life. There's a lot of responsibility involved in that kind of turn, and I begin to worry about some of these distant lives.

Jazz Country ends with Tom, its young white protagonist, wrenchingly deciding to try a year or two of college rather than accept a chance to play jazz full-time. The book's last two lines are: "After all, I could take one year off somewhere along the line. Couldn't I?"

Suddenly, almost seven years after Jazz Country was published, a letter arrives from a young man unknown:

> I read your book, Jazz Country, for the thousandth time last nite. I'm 19. The first time I read it I was 15. And man, I know the answer. Tom's never gonna take off that year. He's lost it--music as life and life as music. He's gonna keep on doing what others, all those others, tell him he's supposed to do.
>
> What should he have done? Well, in answer to that, I lived that ol' book of yours. When I first read it, I

> was a sophomore. I've been playing guitar for 12 years, and my turn around came when I realized one day, when I was 15, that I could just throw away the music and play me. Well, my parents and nobody else would believe me. (They still don't.)
>
> But knowing that led me to leave school. I went to Israel for a year. Just took off and went. I learned a lot; I got some experience you can't get in school; I know where it's at. I went out and did something so I could come back and say something.

He's now in college, I am relieved to see in the next paragraph. I don't believe that "education" need necessarily be a lockstep of years, but I would have been disquieted at having been even partially responsible for so young a fulltime drop out. Yet there's no telling how long he'll stay--there or anywhere.

> There are hip courses and funky professors where I am now, but I've got a whole life full of taking years off here and there. I'm still playing, but nobody's listening. Nobody gives a damn. I've learned that no matter what, I'm alone. I can tear my heart out playing for people talking or drinking or dancing. When my band plays, I just dance and stop in the middle of my solo and laugh because I'm having a good time.

He adds, this reader of mine, that he might take off again any time so long as he finds something to do "with life in it" and that lets him keep playing what and how he must.

> If I can't play music my way, I won't play it their way. Instead I'll run on the edge of the world--move--work--sweat. And wherever I go, I'm gonna carry my guitar or harmonica or trumpet or voice. I'm gonna wail because it's in me.
>
> Well, thanks for writing the book. Did you ever think it could mean so much to someone?

I had hoped it might mean a lot to someone, but I had not expected it to help spur anyone to consider running on the edge of the world.

Keep in touch, I wrote him. Please do keep in touch.

I think of him some nights and I wonder if anyone is listening to him wail. A reader will do that sometimes. If he doesn't like your ending, he'll start creating his own sequel. But he's not likely to let you know about it--unless he's a teen-ager.

PART V

READING INTERESTS OF YOUNG ADULTS

(*trying hard to hear you* ...)

EDITOR'S NOTE

Surveys and studies designed to determine adolescent reading interests have been conducted on a fairly regular basis since the 1890s.[1] Young adults' reading preferences hold a continuing fascination for adults, partly perhaps because we like to be assured that some things really don't change, and partly because those changes which do occur in the reading tastes of the young act as a kind of barometer of the climate in which the current generation is maturing. For teachers, knowing what unassigned reading has captured the attention of their students can provide guidelines for choosing books for assignments that will be more likely to appeal and have something to say. As Corrine Pollan points out, English teachers who know what their students read by choice can build "a common literary ground."

For librarians, the survey can validate (or challenge) the assumptions they make in selecting materials for young adults. In "We Got There ... It Was Worth the Trip!" Los Angeles young adult librarians describe a simple, but effective method of collecting reader feedback.

As *The New York Times Report on Teenage Reading Tastes and Habits*[2] demonstrates, however, it is not only librarians and English teachers who are concerned with young adult reading. In the early seventies, the realization that enormous numbers of high school graduates have failed to learn to read well enough to be considered functionally literate led to a veritable explosion of reading studies, as well as the outcry "back to the basics." While the *Times* report concludes rather optimistically that teenagers are enjoying reading more than ever, the large scale of the survey does lend this assumption some credibility. Moreover, the report validates the findings of smaller surveys conducted during the early seventies in terms of the reading interests identified. Specific interests change all the time, of course, but the *Times* study will remain important, primarily because it identifies a significant trend toward the increasing popularity of the junior novel.

The Hawaii study confirms an observation made by both Stanek[3] and Paul Janeczko,[4] that teenage reading preferences do not vary significantly with geography. What does affect them is what Patty Campbell identifies as "Zeitgeist." The last article in this section, a report on campus reading, echoes Campbell's conclusion that young adults today are concerned more and more with personal survival. It has often been noted that the books read on college campuses today will be picked up in the high schools a year or so later, and therefore The Chronicle of Higher Education's book polls are useful barometers to watch. The effect of movies and television on reading interests is referred to so often, that the point hardly needs to be reiterated.

Notes

1. George W. Norvell's The Reading Interests of Young People (Michigan State University Press, 1973), an analysis of a forty-year study, is perhaps the most exhaustive. The data confirm the thesis that the assignment of literature in schools should be based on interest. While dated, the study is useful for perspective and methodology.

2. Rema Freiberger. The New York Times Report on Teenage Reading Tastes and Habits. The New York Times, 1974.

3. See page 166.

4. See page 400.

REAL PEOPLE, REAL BOOKS: ABOUT YA READERS*

By Lou Willett Stanek

University campuses are haunted by Pirandello characters searching not for an author, but for research topics. A sixteen-year-old girl in Tulsa, Oklahoma, unknowingly saved me from that fate. She also distracted my attention from what adolescents are SUPPOSED to read, re-focusing it on what they read purely for pleasure. I think this anecdote has significance for those of us concerned about the reading interests of young adults.

In 1967 I was directing a demonstration center for students gifted in English. The center was at least democratic or liberal enough to allow students a voice in what they read, or more likely in what they thought they should read. They were reading Faulkner, Camus, Joyce, plays from theater of the absurd, _Hamlet_ ... a very impressive list. Then I heard the first version of what is becoming the Susan Hinton myth ... I think I now know five, but originally I heard and told the students she was walking through a Tulsa park, saw a rumble, a young lad was killed, and Susan was so upset she ran home and started writing it out of her system. Whether Susan Hinton purged her soul in the manner of a Fitzgerald writing _Crack-Up_ or simply was inspired to write a novel about kids she knew is interesting, but what _is_ important is Velma Varner, then juvenile editor at Viking, being insightful enough to publish _The Outsiders_. Adolescent literature could never be quite the same--gangs, violence, poor kids had stolen the spotlight from mundane, middle-class Minnie.

The students at the center read it, loved it, and wanted more (as the earlier generation had wanted more _Seventeenth Summers_). And they were apologetic. These students had been labeled "gifted" and were very self-conscious. So they told me perhaps they should read these teenage books--even though they weren't _great literature_ --because maybe some of them could write a novel like Susan Hinton. And they could get ideas.

I called Zena Sutherland, then children's editor at _Saturday_

---

*Reprinted by permission of the author and publisher from _Top of the News_, (June 1975), 417-425.

Review. She suggested wiggy titles--titles I'd never heard of--The Pigman, Too Bad about the Haines Girl, My Darling, My Hamburger .... The students waited in line for those books, wore them out, ripped them off. This had not been the pattern with Faulkner, Camus, Joyce, and company.

The teachers and I stood in line too. These books were different from those teenage books we had often sneered at--often causing our students to sneer too, I fear. They weren't just different; they were better. Nothing to challenge Beckett, but new to teenage fiction. There was experimentation in style:

1. First-person and multicharacter point of view
2. Stream of conscious narration
3. Non-standard English dialog
4. The setting had left virginal middleville and moved to Spanish Harlem, communes, Appalachia, the Village, and North Beach.
5. Anti-heroes, black kids, Indians, and fat kids were protagonists.
6. The old taboo subjects were themes: mothers had affairs, didn't get married, daughters got pregnant, daddies drank martinis, women went through menopause, girls reached puberty, sons rebelled against their fathers AND a few loved other boys and older men.

There was intrigue here. Questions bobbing like corks--

Aesthetic and literary questions: Propaganda? Socializing tools? or art?
Sociological questions: Were these books barometers of our culture? values? reflecting a quasi-social revolution?
Psychological questions: Did these books aid in the maturation process, or stunt it?
Education and curriculum: Should they be taught or left under the pillow for pleasure?

Pondering these questions, I began to agree with T. S. Eliot when he said that "it is just the literature we read for amusement or purely for pleasure that may have the greatest ... least suspected ... earliest and most insidious influences upon us. Hence it is that the influence of popular novelists, popular plays of contemporary life, require to be scrutinized." AND I HAD FOUND A RESEARCH TOPIC.

Previous studies indicated most adolescent reading lists had been compiled from data collected surveying librarians and English teachers. Seldom were kids polled and the rare cases were students geographically compatible with professors--university lab schools. I wanted a mixture of kids, so I sought my sample from the foothills of Illinois in a rural community to the Gold Coast of Chicago, stopping off at a blue-collar suburb, an inner-city ghetto, a parochial school, and the University of Chicago Lab School.

The study was limited to problem novels published specifically for young adults, and after several pre-tests I had a booklist of 150 titles ranging from a few such as Maureen Daly's Seventeenth Summer, published in the late 1940s, to several such as Go Ask Alice, with the publisher's ink barely dry. Since I was interested not only in WHAT students read, but WHY, I read each book to determine the major fictional problem treated. My contention was that those (Dwight Burton, Robert Carlsen, and others) who thought the young read these books to help solve their personal problems were wrong. I had a hunch fat girls didn't want to read about other fat girls, but preferred the prom queen or a sleek ninety-pound female jockey.

Using Havighurst's developmental tasks of adolescents[1] as the theoretical base for what concerns are significant at this age, I compiled a list of ten categories of real adolescent problems. The students were asked to rank order both the books they most enjoyed reading and their most pressing personal problems as they perceived them. I tested the hypothesis that there was no significant correlation between the fictional problems they enjoyed reading and their perceived personal problems. The results supported my hypothesis so strongly the computer thought that I had cheated. The ten most popular books in ranked order were:

1. Mr. and Mrs. Bo Jo Jones
2. Sounder
3. Fifteen
4. Island of the Blue Dolphins
5. Go Ask Alice
6. The Outsiders
7. My Darling, My Hamburger
8. Lisa, Bright and Dark
9. Jennifer
10. The Soul Brothers and Sister Lou

Real problems rank ordered were:

1. Family
2. School
3. Personal
4. Appearance
5. Boy-girl
6. Concerns about future
7. Money
8. Moral issues
9. Recreation--leisure time
10. World tensions

The concerns that really hassled them were personal, private matters. But generally they read books about abstract, social, all encompassing problems.

What flabbergasted me about the data was the popular booklist.

This study was done in 1973. We were all talking about Man Without a Face, Sticks and Stones, Run Softly, Go Fast, Mom, the Wolf Man and Me, Dinky Hocker Shoots Smack. But the kids were still reading Fifteen and Jennifer. They said they were least concerned about moral issues and world tensions. But they were reading about pregnancy in high school, drugs, gangs, racial tensions, and ecology.

However, if you could all ponder this list for a time, you would probably begin to see some patterns. Why Go Ask Alice, published only a few months before the study, and not The Peter Pan Bag (surely a better drug book)? NEVER UNDERESTIMATE THE POWER OF THE TELLY OR MOVIE HOUSE! I would hazard a prediction that Norma Klein's Sunshine, written from the TV script, will be known to many kids before Mom, the Wolf Man and Me, published in 1972, and that twice as many teenagers know and read John Neufeld's Lisa, Bright and Dark, which has been televised, than the earlier Edgar Allen, which hasn't. Four of the first five choices in my study had either been movies or TV shows before the survey.

Secondly--and this is discouraging--I surveyed the teachers and librarians in the sample schools. Their choices were significantly different from the students' and were even less current. I checked card catalogs and found in some of the Chicago public schools that 1969 was the latest publishing date for a book in the teenage collection. IT SEEMS THAT IT IS A LONG JOURNEY FROM PUBLISHING HOUSE TO SCHOOL HOUSE. Perhaps this explains why kids are still reading Fifteen and Jennifer. Another contributing factor surely is that only three of the professionals in this study had taken a course in adolescent literature, and the majority of the English teachers admitted they did not read reviews of young adult fiction. Their formal educations not only didn't include a bibliography of the journals, most of their mentors had not legitimatized the study of this stepchild of literature, although both MLA and NCTE have recommended the course be included in English teaching programs.

The third trend is not nearly so obvious or significant, but two out of ten, Sounder and Island of the Blue Dolphins, were Newbery winners. Interviews revealed that even teachers and librarians having little respect for junior novels in general will promote award winners. Some kids reported having Island of the Blue Dolphins read aloud to them as many as four times in their short school histories.

The media, availability, and the awards accounted for outside influence, but told little about personal choice. Real insight came when I decided to look at adolescent literature as popular culture. Defining it in social terms rather than aesthetic, this was literature for a nonelite subculture--the young. The literary aspect of pop culture is that it crosses class lines. Perhaps a good comparison is with sports. Polo is a class sport; only the few can afford to play. It is high culture. Football crosses class lines; therefore, it is a part of our popular culture. Finnegans Wake is a class novel--only a few are adequately trained to comprehend; Gone with the Wind, on the other hand, can be read by everyone.

Scholars of popular culture such as John Cawelti, University of Chicago, have been able to make inferences about groups by putting together their cultural products. They have also been able to isolate forms distinctive to types of popular literature. This is not a value judgment. Sherlock Holmes stories are formula literature. The appeal of this formula literature seems to be:

1. People without training can learn how to react to the basic patterns; it becomes a game with all the rules known in advance.
2. Psychologically, it represents fantasy, dreams, or wish fulfillment--a search for gratification we can't get in our own lives.
3. It reaffirms the values of the culture. Les conventional--high culture--Waiting for Godot, The Wasteland, Ulysses QUESTION it.

Formula literature is important because it represents the way cultures have embodied both mythical archetypes and their own preoccupations in narrative form. These formulas of westerns, spy and mystery stories, best-sellers, science fiction ... adolescent literature ... represent a synthesis of several important functions in our modern culture taken over by the popular from religion. May I add that this view does not preclude judging the quality of writing, it just adds another dimension.

Barbara Martinec, University of Chicago researcher, using the four characteristic elements of the formula--type of situation, pattern of action, character roles and relationships, and setting--isolated the pattern of action in the adolescent novel. Use of this formula as a critical tool shed some light into three areas:

1. The novel's appeal for teenage readers
2. Adult concerns in our society
3. The development of the genre

The appeal for teenage readers can perhaps best be understood by looking at the interrelated ideas suggested by the formula:

1. Immaturity (the basic problem of teenagers) is somehow to be equated with isolation from the group.
2. All problems can be solved and will be solved successfully.
3. Adults cannot help you much. They mean well but are ineffectual. True communication, true community is possible only with one's peers.
4. Solutions to problems are found gratuitously, either brought about by others or discovered by chance.
5. Maturity entails conformity. Acceptance equals happiness, and this is the true goal of life. The trick is to conform while maintaining one's own individual identity.

Perhaps these are not the ideas adults would choose to emphasize, but when compared with Havighurst's tasks of adolescent development, the value is more evident, so is the appeal. These tasks include learning new relationships with peers, achieving independence from parents, and acquiring self-confidence and a system of values of one's own. The adolescent novel formula is structured around these problems, and their apparent resolution in the patterned action of the formula helps to explain the popularity with young readers.

These books, in my opinion, don't solve kids' problems, but they offer a super means of escaping them for a couple of hours. The child whose parents don't trust her, hassle her about hours, clothes, keeping her room clean, can read *The Outsiders* and *Island of the Blue Dolphins* and identify with teenagers getting along on their own without adults at all. Or she can read *Lisa, Bright and Dark*, where the kids are all smarter and more capable than the adults. Or *Jennifer*, where it is the mother, not Jennifer, who has the problem. Or read *My Darling, My Hamburger*, where all the young character's problems are the fault of the adults. Or *Mr. and Mrs. Bo Jo Jones*, where a young couple go against their parents and make it. Or *Sounder*, where the young boy is better able to cope than his mother and father. If she's poor or black she can escape to quick and easy fame with Sister Lou and her soul brothers. If she doesn't have a boyfriend but would like one, *Fifteen* will confirm that eventually nice girls always win the "catch of the school." If she has to be home by ten, and the closest she's ever been to a commune or North Beach is a newsreel, she can trip with Alice through the counterculture and when Alice dies from drugs, the young reader can be happy she was only a voyeur.

The second insight from the formula--*the adult social concerns reflected in these books*--seems to be a rich research area, hardly touched. In my more jaded moments I often felt my study probably revealed more of the adult's preoccupations than the kid's interest. At least they certainly do affect the form and development of the books. So I will discuss these issues jointly. From the 1940s to the 1970s the concerns moved:

1. from worrying about adolescents going steady and petting to fear of early pregnancy.
2. from concerns about cigarettes and alcohol to the fear of heroin, marijuana, and cocaine.
3. from concerns about materialistic status symbols--cashmere sweaters and convertibles--to fear of adolescents' rejection of most of our social systems.

I became interested in young adult fiction when the new realism had already been heralded. In 1969 George Woods, children's book review editor at the *New York Times*, said in spite of the new trend the books still plodded through the steps of the foxtrot--if not the minuet. But it wasn't the topics that were out of tune--all of those social issues of the sixties found their way into books about gangs, racial problems, and counterculture life-styles--it was the treatment. The book was still too often used to tell the young HOW to think. When we're fighting a popular war we push patriotism; pacificism when it isn't. Women are THE minority of the seventies. Currently, it is difficult to find a female figure in adolescent fiction who gives a damn about the prom (even though a Skokie, Illinois, librarian recently told me *Cheerleader* was probably still the most popular in her young adult collection). Their fictional mothers are plumbers, doctors, oil field roustabouts, most of them making it without daddy or his paycheck, while the majority of the readers probably still get their allowance from dad when he comes in on the 5:05--even if it isn't chic. Robert Peck's hero in *Millie's Boy* reverses the role and plans to work to send his Amy to medical school. Richard Peck's Super Doll rejects beauty contests, and the Cleavers' Littabelle Lee at six months survives a raging river flood, by sixteen proves she can bring home her own bacon, and finds a boy showing off his manhood a bit "tacky." Currently the women's issue in the genre resembles an adolescent girl's early experimentation with make-up--a bit heavy, applied rather thick, not yet artistic, but showing promise.

It almost seems an understatement to call Watergate a preoccupation. I wondered how this concern would appear in adolescent fiction. Perhaps I'm looking too hard, but the influence seems evident to me in *The Chocolate War* and *Some Sweet Day*. In both books evil is the strong force; the good are taken advantage of and evil is never really punished. If I'm correct this issue has affected the structure of the adolescent novel most dramatically. The racial issue changed the color of the protagonist, perhaps the setting, affected the dialog, but good deeds were still rewarded, evil characters punished. Not so in either *The Chocolate War* or *Some Sweet Day*.

I've been accused of being too harsh, too academic, my standards set too high. I come to you through a circuitous route--I worked my way through *Finnegans Wake*, *The Wasteland*, and *Waiting for Godot*, was and *am* excited by serious adult literature, but I'm equally excited by what is happening in young adult fiction and feel strongly that the standards must be high or too few teenagers will care enough about literature to ever wait for Godot. So let a convert--a late arriver--briefly summarize a long study. The results of my research indicate the following about reading interests of the young.

1. Adolescent literature written to interest the young generally reflects adults' social preoccupations. If we're lucky they come together--not always and *too* often the treatment is heavy. For example, the book I found universally loved by kids was *Mr. and Mrs. Bo Jo Jones*. I learned later it was originally written for adults and then marketed for kids.
2. Not all books written for the young follow the formula, but those that don't are the exception.
3. Kids aren't reading as much as they did a few years ago; girls are reading more adolescent novels than boys and the

only ones indiscriminately read by both are those adapted for the silver screen and cathode tube. And the readers are not generally twelve to sixteen; it's more like eight to thirteen. Teenagers are more often reading adult pop culture.

4. This is timely literature. The major breakdown in dissemination comes in two areas: English teachers, librarians, and parents are often uninformed about adolescent literature --a genre where more experimentation is probably taking place than in any other type of literature. Don't Tom Wolfe and his new journalism friends tell us the adult novel is dead? I don't believe him or them and I *know* junior novelists have not been intimidated. And I'm *glad.* But we need better hotlines to professionals influencing reading choices of the young. Finally, it takes too long for current books to reach the shelves.

But my study was completed a year ago, and this is timely literature. So I looked around for more recent studies, loaned current books to neighborhood kids and elicited their responses.

The most recent study I found was done by Hipple and Schullstrom, University of Florida, with an impressive sample of 308 schools. They also surveyed adults, but the lists are supposedly based on student feedback. Their categories were: MOST COMMONLY REQUIRED NOVELS and NOVELS MOST OFTEN IDENTIFIED AS FAVORITES. The list of forty required novels contained three adolescent books--*The Outsiders*, *The Pigman*, and *Bless the Beasts and Children*. Nine on the fifty favorites list were adolescent; six of the nine were among the ten favorites in my study.

A few weeks ago I rounded up kids who hadn't escaped to The Cape, The Vineyard, or Lake Michigan, and asked them to read a few current books: *Watership Down*, *The Whys and Wherefores of Littabelle Lee*, *A Hero Ain't Nothin' but a Sandwich*, *The Chocolate War*, and *Some Sweet Day*. The books were current books that interest me. Admittedly these were University of Chicago Lab School kids and that might make a difference; however, I found in the more extensive study that geographic area didn't affect topic interest. Bo Jo Jones was as popular on the farms as the Gold Coast, but just read more often because fewer books were available. My recent sample of both kids and books was too small to be significant, but their responses were interesting:

- Littabelle Lee made them uncomfortable, but her Aunt Sorrow turned them on. Their comments included: Littabelle wouldn't have acted that way "way back" in Depression days. "They were trying to make us think a girl can do anything." These kids were so sophisticated. I tried to probe beyond what they thought they should say. Finally one fourteen-year-old professor's daughter said, "Boys would hate Littabelle and well, I couldn't identify much with her because she couldn't get married and feel as she did and I want to get married!"

- Almost universally they liked A Hero Ain't Nothin' but a Sandwich--not for the reasons I predicted, such as the unique multi-viewpoint narration, but they liked Butler Craig, the stepfather who never really lost faith in Benjie, the drug addict. They all tuned in to Benjie's mother's thinking his friend was a better boy than he was, and all told stories about THEIR friends their mothers thought were so nice, but IF THEY ONLY KNEW. All of my subjects just refused to talk about the adult sensuality. It was evident that this was too close to their parents' sexual relationships, which they didn't wish to discuss.

- I expected and got a strong reaction to The Chocolate War and Some Sweet Day, especially to The Chocolate War, but again not where I had anticipated. They could accept adults' being evil with no problem, but they objected to kids' being evil. One girl kept saying 300 kids would not have shown up to see that sadistic fight at the end of the book; some of the kids would have stopped it. Poor little Billy Budd. Wouldn't we like to think she is right, Golding wrong in Lord of the Flies, and that the young are basically innocent and good.

- Watership Down was my real intrigue. When that book arrived--426 pages about rabbits--I thought the entire Macmillan staff had lost their reason. When I realized it was being marketed for young adults, I was certain of it. No teenage hero, no obvious teenage problem, a multileveled plot, symbols, and IT WAS TOO LONG. ... But I read it, liked it, and found kids were reading it and liking it too. Macmillan asked me to write a teacher's guide for it, so I had the opportunity to talk to Richard Adams about his book. He said he wrote it for his teenage daughters, but wanted it to be a "proper" novel like Wuthering Heights was a proper novel, with character action growing out of personality. Everything he said sounded like a proper novelist writing a proper novel. But then I asked him if he thought it realistic for none of the characters--rabbits--to be killed in their freedom flight. He replied, "Yes, I know, but my daughter Juliet wouldn't hear of having any of the rabbits she loved die."

So kids in Chicago can't accept that teenagers could be evil and kids in England can't accept death of those they love. Perhaps the formula shouldn't change; perhaps young adult literature should remain escape literature, a way station, a super way to fantasize, dream, play a game, and be reassured. But it will ... the question is how?

The evolution of a literary genre always seems so logical when viewed in retrospect. The piecemeal steps lock neatly into a crescendo. The gifted writers who took an avant garde tack are heralded for breaking into the new epoch and the second-rate writers who flirted with deviant styles or topics fall into convenient obscurity. But what of tomorrow in adolescent literature? Were the sixties and early seventies simply a watershed before the Watergate? Has our government perhaps created the first generation of European cynics in America's adolescent battalions? Will Go Ask Alice be yesterday's cold tea? What fiction, if any, will interest, delight, inspire, or shock those human beings invading their teens today? The distinguished authors fore and aft of me (Isabelle Holland and Barbara Wersba) may give us some hints. I, for one, am listening carefully. I side for the moment with John Updike, who said in a recent interview: "I have more faith than ever in fiction. I really think it's the only way to say a lot of things. To capture the mermaid live, it's the only net we have."

Mermaid beware!

Reference

1. R. J. Havighurst. Developmental Tasks and Education (University Committee on Human Development, Publications [Chicago: Univ. of Chicago Pr., 1949]).

WHAT HIGH SCHOOL STUDENTS ARE REALLY READING*

By Corrine Pollan

English departments in public high schools appear to be the most adversely affected by current changes in teaching methods. English chairmen and teachers seem to be floundering--attempting to impress upon their students the relevancy of the subject matter they are attempting to teach but not sure themselves of what that relevance could be. In other disciplines, there is an inherent sequence to fall back upon; in English there is the whole body of literature. Once the classics were downplayed as a body of knowledge that must be studied by all students--English departments were left without a body of knowledge. One work became as important as another to read and study. How *does* one choose which books to read. Is it the whim of the English department chairman or the particular English teacher? In many cases it appears to be just that! Some teachers stick with the classics, others teach those books that *they* remembered loving, still others are limited by the books available in the stockrooms.

Perhaps the first, and most important, rule that English teachers should learn is that their own particular literary *loves* will not be *loved* by their students. Books or authors meaningful to them--*Spoon River Anthology*, Thomas Wolfe, Hemingway--may have nothing to say to today's students. Teachers must get over their own personal hurt and become aware of, and come to terms with, the books their students are reading. Teachers can draw upon these books. They can become a common literary ground. Most of these books have their own private language, a mystique that can and should be used by English teachers. They can provide possibilities for yet other interactions between students and teachers.

English departments seem to be obsessed with finding relevancy in their discipline. But in so many cases their ideas of relevancy encompass studying "ghetto" literature, historical backgrounds of literary works, or books with social commentary. For the bright student, this obsession with relevancy becomes totally irrelevant.

---

*Reprinted by permission of the author and publisher from *English Journal*, (April 1973), 573-576.

I wanted to discover which books had an appeal to the high school students--which books they found meaningful and enjoyable. So I devised and circulated a questionnaire, a very simple one, to elicit as many responses as possible. I asked three questions and left sufficient space for the answers:

1. Which books have you read on your own during the past year?
2. Which of these would you recommend to your friends?
3. Name some of the books that you wish to read.

From the results of this questionnaire, I was able to compile a list of most often read books. Through an examination of these titles, some patterns as to why these particular books appealed to adolescent students emerged.

There is, of course, a peer group pressure that to some extent determines the particular books that are being read and there is a faddish element as to which books take hold. But, more importantly, there are certain similarities, similar points of view that may account for the particular appeal of these most often mentioned books. The most popular will change--the element that made them popular may not.

On the basis of my questionnaire, I found the most widely read books were Kurt Vonnegut, Jr.'s Cat's Cradle (Dell, 1963); Hermann Hesse's Demian (Bantam, 1965); and Siddhartha (New Directions, 1957); J. D. Salinger's Catcher in the Rye (Bantam, 1964); Richard Brautigan's The Abortion (Simon and Schuster, 1970); and Ken Kesey's One Flew Over the Cuckoo's Nest (New American Library, 1962).

Tolkien's Lord of the Rings and Golding's Lord of the Flies --books that had enjoyed great popularity a few years ago--seemed to have declined in interest. There was little mention of any "ghetto" literature.

In the category of classical literature, Wuthering Heights, Jane Eyre, and F. Scott Fitzgerald's books were mentioned.

Interestingly, there was little inclusion of the escape type of literature. There were some mentions of The Godfather and Ball Four. Leading all others in the "how to" category was Everything You Always Wanted To Know About Sex, But Were Afraid To Ask.

A list of the books not mentioned is almost as interesting as those books included. There was no mention of Kafka, Dostoevski, Hemingway, Camus (very popular a few years ago), Roth, Updike, Mailer, Malamud, Nabakov (all darlings of the adult literary world).

An analysis of the most mentioned books, Cat's Cradle, Catcher in the Rye, Demian, Siddhartha, One Flew Over the Cuckoo's Nest, and The Abortion, reveals many points of similarity on both a superficial and a more profound level.

Superficially, each of these books has a simplicity to it--an ease of reading. Yet these books offer several levels of meaning. Each is a relatively short work; none contains over 275 pages. And each is readily available in a soft cover edition.

On a deeper level, one realizes that each of these books contains a first-person narrative. This first-person involvement has a direct appeal to the young. It is perhaps connected with their love of witnessing--for "telling it like it is" and hearing it like it is. This may be a carryover from television's immediacy and the you-are-there effect of this medium. A personal witness account creates credibility and drama, and witnessing seems to be the most current of literary urges.

The hero in each of these books is an onlooker of--an outcast from--society. On the factual level they are onlookers due to their particular role in the book. Holden and Sinclair are adolescents who have not as yet entered the mainstream of adult life. Siddhartha is a wanderer after truth. John is a writer, an observer of others. The nameless hero in The Abortion lives in a library that he never leaves. Chief Bromden is an American Indian committed to a mental institution.

But more important than the role these heroes play is their sense of their own uniqueness--of being different from those around them. This feeling of uniqueness is one to which the adolescent can strongly relate. Kenneth Keniston writes:

> The estrangement of youth entails feelings of isolation, unreality, absurdity, and disconnectedness from the interpersonal, social ... world. Such feelings are probably more intense during youth than in any other period of life.[1]

Because the adolescent is the outsider, literature about the outsider has a particular appeal. His growing up into society is best reflected in literature about the hero who needs to grow up into the world.

Each of the heroes in these works is alienated. He cannot accept the world as he finds it. He rejects initiation rights into society. He cannot accept the human condition for what it is.

> The refusal to accept the status quo in the universe marks not only adolescents, it also marks the saints and the mad.... The connection is not accidental but necessary and functional. The young have the clarity and newness of vision, the relentless but two-dimensional logic, and the almost unbearable sensitivity that often characterizes the saintly and the insane. A saint as well as a madman may be an adolescent who has refused to "grow up," unable or unwilling to cover his soul with the calluses necessary for the ordinary life.... All three ... wage war with-the-way-things-are. They are martyrs to the commonplace.[2]

These then are the heroes of these most mentioned books--adolescents, saints, and madmen. They embody the idea of the rebel-victim. They refuse initiation into society as they find it and they suffer.

These heroes are apolitical. They are not for any positive political program. They are rather arguing against the complacency of middle-class values and the ugly phoniness of the materialistic, everyday, nine-to-five world.

> For what I always hated and detested and cursed above all things was this contentment, this healthiness and comfort, this carefully preserved optimism of the middle classes, this fat and prosperous brood of mediocrity.[3]

Suburban youth recognize this condition as their own.

One finds a strong anti-intellectual bias contained within these books. They appeal to feelings, emotions, intuitions rather than to the intellect as a means of "knowing." Siddhartha states that the learned, the established ones do not really know. "Knowledge has no worse enemy than the man of knowledge" (p. 15). Wisdom is not communicable. One must soil oneself with life. Sinclair, in Demian, discovers that the ultimate role of man is to find the way to himself. This knowledge of oneself cannot come from the teachings of others. It must be experienced. Holden must accept the final knowledge that he cannot be "the catcher in the rye."

> The thing with kids is, if they want to grab for the gold ring, you have to let them do it.... If they fall off, they fall off, but it's bad if you say anything to them (p. 211).

Holden cannot save the innocent from the fall into experience. Vonnegut urges a surrender of rationality. For him the human gift is intuition. Kesey utters a cry for in-sanity and un-reason.

Anti-intellectualism is a noticeable trend among the youth of today. There is a strong feeling that truth cannot be learned--it must be experienced. The intellect is suspect. Perhaps these feelings bear some relationship to the drug experience. The wish to "blow the mind," the desire to lose the mind, to go out of oneself.

The theme of the quest is an important one in Demian, Siddhartha, and Catcher in the Rye. In each of these books one finds an adolescent at the turning point--the point of going out into the world. These heroes are on a search for self--a quest for identity.

Childhood in each of these works is a time of innocence. There is an inexplicable sense of loss with the departure from childhood. Childhood is the Garden of Eden. Adolescence is the fall from that Garden. It is a fall from Grace into knowledge of the human condition and into the reality of guilt.

In The Abortion one might view the library as a Garden of Eden. In it the hero lives an existence of innocence, isolated from the world and meaningful relationships with others. Veda enters this world, the sexually tempting Eve (a twist here in that Veda hates her 'playboy' body), and the hero is forced to leave his sanctuary on a quest for an abortion and ultimately he must go out into the real world.

There is a similarity of underlying philosophy in each of these books (except for One Flew Over the Cuckoo's Nest). We are dealing here with a theory of an equilibrium between good and evil. It is a vision of the unity of the world and a rejection of a fragmented, dichotomized world. The Bokonists in Cat's Cradle speak of the unity in every second. Siddhartha learns that in every truth the opposite is also true. Everything that is expressed in words is only half the truth; it is one-sided. But the world is never one-sided. He rejects the idea of the world evolving on a path to perfection. In his view the world is perfect at every moment.

Marshall McLuhan has some illuminating thoughts along similar lines. He is concerned with the possible effects of the printed page on our world view. Since printed words must follow one another sequentially, things for us have become fragmented. We perceive the world in a one-thing-at-a-time, linear, fragmented way. For the young, in the electronic age, it's an all-at-once experience and a simultaneous bombardment of the senses.

These, then, are some of the elements that have appeal to and make these books meaningful to adolescent students. The witnessing effect of the first person narrative; the hero portrayed as an outcast, alienated from society; nostalgia for the lost innocence of childhood; an anti-intellectual bias; a quest for self-identity. These represent some of the real concerns of the adolescent. He turns to books that mirror these concerns. They are not an escapist type of literature. They attempt to cope with and resolve difficulties.

I am not advocating the preceding books as ones that necessarily must be taught in high school English classes. However, a questionnaire of this type is simple enough for an English teacher to administer to her students and the information gained could prove useful. From this she can become aware of those books that do appeal to students and gain insight into the nature of that appeal. An attuned teacher can project this knowledge and introduce books that will in the future attain this underground popularity--books such as Being There by Jerzy Kosinski and Kerouac's novels. There is an added interest in being introduced to not yet popular, esoteric books.

English teachers cannot afford to ignore or dismiss literature that students themselves are into.

Notes

1. Kenneth Keniston. *American Scholar* (Autumn, 1970).

2. Henry Anatole Grunwald. *Salinger* (New York: Harper & Row, Publishers, 1962), p. xv.

3. Hermann Hesse. *Steppenwolf* (New York: Bantam Books, Inc., 1965), p. 31.

WHO LIKES WHAT IN HIGH SCHOOL*

By Anne G. Scharf

The reading interests of adolescents are a significant concern of classroom teachers. The relationship of what adolescents read compared to their intelligence, sex, and grade placement offers significant insights that can guide the classroom teacher in his efforts to provide for the individual reading interests of his students.

In an effort to survey the contemporary reading interests of selected high school students, the writer prepared an interest inventory for high school students. The questionnaire used to determine the reading interests of adolescents in Watseka High School, Watseka, Illinois was a revised form of a questionnaire developed originally for a pilot study of student reading interests. Intelligence testing data and grade point average were determined through analysis of guidance office records. The accumulated data were used to determine the relationships between sex, grade placement, and intelligence variables and student reading interests.

A thorough review of the research literature revealed that several studies had been done on the subject. The studies reviewed were completed between 1937 and 1968. The increase in interest in what students read was indicated by the fact that one study was completed in 1937, eleven studies were reported in the 1950s, and sixteen studies were reported in the 1960s.

The studies encompassed third grade through twelfth grade levels. Five studies involved all high school grade levels; six, junior high grade levels; three, lower grades through high school; and three, lower grades through junior high school. Some of the researchers did not report the grade level at which the studies were done.

All twenty researchers who investigated the sex variable found a relationship between a reader's sex and his reading choice. Seven studies considered intelligence to be significantly related to reading interests; three researchers considered age a determining factor in the choice of reading interests; and two investigators found grade placement to be a significant variable.

---

*Reprinted by permission of the author and publisher from Journal of Reading 16:8 (May 1973), 604-607.

Procedures

This writer wanted to determine if differences existed in the reading interests among students at various grade levels, among students with below average, average, and above average intelligence test scores, and between males and females. In addition, the writer wanted to determine if differences existed relative to the reading of paperbacks or hardbacks.

The questionnaire was administered to 414 high school students. In addition to the questionnaire, intelligence scores on the California Short Form Test of Mental Maturity were obtained from the Guidance Department.

The number of students at each grade level: 122 freshmen, 123 sophomores, 102 juniors, and 67 seniors. Two hundred and five students were male. Two hundred and nine were female. By intelligence test scores, seventy-three were in the below average group, 155 in the average group, and 186 in the above average group.

The data were processed by means of a computer service program library. Programs were run to provide an analysis of each question with the variables. A chi square test was employed to determine any significant differences at the .05 level of confidence.

Conclusions

From the statistical analysis of results, this researcher concluded:

1. Differences in reading interest did apparently exist between grade levels. The seniors appeared to read more materials on a regular basis.

2. Differences in reading interest also existed among various intelligence levels. The higher the intelligence test score, the greater the tendency to read materials.

3. There was a difference in reading interests between males and females. The study showed a statistically significant difference on almost every variable. Males preferred reading about sports, world, war, and crime news, as well as biographies and articles or essays. Males preferred newspapers and magazines. Females preferred books and the borrowing and purchasing of materials. They tended to read books more often than did males. In newspapers, females tended to read book reviews, letters to the editor, columnists, fashion news, local news, movie ads, music sections, society news, television and radio news, and pictures. Females preferred reading poetry, drama, autobiographies, and novels. Magazines read by females included homemaking, romance, and movie magazines.

4. Paperbacks over hardbacks seemed to be the choice of a definite majority.

Implications

The results of this study might prove useful to teachers in similar schools. Teachers could use these findings in ordering material for high school students, ordering more paperbacks than hardbacks, for instance, since paperbacks were preferred by many students. In addition to expanding the paperback classroom library, the librarians of both school and public libraries might consider making more paperbacks available.

The element of personal concern may influence what the students read. For example, the senior may become more interested in world and war news as he nears or reaches drafting and voting age. The interest seniors showed in reading newspapers in preference to books and magazines, and in reading various sections of the newspaper more regularly than did youngsters on other grade levels may reflect a growing interest in everyday affairs.

Between one-third and one-fourth of all students indicated they read a paper at least seven times a week while less than one-fifth never read a paper. Newspapers might, therefore, be used in classrooms to teach many students. Also, libraries should probably have newspapers available for students to read. The order of popularity is magazines, books, then newspapers. Therefore, the librarian or teacher might consider making magazines more readily available for pleasure reading and ordering books and newspapers that might be more attractive to the students.

The use of the school library as a major source for freshmen more than for any other group indicated that perhaps more books and other material on advanced or adult levels are needed. The advanced student did indicate different reading interests.

The relationships between intelligence levels and magazine reading might be of interest to the various publishers of each magazine as well as to teachers and librarians. *Hot Rod*, *True Story* and *Playboy* appealed to those of below average intelligence. The reading of *Reader's Digest* mainly by persons of above average intelligence was interesting. A study might be done using several issues of *Reader's Digest* and analyzing the intelligence levels and the reading of individual articles. The same might be done for *Playboy*.

The higher the intelligence, the greater the tendency to read a newspaper regularly. Satire in the comics may account for their appeal to those of above average intelligence. Perhaps a study could be done to determine the relationship between intelligence and sense of humor. One might wonder why those of average intelligence read want ads more often than did students on other intelligence levels. If one were to conduct this study in an area where school ads are included in the newspapers, a question might be included to see if there is a relationship between intelligence level and the reading of school ads.

The use of the public library by those of higher intelligence on a more regular basis might indicate that librarians need a wider variety of materials to appeal to people of all intellectual levels.

The sex of the reader was related to what he reads. Perhaps males read war news more often because they may some day be directly involved. The male interest in sports can be seen both in the reading of the sports news and in the choosing of sports magazines. Although males preferred newspapers more often than did females, they read fewer sections of them on a regular basis. A study of the relationship between sex of a reader and newspaper sales or newspaper reading in a library might be carried out. The females showed an interest in fashion news and the society page. Since females preferred books and read more books than did males, the female interest in the reading of book reviews logically followed. It would be interesting to pursue the findings that females borrowed and purchased more reading matter more often than males. One might discover whether a teenage male has different spending habits than does a teenage female.

The division of the genres by sex could be used by teachers and librarians in guiding personal reading as well as purchasing books. If one has all male or an all female class, these results might aid in determining materials to be used in the class.

The preference of males for magazines can be seen by the fact that males reported reading more magazines on a regular basis than did females. Most of these magazines were identified by this researcher as being either male or female oriented and were found to be so. However, a few were not so identified. A study might be done to determine why males read _Time_ and _Newsweek_ on a rather regular basis. Perhaps this is related to the male interest in war and crime news in newspaper reading as well as sports news. The female interest in reading _TV Guide_ and _TV Mirror_ might be related to the female interest in reading television and radio news in the newspaper.

This researcher recommends that classroom teachers, librarians, and parents be aware of the differences in reading interests as related to sex, grade level, and intelligence. Knowing and making use of the findings of this study could enable one to accept the reading interests of a particular student, to guide the student in his reading, and to provide materials that would be of interest to him.

WE GOT THERE ... IT WAS WORTH THE TRIP!
A Survey of Young Adult Reading in Los Angeles Public Library*

By Patty Campbell, Pat Davis and Jerri Quinn

Question: WHERE DO YOU WANT TO GO?
Answer: out, to the YA mind.

What books do young adults actually read and what do they think of the books libraries offer them? Who is using the young adult collections and are we meeting their needs? All of us who serve young people have working hypotheses about these questions, but in June 1972 the young adult librarians of the western region of Los Angeles Public Library set out to find some hard data for answers. (Perhaps "semi-hard data" would be more exact, since none of the librarians had statistical training.)

For six months all nine branches of the region put questionnaires in the pockets of every young adult book on the shelves. They collected a grand total of 2,009 responses. The results were both appalling and reassuring, but most of all informative.

The questionnaires were designed to be visually appealing. At the top of the slip was a design of mushrooms and the sun--two "in" items in current young adult symbology. (The design evidently had high eye-appeal, because many slips were returned with the picture colored in.) A list of questions followed:

WHAT DID YOU THINK OF THIS BOOK? (Please circle answers)
GREAT! OK! UGH!
Title ....
What is your age? Jr. Hi/Sr. Hi/College/Adult
Did you read this for assignment (or) pleasure?
Do you use the Young Adult Section ... Often/Never/Where is it?
Do you know that we have current rock and folk recordings? Yes/No
Are there any books you would highly recommend to other young people?
Please leave in this book pocket. Thanks!

*Reprinted by permission of the authors and the American Library Association from Top of the News (June 1974), 403-409.

The nine branches that participated in the survey have a broad spread in the ethnic, racial, and economic characteristics of patrons. Palisades and Brentwood have a wealthy, college-educated, and predominantly white clientele. Westchester, Loyola Village, and Palms-Rancho have patrons who are less affluent, more middle-class. The West Los Angeles Regional Branch, due to its proximity to the University of California, draws many students and a more racially mixed group of patrons. Robertson, whose patrons were formerly almost all Jewish and middle-class has seen a recent influx of middle-class black families. Mar Vista draws from a middle-income neighborhood with some Orientals and Chicanos, and the patrons of the Venice library represent almost every racial, economic, and educational possibility.

Question: HOW DO YOU GET FROM HERE TO THERE?
Answer: it's getting better all the time.

Mechanical details were agreed upon ahead of time by the young adult librarians of the region. The survey was begun on June 1 and ended on December 31, so that a sampling of both spring and fall semesters, summer reading, and the winter term paper rush were all included. The questionnaires were mimeographed on eight-by-twelve-inch sheets, four per page, and then sliced up on a paper cutter. On June 1, every young adult librarian put a date-stamped questionnaire in all the books on her young adult shelves. (At the end of the survey it was found that some books still had this original date on the questionnaire and so had not circulated at all during the six-month period.) Paperbacks were included in the survey if they were an integral part of the YA collection, and Mar Vista branch included the junior high school collection, which is shelved adjacent to the YA section in that branch. Most libraries put up posters or signs explaining the survey and its purpose. As the completed questionnaires were returned in the books, clerical staff removed them from the pockets and put them in a box at the circulation desk. People were asked to place blank questionnaires in the empty pockets as they shelved young adult books. About every two weeks the young adult librarians cleared the circulation desk box and stamped the returned questionnaires with the current date.

Question: WHERE DO YOU END UP?
Answer: in the Top Ten.

Out of the 2,009 responses on books actually read, five titles won hands down.* They were:

1. My Darling, My Hamburger — 19 responses
2. Mr. and Mrs. Bo Jo Jones — 16 responses
3. Go Ask Alice — 16 responses
4. Catcher in the Rye — 15 responses
5. Bless the Beasts and Children — 12 responses

*Only questionnaires returned by junior and senior high people were counted in tallying the survey results.

Heavy assignment use apparently put Catcher in the top five; six of the fifteen responses replied that it was being read for assignment (although all of them rated it "Great!"). Only one of twelve responses was read for assignment on Bless the Beasts and Children, and two out of fourteen on Mr. and Mrs. Bo Jo Jones. All of the responses to Go Ask Alice and My Darling, My Hamburger replied that they were read for pleasure.

What do these books have in common that make them such favorites with young adults? Obviously, they are all fiction. They all have contemporary settings, and the leading characters are young people. But it is our guess that the most important factor is that they all deal with the problems of becoming a whole human being in an honest, realistic, gutsy way. Young people want answers to the vital questions of life, and they are intensely interested in books that will present these real problems on their level of experience without being preachy or condescending.

The top five titles stand above all the rest in number of responses; the next most popular group of titles dropped down to eight and nine responses apiece. In order of popularity, the runners-up were:

6.	Phoebe	9 responses
7.	Brian Piccolo: A Short Season	8 responses
8.	The Other Side of the Mountain	8 responses
9.	Run Softly, Go Fast	8 responses
10.	Lennon Remembers	8 responses

Here we have two contemporary biographies, two realistic novels, and a horror-fantasy (Other Side of the Mountain). The popularity of this last title may reflect the fact that it is a great favorite with the young adult librarians of the western region for use in book talks.

The books that were reported as read in the survey were limited somewhat by the individual young adult sections in each branch and by the books in which the librarians placed the questionnaires. However, the titles recommended at the bottom of the questionnaire represented a free choice by the individual. ("Are there any books you would highly recommend to other young people?") We received a total of 1,257 recommendations.

The top ten most frequently mentioned books were:

1.	The Outsiders	42
2.	The Godfather	37
3.	That Was Then, This Is Now	34
4.	My Darling, My Hamburger	33
5.	Go Ask Alice	30
6.	The Pigman	27
7.	Lord of the Rings	24
8.	Gone with the Wind	18

9.	Love Story	18
10.	Mr. and Mrs. Bo Jo Jones	17

Close runners-up ranged from sixteen to ten recommendations (in descending order): A Tree Grows in Brooklyn, Summer of '42, The New Centurions.

Only three of the most read titles (My Darling, My Hamburger, Go Ask Alice, and Mr. and Mrs. Bo Jo Jones) were included in the top recommended ten. Catcher shows up in the top sixteen, but Bless the Beasts and Children was only mentioned seven times in the recommendations.

There was a high incidence of best sellers and movies in the recommended titles: six movies (The Godfather, Gone with the Wind, Love Story, Mr. and Mrs. Bo Jo Jones, Summer of '42, and The New Centurions) and seven best sellers (The Godfather, Gone with the Wind, Love Story, Jonathan Livingston Seagull, A Tree Grows in Brooklyn, New Centurions, and Summer of '42). Jonathan had not been released as a film nor had Alice been shown on TV when this survey was taken.

YASD Best Books lists for the past five years only included three of the top ten books recommended by the YAs. Of the ten recommended, nine were eligible for consideration by virtue of their publication dates, giving the YASD Best Books a batting average of .333. None of them were titles which appeared in the Best Books for 1972. The 1971 list fared better. Go Ask Alice and That Was Then, This Is Now both appeared in the top recommendations. The 1970 list included Love Story and Bless the Beasts and Children, one of the ten most read books.

Frankly, some of these recommendations by young adults were a surprise to us--notably The Godfather, which we are at a loss to explain as a book with high YA appeal. The two Hinton books, although purchased for young adult usage, we had considered primarily of interest to younger readers. It is our guess that the popularity of Gone with the Wind and A Tree Grows in Brooklyn are the result of nostalgic parental recommendation. The Lord of the Rings phenomenon is of course by now well known; although many other fantasy and science fiction titles appeared, none of them was mentioned with enough unanimity to show up on the top lists. The rest of the ten most recommended books (with the possible exception of Love Story) reflect again that enthusiasm for honest realistic treatment of problems of personal relationship.

Question: WAS THE TRIP ALL FANTASY?
Answer: no, it was real.

Of the above twenty titles, only two are nonfiction; this tends to give the mistaken impression that our YA patrons are not reading this category. On the contrary, almost equal numbers of nonfiction and fiction titles were reported, but there was a broader spread among nonfiction. Certain kinds of books showed consistent popularity: biographies of contemporary sports and rock music stars, love poetry, self-awareness, books by teen-age authors such as Dove and Hey! White Girl, black awareness classics like The Autobiography of Malcolm X and Manchild in the Promised Land, and books based on comic strips--especially Doonesbury and Peanuts.

Question: HOW OLD DO YOU HAVE TO BE TO TAKE THE TRIP?
Answer: old enough to cross the street.

The age of patrons reporting usage of the YA section was equally divided. Three branches had a higher percentage of junior high readers, three had a higher percentage of senior high readers, and three had a higher percentage of adult readers. Two of the branches with higher adult usage have the YA collection adjacent to the recent book and family sections. The region-wide relative proportion of junior and senior high usage was remarkably close--35 per cent of the total usage for junior high and 32 per cent of the total usage for senior high. Only two branches have junior high and YA sections comparatively near each other; most branches house junior high books in the children's room. There might have been even a higher percentage of junior high usage if the two sections were closer in more branches.

Los Angeles Public Library has always defined "young adult" as ninth through twelfth grade, but during the last two years we have been reconsidering these guidelines. Our feeling was that the young adult collections were being used by younger and younger patrons, and the results of this survey would seem to bear this out. After lengthy consideration, a committee decision has been made to redefine the responsibilities of the young adult librarian; we now serve eighth through eleventh grade.

Question: CAN I GO ANY TIME?
Answer: just call: winter, spring, summer, fall.

The tallying of questionnaires was divided by summer and fall reading to see if there would be any seasonal correlation between fiction/nonfiction and pleasure/assignment usage. The overall general trend showed the largest percentage of fiction reading for pleasure in all seasons, although one branch showed 54 per cent nonfiction reading and all others showed at least 40 per cent nonfiction reading. There was not as much increase in use of the YA section for assignments when school began as might have been anticipated; most branches showed only a 10 per cent increase in assignment reading in the fall. Therefore, it can be said that most branches reported no substantial difference between summer and winter reading in the YA section. Fiction reading for pleasure was universally predominant, but only a 10-20 per cent lead.

The statistical answers to the question "Do you know that we have current rock and folk recordings?" ran approximately 70 per cent Yes, 30 per cent No. The written comments were more challenging. There is quite a heavy demand for good recordings of rock and popular music and a high degree of loss and damage. Thus, in many branches, the current recordings are in sorry shape. Many expressive comments were included on the questionnaires in answer to this question. "You've got to be kidding," "Get more," "That's a laugh, they're never in," "Far out," and "Like hell you do" were common answers.

Question: DOES IT FEEL GOOD?
Answer: it was worth the trip!

Although there was no specific area on the questionnaire for extended responses and comments, many YAs took the liberty of telling us what they thought, either venting anger and frustration or adding a few encouraging words. One heartwarming comment from a junior high reader was: "One of the people that work here came to my school. That's how I knew about this book [Mr. and Mrs. Bo Jo Jones]. I seen her here today. I have never came here befor." The majority of salutations simply stated "You're welcome" or "Get more books."

All of the librarians who participated in the survey agreed, even before the results had been tabulated, that it was a valuable experience. As one librarian wrote, "My outlook toward the YA collection has changed; I feel I know more about what the kids are reading and what types of books they like to read."

Another librarian commented, "This was a very worthwhile and stimulating project. I became aware of the merits and faults of my section, as well as the range of taste of my patrons. The project may have a good effect on the patrons also by making them aware of the section as a separate unit. It also may have helped them feel involved in the library because they were able to talk back to us for a few months."

Any library system that tries this inexpensive simple type of survey is going to be in for some surprises, but some enlightenment and encouragement, too.

Books Mentioned

Bach, Richard. Jonathan Livingston Seagull. Macmillan, 1970.
Bernanos, Michel. The Other Side of the Mountain. Houghton Mifflin, 1969.
Brown, Claude. Manchild in the Promised Land. Macmillan, 1965.
Dizenzo, Patricia. Phoebe. McGraw-Hill, 1970.
Go Ask Alice. Prentice-Hall, 1971.
Graham, Robin L., and Gill, Derek. Dove. Harper & Row, 1972.
Gregory, Susan. Hey! White Girl. Lancer, 1972.
Head, Ann. Mr. and Mrs. Bo Jo Jones. Putnam, 1967.
Hinton, S. E. That Was Then, This Is Now. Viking Press, 1971.
________. The Outsiders. Viking Press, 1967.

Malcolm X. The Autobiography of Malcolm X. Grove, 1965.
Mitchell, Margaret. Gone with the Wind. Macmillan, 1936.
Morris, Jeannie. Brian Piccolo: A Short Season. Rand, 1971.
Puzo, Mario. The Godfather. Putnam, 1969.
Raucher, Herman. Summer of '42. Putnam, 1971.
Salinger, J. D. Catcher in the Rye. Little, 1951.
Segal, Erich. Love Story. Harper & Row, 1970.
Smith, Betty. A Tree Grows in Brooklyn. Harper & Row, 1947.
Swarthout, Glendon. Bless the Beasts and Children. Doubleday, 1970.
Tolkien, J. R. R. The Hobbit. Houghton Mifflin, 1938.
________. The Lord of the Rings. Houghton Mifflin, 1967; Ballantine, 1969.
Wambaugh, Joseph. The New Centurions. Little, 1971.
Wenner, Jan, ed. Lennon Remembers. Quick Fox, 1971.
Wersba, Barbara. Run Softly, Go Fast. Atheneum, 1970.
Zindel, Paul. My Darling, My Hamburger. Harper & Row, 1969.
________. The Pigman. Harper & Row, 1968.

YOUNG ADULT FAVORITES: Reading Profiles from Nine Hawaii High Schools*

By Julie N. Alm

A graduate of the University of Hawaii--a young woman of Japanese ancestry--described in an article printed in the Los Angeles Times an experience she had recently in the UCLA personnal office. The receptionist called her to the counter and asked if she had her passport and visa. "But I'm from Hawaii," said my former student. "I'm a U.S. citizen."

This is not an isolated experience for someone from the fiftieth state. Misconceptions about Hawaii abound. We are, most of us, U.S. citizens, and for better or worse, we are very much like mainland residents in every way--including our teen-agers' reading choices.

Spurred by the article "A Decade of Teen-age Reading in Baltimore, 1960-1970" by Linda F. Lapides (Top of the News, April 1971), and fortified with a sabbatical leave for the spring semester of 1972, I surveyed the reading interests of high school students on Oahu, the most heavily populated island, with more than 80 per cent of Hawaii's residents.

Because the State Department of Education was reluctant to approve a comprehensive survey such as that made by the Enoch Pratt Free Library, I had to limit my survey to a sampling of tenth-, eleventh-, and twelfth-graders in five public high schools in four districts on the island of Oahu and in four private and parochial schools in Honolulu.

The survey was modeled on the Baltimore study with the students asked to write the name of their favorite book. In addition, I asked them to check whether or not they liked to read and where they had secured the book. Responses from 2,128 students--1,005 males and 1,115 females--were received. Eight students declined to check male or female or suggested a third category. There were 1,367 responses from public schools and 761 from private schools.

---

*Reprinted by permission of the author and the American Library Association from Top of the News (June 1974), 403-409.

Individual titles listed were many and varied--from Winnie-the-Pooh to War and Peace. In all, 709 books were mentioned, of which 213 were listed more than once. Seventy-six titles were listed five times or more; thirty-two appeared ten times or more. Both fiction and nonfiction titles were recorded. The Hardy Boys and Nancy Drew received one vote each, while at the other end of the scale there appeared the classics, including the most frequently listed title in this category--the Bible.

Six categories were used to classify the kinds of books chosen by students as their favorites: teen-age novels (or junior novels), popular adult fiction, significant adult fiction, classics, nonfiction, and poetry. These categories are used by G. Robert Carlsen in Books and the Teen-Age Reader (Bantam, 1971).

The list presents the favorite books (initial publication date is indicated) of the students polled in the nine Oahu high schools.

Combined Schools--Oahu

1. The Godfather (1969)
2. Love Story (1970)
3. Mr. and Mrs. Bo Jo Jones (1967)
4. The Catcher in the Rye (1951)
5. Lord of the Flies (1955)
6. Lord of the Rings (1954, 1955, 1956)
7. To Kill a Mockingbird (1960)
8. Black Like Me (1960)
9. Flowers for Algernon (1966)
10. The Outsiders (1967)
11. Gone with the Wind (1936)
12. Catch-22 (1955)

Public Schools

1. Love Story
2. The Godfather
3. Mr. and Mrs. Bo Jo Jones
4. Lord of the Flies
5. My Darling, My Hamburger (1969)
6. The Catcher in the Rye
7. Lord of the Rings
8. Gone with the Wind
9. Stranger in a Strange Land (1961)
10. Black Like Me
11. Rosemary's Baby (1967)

Private and/or Parochial Schools

1. The Godfather
2. Love Story
3. The Catcher in the Rye
4. Manchild in the Promised Land (1965)
5. To Kill a Mockingbird
6. Catch-22
7. Flowers for Algernon
8. Summer of '42 (1971)
9. Mr. and Mrs. Bo Jo Jones
10. Black Like Me

At the head of the combined schools' list, each receiving at least twice as many votes as the third choice, were The Godfather and Love Story. The Godfather was the first choice of students in private and parochial schools and was a close second in the public schools. Love Story was the first choice of public school students, second for private and parochial schools. The movie Love Story had been shown in Hawaii before the survey was made; The Godfather had not.

Mr. and Mrs. Bo Jo Jones, eighth on the list of favorites of Baltimore students, was third on the Honolulu list. Predictably, only girls listed this book. As was the case in Baltimore, The Catcher in the Rye, second oldest among the preferred books, is a strong favorite with Oahu students. Lord of the Flies is still widely read, though more often listed as a favorite by public school students than by those in private and parochial schools.

The popularity of the trilogy Lord of the Rings was somewhat surprising. The students made a point of listing all three titles or Trilogy, so there would be no question but that they meant all three books. Three times as many boys as girls reported this a special favorite.

Like students in Baltimore, Oahu high school students are still finding To Kill a Mockingbird, Black Like Me, and Gone with the Wind good reading. Gone with the Wind, published in 1936, is the oldest book among the top favorites on Oahu. Flowers for Algernon (or Charly), The Outsiders, and Catch-22 complete the list of top choices for the combined schools.

When the results from public schools only are tallied, three books--My Darling, My Hamburger by Paul Zindel, Rosemary's Baby by Ira Levin, and Stranger in a Strange Land by Robert Heinlein--appear in the top group, displacing To Kill a Mockingbird, Flowers for Algernon, and The Outsiders.

When titles listed by private and parochial school students are examined, Lord of the Flies, Lord of the Rings, The Outsiders, and Gone with the Wind do not appear in the list of top favorites. Lord of the Flies, however, is in eleventh place. In the top ten, in addition to others listed by public school students, are Manchild in the Promised Land and Summer of '42.

Examination of favorite titles of Oahu high school students by grades shows the usual changes in the kinds of books students find most satisfying as they mature. With the exception of the novel Mr. and Mrs. Bo Jo Jones, the top-ranking junior novels were more popular with tenth- than with twelfth-graders. For example, My Darling, My Hamburger was the favorite of seventeen tenth-graders, three eleventh-graders, and three twelfth-graders; The Outsiders, too, was chosen by sixteen tenth-graders, five eleventh-graders, and three twelfth-graders. Mr. and Mrs. Bo Jo Jones was popular with girls in all three grades, reaching its peak with eleventh-graders.

Significant adult books were read by students in all three

grades, but the number of readers in the eleventh and twelfth grades tended to be higher. For example, *The Catcher in the Rye* was the favorite of seven tenth-graders, ten eleventh-graders, and twenty-three twelfth-graders, while *Lord of the Flies* was the choice of four tenth-graders, seventeen eleventh-graders, and nine twelfth-graders. The only classic listed more than ten times--the Bible--was chosen by one sophomore, five juniors, and eight seniors.

The popular adult favorites show a varied pattern. Some, like *The Andromeda Strain*, *Hawaii*, *Rosemary's Baby*, and *Summer of '42*, are less often mentioned by seniors than by sophomores; with other titles there is no discernible difference. *The Godfather*, for example, was listed by thirty-two sophomores, thirty juniors, and thirty-seven seniors. *Love Story* was chosen by twenty-eight tenth-graders, thirty-seven eleventh-graders, and nineteen twelfth-graders.

Of the 2,128 students responding, 1,287, or 60 per cent, listed a book that was selected by more than one reader. The 213 books chosen by this group of students were analyzed according to kind of book, content, and readership. As is the case with teen-agers on the mainland, Oahu's high school students most frequently find their favorite books in the popular adult category. The two books that received the most votes are in this group. Almost 14 per cent of the readers listed a teen-age or junior novel as a favorite, seniors as well as sophomores. As a group, however, high school students tend increasingly to move to adult books as they progress through high school, with books in the popular adult category being chosen by 51.8 per cent of the readers.

One out of five of the group listed significant adult novels as most rewarding, showing a real growth toward maturity in reading. Roughly 6 per cent listed a classic as a favorite, but since so many of these were assigned reading, it is hard to know whether the book was a favorite or simply a title they recalled.

When only those books mentioned five times or more and, further, those mentioned ten times or more are examined, certain interesting changes emerge. The percentage of students choosing a junior novel or a popular adult novel remains virtually the same. The percentage of students who listed a significant adult book rises slightly from 20.8 per cent choosing a book listed more than once to 25 per cent selecting a book listed ten times or more. Poetry disappears from the list entirely. From twenty-one classics chosen more than once by 5.8 per cent of the readers, the number declines to one book, the Bible, chosen more than ten times by 2 per cent of the total number of students responding.

In addition to writing the name of their favorite book, students were asked (1) whether they liked to read or did not like to read and (2) where they found their favorite book. Almost two-thirds of the students reported that they liked to read. Although a "sometimes" option was not included on the questionnaire, 107 students wrote in "sometimes," so those responses were tabulated separately. There was no observable difference between public school students and those in the private and parochial schools in enjoyment of reading.

The most interesting finding among sources of books was that one of every four students (the highest single ratio) had bought the book that was his favorite. Another sizable group had borrowed the book from a friend. When offerings of two popular book clubs --Teen-Age Book Club and Campus Book Club--for the last year were checked, the likelihood of book club purchases of favorite books seemed high. Also, paperbacks are readily available, of course, in book stories, supermarkets, drugstores, and a variety of other places.

When public and private and parochial school tallies were examined, the major difference seemed to be in the number of students whose favorite book had been a class assignment. Among public school students, 7 per cent reported that favorite books had been assigned; among private and parochial school students, 15 per cent listed assigned books as top choices.

Titles Listed by Oahu Students

Title/Author	Number of Times Mentioned
Titles Listed Ten Times or More	
The Godfather, Mario Puzo	99
Love Story, Erich Segal	84
Mr. and Mrs. Bo Jo Jones, Ann Head	42
The Catcher in the Rye, J. D. Salinger	40
Lord of the Flies, William Golding	30
Lord of the Rings, J. R. R. Tolkien	28
To Kill a Mockingbird, Harper Lee	26
Black Like Me, John Howard Griffin	25
Catch-22, Joseph Heller	24
Flowers for Algernon, Daniel Keyes	24
Gone with the Wind, Margaret Mitchell	24
The Outsiders, S. E. Hinton	24
My Darling, My Hamburger, Paul Zindel	23
Summer of '42, Herman Raucher	23
Stranger in a Strange Land, Robert Heinlein	21
Manchild in the Promised Land, Claude Brown	21
The Hobbit, J. R. R. Tolkien	19
The Andromeda Strain, Michael Crichton	16
Rosemary's Baby, Ira Levin	16
The Bible	14
The Pearl, John Steinbeck	14
The Sensuous Woman, "J"	14
A Separate Peace, John Knowles	14
The Good Earth, Pearl Buck	13
The Illustrated Man, Ray Bradbury	11

Johnny Got His Gun, Dalton Trumbo	11
The Crystal Cave, Mary Stewart	10
Future Shock, Alvin Toffler	10
Hawaii, James Michener	10
Joy in the Morning, Betty Smith	10
The Mephisto Waltz, Fred M. Stewart	10
2001: A Spacy Odyssey, Arthur M. Clarke	10

Titles Listed Five Times or More

Black Boy, Richard Wright	9
Instant Replay, Jerry Kramer	9
Siddhartha, Hermann Hesse	9
Christy, Catherine Marshall	8
Dibs in Search of Self, Virginia M. Axline	8
The Love Machine, Jacqueline Susann	8
My Sweet Charlie, David Westheimer	8
Of Mice and Men, John Steinbeck	8
The Old Man and the Sea, Ernest Hemingway	8
The Prophet, Kahlil Gibran	8
Animal Farm, George Orwell	7
Bless the Beasts and Children, Glendon Swarthout	7
Coffee, Tea, or Me, Trudy Baker and Rachel Jones	7
Death Be Not Proud, John Gunther	7
A Farewell to Arms, Ernest Hemingway	7
The Greening of America, Charles Reich	7
Moby Dick, Herman Melville	7
The Pigman, Paul Zindel	7
Anthem, Ayn Rand	6
Ball Four, Jim Bouton	6
Foundation Trilogy, Isaac Asimov	6
I Never Promised You a Rose Garden, Hannah Green	6
Nigger, Dick Gregory	6
One Flew Over the Cuckoo's Nest, Ken Kesey	6
Red Sky at Morning, Richard Bradford	6
When Michael Calls, John Farris	6
Where Eagles Dare, Alistair MacLean	6
Airport, Arthur Hailey	5
The Autobiography of Malcolm X, Malcolm X with Alec Haley	5
A Canticle for Leibowitz, Walter M. Miller, Jr.	5
The Chosen, Chaim Potok	5
The Cross and the Switchblade, David Wilkerson	5
Dune, Frank Herbert	5
Fahrenheit 451, Ray Bradbury	5
Light in August, William Faulkner	5
1984, George Orwell	5
Run Baby Run, Nicky Cruz with Jamie Buckingham	5
The Scarlet Letter, Nathaniel Hawthorne	5
Seventeenth Summer, Maureen Daly	5
Soul on Ice, Eldridge Cleaver	5
Tales of the South Pacific, James Michener	5
To Sir, with Love, E. R. Braithwaite	5

Troutfishing in America, Richard Brautigan	5
Valley of the Dolls, Jacqueline Susann	5

Hawaii's young adults, then, read the best sellers and see the movies based on them, though not necessarily in that order. They like books that reflect honestly the problems they know in growing up. They are concerned about the problems of the society around them. They are catholic in their taste. They still like junior novels, but they are also reading significant modern classics. Most of the top favorite books are in some way or other controversial in the eyes of some adults. They are not, obviously, taboo among the young adults themselves. In short, though surrounded by sun and surf for most of the year, Hawaii's teenagers--with ancestors that may be Hawaiian, Chinese, Japanese, Filipino, Black, Korean, Samoan, Caucasian, and/or Indian--are reading and enjoying the same kinds of books their counterparts on the mainland are.

SE HABLA Y. A. AQUÍ

By Patty Campbell

Bruce Lee and the Bermuda Triangle, ESP and weight-lifting, tai chi and euthanasia, satanism, Betty Boop and vegetarian cooking, sharks and meditation, love stories and Frankenstein, King Kong and reincarnation, the fifties, karate.

What is this word salad? Any YA librarian would recognize it instantly as a mixed bag of current young adult reading interests. We can all rattle off our own variants of this list, modified by geographic, cultural, and economic differences in the kids we serve, but by and large we would produce similar lists at any given point in time. What sense can we make out of this conglomeration of fascinations? Is there a unifying theme, a meaning or direction?

In past decades, at least to the clear eyes of hindsight, the Zeitgeist was obvious. In the early sixties the spirit that made every teenage heart beat faster could be expressed in that dear old phrase "We shall overcome!" And we really--oh, yes, we really did believe, that if only everybody could get together and organize and act, then it would all come out right once and for all. So we had the young activists, the underground newspapers, the absorbing interest in everything to do with black culture.

In the mid-sixties, reaction set in. Kids discovered that political action sometimes got people shot, that freedom was not as simple as everybody had thought. And Vietnam made no sense at all. But hash and LSD seemed to offer instant enlightenment, and strange and beautiful vistas of total truth and happiness were just over the horizon. The watchwords: "peace and love and do your own thing!"

And then into the seventies--glassy-eyed, bummed out, and hung over. Doom in every direction: the ecology disintegrating, world population growing insanely, the military-industrial complex out of control, the nuclear holocaust always threatening, the Nixon caper revealing obscene corruption in powerful places. What hopeful catch phrase, what word to live by summarizes the spirit of the teens of the seventies?

---

*Reprinted by permission of the author and publisher from Bookleg-ger, no. 10 (July/August 1975), 35-36.

The word is--"Survive." Not the grey flannel shut-up-and-conform survival of the fifties. Not the fighting give 'em hell survival of the frontier. But the acceptance and survival of the Orient. This survival is spiritual, individual, even mystic. There is a turn ing in, a search for new answers inside oneself. Salvation is individual, and not to be found in group action nor in relationships. The search is not a frantic one; this is a time of waiting, of action and decision suspended. There is no sense of time running out because it has already run out....

An impatience with irrelevance is characteristic--an annoyance with outworn values, hypocrisy, and sterile intellectualizing. An appropriate metaphor comes from zen: A young person hangs from a cliff by the fragile, breaking branches of a little bush. At the bottom of the cliff is a hungry crocodile, at the top a snarling tiger. Is that person in any mood to respond to questions like "Do you have hope?" or "What does this mean for the future of society?" Yet (the zen master continues) there are berries on that bush and as the young person hangs there s/he snatches some of the berries, eats them, and enjoys them. And that is the kind of cool people our YAs are in 1975.

Now, how do the separate threads of reading interests fit into this tapestry of survival? The occult, Eastern religions, the supernatural, any religious cult or spiritual system except the "ordinary" Judeo-Christian ones are part of the search for new answers through inner awareness. The Oriental martial arts, certainly survival techniques, with the added attraction of Eastern spiritual enlightenment. ESP, the Bermuda Triangle, gods from outer space: can the answers for survival be found in the Unknown? Organic gardening, vegetarian cooking, return to the land, natural living, nostalgia for the thirties, the fifties: can survival be recovered by returning to simpler ways? Karate, weight-lifting, a less sophisticated manifestation of the survival impulse, often found in inner city neighborhoods. Realistic junior novels--knowing what to expect from the realities of life is a necessary tool of survival. Didactic poetry in the Celestial Arts style--pseudo-wisdom, but uncritically accepted by young seekers for life knowledge.

The reverse side of the coin, anti-survival, also generates a set of interests. YAs are fascinated with the ways their contemporaries can fail to survive: alcoholism, satanic possession, witchcraft, suicide, terminal illness and all other aspects of death. (Interestingly enough, insanity is not seen as tragic or a failure to survive. YAs tend to rather idealize the insane as people who have found an individualistic way to enlightenment. Or else they see madness as a political definition.)

I could go on and on playing with this concept of survival as the seventies YA Zeitgeist, but like all broad generalizations, it can be stretched too far. There are always yes-buts, bits and pieces that don't fit. How about the continuous popularity of S. E. Hinton's The Outsiders? What has a semi-fantasy about gang wars in Oklahoma City got to do with survival? How about hang gliding, motorcycling--a flirtation with death? Is Jaws enough to explain the overwhelming interest which has stripped our shelves of everything about sharks? And what explains the phenomenon of media tie-ins? Why do YAs rush to read a book they have already seen on tv? Another round of Zeitgeist analysis, anyone?

CAMPUS QUIETUS*

By the New York Times

All's quiet on the campuses with the Vietnam War over and a shrunken job market turning students into greasy grinds. Although this hasn't brought back panty raids, goldfish swallowing and other frivolities (as far as we know), it has had an interesting effect on the books students are reading for their own pleasure. Every month a list of campus best sellers is compiled by The Chronicle of Higher Education, an au courant weekly newspaper covering the campus beat, and we have taken note of its findings here from time to time.

The titles on the most recent list are a far cry--well a pretty far cry--from those on the lists of a few years back, and will be familiar to any reader of the Book Review's own best seller lists, especially the paperback lists. There is only one hardcover present, which is not unusual, students' budgets being what they are, and that is Woodward-Bernstein's The Final Days, at number two; number one is the paperback All the President's Men, having a revival thanks to the movie. Indeed, movies and TV influence college reading just as they do civilian reading--witness the presence of One Flew Over the Cuckoo's Nest, a movie-made favorite (and ironically a long-ago counterculture favorite), and Helter Skelter and Rich Man, Poor Man, which were television specials. Two other titles are national best sellers, Looking for Mr. Goodbar and Winning Through Intimidation. Two titles have a slightly more youthful aura, but also a practical slant, Our Bodies, Ourselves and The People's Almanac. Only Robert Pirsig's Zen and the Art of Motorcycle Maintenance qualifies as exotic, but even that one is more about madness and, well, motorcycle maintenance than Zen.

We asked Edith H. Uunila, who is in charge of compiling the Chronicle's list from reports sent in by 180 campus bookstores, what changes in student reading tastes she's noted in the five years she's been at it. Her overall comment was that current lists reflect a "dreadful narrowing of vision," and that the dominant themes are "pure escape" and "personal advancement." Escape is reflected in the higher percentage of fiction on the lists these days; when the counterculture was in flower, students read Hesse, Vonnegut and

*Reprinted by permission from "Book Ends," New York Times Book Review, September 12, 1976, p. 53.

Tolkien, plus a few sentimental outsiders like Love Story and Jonathan Livingston Seagull, but that was it. They're still reading H., V. and T. but are more into commercial best sellers; science fiction seems to have "fallen by the wayside."

In nonfiction such "social-issue" books as Bury My Heart at Wounded Knee, Future Shock and The Female Eunuch have given way to the hustling of Winning Through Intimidation and the make-Daddy-love-me marital manipulations of The Total Woman (a recent favorite). Gone are counterculture concerns such as drugs, the occult, Castaneda, Euell Gibbons's living-off-the-land books, "touchy-feely" pop-psychology of the Esalen school, I'm O.K.--You're O.K. self-help, The Whole Earth Catalogue and environmental books in general. Where once there had been "the celebration of touching and loving the earth," Miss Uunilla recently wrote, now there is "celebration and isolation and assertion of self." Or as comedienne Lily Tomlin remarked recently, "We're all in this together--by ourselves."

PART VI

CENSORSHIP

(*catch-22* ...)

EDITOR'S NOTE

The perennial problem of censorship has become increasingly complex of late. As Kathleen Molz points out, stereotyping, violence, misrepresentation of racial, ethnic, and religious groups in books are just as likely to cause problems as the familiar targets--sex and profanity. The issues raised in the Council on Interracial Books for Children's _Human (and Anti-Human) Values in Children's Books_ deserve serious consideration. We need to be more sensitive to our own blind spots and biases, and more aware of the concerns of minorities regarding their image in the media.

On the other hand, where do we draw the line between avoiding books that may hurt the feelings or damage the self-image of a young person and obstructing freedom of expression? There are no easy answers and certainly none is offered by the writers of the articles in this section. The underlying theme, however, is that we need to be conscious of the personal biases we bring to the selection process and to understand the real, not necessarily the expressed, objections of the would-be censor (Broderick's insight that sensuality, not sex per se, is the taboo, for example).

Above all, we should trust and respect young readers. As Enid Olson puts it, "the solution lies in more reading, not less; in greater availability of many books and materials, not in curtailment. Because only with more reading does the mind begin to sift and weigh and determine for itself."[1]

Note

1. See page 231.

REALITY AND REASON: Intellectual Freedom and Youth*

By R. Kathleen Molz

From June 21, 1973 to June 24, 1974 encompasses by any man's reckoning little more than a year of time. But in that twelve-month period, the nation's highest court handed down a series of opinions regarding First Amendment rights that created some confusion.

Last year the U.S. Supreme Court in an opinion affecting five cases ruled that national standards could no longer be called for in determining what is or what is not obscene. Community standards, presumably those of any of the 78,000 governmental jurisdictions of the United States, were to prevail. Within a few days of the decision, the Supreme Court of Georgia held that the film Carnal Knowledge was obscene according to local standards, and the appeal defending the film was submitted to the U.S. Supreme Court, which on June 24, 1974 overturned the Georgia decision holding that these same community juries so extolled a year ago do not "have unbridled discretion in determining what is patently offensive." One cannot say today that we have come full circle; we have not even come half circle; we seem to be standing up straight in the midst of muddle.

The court's newest rulings have left us with ambiguity as a guideline, which is to say that we are left with what Justice Brennan so rightly characterizes as the "mire of case-by-case determination" of what is licit or illicit in books, films, illustrations, etc.

The legislators who look to the jurists for guidance have been at work in the states to up-date their own state obscenity statutes and bring them into conformity with the high court's rulings of 1973. As a result, thirty-eight state legislatures have this year considered over 150 bills relating to the obscene. Some of these measures contain exemptions for libraries; others do not. Many make special provision for the protection of minors.

The word "obscene" is an interesting one. Etymologically,

---

*Reprinted by permission of the author and the American Library Association from Newsletter on Intellectual Freedom (September 1974), 105, 125.

the word is said to have derived from a Greek word meaning that which was off the scene, that is, the part of the drama or play that could not be shown upon the stage. In that sense, it is related to the phrases we use ourselves when we speak of something beyond the pale or off-limits. The problem comes, of course, when one person tries to determine for another the precise demarcation point for those limits. Here the matter gets fuzzy, so fuzzy in fact that one Supreme Court jurist said that he couldn't define hard core pornography, but he knew it when he saw it.

I wager that most of us would be happy to have our own value judgments in such matters left to ourselves. Live and let live is not a bad axiom in questions of intellectual and aesthetic taste. The rub comes when the question of minors is introduced--because adults make many things off-limits to youth. Society makes liquor and tobacco unpurchasable by them; it enforces laws requiring them to attend school and protects them from exploitation in the labor market. Society will even protect them from their parents if they are shown to abuse them or cause them harm. Society's view is a little like Wordsworth's in that children are seen as innocents and that such innocence should be protected until some chronological point when the child is no longer a child but an adult.

Somewhere in between these two points in time the maturation process is supposed to occur, and one vehicle for that process is education which involves books and reading. Now we come to the sticky part--for are there limits to a child's vicarious exposure to experience? For them, what cannot or should not be shown upon their stage? And if there are such things better left unrevealed, then who is to determine what they are: their parents, their teachers, the librarians from whose collections they borrow?

I am not a specialist in the literature of youth. All I can do is detail for you briefly some of my observations after reading some of the correspondence received by the youth divisions of ALA and some of the commentaries which have appeared in journals devoted to the concerns of youth and their books.

The limitations appear to be these:

First, offensive language: A school library supervisor writing to ALA comments:

> I realize that profanity is often a very large part of the spoken language, but to see it in print in an elementary school library book is offensive and rather shocking....

The book: _The Drowning Boy_ by Susan Terris.

Second, candor in the treatment of sexual conduct: A classroom teacher comments:

> I do not believe a book that presents a story based on a thirteen-year-old girl's marriage to a retarded boy and includes a scene where he attempts to mate with her should be placed on library shelves with the seal of the Newbery

Award on its cover....

The book: Julie of the Wolves by Jean C. George.

Third, violence: The book "appeals directly to any latent sadistic impulses in its young readers, giving explicit accounts of the wounds and blood of both man and beast."

The book: Shadow of a Bull by Maia Wojciechowska.

Fourth, stereotyping: "I do not feel that a distinguished award should portray policemen as 'pigs'. With all the present day feelings about policemen, a book especially a children's book, should not help to emphasize this ill-feeling."

The book: Sylvester and the Magic Pebble by William Steig.

Fifth, misrepresentation of racial, ethnic, and religious groups:

> The author makes false statements which are very offensive to Jews and to thinking, sensitive Christians.

The book: The Tale of Ancient Israel by Roger Lancelyn Green.

> America knows the wrongs of history perpetrated on minority races, and we feel that this book is a bitter comment of man's inhumanity to man. How can such a book do anything for young children, except increase the hatred and violence already carried to the extreme?

The book: Sounder by William H. Armstrong.

> It is beyond our comprehension how a book like this is still being published. It is biased and filled with half-truths concerning the lives of Mexican-Americans.... We are demanding that the book be banned from all libraries supported by public monies.

The book: Bad Boy, Good Boy by Marie H. Ets.

Profanity, violence, sexual candor, stereotyping, and misrepresentation of ethnic, religious, and racial groups--these seem to be the principal areas of concern and all of them seem to bear on the key words that introduce this program this morning: Reality and Reason.

Is realism conveyed by a liberal sprinkling of four-letter words? Is it reasonable to expect that children can be left innocent of sexual matters when the advertising world exploits sex in almost all of the mass media? Is it rational to expect that the ghetto or the barrio can be depicted without giving some offense? These are the ponderables that will be considered this morning.

SEX AND THE SINGLE CHILD: Innocence Is a Cop-Out*

By Joan Bodger Mercer

A. S. Neill of Summerhill writes of his belief that a child who pokes into drawers and purses, opens cupboards, peers into boxes, and takes toys or watches apart is a child who is looking for answers to life's sexual mysteries. "Do you want to know where babies come from? I'll tell you!" he says is the swiftest cure for snoopiness. Perhaps the reason that generations of little girls have identified with flat chested Nancy Drew is that instinctively they know she is looking for something more exciting than The Secret of the Old Clock. In vain we point to vulgar style and shallow character development as reason to shun that perennial challenger to our professional infallibility. But what do we offer in Nancy's place? Perhaps it is not better style or characterization that children need and search for, but recognition of an ultimate mystery.

In all my travels in this past year, the book that non-professionals have asked me about most often has been The Godfather. I began to get the feeling that in 1970-71 an uncommon number of thirteen-year-olds were reading not Segal, but the tender love story of Sonny Corleone, his oversized sex organ, and his similarly abnormal mistress.

The parents who volunteered the information about their kids' reading habits were quite ordinary people, really, not far removed from the minor characters in Mario Puzo's ethnic Forsyte Saga. One was a Detroit housewife who said her daughter had read the book and discussed it with her, but she had abjured her not "to let father know." Of the men, one was "in dogfood," the other "in dispensers." Each of them opened up when he learned I was "in children's lit." I got the feeling they were a little anxious but a lot more proud about their sons' choice of reading. None of the three discussed any other part of the novel so perhaps their children didn't either. After all, there is a sort of folk tale grandeur to it, fabulous yet explicit, that lends itself to speculation. Unlike most books for thirteen-year-olds, it leaves no doubt about the

*Reprinted by permission of the author and publisher from Wilson Library Bulletin (October 1971), 144-146.

nature of the sexual act nor that sex is essential to a loving relationship between man and woman. But what strikes me most forcibly is that the adults who confided in me represent the very kind of parent upon whom we project our professional paranoia. However, the moral of The Godfather (if there is one) is that Father knows best. This lends support to my belief that it is not sex that makes the would-be censor, but challenge to authority.

Once, when I was involved in a library censorship case, I found myself answering to a group of my fellow workers--everyone from professionals to the maintenance man. Questions were hurled at me and I tried to answer them intelligently. I felt terribly stupid because I didn't seem able to grasp the politically-oriented questions being pressed upon me by a middle-aged clerk. Her color was high, her eyes glazed bright blue. She looked enamelled. Then I remembered: the only other time I had ever seen her look like that was when she was discussing her hot flashes!

Right then I realized that we were not discussing Communist influences in the SDS. We were discussing sex! Yet later, when the arguments turned explicitly to sex and pornography, I noticed that the conversation flipped again. Suddenly we were discussing Communism, or what passed as a definition of Communism. For a moment the fog lifted and I glimpsed the battlefield whole. Anything new is taboo. "Communism" is anything new. Therefore, Communism is anything that is taboo. Sex is taboo. Therefore, sex is Communistic and Communism is sexual.

Sex, sexualism, and sexism in children's literature have been around for a long time, covert but powerful. Sex is power. One has to grasp only the rudiments of anthropology to perceive that whole religions and priesthoods have been attempts to explain and control the energy of propagation, the mysterious life force. "What do the simple folk do?" asks Guinevere, having just tasted the joys of love. Innocent, yet callous, she assumes any experience so delicious must surely be reserved for the ruling classes. What do the children do? Freud has tipped us off to the fact that they are sexual little beggars but we have used our own innocence and theirs as a cop-out. We have refused to see what we did not want to see. Philippe Aries, in his fascinating study, Centuries of Childhood, points out that the concept of childhood is a recent invention that came into being at the onset of the Industrial Revolution. Perhaps we should face up to the fact that it was conceived as much for the benefit of adults as for the children. Teachers and librarians make a living by keeping children in their place.

How long is it since you read Black Beauty? The swinging intellectual's stance is to despise the book's mincing prissiness, yet to tolerate shelf room for it because mothers and grandmothers come looking for it to hand on to another generation. Even more damnable, it has become a fixed "classic" on school lists. Despite these formidable handicaps, little girls still read the book eagerly and buy cheap fuzzy-papered editions of it even while the book loses ground in sophisticated book selection circles.

Black Beauty is a funny book, hilarious if you read long passages of its Victorian prose aloud. Who wants it? Who needs it? But why did I remember--not the book, but the *feeling* of the book--so vividly? So Helen Sewell was revisited and Ginger resurrected. No wonder I was sexually aroused as I read my favorite chapter! Poor broken Ginger was put out to pasture because she had been ridden all night by the squire's son! I don't consider myself particularly precocious, but somehow I had known without knowing I knew what the book was about. Tell me, gentle reader, am I the only one?

I suppose that my confession now furnishes evidence that children's books stir prurient interests. But how to predict which book will stir which child when? We can no more do that than predict the right book for the right child, professional arrogance to the contrary. Even supposing we withhold books, how are we to prevent our patrons from receiving stimuli elsewhere? Ah, the Devil whispers, that is hardly our concern. All we have to worry about is that no child point to the Children's Room and make claim he/she found excitement there.

Last summer (1970), having several hours to spend in a large city library before going out to the airport, I asked the Young Adult librarian if I could browse through some of the new books, among them, *Girls and Sex* (Pomeroy). The book had been rejected, she explained, because it encourages girls "to sneak behind their parents' backs." An hour later I left the library by the front door, picking my way down the broad shallow steps and across the famous square that fronted the building. Then I began to laugh.

The reason I was stepping so carefully, blushing prettily, and murmuring, "Oh, excuse me!" so many times was that the whole scene was carpeted by young couples sitting, standing, lying in close embrace. Any fourteen-year-old who came to the library that day would have had to run the same gauntlet that I did. He or she might do worse than to have a copy of Pomeroy in hand. Later, I interpreted Pomeroy's remarks to mean that if any young girl were determined to have intercourse she should face up to her decision, find some place where she and her lover would not be interrupted accidentally-on-purpose. In other words, don't involve the parents or use the action as a weapon against them. This seems like old fashioned prudery as compared to the action on the library steps!

There are many ways to hide books that have been written and published for children or young adults. One way, of course, is not to buy the book in the first place. Book budgets are tight; book selection is highly professional (read static); we must limit ourselves to the flawless. Take no chances on the Harlan Quist publications, for instance. *Book No. 1* (Ionesco) is unpleasant and upsetting. We do not eschew books because they are controversial but because of poor literary quality, weird illustrations or--favorite cop-out--disrespect to parents.

Books that are not specifically sexual are sometimes treated as though they were because of challenge to parental authority. However, as I have pointed out elsewhere, I feel that the struggle to *be* sexually, politically, individually is all intertwined. In one city I visited, Steptoe's *Uptown* was too well reviewed to be excluded from purchase but ingenious ways have been found to hide it from the kids. The modest little picture book, originally meant for five- to ten-year-olds, is relegated to the adult section because "the father drinks beer and the grammar is substandard." I am happy to report that in a branch library in that same city (in a neighborhood where the fathers drink beer and the grammar is substandard), the librarians just never seem to get around to hiding the book by reclassifying it. Meanwhile, in the opposite corner of the country, the Pacific Northwest, *Lisa, Bright and Dark* (Neufeld) is hidden away in the adult psychology section. The reason is not that young people cannot understand a psychotic break (after all, the same kids can buy *You Never Promised Me a Rose Garden* in paperback) but because the book makes adults look stupid, ignorant, and neglectful.

Little old ladies still trot into the library and ask for YA titles, "a nice love story without too much sex in it," but they are in for a shock these days. Eleven-year-olds are better able to dig sex, drugs, out of wedlock pregnancies, and bumbling parents than are their escapist elders. Young adults read adult books. If they are not allowed to use the adult section of the library or if the YA section is too timid in its selection they turn to paperbacks. But younger and younger children are reading the books that authors and publishers assumed were for young adults. Hinton's *The Outsiders*, considered a little racy for young teenagers in the early 1960s, is the hottest title for nine-year-olds in Vancouver, Wash.

In the good old days the best children's books got rid of the parents early. They either died, were already dead, were sent on a trip or were conveniently lost. From *Children of the New Forest* to *From the Mixed Up Files of Mrs. Basil E. Frankweiler* children have found vicarious delight in the Robinson Crusoe dilemma of making it on their own. Whenever parents came on the scene they were so wise and strong and good that we longed to get rid of them again. One of the most frightening characters in children's literature, to my way of thinking, is the omnipotent mother in *The Runaway Bunny* (M. W. Brown). Sometimes I find myself comparing her to the Victorian briskness of Beatrix Potter's estimable Mrs. Rabbit. If Peter had been born in the 1950s his mother would never have left him. There would have been no Mr. MacGregor, no camomile tea. In short, no adventure.

In May, 1970, I was in Anaheim, California, attending an International Reading Association convention. It happened to be the week that Cambodia was invaded, when students were being killed at Kent and Jackson State. There was almost no mention of these things made in the speeches and workshops although the several thousand of us attending there were directly involved with the welfare and education of the young. When, at intervals, we came out of the Plato's Cave of the convention hall it was into the surreality of Disney's land. The plastic Matterhorn glittered in the smog. We did it all for the children.

I am convinced that, as usual, the conservatives and the reactionaries see the situation clearly. If we step down from our height or the children are allowed to be more free, the tension of the whole structure will be threatened. If we persist in opening up the children's section to "adult" feelings and ideas, if we let children read where and what they want to there is no predicting what may happen. To pretend otherwise is a cop-out.

A DIFFERENT LOOK AT THE DIVINERS*

By Dorothy Broderick

Everybody seems to have an opinion about Margaret Laurence's _The Diviners_ as appropriate reading for grade thirteen students. But so far, I have yet to read anything that goes beneath the surface and tries to determine what is really at issue in these attacks upon one of the finest novels of the twentieth century.

I cannot, of course, _prove_ what is at issue, but I can hypothesize. Every case of censorship that I know about in depth, has proved to be about something other than what the censors claimed, and I think _The Diviners_ is a perfect example of my hypothesis.

First of all, there are many more books with sex and dirty words in them that cause no one any trouble. So when a book causes trouble, the question arises: why this one and not ten others?

In the case of _The Diviners_, the answer seems surprisingly simple to me. Morag is a sexually healthy woman who _enjoys_ sex. That is a no-no. A woman who refuses to experience guilt over having a child out of wedlock is a no-no. It is not the sex in _The Diviners_ that causes trouble, but the sexuality, which is an entirely different thing.

The only time Morag does feel shamed, she reaches the conclusion that she will never have sex with a man whom she would not wish to be father of a child. From my point of view, that is one of the highest moral standards anyone could choose to live by, but my standards aren't everyone's, as the censors make clear.

Then there is the question of the racial identity of the man Morag loves throughout her life. Skinner Tonnerre is a "breed," part Indian, part French. Some people might forgive Morag her healthy sexuality if only she had selected a more suitable man, but make no mistake about the depth of racial and ethnic bias that exists in Canadian society. The bigotry is there, the lines carefully drawn, and people who cross those lines should pay a price. Morag doesn't pay, and that is another no-no.

---

*Reprinted by permission of the author and publisher from _Emergency Librarian_, 4:2 (November/December 1976), 14-15.

As for the *dirty* words, well, they are used only in connection with Christie, *and* people who were literate (and censors never are) would appreciate how skillfully Laurence varies the tone and style throughout the book to reflect the people she is telling us about. There is no point in the book when the *Memory-bank* scenes are confusing to a perceptive reader. We know from the tone and style precisely where we are in Morag's life. It is easy to see why someone teaching literature would delight in this book since analysis of it would go far toward helping people learn how to read a novel.

Finally, there is the fact that Morag has let Pique go out on her own. I still remember the flak Jean George took when *My Side of the Mountain* was published. Parents do not want to be told directly or indirectly that true love of children consists of letting them live their own lives, making their own mistakes and their own decisions.

A book is attacked in direct proportion to how much truth it tells that people do not want to hear. In *The Diviners*, Margaret Laurence has moved beyond looking at the truth of one person's life, which she did so superbly in *The Stone Angel*, for example, and looked at the truth of Canadian society. This is her first genuinely Canadian novel and the attacks on it, rather than discouraging Laurence, should tell her than she has succeeded admirably.

If we are to do battle with the censors inside and outside the profession, we need to think through how we stand on the question of *truth*. The censor's approach is to *judge*--that is, truth is divided up into good truth and bad truth. The censor is always willing to hear the good truth; never willing to hear the bad. To acknowledge defects in society, is to be faced with the idea that maybe we should do something about them. It is easier for many people to deny those defects than to work to eliminate them.

The other way of looking at truth is simply to accept it. If we do that, we can settle for being grateful for having been offered another insight into the human condition. And each such insight brings us a little closer to being personally free. The trouble with being personally free is that it shifts the burden of responsibility from some amorphous entity called society or religion or some *ism*, onto our shoulders.

We in western society talk too glibly about freedom and liberty and act as if they were unmixed blessings. They aren't. As Ursula LeGuin says about Tenar in *The Tombs of Atuan*:

> What she had begun to learn was the weight of liberty. Freedom is a heavy load, a great and strange burden for the spirit to undertake. It is not easy. It is not a gift given, but a choice made, and the choice may be a hard one. The road goes upward towards the light; but the laden traveler may never reach the end of it.

Censors not only do not want to choose liberty for themselves; they want to keep us from choosing it for ourselves. That is why, no matter how frustrating and discouraging it is to fight the same old battle week after week, month after month, we must challenge the censors. Not for some lofty statement of democratic principles, but because our personal right to choose and to grow is at issue.

COMICS, COKES, & CENSORSHIP*

By Norma Fox Mazer

When I was growing up, my mother didn't allow comics in our house. My parents were readers, and nothing else printed was off limits. I read everything, without discretion, as long as it contained words: my parents' books, the Sue Barton nurse series from beginning to end, *Gulliver's Travels*, and dreadful *Pollyanna* whom I adored, all in the same big gulp. But no comics. I had to go across the street to Buddy Wells' house and read his *Wonder Woman* and *Elastic Man* on the sly. I guess my mother thought comics would corrupt my sisters' and my brains the same way she firmly believed Cokes would poison our insides.

When my children began to read, I decided they could read anything, including comics. I hewed to the line that no printed word, sentence, or story ever killed or maimed anyone, that reading leads to more reading, and that, finally, given time, the kids would develop their own tastes which, hopefully, would include much more than comics.

All this was fine and liberated, but I didn't anticipate some of the reading material my four offspring would choose. Comics of all kinds, war comics, horror comics, even funny comics, were big in our house. My nine-year-old son had a collection that stood taller than he did, and which he read avidly, day after day after day. Despite my theories I had never shaken off a faint queasiness about comic books, a feeling that they were, yes, bad for you. (In the same way I've never been able to really relish a nice frosty Coke without a pang of guilt. It tastes good, but what is it doing to my insides?)

One day I went into my son's closet where he kept his comic collection and leafed through a few. I had forgotten, or maybe, as a child, had never recognized, how lurid, violent, racist, and sexist comics could be. (Besides, their literary style was a bit purple. "Alone ... so terribly, hideously alone! The surrounding silhouettes of mountains ripple in the heat ... the moon is a fading ember ... the wind whispers DEATH ... a shadow blackens the sky ... as the dread BATMAN awaits a doomful destiny along the HIGHWAY TO NOWHERE!")

*Reprinted by permission of the author and publisher from *Top of the News* (January 1976), 167-170.

Reading my son's comics, so far removed from the mixture of approved classics and bland kids' fare I'd been nurtured on, I grew definitely uneasy. What sick festering notions were already rotting in his young mind? He was a delicious looking little boy, round cheeked, rosy faced, a bit plump, the sort of kid you like to hug and squeeze. But you couldn't tell anything by that, could you? The comics could really be mucking up his mind. Good Lord, what would be the use of all my efforts about nutrition and diets, enough sleep, yearly checks with the pediatrician, and always the right shots and shoes if it were all sabotaged by these miserable comic books? With a wave of guilt, I took a huge armful straight to the garbage can. I never opened it. I stared at that big pile of pulpy words and lurid pictures and chose again the principle of no censorship. My son could have his comics.

I was put to another test when one of our daughters brought home a book that was, by anyone's standards, pornographic. This daughter was only fourteen at the time, and I still felt terrifically protective toward her about all sorts of things, most of which I already realized I could no longer control.

There was the usual mental struggle--Should I make her take the offensive book out of the house immediately? Should I ignore it? Should I read it? Should I say something, but lay down no law? I was not happy that she was getting any of her sexual education this way, but a little thought convinced me that banning a book from our house didn't mean banning it from her eyes and mind. In fact, she and a whole group of girlfriends were passing this book around, generally secretly as far as parents were concerned.

More recently, I discovered a young daughter reading scenes from *Sybil*, scenes which had so distressed me that I had felt an actual physical shock to my system. By this time, after passing through all this and more with three other children, I ought not to have felt even a jolt. But I did. My first impulse was to throw out the book, protect her from the knowledge that such a terrible thing as a mother's attacking her infant daughter could happen in this world.

Once again, although I spoke to her about what she was reading, I refrained from taking the book from her.

Enough time has passed for me to feel more strongly, not less so, about my position on the matter of reading. My son, the comic book freak, has grown up to be a young man who doesn't seem to have a violent bone in his body and whose mind is clear and capable. Along with a variety of material that ran the gamut from Tolkien to Tolstoy, interestingly enough he was still also reading comics right into his late teens. I've noticed the same thing not only in my daughters but in a lot of young people. Comics--*Mad Magazine* and *National Lampoon*, for instance--are an accepted part of their culture.

Today there's a rather strong current alive in our country devoted to screening, censoring, banning, and in some cases even burning books that our children read. And the cry for censorship rings out not just against sex, for instance, but against books which contain certain words people find offensive, certain attitudes and points of view.

As a writer for the young, as a reader, a parent, I despise all censorship, even including things that enrage and pain me. I want to bite nails when I read yet another portrait of a silly, simpering, weepy, noncapable girl. I find, even in a book for the young that I otherwise admire, a gratuitous, racist remark about Jews. And in a book which has been widely acclaimed, a black woman character who might have come off the pancake box: unmarried, working faithfully for a white family, deeply understanding, and always there when needed by the white children.

I don't like these things, I hate the blindness that persistently ties us to such stereotypes, but I wouldn't keep these books out of the hands of children who want to read them. And this is because I believe that children are people with as much sense and an equal ability to sort out things for themselves as adults.

Children are not imperfect copies of ourselves who magically come into the possession of our superior adult reasoning powers at a certain fixed age. Children, in fact, have remarkable sense from quite a young age and lack, most of all, experience. It's experience, I believe, which separates "us" from "them."

Of course there are other differences. The young are more intense, emotional, impatient, lusty, and zestful. Their time sense is quite different. And they can throw themselves into life in a wonderful way which we adults gradually lose. When my youngest daughter reads, for instance, I have to shout in her ear three or four times to pull her out of that world she's so blissfully fallen into.

Today, writers for adolescents are giving them stories about things that used to be verboten. Growing up, I read saccharine Pollyanna. My kids can read M. C. Higgins the Great and Pocketful of Seeds. Two marvelous books. There are a lot around. Writers are discovering that death, sex, love, war, divorce, and so on are part of the lives of the young. Some books, it's true, are written, it seems, merely to be in the swim, to be realistic because "realistic" is in vogue. But others are literature; they're real, passionate, felt books. They may deal, on one level, with social problems, but they are primarily about the human condition, about the way we feel and how we live with others.

When I write, I hope not to write for "children"--that is, for the fictional dear little innocent some of us seem still to believe in --but for readers. Younger readers, yes, who will respond to the characters I create--characters like themselves, also young, with the same limitation of experience. For me, all readers are equal.

This point of view, however, raises certain thorny questions. We are back to square A. Does this mean that there are no limits to what can, or should, or will be written for children? Where do we draw the line between discretion, taste, and censorship? As guardians of the young do we protect them from certain ideas, certain types of literature, the way we try to protect them from bad food and dangerous ventures? Is there material that is inappropriate for the young, or is this, too, censorship?

And if we are censoring, however discreetly, whether as parents, readers, teachers, librarians, or writers, what are we risking?

CONTROVERSIAL FICTION FOR YOUNG ADULTS: A Few Thoughts and a Bibliography

By Jane Ameline

Most librarians doing young adult work sooner or later run into the question of "controversial" fiction. What is suitable (so-called) reading for this age group? Who decides? My library system follows the ALA guidelines for young adult services: "Young adults are entitled to open and equal access to all materials and services--regardless of cost, location, or format--and the right to a confidential client-librarian relationship, a non-judgmental attitude, respect, and participation in the decision-making process of the library.... Young adults should have full access to materials in order to permit individual decisions to be made with a full understanding of options and alternatives.... The special needs and interests and the uniqueness of young adults must be recognized in library services and materials." (Community Library Services--Working Papers on Goals and Guidelines, *School Library Journal*, September, 1973, p. 24-5)

Surely these are fair and reasonable goals. After all, we are thinking of an age group that was considered fit for adult responsibilities in pioneer days, and we are frequently reminded that the idea of adolescence as just a more advanced category of childhood is a 20th century invention.

And so I surprised myself a few months ago when I found myself hoping my grade seven daughter wouldn't read a novel her contemporaries were reading, and which was in my library. The double standard in a new variation--a special dose of censorship for my own child! After thinking it over, I decided that I didn't want her reading about anything unpleasant at all. This patently unreasonable wish led me to think of the needs of parents, and those of their children, and to the realization that all too often these needs do not coincide. When I am being a librarian, I am thinking first of all the young people who are my clients, and their special requirements: their need to find out, to understand, to stretch their minds as far as possible, and to grow. When I was worrying about my daughter's reading, it was closer to being part of that whole anxiety package of parenthood; I wanted her to be a happier, better

*Reprinted by permission of the author and publisher from *Ontario Library Review* (December 1974), 250-254.

person than her mother, as well as smarter and safer. As a corollary to these edifying emotions, I wanted to be able to relax from worrying about her.

I suspect that other parents who worry about their children's reading are feeling somewhat the same. I am not speaking here of pornography and atrocity accounts, but of the themes so often found in the fiction lately being written for teenagers--parental fallibility, alcoholism, divorce, episodes of sex and discussions of death. Some of these books are as full of formulas and stock answers as their boy-meets-girl counterparts of the 1940s and '50s. Certainly there are a great many of them being written, and it would be pleasant to see more books with unusual settings and imaginative qualities. However, the best of these realistic novels for young people are quite well done, and the quality seems to be improving.

Non-fiction of an informational nature can give facts, but not an understanding of, and sympathy with, the problems and predicaments of others. For that we need fiction and autobiography. We need books which depict young people coming to an understanding of their own natures as sexual and social beings, realizing that they must take responsibility for their own lives, knowing that we all must grow old and die, and that nobody is perfect, including parents. Of necessity, such themes must involve discussion of sex, death, and human imperfection.

Good readers among this age group are apt to skip the teenage novel altogether. But I have noticed that young people who are only average readers, when they do not find these themes in fiction written for them, will seek out books written for adults containing young adult characters. Two recent examples are Herman Raucher's Summer of '42 (Putnam, 1971) and Ruth D. MacDougall's The Cheerleader (Putnam, 1973). (The starred items in my bibliography are other examples of this category.)

It is easy to see why many parents might object to their children reading this type of material. (In my case, I hate to see my children exposed to examples of cruelty or unkindness--to watch them growing older and sadder.) In families from certain other countries, special cultural differences may arise: their children are growing up following many of the customs of their Canadian school friends, but in their homes discussions of sex and criticisms of their parents are not encouraged. One also runs into any number of other factors--sexual prudery, an overly-protective attitude, and/or the conviction that if you don't think or talk about a subject it will go away.

Under pressure from parents or community, it is certainly possible to censor the contents of a public or a school library, but in so doing we ought not be fooled into thinking that we can censor what the children in fact read or discover. We are only making sure that we don't know what it is, or where they get it. If the library does not contain material that young people want and need, they will not come to the library. They will get their stories and information from news stands and book stores, and watch television by the hour instead. Surely these alternate sources of information exert a sufficient pull on their time and attention as it is. In my neighbourhood, it is a status symbol among the 9 and 10 year-olds to watch baby blue movies!

I don't think it is possible to keep children much more innocent (if that is the correct word) than the culture of which they are a part. What we can do, as librarians, teachers, and/or parents, is be aware of the type of books they enjoy, review them, buy the good ones (yes, there are some good ones) and keep our collections up-to-date. If the library is a pleasant helpful place to visit, and the librarian equally so, young people will come, at first for information and school projects, and some of them will develop the habit of reading fiction for pleasure.

As a postscript and an example of the type of book mentioned, I have appended a brief and personal list of fiction titles. They vary considerably in difficulty and appeal, and, except for the starred items, were all written with the young adult reader in mind. I believe they all have more than enough interest and literary merit to justify their presence in a popular collection. They all contain themes or elements which some people would consider unsuitable for young adult readers.

Bibliography

Arundel, Honor. A Family Failing. Nelson, 1972.

A family's carefree existence is shattered when the father becomes unemployed--a thoughtful look at sex roles and how misfortune can change the characters of even those we feel we know best.

Blume, Judy. It's Not the End of the World. Bradbury (Oxford) 1973.

Some of Blume's novels are rather close to bibliotherapy, but this story of a divorce and its effects on the three children of the family is true-to-life and unsentimental.

*Bradford, Richard. Red Sky at Morning. Lippincott, 1958.

When his father joins the navy in World War II, Joshua Arnold and his mother move from Mobile, Alabama to Corazon Sagrado, New Mexico. In this hilarious and sad story Josh learns Spanish, grows older, falls in love, and learns to be the head of his family.

Branscum, Robbie. Me and Jim Luke. Doubleday, 1971.

Two boys discover a murder and become involved with the feared Ku Klux Klan. As well as their adventures there are warm descriptions of family relationships and a considerable understanding of the complexities of life.

Cleaver, Vera and Bill. The Mock Revolt. Lippincott, 1971.
Ussy Mock is a rebellious and courageous 13-year-old--a potential winner cooped up by his environment. He has saved up quite a bit of money (with a view to leaving town) when he is unfortunate enough to run into a loser, who, little by little, borrows all his money. Ussy finds that there is no easy solution to being one of nature's victims, and that such people can be very difficult to help. Excellent characterizations.

Donovan, John. Wild in the World. Harper (Fitzhenry), 1971.
On one level, this book is pathetic and implausible. The hero, John Gridley, is the last living member of a family of 13 people: mother, father and 10 other children, all of whom die prematurely (haven't they ever heard of doctors?). At the end, after befriending a wild dog, John dies too. On a realistic level, this is unlikely. But as an allegory of human solitude, of being in God's hand, it is very well done indeed--well-constructed, and well-written.

Engebrecht, Patricia A. Under the Haystack. Nelson, 1973.
Sandy, a mature 13-year-old, tries to hold her family of two younger sisters together after her mother and stepfather have deserted them. When her mother finally returns, Sandy is able to understand what compelled her to run away, and even to feel compassion for her.

Garfield, Leon. The Drummer Boy. Pantheon (Random) 1970.
A wonderfully talented historical novel which attacks the obscenity of war by contrasting metaphors of love and lust. The handsome golden young drummer boy is pitted against a cruel general, who, from a perverted love of glory, longs for the death of his soldiers.

George, Jean. Julie of the Wolves. Harper (Fitzhenry) 1972.
Julie, a young Eskimo girl, stands halfway between the old ways of her people (which she prefers) and the 20th century. When she becomes lost in the wilderness, her remembered skills and the friendship of a wolf pack enable her to survive. Upon her return to civilization, she feels betrayed by her father and irrevocably separated from the dying customs of the Eskimos. Essentially a tragedy.

Holland, Isabelle. Heads You Win, Tails I Lose. Lippincott, 1973.
"One moment I'm almost an adult and shouldn't behave like a child. The next minute, when I try to talk to you as though I were an adult, all of a sudden I'm a child and mustn't be rude to my elders. You can't have it both ways."

Jordan, June. His Own Where. Crowell (Collier-Macmillan) 1971.
Two young black teenagers Buddy and Angela fall in love and run away from all the circumstances of their lives which separate them. The story ends with their setting up housekeeping in a deserted corner of a cemetery, and hoping Angela is pregnant so they will not be separated. Beautifully written in a heightened form of Black Language which many of our readers may find difficult.

Kerr, M. E. Dinky Hocker Shoots Smack. Harper (Fitzhenry), 1972.

All about having friends, being a fat food addict, having a mother who is a good person but bad for you, and learning to be polite in the face of opinions you really disagree with.

Klein, Norma. Mom, the Wolf-Man, and Me. Pantheon (Random) 1972.

"Mom" is liberated, unmarried, and talented; the "Wolf-Man" is her lover and friend, and "me" is her 12-year-old daughter. A well written and sympathetic look at an unorthodox (at least by the standards of YP fiction) family arrangement.

Neufeld, John. Lisa Bright and Dark. Phillips (Saunders) 1969.

A moving account of the attempts of three teenaged girls to get help for a friend who is mentally ill and getting worse. The author's characterizations of the adults who should have helped her --parents and teachers--are perhaps excessively harsh and two-dimensional, but (I am assured) not untrue to life.

Peyton, K. M. Pennington's Seventeenth Summer. Crowell (Collier-Macmillan), 1972. The Beethoven Medal. Crowell (Collier-Macmillan), 1972. Pennington's Heir. Oxford, 1973.

This trilogy takes Patrick Pennington from his last year of high school, through jail, a love affair, a shot-gun wedding (with his love) to the beginnings of a career as a concert pianist. Well-written, very funny and exhilarating.

*Salinger, J. D. The Catcher in the Rye. Little, 1951.

Holden Caulfield is the archetypal rebellious and intelligent teenager who sees too clearly the faults of the society in which he must live. Although this book was published in 1951 and has been on school reading lists ever since (enough, you would think, to draw the sting of the most subversive book!) it still has power to rouse the wrath of the occasional authority figure.

*Swarthout, Glendon. Bless the Beasts and Children. Doubleday, 1970.

Society can be cruel to children in many ways. The heroes of this novel are The Bedwetters, a persecuted cabin group of boys at a camp which is supposed to make "men" of them. How they turn on their tormentors makes the moving (although overdrawn and bloodthirsty) climax of this exciting story.

Townsend, John Rowe. Good Night, Prof. Love. Lippincott, 1971.

"Prof. love" is a bespectacled 16-year-old freed for the first time in his life from adult authority. While his parents are away on a holiday, leaving him at home, he meets a charming and socially unsuitable girl whom he wishes to marry so that they may both escape from their uncongenial backgrounds.

Wersba, Barbara. Run Softly, Go Fast. Atheneum (McClelland), 1970.

David Marks has always found it extremely difficult to get along with his father; for all their lives together they had virtually nothing in common. One sympathizes with them both, and understands that some parents and children cannot come to terms with each other.

Windsor, Patricia. The Summer Before. Harper (Fitzhenry), 1973.
Bradley and Alexandra were the best of friends, and when Bradley is killed in a car accident for which Alexandra feels partly responsible, she finds it almost impossible to accept his death.

REASON, NOT EMOTION*

By Elaine Simpson

Reason, the application of logical processes to accomplish a desired end, and the selection of materials for young adults sounds so obvious, doesn't it? All of us are sure that clearness of thought, soundness of reasoning, and freedom from bias underlie our decision to buy or not to buy a book, a film, a record.

However you may word your criteria for selection, they are probably encompassed in these broad considerations suggested by John Rowe Townsend: (1) "popularity or potential popularity"; (2) "relevance," that is "the power, or possible power, of theme or subject matter to make the [young adult] more aware of current social or personal problems or to suggest solutions to him" or her --to have significance in any way for the prospective audience; (3) "literary merit"; (4) "suitability," that is, the "appropriateness to the supposed" user.[1]

This last area for appraisal, suitability, has always been one which has posed problems and touched off arguments among selectors of materials for any age group, but particularly among those who select for children and young adults. The problems seem to have been intensified within the past few years. Librarians are having to pass judgment upon materials which, because of subject, style, story line, language, or other element, disturb some to the point that emotion overrules, or at least seriously affects, reason.

For years librarians and others have criticized junior novels saying they are written to a formula; they all have pat, sweetness-and-light resolutions that instill false conceptions of life; they fail to deal with fundamental problems of personal and societal adjustment that are of immediate concern to young adults, etc, etc. But, they would continue, teenage fiction does serve a purpose. It is good transitional material for the younger readers; it helps them move on to adult books. And, besides, it's all we've got.

Then juvenile authors and editors began giving us such books as Go Ask Alice, Run Softly, Go Fast, Admission to the Feast,

---

*Reprinted by permission of the author and the American Library Association from Newsletter on Intellectual Freedom 23:5 (September 1974), 128-129.

Run, Shelley, Run, The Chocolate War. I could go on and on naming both fiction and non-fiction.

And what happened? All too many of these same people who had been asking for an honest story about serious teen-age problems began protesting: language like that in a book for young people? Are rape, abortion, homosexuality, unwed mothers, suicide, drugs, unsympathetic portrayal of parents, and violence appropriate subjects for junior novels? Are young people ready for such explicit realism; Would you want your daughter to read one?

Several years ago Clifton Fadiman wrote, in essence: If a young person cannot understand what he reads, it will not harm him; while if he can understand, he is ready to read of life situations truly presented. It is a disservice to the young, who mature at different rates, to limit them to "puerile interests and simplified writing" when there is a desperate need for the young to expand their experience with the world.[2]

The reaction to and interpretation of a book by a twelve-to-fourteen-year-old is not the same as that of an adult. Each of us, adult and young adult, brings different and varying degrees of experience, different backgrounds and pasts to a book. These diversities affect our responses to what we read. We adults may read more into an event than is actually there. One of my students in talking about Mrs. Klein's It's Not What You Expect said that the mother's job handing out flyers in a shopping center had unconscious sexual implications unfitting for young adults to read about.

Sometimes one might think we are reading different versions of the same book because we disagree about what has been written. An example of such a disagreement occurred in one of my classes two or three years ago during the discussion of Journey All Alone by Deloris Harrison. One student said Mildred had been raped; another said she had not and thought the book pointless because she could see no reason for Mildred's thinking she had to make a sad journey through life all alone. Each student was so positive of the correctness of his or her interpretation of events that everyone in class read the book in order to make up his or her own mind about the question.

This episode is also an example of an unfortunate reaction some adults have to these realistic junior novels: their attention is so caught by language or an incident which they find shocking that they focus on that element alone; they cannot accept the story as a unified work which ought to be judged in its totality, not by some isolated parts. In I'll Get There, It Better Be Worth the Trip, for instance, there is a brief, not really explicit, homosexual experience. In letters to Library Journal and in other comments this experience was so exaggerated in importance that it was made to seem the issue on which the whole story depends. Actually it was only one of the many experiences in the life of a young boy adapting himself to grief, change of life-style, and growing up.

Especially in the areas of sex and drugs, as Barbara Wersba has pointed out, adults think they are considering whether or not teenagers should read about these subjects; but actually they are judging what they think a teenager should do about them.[3]

As for the language--I think that young adults have two vocabularies, one that they use around most adults and another, much freer one, that they use among themselves. I think that many adults are ignorant of, or refuse to accept, the fact that teenagers in white, middle class communities as well as in the inner city know and use this second vocabulary.

For a book to meet the needs of today's young people, its characters should speak in their language; its problems be those currently most pressing to them; details of action and of reaction to events and attitudes toward life should agree with psychologically valid patterns of behavior among them.

If we feed children and young adults a steady diet of pap--of the false, the trivial, the phoney--we will produce adults who will continue to believe lies and cheap sentimentalities because they do not know truth.

We seem to have an innate compulsion to protect those who are younger and more innocent than we. Repeatedly the teenagers who review books for me say, in effect, "This is an honest book, and I got a lot from it; but I would not recommend it for younger readers." We adults too often bring this same over-protective attitude to our judgment of what is or is not suitable for young adults to read. This is not protection; it is betrayal.

Those who teach in library school or argue for the young adult's freedom to read or urge you to use reason, not emotion, to judge all books cannot teach you commitment to the ALA policy stated in "Free Access to Libraries for Minors."

One day I left the classroom too closely upon the heels of the departing students and heard one say to another, "Humpf! She can argue all she wants about that kind of book. I'm not going to have them in my library!" She had already made her commitment, and I could only hope that she would never hold any library job that would involve materials selection for any age group.

Do not, please, assume that I am saying that all of the current books being published for young adults are desirable additions to your collection. Among them you will find propaganda and case studies thinly disguised as fiction; distorted and exaggerated personal problems; amateurish sociology and psychology; incident and language that seem to have been dragged in for shock value and are not an integral, enlightening element of plot or character. And even the most innovative ideas can become shopworn cliches.

Let us not be panicked into reverting to the early concept

that librarians, as the arbiters of morality, should control materials provided for their public.

Let us, instead, use reason, not emotion, in selection. Let us recognize that we are living in a changing world with changing values and crucial problems and that a book about today, to be honest, must reflect this world.

Notes

1. Quoted and paraphrased from "Standards for Criticism for Children's Literature" by John Rowe Townsend. *Top of the News*, June 1971, p. 380.

2. Fadiman, Clifton. "Children's Reading" in *Party of One: Selected Writings of Clifton Fadiman*. World, 1955.

3. Paraphrased from "Sexuality in Books for Children" by Barbara Wersba. *Library Journal*, February 15, 1973, p. 620.

4. Paraphrased from "Real Adventure Belongs to Us" by Ivan Southall. *Top of the News*, June 1974, pp. 383-384.

"THE KIDS KNOW WHEN THEY'RE BEING CONNED"*

By Enid Olson

Here we are again: English teachers talking to English teachers about censorship. ("What did the minister preach about?" "Sin." "What did he say?" "He's against it.") It's like sending Clark MacGregor to Lockheed to tell them why they should vote for Richard Nixon. But, here we are _again._ For, as Jim Lape said when he asked me to be a consultant on this program, "The problem hasn't gone away." Or, as Ken Donelson says in _The Students' Right to Read_ (NCTE, 1971), "The fight against censorship is a continuing series of skirmishes, not a pitched battle leading to a final victory over censorship" (p. 1).

But here we are again: English teachers talking to ourselves or to each other, when there are so many other people we should be talking with. The librarians and we have done pretty well in exchanging meetings at NCTE and ALA. Occasionally, we have talked about censorship with organizations of school administrators. Less often, we've met with school board associations to discuss the problem. At times, but not often enough, we've shared ideas with parent-teacher congresses, likewise with the NEA and the AFT, though both of those organizations are now as vitally and actively concerned as NCTE has been.

But we should be talking with associations of newspaper editors, booksellers, directors of radio and television stations, with bar associations and church synods. (National boards of parish education now and then find local congregations censoring church curriculum materials.)

Building a national or even a regional awareness of the dangers of censorship among all these groups would help to marshall unified responses to would-be censors whenever, wherever, and however they attack. If we don't yet do it nationally, through our organizations, we should do it locally. Again, _The Students' Right to Read_ says: "... No community is so small that it lacks readers who will support the English teachers in defending books.... Un-

---

*Reprinted by permission of the author and publisher from _English Journal_ (May 1973), 779-783, 816.

happily, English teachers too often fail to seek out these people and to cultivate their goodwill and support before censorship strikes" (p. 15). We can explore this further during the discussion period if anyone wishes. Now let's look at the topic of this program.

Implications of the past. What do they mean now? In 1965 a school librarian from Alaska told me they had had no censorship incidents there. "We work so hard to buy books to put in our classrooms and libraries," she said, "that no one is about to take them out." Yet, since then, Alaska has learned what would-be censors try to do.

That same year I met with an NDEA institute for school librarians in Oklahoma. The director said that political censorship had not yet reached most of the school libraries in the South and Southwest, but he could see it coming, particularly from forces of the far right. He spoke truly. In the past three years, just from records in my own clipping files, nine states in the South and Southwest have experienced one or more censorship incidents each. Regionally, the East came second, with six states involved. During the same time, five Midwestern states got into censorship news, and two in the Far West. Twenty-two states with censorship incidents that reached the national press! And that's only in a private, unofficial count.

Implications of the present. At times I think the situation might improve. Court decisions have been granting more student rights. The student underground press has been wresting some freedom in which to flourish, with concomitant benefits to regular student publications. Dress codes are being abolished. It seems that the few schools still foolish enough to have them are trying to use them as a weapon against minority children; that, too, though painful now, will pass away. Teacher organizations have been bargaining more successfully for the rights of individual teachers than in the past.

But we can't relax. This coming year several state legislatures will be considering abolishing teacher tenure laws. Our Federal administration seems to condone, and at least must acknowledge, widespread surveillance of Congressmen, students, immigrants, dissenters, any individuals who may simply "disagree" openly. The USIA in 1969 barred from its overseas libraries books which raised questions about American policy. The IRS in 1970 tried to confiscate and search public library circulation records. Also in 1970 the House Internal Securities Committee blacklisted sixty-five "radical" campus speakers. The Justice Department in 1971 sought to stop publication of the Pentagon Papers, and the House Commerce Committee recommended that CBS be cited for contempt in regard to its documentary "The Selling of the Pentagon."

Our courts can jail both Angela Davis, teacher, and Peter Bridge, reporter. Our prisons apparently have more political prisoners in them than felons. The present U.S. Supreme Court has an erratic record--granting demonstration rights on Capitol Hill, yes, but also requiring reporters and Congressmen to reveal their confidential sources of information while extending executive privilege to that branch of government. Just this month it refused to review a school censorship case in which a book was banned. And we don't know what implications the proposed mini-Court, if established, will bring.

Apparently, to judge from the current climate, our government does not believe that "great power demands great restraint by those who hold it" (Publisher's Weekly, June 1, 1970, p. 49), or, as Stuart Little has said, "... to be hospitable to hostile opinion is an even more convincing demonstration of power than to promote one's own" (Saturday Review, September 12, 1970, p. 96). Repressiveness in government is contagious among the grass roots, especially after a landslide election. Our government would do well to heed the editor of Al Ahram in Cairo: "Unless we allow all ideas to be expressed freely--unless we allow this ferment, conflict, dialog--we will remain a society in a test tube" (Edward R. F. Sheehan, "The Second Most Important Man in Egypt," New York Times Magazine, August 22, 1971, p. 12).

No, the future does not look good. Yet, we must continue to fight the good fight. Why? For the sake of our students, the real victims of censorship, as Donelson says (p. 10). He also warns us that English teachers under censorship "are placed in the morally and intellectually untenable position of lying to their students about the nature and condition of mankind" (p. 9).

I worked for two years in a commercial publishing house, where I soon discovered a most censorious atmosphere imposed from the top. Its officers were afraid--afraid of ideas, afraid of trying anything they had not tried before. I found that they were afraid of people, especially new people, those whom they themselves had not trained since early adulthood. Yet that firm should have felt all the security which money, prestige, popularity, and political clout could buy. A curious state of affairs, and we might well wonder if their fear arose from trying to fool all of the people all of the time.

This publisher produced educational materials. A teacher told me one day why his students rejected those materials. They resented, he said, the smug, all-knowing tone, the loading of questions, and the assumption that each question had only one answer. "This is no good," they said; "there's no room to discuss anything." Then he added, "The kids know when they're being conned."

We talk about the credibility gap. I like better the term used by a former director general of the Vietnam Press Bureau (before 1962)--the "gap of truth": an opening in an authoritarian pattern of thought control by increasing exposure to other sources of information. The kids know when there's a gap of truth.

John Leonard in the New York Times Book Review (March 1, 1970, p. 34) commended the editors of two short story books for young people--John Simon for his Fourteen for Now (Harper, 1970) and L. M. Schulman for his The Loners (Macmillan, 1970). "Neither," he wrote, "has compromised with quality in these selections. Which is admirable, for quality means ambiguity, and if there is one thing the Now Generation needs today ... it is a decent dose of ambiguity.... It would be preposterous to pretend that our adolescent subculture consists wholly of innocent mushrooms. Anxious, yes; innocent, no ... the sense of ambiguity, a prerequisite for wisdom, must be transcended, not denied...."

Three years ago hundreds of teenagers were surveyed for their opinions on reading, viewing, listening (Nancy Gilbert, "What Young People Think," Ossining [N.Y.] Citizen Register, September 11 and 18, 1969). Eighty-one per cent of those surveyed claimed to have seen hard-core pornography; of those, 79 per cent claimed it had absolutely no effect on their morals. One third of the boys said it amused them; 20 per cent said it bored them. Of newspapers, one teenager said, "What I want is the truth ... the straight publication of facts, not some reporter's interpretation of them." Another said, "I'd like to hear radio discussions of abortion, drugs, smoking, alcohol, the things that pertain to us." Are these young people afraid of ideas? Hardly. Censorship would con them, and they know it.

By way of further illustration, here is another area in which children and adolescents are way ahead of adults. That is in the acceptance of death and its presentation in literature, theater, television.

When Rod Steiger was filming in Spain in 1971, he told interviewer Bernard Drew this (about our adult mentality): Funny, sex is the only subject you can discuss on the screen today. Funny that you can discuss sex but not atomic energy; that in an age where total destruction is possible at any moment, you can't even talk about it ("Showtime," March 24, 1971). About the same time, a minister told a gathering of the clergy in Iowa that "Dying used to be discussed in our society, but sex was obscene. Now sex is openly discussed and dying is obscene."

I thought of these comments the day an editor of a reader for children changed a story's unhappy ending to a happy one. "There's enough unhappiness in the world without making children read about it," she explained.

But do you recall Flora Arnstein's article in the September 1972 English Journal, "'I Met Death One Clumsy Day'"? Remember how she wrote: "During all but the last two years [of my teaching] few poems, at most four or five, have been written on war and death, although the early years of my teaching were inclusive of World War II.... In contrast, during these last two years more than fifty-two poems have been written on these subjects." And the title of her article was a line from a ten-year-old's original poem.

What do we do when we use only stories with happy endings, even for the young? Don't we end up telling them that literature doesn't reflect their life, that they must be out of the mainstream because for characters in books things always turn out well? Aren't we conning them?

How can we pretend that children don't know death. When the average eleventh-grader has known the war in Vietnam during all his school years? And the elementary school child and the junior high student have known it all their lifetimes? Isn't death real to children in such disparate places as Birmingham, Detroit, Corning, Rapid City? When death is not even an act of God as it comes to Emmett Till, age 14, or when a North Carolina jury convicts of first-degree murder and condemns to death Marie Hill, age 15? When Angela Davis says of her people: "We buy caskets more often than any other U.S. citizens ... our death rate is higher and earlier, and shrouds have now become teenage wearing apparel" (If They Come in the Morning [New American Library, 1971], p. 281).

Paula Fox wrote in Saturday Review (September 19, 1970, p. 34):

> The major fact of life has already been learned by any five-year-old, though he lacks the self-consciousness to utter it: Life is hard. It's a struggle, as well as a joy, to learn to see, to hear, to walk, to speak, to explain oneself.... Read the poems of black children, poor children; look at drawings by the abandoned and orphaned; read the ordinary compositions of any random group of fifth-graders. They already know about disappointment and dread, about longing and hope.... [But] if what is taught is banal and fatuous, a child will learn to be banal and fatuous too, even at the expense of his hard-won experience. Perhaps it is at the point where a child learns to dissimulate that he at last joins the "grown-ups."

The kids *do* know when they're being conned!

A most troublesome area for the teacher, though, is the problem of what to do with hate literature or literature laced with racial or ethnic or religious prejudice, either advertently or by interpretation. Here is where all my personal convictions against censorship begin to shatter, for I want to take all "hate lit" out and burn it.

But even here the lines blur. We don't all react with the same sensitivities. And who is any of us to tell another what he should or should not be sensitive to? We're familiar with long-time feelings against *Adventures of Huckleberry Finn*, for instance, and The Merchant of Venice and Little Black Sambo. More recently we've become aware of such cases as the Italian-American Civil Rights League and The Godfather, the Anti-Defamation League of B'Nai B'Rith and Lansky by Hank Messick, and the Equal Employment Opportunity Commission's ruling against Polish jokes.

A few years ago, two Indian women of Minnesota, working through the Duluth Civil Rights Committee and the American Indian Historical Society, asked the Minnesota State Board of Education to withdraw from use in the state's schools a textbook found offensive and derogatory to American Indians. During the discussion, a State Committee member remarked that the Committee goes to great pains to avoid being censors, to avoid telling teachers what to teach and what texts to use. The American Civil Liberties Union, at the same time, took the position of opposing censorship--and the Indians--in the interests of free speech. The Indian Historical Society commented: "There is no trouble in getting racist literature into the schools. The problem is getting the truth into the school books, and into the minds of school children" (Rupert Costo, ed. Textbooks and the American Indian [Indian Historian Press, 1970], p. 235). The State Board finally agreed to withdraw the book.

Teachers who want to fight censorship and who don't want to offend minority group readers may feel caught in a dilemma. In *selecting* books, how can they avoid charges of censorship? Will they omit so many books from their lists that their students end up with pabulum as surely as if the teachers censored against politics and sex?

I struggled with this question for years. Now I have come across a statement which I think resolves the dilemma. It appears inside the front cover of Textbooks and the American Indian and is written by the American Indian Historical Society. It says:

> Everyone has the right to his opinion. A person has also the right to be wrong. But a textbook has no right to be wrong, or to evade the truth, falsify history, or insult and malign a whole race of people. That is what the textbooks do.
>
> There is a difference between a book for general readership, and one accepted for classroom use. In the first case, the individual has a choice, and this choice we must protect. The student has no choice. He is compelled to study from an approved book, and in this case, we have a right to insist upon truth, accuracy, and objectivity.

Here we have some guidelines. If a course uses a basic text, in which editorial exposition and comment accompany literary selections or original documents, and that text is required study for all students in the course, such a text is the textbook that "has no right to be wrong." We should submit those textbooks to the most rigorous scrutiny, making sure they conform not to mere opinion but to documented facts and research findings. We should watch especially for textbook treatment of minority groups, knowing that the majority has had its day in court for generations. Students should have access to more than one text in a subject if need be in order to find counterbalance of ideas.

Regarding literary works and supplementary texts and readings, the solution lies in more reading, not less; in greater availability of many books and materials, not in curtailment. Because only with more reading does the mind began to sift and weigh and determine for itself. Only with continued and wider reading and viewing does the mind stay open to receive new ideas, to assimilate, or to reject.

If teachers and schools grant to students' minds such trust, they will, for today and for tomorrow, earn the respect of their students. What more honorable reward?

PART VII

MINORITIES IN YA LITERATURE

(the outsiders ...)

EDITOR'S NOTE

Somewhere in the sixties we woke up to the realization that minorities had been grossly misrepresented--when represented at all--in literature for young people. That situation has improved considerably. Caren Dybek's "Black Literature for Adolescents" illustrates the distance traversed and draws attention to the fact that "the most successful books do not present their characters in the perspective of black-white conflicts.... Today, black characters are looking into _themselves_, rediscovering their mythology, redefining their history, celebrating their language, their music, their art, their ethos."[1]

The analysis by Kraus of some of the earlier, well-intentioned but unrealistic young adult books about Blacks serves as a reminder that until recently it was usually the conflict between races which gave these books their focus. Kraus shows how most of these books "opted for accommodation" and delivered simplistic messages.

In her _Image of the Black in Children's Fiction_, Dorothy Broderick goes somewhat further, pointing out that "the major problem with the books ... is that they personalize the race issue instead of recognizing it as the social-economic-political problem it is."[2] She calls for books in which "the battles being fought must be those that are being fought--not one black against one white bigot, but the black community fighting the structure of white society."[3] According to Broderick, reviewers of young people's books about Blacks must read widely in adult literature by Blacks in order to develop an awareness of current attitudes and therefore the ability to spot the false and simplistic in books for youth.

Her point about the need for reviewers to become more sensitive has been made ad nauseam, but is particularly well illustrated by Alice Brooks McGuire's selection of reviews of _Sounder_ and _The Cay_.[4] While many critics praised these books as fine literature with admirable moral values, others found them racist and offensive. McGuire offers some criteria for evaluation and agrees that materials about minorities should be reviewed by members of the minority. But she "deplore[s] the possibility of banning books as unacceptable for certain readers, especially if they have been subjected to biased criticism."[5]

Augusta Baker notes that _Sounder_ and _The Slave Dancer_ have been attacked for their lack of militancy, but goes on to say:

> Courage is shown in many ways and by many different reactions under stress. Will we deny children books about the past, books about the ugliness, the humiliation, the cruelty, and the destruction of human dignity that existed during slavery days when the Ku Klux Klan rode openly and often? I hope not--for all children, black and white, deserve the truth.[6]

This controversy about the Black image in literature for young people of course extends to the treatment of other minorities. Articles on women and gays in literature for young adults are reprinted in this section, but similar ones on the treatment of Native, Mexican, Puerto Rican and other American ethnic groups might have been included. Reading periodicals devoted to the literature of specific groups and the _Interracial Books for Children Bulletin_ in addition to the usual reviewing sources is one way to increase one's sensitivity to the issues.

Notes

1. See p. 245-246.

2. Dorothy Broderick. _Image of the Black in Children's Fiction._ Bowker, 1973. p. 179.

3. _Ibid._, p. 180.

4. Alice Brooks McGuire. "The Minority Image in Books for Youth: Evolution and Evaluation" in _Reading, Children's Books, and Our Pluralistic Society_ ed. by Harold Tanyzer and Jean Karl, International Reading Association, 1972. p. 55-57.

5. _Ibid._, p. 59.

6. Augusta Baker. "The Changing Image of the Black in Children's Literature," _Horn Book_, February 1975, p. 88.

FROM STEPPIN STEBBINS TO SOUL BROTHERS: RACIAL STRIFE IN ADOLESCENT FICTION*

By W. Keith Kraus

The recent plethora of adolescent novels about racial strife appears to be the culmination of an evolutionary pattern that has its parallel in the civil rights struggle that began in the early 1960s. Prior to this time adolescent novels were almost exclusively oriented toward a white middle-class audience. Even as late as 1965 there was an "almost complete omission of Negroes from books for children." (Nancy Larrick, "The All White World of Children's Books," Saturday Review, September 11, 1965, p. 63.) Those books which did exist tended to be typical adolescent romance novels except that the hero or heroine was black. No racial prejudice existed and the protagonist succeeded in a white world without any real problems. "The protagonist is usually female, and an attractive, understanding, safe boyfriend of the same color hovers in the background and makes unnecessary any worries about miscegenation." (Susan Peters, "The Black Experience in Books," Top of the News, June 1969, p. 386.)

Typical of the type of innocent racial romance novel available during the 1950s are Hope Newell's A Cap for Mary Ellis and a sequel, Mary Ellis, Student Nurse. In these two books, which are basically career novels, the heroine is presented with integration situations that are never fully examined.

In A Cap for Mary Ellis, a black teenage girl begins her first year at an all-white nursing school in upstate New York, but for all practical purposes, her color is of no consequence to the plot, and the "problems" she faces are how to give a bed bath and take a patient's temperature.

Mary Ellis Stebbins lives in Harlem, but the description of her mother's apartment is hardly typical.

> The Stebbins lived in one of six Harlem apartment houses grouped around a tree-shaded garden. Steppin had moved them there soon after he got his first job as a professional dancer. That was 'way back when Mary Ellis

---

*Reprinted by permission of the author and publisher from Arizona English Bulletin (April 1976), 154-160.

> was in grade school, but she had never gotten over the wonder of these sun-drenched rooms with the cleverly built-in cupboards, bookcases, and dining nook. Above all, she loved the modern bathroom, immaculate in pale-blue tile porcelain and gleaming nickel fixtures. (Hope Newell, A Cap for Mary Ellis, NY: Berkley, 1963, p. 14.)

Mary Ellis is persuaded to train at Woodycrest because she will "be opening a door to others of her race." Once there she makes friends among the other students and enjoys her work. She is nick-named "Tater" because she is like a "little brown potato," and the only girl who seems to snub her is Ada Belle Briggs, a slothful, grumpy girl from "the South." Later, Mary Ellis becomes home-sick and decides to leave; however, when a food poisoning epidemic breaks out she "comes-to-realize" she is needed and goes on to become "capped" as a nursing student by novel's end. The only hint of racial problems is an allusion to a restaurant that "serves colored people without any fuss or bother" and the seldom-seen Ada Belle Briggs, who is disliked by everyone at the school and eventually flunks out and leaves in a huff. Actually, the kind of racism which appears in the novel is the unconscious racism on the part of the author when she names her characters "Tater" and "Steppin Stebbins" without a hint of the pejorative nature of these terms.

Occasionally, a rare book did appear before 1960 that directly confronted the problem of racial integration. Certainly one of the first adolescent novels to treat this theme was Call Me Charley, by Jesse Jackson published in 1945. This simply written novel tells the story of a Negro boy whose family moves to an all-white suburb from the "Bottoms," where the "railroad tracks run right across the streets." The protagonist encounters racial slurs from other boys, is ignored by the English teacher in the casting of the junior high play, and refused admittance to the community swimming pool. But in the end everyone does a guilty turnabout as the most bigoted boy is converted and Charley is accepted. (Later books by Jesse Jackson follow the same character through his high school graduation to an Olympic tryout. These sequels are essentially sports books for boys and the protagonist's color has little to do with any of the stories.) Charley's mother provides the theme of the novel when she states: "'As long as you work hard and try to do right ... you will always find some good people like Doc Cunningham or Tom and his folks marching along with you in the right path. And fellows like George may come along too, sooner or later.'" (Jesse Jackson, Call Me Charley, NY: Dell, 1945, p. 156.) The happy ending is unrealistic and forced and the protagonist is somewhat unbelievable in his easy acceptance of the situation; still, the book is a milestone in that it is one of the first novels to confront the problem of racial strife.

One of the more realistic adolescent novels about racial problems to appear in the 1950s is Hard to Tackle by Gilbert Douglas. Basically a boy's sports book, the story is about a Negro football player who encounters difficulties when his parents move into an all-white neighborhood. The story is told from the point of view of Clint Thomas, a white student, who encourages Jeff Washington to try out for the football team. He organizes team members to help repair the Washington house after the windows are broken, and finally when the house is partially burned the neighborhood feels sorry for the black family and offers them some measure of acceptance. At different times in the novel, Jeff Washington talks to Clint about the prejudice he encounters and this serves to present the plight of Negroes struggling to advance in a racist society. At a rally held by the anti-housing group, the white minister gives an impassioned speech about brotherhood and the team coach expresses the novel's theme during a locker room talk after he has kicked four boys off the team because of their attitude.

> 'I'm glad you're not quitting, Jeff. But whether you quit or not, the others aren't coming back. Not while I'm coach. The majority of fellows are on your side, Jeff. You're one of the few Negro students in our school. You're so much in the minority that it looks as if only white boys are capable of cruelty and prejudice. But deep down, people are pretty much the same everywhere. There are people of your race who have the same faults as some of us. So don't go judging all of us by what a few do. That's not fair, either.' (Gilbert Douglas, Hard to Tackle, NY: Dell, 1971, p. 138. The novel was first published in hardcover in 1956.)

What makes this novel more realistic than some other books published at this time is that there are no quick character conversions to bring about a satisfying ending. The Vanderpool family, who lead the opposition, become resigned to the situation but are unchanged in their attitude to Negroes, and the houseburning works to make the community realize what racism can lead to even though as individuals the people remain the same. In short, no easy solutions are offered in the book.

But for the most part adolescent novels about racial strife published during the 1950s opted for accommodation. In Hold Fast to Your Dreams a Negro girl works to become a ballet dancer and her talent alone overcomes white racism. (In a biographical note the author, Catherine Blanton, states that "if we could know all the people of the world as our next door neighbors, our problems could be quickly solved in friendly disagreement.") In South Town the white racist reforms and a white doctor states that "progress is being made all the time.... In spite of what happened last week, things are better now than they were; and in some places, I understand, you might be very comfortable, and the children could grow up to forget this." (Lorenz Graham, South Town, NY: NAL, 1958, p. 132.) Thus, the message for Negroes in these novels tends to be "pull yourself up by the bootstraps" and whites will grant acceptance; for whites the moral is to treat people as individuals and learn that "they're just as good as we are."

But then in the 1960s--and probably tied as much to the civil rights movement as to changes taking place in adolescent fiction--a number of novels appeared that dealt more directly with racial problems. After 1966 as high as "19.5 per cent of the recommended fiction and nonfiction books contained some concern for racial strife," (Janet K. McReynolds, "A Study of Common Aspects Found in Selected Literature for Adolescents, 1966 to 1970," unpublished Ph.D. dissertation, Southern Illinois U., 1971, p. 89.) but still many of these novels were unrealistic and simplistic in their solutions. One of the most popular 1960 adolescent-problem novels that treats an integration theme is A Question of Harmony. Still, this book is essentially an adolescent romance with a superimposed racial incident. Fully one half of the novel deals with a white high school girl's "problems" of dating a doctor's son. The story is set in "Valley City," a midwestern city with all the trappings of small town life. Jeanne Blake, the girl of the story, meets Dave Carpenter at a picnic, but she is forced to call her father when two of the boys begin drinking.

> 'Two of the boys were awful,' she said. 'It was bad enough when they started to spike their Cokes, but then they tried to make me drink some of it too.'
> 'Irresponsible young louts!' her father grumbled.
> Tears stung Jeanne's eyes. 'I don't suppose I'll ever hear from him again after this mess.'
> 'I shouldn't think you'd mind,' her father said.
> But I do mind, she thought unhappily. I liked him. (Gretchen Sprague, A Question of Harmony, NY: NAL, 1969, p. 18.)

After that the couple go for butternut sundaes, play badminton together, share the thrill of going to new classes during the fall of their senior year, and participate in classical music concerts. Jeanne Blake plays the cello while her budding boyfriend plays the piano, and much of the story revolves around the description of orchestra rehearsals and the challenge of moving up to "first chair." Major decisions are what pieces to play for scholarship auditions, and the big dance and the big concert are equally climactic scenes at the end of the novel.

The racial issue is introduced when Jeanne, her boyfriend, and Mel Johnson begin a classical trio. Mel is a Negro who plays the violin and is also the star football player on his high school team. They are asked by the Garden Club to play at a dinner at the local hotel, and after they finish they go to the hotel dining room for chocolate eclairs. There they are refused service, and at first they do not understand why.

> 'I must ask you to leave.' the hostess repeated.
> 'But why?' Jeanne demanded.
> Two or three boys left their booths and strolled, with ill-concealed curiosity, past the end of the aisle.
> Dave turned his head and looked at Jeanne. 'Don't

> you know?'
>
> 'It's me, Jeanne,' Mel said gently.
>
> Jeanne stared at him in astonished silence. Presently she became aware that her mouth was open. She closed it. Mel. He's a Negro. I'd forgotten. (Sprague, p. 91.)

This leads to a spontaneous sit-in by the three teenagers and the manager is called. He wants to avoid a public scene, but still he is adamant that the group not be served. A newspaper reporter takes pictures and Jeanne's parents are called. At this point Jeanne learns about racial segregation. The Blake family "hasn't met any Negroes" and Jeanne "never even thought of Valley City's having a Negro section"; now, Jeanne believes she is snubbed at school simply for having taken part in the sit-in.

The hotel manager is secretary of the Civil Club and he is in charge of selecting judges for the music auditions which determine the town's college scholarships. At the restaurant the manager had hinted that Mel's father would lose his janitor's job, and now the group is sure he will see that Mel fails to win an award. But a number of the townspeople side with the teenagers and stop going to the hotel for Sunday brunch. The paper has a supporting editorial, and eventually the owner writes a letter of apology to the three musicians.

On the day of the scholarship auditions Mel not only wins a scholarship but the hotel management adds a special five-hundred dollar award to go with it. (The hotel manager himself presents the scholarship gift.) At first Mel wonders if he should accept the award, reasoning that "he gave it to me because I'm a colored boy and all of a sudden it's good business to be nice to colored boys." But Dr. Carpenter persuades Mel the offer might have been given in good faith because "he wants to encourage string music."

The one theme in the novel is that people should listen more to each other and not jump to conclusions, all of which neatly sidesteps the racial issue. But the fact is that Mel was not served because of his color and the hotel gave him the award because it was indeed "good business." The novel's central theme is that racial problems can be solved easily with a little trust and understanding, hardly in keeping with events in the story. Earlier Jeanne believed she was being snubbed by people for her participation in the sit-in, but she learns that her girlfriend had really been upset over a boy, that the couple who canceled her as a babysitter really had a sick youngster, and that her former boyfriend was not upset over her behavior. "Nobody took you at your word," Dr. Carpenter tells Mel at the end of the novel, "and there's where all the trouble started." This advice is offered as the all-too-neat solution for racial strife and dating problems as well.

In the final chapter the novel shifts gears and presents a different didactic message about a "fast crowd" leading to trouble. As the group is sitting around the Carpenter kitchen there is a crash outside and everyone rushes out to discover that the "irresponsible young louts" from the picnic have had a car accident. Dr. Carpenter saves a girl's life with a new medical technique he has just read about, and then everyone returns to the house. The racial problem is forgotten with this final piece of unbelievable melodrama, and a few pages later the story returns to its romantic plot as Jeanne receives her first kiss from Dave. ("Warm and gentle, his lips touched hers. Roman candles; skyrockets. Drums beating, and the far, soft music of flutes.") Thus, the novel hardly does more than mention racial segregation and gives an oversimplified impression about how easily the problem can be solved.

One of the few adolescent novels to treat interracial dating also appeared in the early 1960's. (M. E. Kerr is currently completing an adolescent novel on this subject which should be available this year.) Anything for a Friend is about a white teenager who is tricked into asking a Negro girl to the senior prom. The situation is dealt with humorously and the white protagonist's predicaments are reminiscent of Max Shulman's books. The novel is not so much concerned about integration as it is with such perpetual teenage problems as the generation gap and the search for identity. But the novel does try for a tragic ending when the protagonist finds he lacks the courage to continue his relationship with the girl. In a sense both these books could be called racial novels for a 1960s white adolescent audience--arrived at by adolescents acting as the conscience for the community.

Because of the popularity of A Question of Harmony in the Xerox Education Secondary Book Club other novels were offered in paperback that dealt with racial strife. A few of these novels were told from the point of view of Negroes and provide "a valid portrayal of the values and life styles of American ethnic minorities." (G. Robert Carlsen, Books and the Teen-age Reader, NY: Bantam, 1971, p. 209.) For the most part novels with a Negro as narrator did not sell well, but this is perhaps due to the nature of the book club's adolescent audience. Their market is predominantly small town, suburban and rural districts, and Catholic schools that lack black/minority representation. (Information in a personal letter from Earl A. French, former editor of Xerox Education Publications Secondary Book Clubs, March 9, 1974.)

Beginning in the 1970s adolescent novels appeared that treated the black ethnic experience itself and in which "young characters ... define their own world and establish their own values, often at variance with society's demands." (Caren Dybek, "Black Literature for Adolescents," English Journal, January 1974, p. 64.) One of the more popular of these books that use a black protagonist is The Soul Brothers and Sister Lou. In this book fourteen-year-old Louretta Hawkins lives with her mother and seven brothers and sisters in a northern ghetto. She shares her bed with two sisters and the family subsists on an older brother's post office job. Louretta's father has left home and her mother is proud of the fact that they have never had to go on welfare. In any number of ways the girl's ethnic experience is recounted, even to the food the family eats.

> Louretta didn't mind having beans and greens for supper because Momma flavored them with cured neck bones that gave them a delicious meaty taste. She thought they were lucky to have meat once a week; most of the Southside kids, especially the ones on Welfare, never had meat at all, except the nasty, cardboard-tasting canned meat they gave away at the Surplus Food Center. (Kristin Hunter, The Soul Brothers and Sister Lou, NY: Avon, 1969, p. 27.)

Louretta has an older sister with an illegitimate child who is cared for by Louretta's mother, but her situation is really not a social stigma in Southside culture. Hair straightening is mentioned as well as the meaning of the various shades of darkness among Negroes. Louretta has light skin and slightly red hair, and some of the neighborhood boys imply that her real father was white. (It is later explained there is "white blood" in her father's family dating from slave times.) The handclapping and "Amen" evangelism of the black Baptist Church is introduced into the novel when the Reverend Mamie delivers a eulogy for one of Louretta's friends. Unlike the Mary Ellis nurse stories and A Question of Harmony, this novel is realistic in terms of its depiction of a typical black family recently relocated in a northern city. The author, Kristin Hunter, has said she "tried to show some of the positive values existing in the so-called ghetto" in an attempt to "confirm young black people in their frail but growing belief in their own self-worth." ("The Soul Brothers: Background of a Juvenile," Publishers Weekly, May 27, 1968, p. 31.)

Louretta's brother opens a printing shop and Lou persuades him to let her friends use a portion of the building as a clubhouse. Lou and her "gang" meet at the shop where they compose and sing soul music. They are helped by a famous blues singer and by some of the teachers from their school; however, a number of the boys are still more interested in fighting the Avengers, a rival street gang. One of the boys is particularly rebellious and his hatred is directed toward all whites. His desire is to print a radical paper denouncing the white racist establishment.

The novel's villain is Officer Lafferty, a brutal white policeman who constantly harrasses Lou and her friends.

> In school they taught that the policeman was your friend. Louretta and all the other Southside pupils smiled wisely whenever a teacher said this, because they knew better. They knew that all policemen were not *their* friends, even if they might be the friends of children on the other side of town, and that some policemen, like Officer Lafferty, were their worst enemies. Officer Lafferty's favorite sport was to catch groups of Southside boys in out-of-the-way places like vacant buildings and

> alleys, where there would be no witnesses to what he did. He would call them names and accuse them of committing crimes, just to provoke them into saying something back or hitting him or running away. If they ran away he would shoot them. If they did anything else, he would beat them up with his club and take them to the police station and charge them with resisting arrest and assaulting an officer. (Hunter, p. 11.)

When Lou and her group hold a dance at the print shop, Lafferty and a group of policemen break in and search the members. In the ensuing scuffle one of the group is shot by a policeman and both Lou and her brother William become more militant in their attitudes.

> 'Lou,' William said seriously, 'I learned something tonight. These cops can't tell the difference between a respectable Negro and an outlaw. They treated me just as rough as everybody else. So that makes us all outlaws, at least in their eyes.' (Hunter, p. 110.)

For a brief time Lou decides to join a black African group which denounces all whites, but she realizes this approach is filled with too much hate and is merely another form of racism.

Up to this point the novel is honest and uncompromising in its depiction of a particular segment of Negro existence; however, the ending is unrealistic and unsatisfactory. At the funeral of the boy killed at the dance the members of the Cheerful Baptist Church sing a "lament for Jethro," a part of which is aired on an evening television news show. The next day representatives of a musical recording company call at the club house and offer the group a contract with a "nice little sum in advance for each of you, and more if the record is a success." The recording representatives ask the kids to "please run through the number you did at the church. The one about the boy who died." Eagerly the group sings and plays "Lament for Jethro," and the Soul Brothers and Sister Lou are born.

In a concluding chapter readers learn that the record is a hit and that Lou is banking her money, except for enough to buy her mother a washer and dryer. The most incorrigible member of the gang begins "saving every cent for college" as he unbelievably turns from "an ardent revolutionary ... to an enthusiastic booster of business, free enterprise and capitalism." (Hunter, p. 187.) And to complete the fairy tale ending it is revealed that Officer Lafferty has been suspended.

In a sense it could be argued that The Soul Brothers and Sister Lou is no different from other "safe" adolescent romance novels. Lou is basically a "nice" girl who studies hard, gets good grades, and dreams of going to college. "In fact, she's so WASP-ish inside, one gets the impression that she wouldn't eat a slice of watermelon if you paid her." (Nancy Mack, "Youth Books: They Aren't What They Used to Be or Are They?" Hartford Currant,

July 8, 1973, p. 6.) Further, the all-too-convenient ending is used to solve the novel's racial problems and provide a happy and successful future for the story's characters. Still, this novel honestly depicts lower class ghetto life and shows the conditions which can produce racial hatred. In this sense the novel is much more mature and realistic in its approach to racial strife than most of its predecessors.

Recently a number of books have been promoted and sold through teenage book clubs which were not written specifically as adolescent novels. For the most part these are more realistic in their treatment of the black ethnic experience than are traditional adolescent novels. One of the most successful of these new books is Daddy Was a Number Runner, by Louise Meriwether. Here life in Harlem is depicted as degrading and unfair. There is no escape from the world of perversion in which twelve-year-old Francie Goffin finds herself. Good grades in school, obedience to parents and the law, avoidance of cursing all fail to help Francie in a culture filled with rapists, gang fighters, homosexuals, and rioters. She encounters men who give her nickels to feel her legs and who pay her a quarter to drop her panties. She is involved in an attempted rape, witnesses another rape, and is acquainted with a street whore. In a foreword James Baldwin calls the novel "the American dream in black-face, Horatio Alger revealed, the American success story with a price tag showing." (Louise Meriwether, Daddy Was a Number Runner, NY: Pyramid, 1971, p. 7.) In the end Francie is on the street in front of her tenement and we hear her spell out the truth of the story. "We was all poor and black and apt to stay that way, and that was that." Even the final word of the novel, "shit," denotes Francie's despair and anguish that will be present for the rest of her life.

Among the most recent novels to deal with racial strife that is being sold by the Xerox and Scholastic Book Clubs is A Hero Ain't Nothin' But a Sandwich, by Alice Childress. This account of a thirteen-year-old boy hooked on drugs is told from different viewpoints by people who affect the protagonist's life in some way. (One chapter is written from the point of view of a drug pusher.) Although the book is well written, there is very little "story" to it and much of the novel is an indictment of schools, teachers, and social workers for their lack of concern and knowledge of the drug problem. At the end of the novel the protagonist is saved by a black father figure who is "supporting three adults, one child, and the United States government." (Alice Childress, A Hero Ain't Nothin' But a Sandwich, NY: Avon, 1973, p. 126.) The implication is that rather than white do-gooders or black militants, love and sincere concern are needed to rescue boys like Benjie Johnson.

It will be interesting to see the direction of future adolescent novels that treat racial strife. So far these books have paralleled the civil rights struggle from the 1950s to the present, and it is difficult to guess what subjects are left to be explored. (It is possible that events like the recent Boston school controversy might be the subject of fiction.) What is hoped is that the better novels now available will be used in school classrooms and made a part of library collections. Because many of the books use generalizations and stereotypes, it is necessary for adolescents--especially white adolescents--to read as wide a range of books as possible. Although this approach may not bring about any lasting solutions it is at least possible that the nature of the problem of racial strife may be understood.

BLACK LITERATURE FOR ADOLESCENTS*

By Caren Dybek

> We now know that we are, in spite of the racists and the politicians, of the false prophets, and the hustlers, embarked on a voyage of self-discovery. --Orde Coombs

"The last thing the English Journal needs in 1974 is another article on Afro-American literature." "Black studies programs are already established--or not going to be." "Black literature is a dead issue; it's time for other things."

One could be comfortable with those assertions if it were not for the fact that black authors have, in the last five years, been producing fiction, non-fiction, poetry, and drama of astounding virtuosity and energy. This bibliography begins to explore an important development in literature: black literature with direct appeal to adolescents. Many of the most interesting books mentioned here were written specifically for adolescents; others have a more general audience. What they all have in common is that they were written by black writers dealing with the black experience.

If any generalization can be made from this sampling, it is that the most successful books do not present their characters in the perspective of black-white conflicts. In the introduction to What We Must See: Young Black Story Tellers, Orde Coombs makes a statement that is applicable to much of the writing of young black authors today:

> In none of these short stories is the specter of white oppression ... more than merely menacing ... these brothers and sisters have gone beyond terror to find love ... a celebration, as it were, of the infinite variety of the black life style.

These books are quite different from the novels Jesse Jackson wrote in the '50s and '60s about black teenagers trying to succeed in a white world. Today, black characters are looking into

*Reprinted by permission of the author and publisher from English Journal, 63:1 (January 1974), 64-67.

themselves, rediscovering their mythology, redefining their history, celebrating their language, their music, their art, their ethos. Writers like June Jordan, Julius Lester, Toni Cade Bambara, Sharon Bell Mathis, Nikki Giovanni, and Virginia Hamilton are describing a black consciousness of self-celebration rather like that which flowered during the Harlem Renaissance and was somehow lost, at least in literature, in the intervening years of social upheaval.

There seem to be three major identifiable sub-genres in recent black prose. Some of the new writing has its roots in the angry realism of Richard Wright (Ronald Fair, *We Can't Breathe*; Louise Meriwether, *Daddy Was a Number Runner*). Many of the new writers, however, are developing the satiric and anti-realistic conventions of Ralph Ellison's *The Invisible Man*. June Jordan's *His Own Where*, Virginia Hamilton's *The Planet of Junior Brown*, Nolan Davis's *Six Black Horses*, and Barry Beckham's *Runner Mack* all blend elements of fantasy and realism. Their dream-like quality and impressionistic style get at the terror of urban life or the joy of being young and black in a way that realism alone cannot.

The third emerging force in black literature is a rediscovery of the historical and mythical past as seen in Ernest Gaines' *The Autobiography of Miss Jane Pitman*, Arna Bontemps' *Young Booker*, Jay David's *Black Defiance*, and Julius Lester's *To Be a Slave*, *Long Journey Home*, and *Black Folk Tales*. The issue of dialect, so burning for earlier black writers, seems to have been resolved by extending the concept of dialect to language and style. In much of the current fiction, not only is the integrity of black English as a linguistic unit realized, but its energy and creativity is celebrated. Toni Cade Bambara (*Gorilla, My Love*) and June Jordan are the best of the writers using black English to create a style that is an extension of a consciousness.

One of the most interesting trends in current black adolescent fiction is the new trust the authors are putting in their young characters to define their own world and establish their own values, often at variance with society's demands. *His Own Where*, *The Planet of Junior Brown*, Sharon Bell Mathis' *Teacup Full of Roses*, *Six Black Horses*, and even Jesse Jackson's most recent book *The Fourteenth Cadillac* are notable examples.

The importance and intrinsic interest of these books to young people is obvious. One has only to read the Newbery Award-winning *Sounder* by William Armstrong to perceive the distorted picture of black personhood and the unconscious racism that is sometimes present in even the best intentioned work on black themes by a white author. (See also Theodore Taylor's *The Cay*.)

But I would argue that even though many of these authors express no interest in communicating with a white audience, white adolescents will find an affinity with the perceptions and feelings of these books, which chronicle the same alienation from the mainstream of adult values and authority figures that many young people feel. The values of these writers are the values of freedom versus constriction, sensuality versus puritanism, living for others versus living for success. The black movement through literature is a voyage of self-discovery--the same voyage that all adolescents are embarked upon.

Bibliography

Novels

Runner Mack. Barry Beckham. William Morrow & Company, Inc. 1972.

Offers both an allegorical confrontation with black history and a Kafka-like encounter with the nightmare side of the American dream. It is most accessible and enjoyable on the narrative level as a story of baseball, war, love and radical politics.

Six Black Horses. Nolan Davis. G. P. Putnam's Sons. 1971.

Out of Charles Dickens by Ralph Ellison comes Laurence Xavier Jordan who wants to become a sculptor, but instead becomes the leading black mortician in Kansas City. Includes some of the most delightfully eccentric characters to appear in recent fiction. The novel is both a satiric look at the black middle class and a serious examination of the theme of self-realization.

We Can't Breathe. Ronald Fair. Harper & Row. 1972.

Ernie and Sam are determined to survive both the Depression and the South Side of Chicago: one to lead his people; the other to tell their story. The leader is killed; only the writer survives to make this bitter, lyrical statement.

The Autobiography of Miss Jane Pitman. Ernest Gaines. The Dial Press. 1971. Bantam. 1973.

At twelve, Miss Jane escapes from slavery and at a hundred and twelve, she is a freedom-rider. Ernest Gaines has created in Miss Jane Pitman a fictional voice expressive of the whole sweep of black American history.

The Planet of Junior Brown. Virginia Hamilton. The Macmillan Company. 1971.

Fourteen-year-old Junior Brown, his friend Buddy, and the school janitor spend their days in a secret room of their junior high school constructing a huge model of the solar system. Through their ingenuity and humanity, the boys create a "planet" whose only law is that people live for each other. Junior high level.

The Fourteenth Cadillac. Jesse Jackson. Doubleday & Company. 1972.

The family of seventeen year old Stonewall Jackson is trying to steer him along the path of middle class respectability, but Stonewall has other ideas. How he launches himself on a career is told with humor and a style that will appeal to a slow reader. Junior high, easy reading.

His Own Where. June Jordan. Thomas Crowell. 1971. Dell. 1971.

Buddy, sixteen, and Angela, fourteen, escape from their brutal or abandoning parents, their deadening schools and create "their own where." There are moments of high comedy, deep sensual love, and loss expressed in a black idiom of wit and poetry.

Teacup Full of Roses. Sharon Bell Mathis. The Viking Press. 1972.

The title describes a fantasy place Joe creates for his girlfriend that is in grim contrast to the realities of their lives. This is a celebration of black family life, not of the stereotypical enduring parents, but of the children who find their strength in giving to each other. Junior high, easy reading.

Daddy Was a Number Runner. Louise Meriwether. Prentice Hall, Inc. 1970. Pyramid Books. 1971.

For Francie Coffin, twelve and growing up in Harlem during the Depression, the hope and faith of childhood are gradually worn down by the pimps, child molesters, welfare workers, and disintegrating families that people her world. It is a child's freshness of perception that makes this a very angry book.

Snakes. Al Young. Holt, Rinehart and Winston. 1970. Dell Publishing Co. 1971.

Music--blues, jazz and soul--forms the world for MC and his friends growing up in Detroit. When MC's band cuts a single that is a local best seller, he begins to sort out his identity from the forces of school pressures, family ties, love, sex, drugs, and friendship that surround him.

Short Story Collections

Gorilla, My Love. Toni Cade Bambara. Random House. 1972.

Toni Cade Bambara possesses one of the finest ears for the nuances of black English. Her short fiction is filled with the voices of old people and children, the sophisticated and the simple. Each story is a celebration of the possibilities of language. Advanced.

What We Must See: Young Black Story Tellers. Orde Coombs. Dodd, Mead & Company. 1971.

The short stories in this collection are affirmations of the black life style, such as how to live on nothing with elegance and dignity, and how to conduct a funeral that is a celebration of life. They speak frankly of sex and violence and of their characters' brilliant strategies of survival.

Black Folk Tales. Julius Lester. Illustrated by Tom Feelings.

Richard W. Baron Publishing Company, Inc. 1969. Grove Press, Inc. 1969.

Includes animal fables and stories of magical love from Africa, stories of slavery and city life from the United States. The idiom is contemporary: God reads the TV Guide, snakes do their washing in the laundromat, and Ole Massa gets Excedrin headaches. Junior high, easy reading.

Long Journey Home. Julius Lester. The Dial Press. 1972.

These stories chronicle the archetypal heroes of black history: the run-away slave, the blues singer, the cowboy. Junior high, easy reading.

Two Love Stories. Julius Lester. The Dial Press. 1972.

Lester explores the interracial friendship of two fourteen-year-olds against a backdrop of contemporary southern mores and the awakening of love between a young dancer and her summer camp counselor.

Hue and Cry. James Allen Mcpherson. Macmillan. 1969. Fawcett.

Winner of the Atlantic Prize Grant, Mcpherson sees his stories as "... about people, all kinds of people, old, young, lonely, homosexual, confused, used, discarded wronged."

Non-Fiction

Young Booker. Arna Bontemps. Dodd, Mead & Company. 1972.

One of the deans of Afro-American writing has vividly portrayed the hardships Washington endured to attain his own education and build Tuskegee. The complexities of Washington's character recently revealed in Louis R. Harlan's works are not dealt with.

Black Defiance: Black Profiles in Courage. Edited by Jay David. William Morrow & Company. 1972.

Sojourner Truth, William Wells Brown, Daniel Hale Williams, James Baldwin, Eldridge Cleaver and fourteen other voices offer a personalized history of black defiance in America from the eighteenth century to the present.

Black Pilgrimage. Tom Feelings. Lothrop, Lee & Shepard Co. 1972.

Prize-winning illustrator Tom Feelings draws and speaks his pilgrimage from Harlem across rural America, to his roots in Africa.

Gemini. Nikki Giovanni. Bobbs-Merrill Company, Inc. 1971.

This collection of autobiographical and critical essays offers an intimate view of Ms. Giovanni as an artist, revolutionary, and private person.

No Time for Dying. Eddie Harrison and Alfred V. J. Prather.

Prentice Hall. 1973.

This account written by a teenager convicted of murder offers a devastating look at the inequalities in our judicial system.

Dry Victories. June Jordan. Holt, Rinehart and Winston. 1972.

This is a biting discussion in the form of a dialogue between two boys of Reconstruction and the Civil Rights Movement, the "dry victories" of black history.

To Be a Slave. Julius Lester. Illustrated by Tom Feelings. The Dial Press. 1968. Dell.

Lester has collected these slave narratives to give a balanced, yet impassioned overview of the institution and its impact on individual lives.

Notes of a Processed Brother. Donald Reeves. Pantheon Books. 1972. Avon Books. 1971.

Reeves tells of the making of a student revolutionary in the New York City schools.

Savior, Savior, Hold My Hand. Piri Thomas. Doubleday & Company, Inc. 1972.

In this sequel to Down These Mean Streets, Piri Thomas writes of his adjustment after six years in "El Sing Sing," in his unique style of Afro-Latin English.

THE FEMINIST INFLUENCE*

By Alleen Pace Nilsen

Over 500 book titles listed in the 1973 Books in Print begin with a form of the word woman. In 1969 this figure was 223, while in 1967 it was only 181. Statistics about book titles beginning with the words girl or female show the same trend. Without a doubt, the women's movement has influenced the publishing world and many of the books which have resulted will be welcome additions to high school libraries.

Rosa Guy's book The Friends (Holt, Rinehart and Winston, 1973, 203 pgs.) is an honest and serious treatment of friendship between two girls. It presents the story of Phyl and Edith who live in Harlem. Although they are the same age, one is very much the daughter in her family while the other plays almost the parent role in her family. It is an unlikely friendship, but entirely believable and very moving.

Pamela Walker's Twyla (Prentice-Hall, 1973, 125 pgs.) utilizes the overworked gimmick of amateurishly typed letters. Nevertheless it is a powerful story about a high school girl whose emotions and thoughts are made to seem very close to those of the reader even though Twyla is mentally retarded.

A book for mature readers is Margaret Atwood's Surfacing (Simon and Schuster, 1972, 224 pgs.). A young woman returns to her childhood home in the Canadian wilderness to look for her father who is missing. The book is a deep exploration of the meaning of life. It is unusual in that treatment of such a serious subject, i.e. the relation between "man" and nature, has traditionally centered around male, rather than female, characters.

Ironically, a few of the things which have happened to books because of women's liberation may harm rather than help the movement. For one thing, people who disagree now feel pressured to loudly voice their opinions as a counterbalance to the wave of feminist writing. For example, the message in Elliot Roosevelt's controversial book about his parents' marriage (An Untold Story, Put-

---

*Reprinted by permission of the author and publisher from English Journal (April 1974), 90-92.

nam, 1973, 308 pgs.) is that his mother, Eleanor, was wrong in seeking a career outside the home.

Another disturbing factor is that many books which would have previously been offered to a general readership are now packaged as "feminist" books. This means that although they are more apt to be read by interested girls and women, they are less apt to be read by the general public, males in particular. As a high school girl said about one of the recent novels, "What this book needs is a new title and a new cover!" The book she was talking about was Lives of Girls and Women by Alice Munro (McGraw-Hill, 1972, 250 pgs.). It is an interesting and revealing story of a young girl's growing up, but in the words of the high school girl who criticized the cover, "What it looks like from the outside is one of those collections of dull biographies!"

Her assumption that biographies are dull is debatable since some very fine ones have appeared within the last couple of years. Probably the crucial determinant in the interest factor is whether or not the reader already knows and likes the subject of the biography. Good books which are biographical in nature concerning contemporary women include Margaret Mead's Blackberry Winter (Morrow, 1972, 297 pgs.), Jane van Lawick-Goodall's In the Shadow of Man (Houghton Mifflin, 1971, 286 pgs.), Shirley Chisholm's The Good Fight (Harper and Row, 1973, 163 pgs.), Anne Morrow Lindbergh's Hour of Gold, Hour of Lead (Harcourt Brace Jovanovich, 1973, 325 pgs.), Sheila Burnford's One Woman's Arctic (Atlantic Little Brown, 1973, 224 pgs.), Lona B. Kenney's Mboka: The Way of Life in a Congo Village (Crown, 1972, 264 pgs.), Shirley MacLaine's Don't Fall Off the Mountain (Norton, 1970, Bantam paperback, 1971), and Margaret Parton's Journey through a Lighted Room (Viking, 1973, 248 pgs.).

Younger readers not quite ready for a whole biography might prefer to browse through anthologies or books written about several women, reading only those selections they find interesting. A good book for high schoolers is Eve Merriam's Growing Up Female in America: Ten Lives (Doubleday, 1971, Dell Paperback, 1973, 352 pgs.). And for readers in junior high, a good book is Pat Ross's Young and Female: First Person Accounts of Turning Points in the Lives of Eight American Women (Random House, 1972, 104 pgs.). One of the most natural of the many books written about the variety of occupations now open to women is Saturday's Child: 36 Women Talk about Their Jobs (J. Philip O'Hara, Inc., 1973, 152 pgs.). This is a collection of interviews accompanied by full page photographs. It is geared to junior high readers.

Some good anthologies of fiction include Stephanie Spinner's Feminine Plural: Stories by Women about Growing Up (Macmillan, 1972, 236 pgs.), Stephen Berg and S. J. Marks' About Women: An Anthology of Contemporary Fiction, Poetry, and Essays (Fawcett Paperback, 1973, 400 pgs.) and Alice Walker's collection of her own stories In Love and Trouble: Stories of Black Women (Harcourt Brace Jovanovich, 1973, 138 pgs.).

One of the most revealing and interesting anthologies for mature readers is Plays By and About Women edited by Victoria Sullivan and James Hatch (Random House, 1973, 421 pgs.). As the dust jacket says, the theater has always been considered a mirror of its time. These plays by Alice Gerstenberg, Lillian Hellman, Clare Boothe, Doris Lessing, Megan Terry, Natalia Ginzburg, Maureen Duffy, and Alice Childress were chosen because of their readability and because they mirrored an image of women as seen by themselves in this century.

An old bugaboo in the English classroom which feminists resent is the idea that boys are not interested in material by or about females. Therefore when books are chosen for common reading or when selections are made for anthologies, stories about boys rather than girls are chosen. Feminists argue that this is not only unfair, it is dishonest and it perpetuates an indefensible prejudice. They say that in reality the emotions and feelings of males and females are not all that far apart. For example, millions of boys have read and enjoyed books by D. N. Ahnstrom, E. M. Almedingen, H. F. Brinsmead, Nicholas Charles, John Clarke, E. Nesbit, J. A. Evans, C. H. Frick, Wilson Gage, S. E. Hinton, E. L. Konigsburg, A. M. Lightner, Ellsworth Newcombe, Andre Norton, K. M. Peyton, Henry Handel Richardson, R. H. Shimer, and P. O. Travers.

The excitement, adventure, and conflict in the dozens of books written by these writers is undoubtedly a part of the female psyche because these writers are all women. They have hidden their femininity under masculine sounding initials or pen names in order to fit the cultural stereotype which says that adventure and excitement is in the male rather than the female domain. Hopefully with today's rejection of falseness and young people's demands that we "tell it like it is," this kind of hypocrisy is on its way out.

In most cases it is a needless kind of deception anyway because boys aren't all that prejudiced against either female writers or characters. They will read books by or about females when the subject is something they are interested in. They read Billie Jean King's book Tennis to Win because they want to improve their tennis. They read Go Ask Alice because they want to find out about the drug scene and they read Lisa Bright and Dark because they are interested in mental illness. And for years they have been responding to The Diary of Anne Frank and To Kill a Mockingbird.

The books they don't like are the so-called girl stories or romances--the kind of love stories found in some women's magazines. I suspect that one reason boys resist these books is that the male characters in them are so false and so romanticized that no boy wants to picture himself playing that role. As Erich Segal's Love Story proved, it's not that boys are automatically "turned off" by the idea of romance. When both male and female characters ring true then readers of both sexes respond to the story.

Although the kind of love stories that appear in some men's magazines are so socially unacceptable that they don't find their way into the curriculum, it is interesting that girls reject these pornographic stories as unrealistic in the same way that boys reject the romances. This is a troublesome area. Apparently males and females are still a long way apart in what they expect from each other. If this is true for adults, we might expect it to be even more true for teenagers who are just emerging from a six or seven year period in which boys and girls have been virtual enemies. As they begin to tentatively reach out and re-establish diplomatic relations they are understandably hesitant to complicate matters by experimenting and breaking out of established social roles. This might be one of the reasons that high school students are slow in coming to an appreciation of the ideas behind the women's movement.

I've heard teachers and librarians express utter amazement at how little attention most high schoolers have paid to the underlying causes of the movement. In one class where the students read The Stepford Wives by Ira Levin (Random House, 1972, 145 pgs.), a boy appalled his feminist oriented teacher by concluding that the book gave a good plan for society. What happens in the book is that the super scientific husbands in the New York suburb of Stepford get together and, through a process not entirely clear, either change their wives or completely destroy them and make new Disneyland-type replicas who function faultlessly in their dual roles of servants and mistresses with never a personal need or demand for self-fulfillment. Notwithstanding the boy who thought this an excellent idea, most readers of The Stepford Wives get new insights into what the women's movement is all about.

A more direct but less exciting book which will help teenagers develop awareness is The New Feminism by Lucy Komisar (Franklin Watts, 1971, Warner paperback, 1972, 190 pgs.). This book has been especially prepared for young people. Some chapters that are particularly relevant include "Teen-Agers Talk About Themselves," "Sexism in High School," and "Barriers in Higher Education."

Another new book, Male and Female Under 18 (Edited by Nancy Larrick and Eve Merriam, Avon Paperback, 1973, 188 pgs.) has the advantage of being written by and for both boys and girls. Last year the editors solicited through schools and libraries personal statements in response to such questions as "What does it mean to be a girl in 1972? Or a boy?" and "How can I make the most of myself as a male or as a female?" They received 2,500 replies from which they selected 165 by-lined items which could be very useful in stimulating class discussion and writing. Some of the comments include one-liners such as this question from fourteen-year-old Mia Winter:

> What's the sense in life if you can't be what you expected to be?

Others are poetry, some bitter and some funny. And still others are thoughtful little essays. Sixteen-year-old Tom Farrier started his with:

> 'A boy's life.' That sounds a lot like 'a dog's life,' doesn't it? In a way, the relationship isn't exactly a coincidence.

Sixteen-year-old Nina Wormser concluded her paragraph with:

> If I don't fit into any set image of what a young lady is, that is too bad for all the people who like to categorize since I don't want to be anyone's ideal woman except my own.

The variety, the sincerity, and the perceptiveness of the comments make fascinating reading and bring home the point that the influence of the feminist movement is not limited to only one sex or one age group.

WOMEN: A RECOMMENDED LIST
of Print and Non-Print Materials*

By Members of the ALA Social Responsibilities
Round Table Task Force on Women**

One of the marked contributions of the women's movement has been its realization that schools, teaching materials, literature, and media can contribute to the limitation of human potentialities. Over forty studies of the impact of sexism and sexist conditioning are anthologized in Sexism and Youth by Diane Gersoni-Stavn (R. R. Bowker, 1974). We recommend this collection as required reading for any educator or librarian interested in an educational process free of sexual programming. The studies of children's books and media collected in Stavn are probably largely responsible for what seems to be increased sensitivity by publishers to the treatment of women in literature.

On the other hand, studies of non-print media are few, perhaps reflecting the overall emphasis of our educational system towards print. This is unfortunate. We found the quality of nonprint media sorely lacking in many areas. While lack of sensitivity and lack of comprehensiveness are present in print and nonprint, we found the latter insensitive, trite, and unaware in most of the materials examined. In general, nonprint materials reflect the worst kind of tokenism. An example we viewed of this was a film on women narrated by a man with the only woman speaker in the film being one who spoke against the equal rights amendment.

Sexist programming is an underlying cultural bias, a mythology which is difficult to counteract. We have all been subject to it--authors, editors, librarians, teachers, publishers, producers, and we tend to perpetuate it without awareness. This is particularly true of the materials with which we stock our classrooms and libraries. But, if we are going to change such horrifying facts like: forty per cent of families headed by women live in poverty, or that female college graduates can expect to earn only one hundred dollars more than men with an eighth grade education, then we must change

---

*Reprinted by permission of the authors and publisher from Media-center (May 1975), 36-41.

**Members of the group were Phyllis Cantor, Kay Cassell, Mary Kay Chelton, Renee Feinberg, Joan Marshall, Patricia Glass Schuman, Betty-Carol Sellen and Susan Vaughn.

our view of "reality" and the natural order of things. To wit, women are beautiful, passive creatures, altruistic, loving and kind. They are fulfilled by roles of wife and motherhood.

Aspirations are very much affected by conditioning. A desire to be a doctor is not a genetic characteristic. Psychology plays a very significant part in determining destiny, and the materials we choose must offer a wide enough choice of role models and options to insure individual fulfillment. Author Scott O'Dell has said that his prizewinning Island of the Blue Dolphins was rejected by one publisher because he refused to change his central character to a boy. Girls will read books about boys, but boys will not read books about girls, goes the conventional wisdom. We must avoid that trap of facile rationalization.

The key to keep in mind is that as purchasers of materials --we--and our users--are consumers. We have some power--the power of the dollar, and publishers will listen--if only we speak out. The Task Force Committee agreed to prepare this bibliography as one way of speaking out. During the past five years we have seen a great explosion of material on women, and as a result of severe time and space constraints, we have largely limited our selection to that period. There is certainly good material available with earlier publication dates, and we hope our "Professional" section will help lead you to these. On the whole, though, we must observe that despite the number of items available currently, selectors will still have to weed carefully through the garbage to find the gold.

While this list can easily be interpreted as one to be used in the education of girls and young women, a word of warning: it would be perpetuating our sex-classed society to limit the use of these materials. It is just as important that males be aware of them and exposed to them, that we do not catch ourselves in the time-honored trap of books for boys and books for girls. Our goal must be to open options and understanding for all.

This list should be viewed as a beginning, and certainly not as an end--either for print or nonprint. Materials selectors should continually keep informed of new materials, review them, exchange information with each other, and relay their concerns to publishers. McGraw-Hill's guidelines on non-sexist terminology are a good start, but many publishers still have a long way to go.

Criteria or Questions?

We have been requested to clearly state criteria for the selection of non-sexist materials included in this recommended bibliography. Instead we have continuously come up with questions which hopefully suggest the complexity and pervasiveness of the problem. We hope that these questions will serve as guidelines that will be helpful to other materials selectors and that they can be revised and amended to suit specific needs.

Some critical questions to consider in appraising the value of materials are:

What activities are the characters engaged in? What is the male-female ratio of characters? Is it a realistic and valid one? How traditionally are the characters portrayed? Are the girls cute and the boys adventurous, or is each character defined by his or her own individuality? Who are the adult role models? Are females portrayed within a limited range of activities (mother, teacher, nurse), while males are anything from garbage collectors to astro-physicists? Are illustrations male-dominated, e.g. pictures of doctors, lawyers, thus implying that their professions are also male-restricted?

How is a woman defined in the story-line? What is her role in the plot? What are her ambitions--is she simply an appendage--someone's wife, mother, sister, etc. or is she an independent person as well as--or instead of--one of these? Is the male character's search for himself based on what he will be as opposed to the female "Who will I marry?" Are women merely helpmates or are they creative in their own right. Are females dependent on males or are both interdependent? Is there a non-stereotyped principal character surrounded by characters still in traditional roles? Are female characters praised for their attractiveness, or described in physical terms, while males are noted for their achievements. Does one find sentences like "Despite her beauty, she was a clever woman?" How often is a bright and active woman considered somehow "unique" and held above the rest of her sex, either implicitly or explicitly? How much sameness (with or without comments on quality) are there in female as opposed to male roles?

Language is often a very subtle, but very real sexist conditioning factor. The word man can stand for male or female, but there is no female noun which can represent man. As a result, writers often fall into the trap of using the masculine gender with the best of intentions, but with a net effect which places many activities, professions, feelings, etc. in purely male contexts. How much assumption is there in the use or choice of pronouns: "The doctor asks <u>his</u> nurse if <u>she</u> will...." Do they reinforce stereotypes? It has been noted that most animal books for children contain mostly male characters. This may be as much as an unconscious use of man, in lieu of an acceptable neuter pronoun, as direct awareness of the author. Is the word "girl" used to refer to women over 16?

Where is the work set? Is it realistic or are sexist mythologies being perpetrated. For example, one book we looked at dealt with a boy and his father keeping house <u>until mommy came home from a trip</u>. Do all children have mothers who keep house? Do they all live in a pretty apartment? Do only strong little girls have strong mothers? Is class, as well as sex, dealt with?

Are the so-called controversial issues discussed realistically or moralistically? Is being a tomboy all good now? (If so, why is the term used at all?) Does a pregnant teenager always have a male baby? Can a teenager have an abortion and not almost die--physically, or out of remorse?

Is friendship between female protagonists genuine or based on competition alone? Are the women described or pictured in stereotyped clothing (e.g. members of the movement all wear jeans, are all young, etc.)? Are alternative lifestyles treated sympathetically or merely as an aberration? Are women characters--or biographees--treated as "superwomen" rather than realistic role models?

One cannot always judge a book by its cover--or by its title. The Boys Book of Fishing, for example may be perfectly acceptable for anyone interested in the subject ... but its title alone can limit it. A book on Modern World History which omits mention of women, except as luggage ("the pioneers brought their wives and children"), is not Modern World History. And it does not help a great deal if the authors have added a single chapter on women. Women are 51% of the human race and their contribution to it should be an integral part of any text, not an addendum.

Keeping Up

Selection of materials is a full-time job. Until we live in the perfect society, we are going to have to pay special attention to non-sexist materials and materials about women. In addition to the many commercial publishers of books, there are many women's presses publishing for, by, and about women and non-sexist children's books. Cynthia Ellin Harrison's Women's Movement Media: A Source Guide (Bowker, 1975) lists and annotates over 500 publishers, periodicals and organizations, many of which provide books, tapes, pamphlets, and nonprint media. The Clearinghouse on Women's Studies, an educational project of the Feminist Press, publishes several pamphlets and books on elementary and high school feminist studies as well as a quarterly Women's Studies Newsletter (c/o SUNY at Old Westbury, Box 334, Old Westbury, New York 11568). KNOW, Inc. is a feminist publishing and distribution collective which is an excellent source of women's movement materials, for children and adults. KNOW News, published ten times per year, is an efficient way to keep up to date, (P.O. Box 86301, Pittsburgh, Pennsylvania 15221). The National Organization for Women has local groups set up all across the country, many of whom sponsor task forces on schools and materials (see Harrison or write to NOW, 1952 East 73rd Street, Chicago, Illinois 60645). Some other groups working in this area include the Women's Rights Committee of the American Federation of Teachers (1012 14th Street, N.W., Washington, D.C. 20005) and Feminist Resources for Equal Education (Box 185, Saxonville Station, Framingham, Massachusetts).

Small recommended publishers of pamphlets and some books include:

Joyful World Press, 468 Belvedere Street, San Francisco, California 94117

Lollipop Power Inc., Box 1171, Chapel Hill, North Carolina 27514

New Seed Press, Box 3016, Stanford, California 94305

Times Change Press, Panwell Road, Washington, New Jersey 07882

New England Free Press, 60 University Square, Somerset, Massachusetts 02143

Some media sources are:

Media Plus, Inc., 60 Riverside Drive, New York, New York 10024

New Day Films, Box 315, Franklin Lake, New Jersey 07417

Pacifica Tape Library, 5316 Venida Boulevard, Los Angeles, California 90010

Women's Film COOP, 200 Main Street, Northampton, Massachusetts

Miscellaneous Resources:

Aphra (The quarterly on arts) 4 Jones Street, New York, New York 10014

Everywoman (general--issued every three weeks) 10438 West Washington Boulevard, Venice, California 90291

Ms. (slick general monthly), 370 Lexington Avenue, New York, New York 10007

Off Our Backs (biweekly women's news journal), 17724 20th Street, N.W., Washington, D.C. 20009

Spokeswoman (monthly news and currents on women), 5464 South Shore Drive, Chicago, Illinois

Up From Under (issued five times a year includes material aimed at women workers), 339 Lafayette Street, New York, New York 10012

Women: A Journal of Liberation (a thematic quarterly, e.g. Sexism, Women in History), 3028 Greenmount Avenue, Baltimore, Maryland 21210

Women's Studies Abstracts (a quarterly abstracting service to over 200 periodicals), Box 1, Rush, New York

And last but not least, in honor of the first women's college basketball game ever held in Madison Square Garden: *Sportswoman*

Magazine, Box 7771, Long Beach, California and Women Sports, 1660 South Amphett Boulevard, Suite 2666, San Mateo, California 94402.

WOMEN: a recommended list of print and non-print materials

Art

Tucker, Anne. The Woman's Eye. Alfred A. Knopf, 1973. Grades 10 and up

The works of ten American women photographers from the turn of the century to the present are represented.

Biography

Brent, Linda. Incidents in the Life of a Slave Girl. New Edition. Harcourt Brace Jovanovich, 1973. Grades 10 and up

Autobiography of Brent, a mulatto--the great-grandaughter of a South Carolina planter--who escaped from slavery at the age of 27.

Chamberlin, Hope. A Minority of Members: Women in the U.S. Congress. New American Library, 1974. Grades 9 and up

Succinct profiles of 80 women who served in Congress from Jeannette Rankin to the present. The biographies are arranged in chronological order with notes describing the status of politics in the U.S. when the women were elected.

Chisholm, Shirley. Unbought and Unbossed. Avon Books, 1971. Grades 9 and up

A candid autobiography of the first black woman elected to the U.S. Senate. She is outspoken on politics, poverty, racism and the women's movement.

Clapp, Patricia. Dr. Elizabeth: The Story of the First Woman Doctor. Lothrop, Lee & Shepard, 1974. Grades 6-10

A fine biography of the first woman to get a medical degree in the United States. The book describes her difficulties in being admitted to medical school, in getting postgraduate training, and in being accepted as a practitioner. An epilogue describes the doctor's last years.

Felton, Harold W. Mumbet: The Story of Elizabeth Freeman. Dodd, Mead, 1970, 63 p. Illustrations by Donn Albright. Grades 3-7

A brave black woman wins her freedom in a Massachusetts court in 1781, proving all are "free and equal."

Harnan, Terry. African Rhythm-American Dance: A Biography of

Katherine Dunham. Alfred A. Knopf, 1974. Grades 5-6
Biography of the black dancer and choreographer who specialized in dances originating from African and Caribbean sources.

Hautzig, Esther. The Endless Steppe: A Girl in Exile. School Book Service. Grades 6-10
A young woman, taken as a child from her home in Vilna, Poland, tells how she survived in wartime Siberia.

Holiday, Billie. Lady Sings the Blues. Lancer Books, 1972. Grades 9 and up
An oral history of a black female artist which documents the oppression of poor black women in America. Holiday's life was a struggle against racism, drugs, poverty and men.

Jackson, Jesse. Make a Joyful Noise unto the Lord: The Life of Mahalia Jackson, Queen of Gospel Singers. Thomas Y. Crowell, 1974. Grades 5-6
Story of the famous black gospel singer who hoped to break down barriers between black and white people. The Thomas Y. Crowell biography series has other fine titles.

Klein, Mina and Arthur Klein. Kathe Kollwitz: Life in Art. Harper & Row, 1972. Illustrations. Grades 10 and up
Biography of one of Germany's foremost 20th-century artists --a master of graphic technique--whose work was ultimately suppressed by the Nazis. Black and white drawings and photographs of Kollwitz's work are included.

Kosterina, Nina. (Translation by Mirra Ginsburg). Diary of Nina Kosterina. Avon Books. Grades 9 and up
Diary of a Russian girl from age 15 to 20 when she left to fight against the German invasion of Russia. A record of the life of young people during the Stalin regime.

Lupton, Mary Jane. Elizabeth Barrett Browning. The Feminist Press, 1971. Grades 9 and up
A feminist biography of one of England's nineteenth-century women poets.

Merriam, Eve, Editor. Growing Up Female in America. Dell. Grades 9 and up
The lives of ten extraordinary but little-known women who pioneered in such areas as social reform, politics, science and the labor movement as seen through their letters, diaries and autobiographies.

Moody, Anne. Coming of Age in Mississippi. Dell, 1970. Grades 9 and up
A young black woman risks her life and endangers her family in her struggle for black liberation.

Munro, Alice. Lives of Girls and Women. New American Library.

Grades 9 and up
An autobiographical account of a girl growing up in a small Ontario town with a cast of mainly female local characters.

Nathan, Dorothy. Women of Courage. Random House, 1964. Grades 7 and up
Five biographies of well-known women--Margaret Mead, Jane Addams, Susan B. Anthony, Mary McLeod Bethune and Amelia Earhart.

Oakley, Mary Ann B. Elizabeth Cady Stanton. 2nd Edition. The Feminist Press, 1972. Grades 7 and up
A feminist biography of one of the early leaders of the women's rights movement in the United States.

Petry, Ann. Harriet Tubman. Pocket Books, 1955. Grades 6-8
A biography of Harriet Tubman, the "Moses of her people," who led more than three hundred blacks up from slavery to freedom in the North.

Ross, Pat, Editor. Young and Female. Random House, 1972. Grades 6-8
The personal accounts of the turning points in the lives of eight women including Shirley Chisholm, Dorothy Day, Margaret Sanger and Margaret Bourke-White.

Shulman, Alix. To the Barricades: The Anarchist Life of Emma Goldman. Thomas Y. Crowell, 1971. 225 p. Grades 7 and up
A lively biography of a woman anarchist who defended pacifism, birth control, free love and women's suffrage.

Stiller, Richard. Commune on the Frontier: The Story of Frances Wright. Thomas Y. Crowell, 1972. Grades 7-12
Frances Wright crusaded against religion, marriage and slavery. She went on to found a commune where slaves could earn their freedom.

Zassenhaus, Hiltgunt. Walls: Resisting the Third Reich--One Woman's Story. Beacon Press, 1974. Grades 10 and up
The author tells her true story of resisting the Third Reich by helping the Scandinavian prisoners held in Germany during the war.

Career Education

Campbell, Margaret A. "Why Would a Girl Go into Medicine?" Medical Education in the United States: A Guide for Women. The Feminist Press, 1973. 116 p. Grades 10 and up
A highly useful book on attitudes about women in medical schools taken from a questionnaire sent to women students. Indirectly comments on male doctors' attitudes towards women patients.

Career Opportunity Series. Catalyst (6 E. 82nd St., N.Y. N.Y. 10028).

A series of career pamphlets for women.

Goldreich, Gloria and Esther Goldreich. What Can She Be? An Architect. Lothrop, Lee & Shepard, 1974. 48 p. Grades 2-4

One of a series of books that show professional woman in various careers, this volume shows the facets of the profession, the skills required of the practitioner, and the satisfaction it brings to her.

Goldreich, Gloria and Esther Goldreich. What Can She Be? A Newscaster. Lothrop, Lee & Shepard, 1973. 48 p. Grades 2-4

One of a series of books that show contemporary women in various careers. This describes the day-by-day activities of Barbara Lamont, newscaster on the New York program, "Black News."

Goldreich, Gloria and Esther Goldreich. What Can She Be? A Veterinarian. Lothrop, Lee & Shepard, 1972. 48 p. Grades 2-4

One of a series of books that show contemporary women in various careers and professions. This book describes the training and the skills needed to care for and to cure animals, a particularly rewarding profession for a woman who loves them.

Klein, Norma. Girls Can Be Anything. E. P. Dutton, 1973. Grades 7-12

A little boy tells a little girl that girls cannot be doctors. Upset, the girl approaches her parents, who relate in a series of episodes that females can indeed be doctors and pilots and presidents.

Lasker, Joe. Mothers Can Do Anything. Albert Whitman & Company, 1972. Grades K-12

The author demonstrates the concept that women "can do anything" by depicting mothers in some occupational and recreational roles which they often play and in others that they seldom play. Some of these are plumber, train conductor, astronaut and ditch digger.

Maury, Inex. My Mother the Mail Carrier/Mi Mama La Cartera. The Feminist Press, 1973, 32 p. Grades 4-9

Five-year-old Lupita's mother not only loves her--she also loves her job. In both the English and Spanish text, Lupita clearly feels good about her mother and herself. The warmth of their relationship illuminates Lupita's account of their shared experiences.

Seed, Suzanne. Saturday's Child. Bantam Books, 1974. Grades 9 and up

Successful women in a variety of fields discuss their life and work styles.

Splaver, Sarah. Nontraditional Careers for Women. Julian Messner, 1973. Grades 10 and up

A survey of more than 500 job opportunities for women giving the history of women in the occupation, qualifications and education needed, advantages and disadvantages. It includes law, health, education, social sciences, sciences, business and government and sources of additional information.

Health And Self-Protection

Boston Women's Health Collective. Our Bodies, Our Selves. Simon & Schuster, 1972. Illustrations. Grades 9 and up

A comprehensive work on every aspect of gynecological health including information on birth control, reproduction, abortion, venereal disease, rape and childbirth. Especially valuable for teenagers.

Ehrenreich, Barbara and Deidre English. Witches, Midwives and Nurses: A History of Women Healers. The Feminist Press, 1973. Grades 10 and up

Women's history as healers through the ages is described. They were abortionists, nurses, counsellors, pharmacists and midwives. The male takeover of medicine and the suppression of the witches are also discussed.

Frankfort, Ellen. Vaginal Politics. Bantam Books, 1972, 224 p. Grades 10 and up

A frank discussion of women's health problems and how they are treated by the medical profession. Abortions, breast cancer and VD are among the issues discussed.

Medea, Andrea and Kathleen Thompson. Against Rape. Farrar, Straus & Giroux, 1974, 150 p. Grades 10 and up

This is a basic book on rape which deals with the myths about rape, precautions and preventions of rape, self-defense and what to do if raped.

Planned Parenthood of New York City, Inc. Abortion: A Woman's Guide. Abelard-Schuman, 1973. Grades 10 and up.

A responsible guide to every aspect of pregnancy termination.

Seaman, Barbara. Free and Female: The Sex Life of the Contemporary Woman. Fawcett World Library, 1972. Grades 10 and up

Everything you always wanted to know about the sex life of the contemporary woman, but "they" were afraid to tell you. Forthright intelligent data on sex, marriage, venereal disease and birth control.

Tegner, Bruce and Alice McGrath. Self-Defense for Girls and Women: A Physical Education Course. Thor Publishing Company, 1969. Revised Edition. Grades 9 and up

Provides instruction for self-defense in the home, in elevators, walking alone in streets, etc. Practical, simple techniques that anyone can learn.

Language Arts: K-6

Blume, Judy. Are You There, God? It's Me, Margaret. Dell, 1972. Grades 5-9

Margaret Simon is worried about boys, dances, parties, school projects, making friends, and choosing a religion. When she's alone, she has long and sometimes exacerbating conversations with God.

Boccaccio, Shirley. Penelope Goes to the Farmer's Market. Joyful World Press. Illustrations by the author.

Penelope and her brother, Peter, are orphans and live with Sally, the salamander, and Rac-Rac, the racoon in a house in the city. The problem is how to secure food and Penelope applies her resourcefulness and imagination at the Farmer's Market.

Chorao, Kay. A Magic Eye for Ida. Seabury Press, 1973. Illustrations by the author. Grades K-3

The palmist, Madam Julia, sees that Ida's poetic soul lends her more distinction than owning a dolly-wetse-bye.

Clifton, Lucille. Don't You Remember? E. P. Dutton. Illustrations by Evaline Ness. Grades K-3

Four-year-old Tate remembers the promises her family makes to do something "next time." It's always wait till next time.

Danish, Barbara. The Dragon and the Doctor. The Feminist Press. Illustrations by the author. Grades K-3

This is the story of a girl doctor and a boy nurse who cure a dragon's sore tail with the help of an X-ray machine.

Dragonwagon, Crescent. Strawberry Dress Escape. Scribner, 1975. Illustrations by Ann Powell. Grades K-3

This is a story full of magic. Stiffled in her hot school room, Emily slips out and is soon flying across a meadow finding food and shelter. The pastel drawings are enchanting.

Fine, Esther and Ann Powell. I'm a Child of the City. Kids Can Press (Distributed by Canadian Women's Educational Press, Toronto), 1973, 32 p.

This child of the city bubbles over with mischief and fun, and, for her, city life is great.

Fitzhugh, Louise. Nobody's Family Is Going to Change. Farrar, Strauss & Giroux, 1974. Grades 4-6

The Sheridan family is black and middle class. Emma is elevan, fat and obsessed with eating and becoming a lawyer. She is a child of great resourcefulness and preception, and she realizes that she will have to change and develop her own life style which is far from what her parents want for her.

Flory, Jane. The Liberation of Clementine Tipton. Houghton Mifflin, 1974. Illustrations by the author. Grades 3-6

Spunky Clementine is convinced that there are more important things to learn than how to balance a tea cup. At the age of 10 she is caught up with the excitement of Philadelphia in 1876.

Gauch, Patricia Lee. Christina Katerina and the Box. Coward, McCann & Geoghegan, 1971. Illustrations by Doris Burn.

The box becomes a castle becomes a clubhouse becomes a racing car becomes a dance floor when imaginative Christina Katerina rescues it from a mundane fate as a trash bin.

Goffstein, M. B. Two Piano Tuners. Farrar, Strauss & Giroux, 1970. 65 p. Illustrations by the author. Grades PS-3

This persistent little girl convinces her grandfather of the nobleness of her life's ambition--to be a piano tuner like him.

Greene, Bette. Philip Hall Likes Me. I Reckon Maybe. Dial Press, 1974. 135 p. Picture by Charles Lilly. Grades 5-6

Beth Lambert loves Philip Hall, the cutest, smartest boy in class who is always beating her in everything--until she realizes she is letting him win.

Grifalconi, Ann. The Matter with Lucy: An Album. Bobbs-Merrill, 1973, unpaged. Illustrations by the author. All ages

Lucy, her mother's helper, her brother's comforter, has a passion for questions, though she has not been asked what school she wishes to attend. But Lucy is determined and becomes a world-famous scholar. The graphics are exciting collages of turn of the century portraits, drawings, cut-outs and paste ups.

Grosvenor, Kali. Poems by Kali. Doubleday, 1970. 62 p. Photographs by Joan Halifax and Robert Fletcher. Grades 3-6

"Black is Black/I am Black."

Herman, Harriet. The Forest Princess. Over the Rainbow Press, 1974, 48 p. Illustrations by Carole Peterson Dwinell.

Although the princess rescues the prince, there's no easy solution to the problems of sexism, and so the ending has more truth than most.

Hochschild, Arlie Russell. Coleen the Question Girl. The Feminist Press. Illustrations by Gail Ashby. Grades K-4

A captivating story of Coleen, a little girl who loved to ask questions. The more she asked, the more she felt like asking.

Katz, Bobbi. Nothing But a Dog. The Feminist Press, 1972. Illustrations by Esther Gilman. Grades K-3

Our young hero is full of vitality. She flies kites, climbs trees, rides a bike and builds things, but her life is not complete until she gets a job.

Kindred, Wendy. Ida's Idea. McGraw-Hill, 1972. Illustrations by the author. Grades K-4

If your maple sugar candy doll that you savored in small

bites started disappearing in large bites, how would you save it (for yourself)?

Klein, Norma. Mom, the Wolf Man and Me. Avon Books, 1972. Grades 4-6

An 11-year-old, Brett, tells about growing up with her 31-year-old photographic mother whose boy friend sleeps over on weekends. It's the story of a contemporary lifestyle with real people.

Lisker, Sonia O. I Am. Hastings House, 1974.

An energetic little girl plays a fast-paced game of "Careers" in which she can do anything--she's a daredevil photographer, astronaut, etc.

Miles, Miska. Annie and the Old One. Little Brown, 1971. Illustrations by Peter Parnell. Grades 1-3

A young Navaho girl cannot accept the fact that her grandmother is going to die. She tries to hold back time as she slowly unravels her day's weaving.

Montgomery, Constance. Vermont School Bus Ride. Vermont Crossroads Press, 1974. Photographs by Larry Barns. All ages

This is an attractive book which presents the charm of the Vermont countryside, a round barn, a covered bridge, horses, snow. Sally is the hearty bus driver who maneuvers the big vehicle through the back roads.

Ness, Evaline. Do You Have the Time, Lydia? E. P. Dutton, 1971. unpaged. Illustrations by the author.

Lydia, who sews and bakes but also hammers nails and builds racing cars, learns to include her unhappy little brother in her hyper-active daily routine.

Parents' Nursery School. Kids Are Natural Cooks. Houghton Mifflin, 1972. Illustrations by Lady McCardy. Grades K-6

Classroom tested fun-to-follow recipes encouraging cooking skills and awareness of organic foods and nutrition.

Phillips, Lynn. Exactly Like Me. Lollipop Power, 1972, 27 p.

This young lady says exactly what she thinks and celebrates herself as she is.

Poix, Carol de. Jo, Flo and Yolanda. Lollipop Power, 1973, 32p. Illustrations by Stephanie Sove Newy. Grades 3-6

These triplets, while they look alike, have very different career aspirations. The setting is a Puerto Rican neighborhood in New York City.

Preston, Edna Mitchell. Horrible Hepzibah. Viking Press, 1971, 48 p. Illustrations by Ray Cruz.

The only person meaner and uglier than Hepzibah Smith is her old aunt. Funny/nasty pen-and-ink drawings follow the evil twosome as they cow a Horrible Ugly, unnerve Mr. and Mrs. Smith, and vanquish painfully prissy Beautiful Vanilla.

Raskin, Ellen. The Mysterious Disappearance of Leon (I Mean Noel). E. P. Dutton, 1971. Illustrations by the author. Grades 4-6

A wacky heiress would be in the soup if not for the efforts of her two young traveling companions: earnest, well meaning, if indecisive, Tony and terribly clever, cool-headed Tina.

Rich, Gibson. Firegirl. The Feminist Press, 1972. Illustrations by Charlotte P. Farley Burrington. Grades K-6

In her determination to be a fireman, eight year old Brenda comes to the daring rescue of a pet rabbit in a smoke filled attic and lands a job as official Firegirl.

Scott, Ann. On Mother's Lap. McGraw-Hill, 1972. Illustrations by Glo Coalson. Grades K-3

A small Eskimo boy wonders if there's room on mother's lap even for the new baby.

Shulman, Alix Kates. Finders Keepers. Bradbury Press, 1971, unpaged. Illustrations by Emily McCully.

Hawk-eyed Lisa always finds lost toys and new trifles in the playground for her friends; one day, she stumbles on an old wagon and, with a healthy display of ego, decides to keep it for herself.

Tallon, Robert. Rhoda's Restaurant. Bobbs-Merrill, 1973. Grades K-5

Rhoda's Restaurant is great fun. Only a CanGenie can help a rotten cook like Rhoda save her unsuccessful restaurant.

Thomas, Ianthe. Lordy, Aunt Hattie. Harper & Row, 1973. Illustrations by Thomas Di Grazia. PS-3

This picture book stresses the warm relationship between a small black girl, Jeppa Lee, and her beloved Aunt Hattie. The nostalgic scenes depict the simplicity and beauty of a rural southern summer.

Thomas, Marlo. Free to Be ... You and Me. McGraw-Hill, 1974. Grades K-6

Feel free to be who you are and who you can be, not who you should be.

Udry, Janice May. Angie. Harper & Row, 1971. 64 p. Illustrations by Hillary Knight. Grades 4-6

In a brisk, funny series of chapter episodes, Angie outmaneuvers an obnoxious schoolmate, fools a couple of bigshot boys, goes into business selling rides, and even befriends her school principal.

Van Leeuwen, Jean. I was a 98-Pound Duckling. Dell. Grades 3-6

Kathy finds being thirteen is a disaster. She has problem hair, is taller than everyone except her father, and weighs only 98 pounds.

Williams, Jay. The Silver Whistle. Parent's Magazine Press, 1971, unpaged. Illustrations by Friso Henstra.

Prudence is constitutionally blase but her ample spunk, quick thinking, and clever use of a magic whistle enable her to save a kingdom and wed a very likeable prince.

Wells, Rosemary. Benjamin & Tulip. Dial Press, 1973. Illustrations by the author. Grades PS-2

A bully named Tulip terrorizes poor Benjamin--until she gets her just desserts.

Language Arts: 7-12

Adams, Elsie and Mary L. Briscoe, Editors. Up Against the Wall, Mother ... on Women's Liberation. Glencoe Press, 1971. Grades 10 and up

An anthology about issues in the women's movement from the traditional view of women to women's liberation writings including short stories, poetry and non-fiction.

Angelou, Maya. I Know Why the Caged Bird Sings. Bantam Books, 1971. Grades 9 and up

The author, an actress and poet, traces her life as a black woman from rural Arkansas to San Francisco.

Arnow, Harriette S. Dollmaker. Avon Books. Grades 10 and up

An indomitable mountain woman follows her husband to war-industry rich Detroit, only to be crushed by her alien urban life.

Bambara, Toni Cade. Gorilla My Love. Random House, 1972. Grades 7 and up

Fifteen short stories portraying the lives of black women.

Chester, Laura and Sharon Barba. Rising Tides: 20th Century American Women Poets. Washington Square Press, 1973, 410 p. Grades 10 and up

An anthology of twentieth-century women poets from Gertrude Stein to Erica Jong. There is a photograph of each poet and a short biographical sketch.

Gaines, Ernest J. The Autobiography of Miss Jane Pitman. Bantam Books, 1972. Grades 9 and up

Although her past stretched back into slavery, her rich life helped her understand and join the struggle for black people to be free.

Green, Hannah. I Never Promised You a Rose Garden. Holt, Rinehart and Winston, 1964. Grades 9 and up

A young woman's struggle for sanity is the theme of this haunting autobiographical novel.

Howe, Florence and Ellen Bass, Editors. No More Masks: An

Anthology of Poems by Women. Doubleday, 1973. Illustrations. Grades 10 and up

An attempt on the part of the authors to publish a work on women poets as a group. Eighty-seven modern women poets are represented. All but 8 are living. Poems cover a wide variety of themes.

Knudson, R. R. You Are the Rain. Delacorte Press, 1974. Grades 6 and up

Stranded together in the midst of a hurricane in Florida, two teen women who are total opposites, find they have more in common than they thought.

Knudson, R. R. Zanballer. Dell, 1974. Grades 8 and up

Thwarted in her efforts to play "girls' sports" teenage Zan Hagen learns how to play football--to win!

Laurence, Margaret. Stone Angel. Alfred A. Knopf, 1964. Grades 11 and up

A ninety-year-old woman, about to be dumped in a nursing home by her children, reminisces about her life and its meaning.

Logan, Jane. Very Nearest Room. Scribner, 1973. Grades 9 and up

A teenage woman's struggle to come to terms with her mother's slow death.

MacDougall, Ruth D. Cheerleader. Bantam Books. Grades 9 and up

A high school woman in the 50's tries to conform to the expected social roles, only to discard them as she leaves for college in this scathing satire of nostalgia.

Miller, Isabel. Patience and Sarah. Fawcett World Library, 1973. Grades 10 and up

The story of the love relationship between two young women who lived in Connecticut in the early 19th century.

Mohr, Nicholasa. Nilda. Bantam Books. Grades 9 and up

A Puerto Rican girlchild comes of age in the New York barrio in the 1940's in large part because of the sacrifices of her mother.

Morrison, Toni. The Bluest Eye. Holt, Rinehart and Winston, 1970. Grades 9 and up

A novel which deals with the effects of racism and poverty on young black women.

Murray, Michele, Editor. A House of Good Proportion: Images of Women in Literature. Simon and Schuster, 1973, 379 p. Grades 10 and up

Divided into the twelve chronological stages and roles of women, this collection uses short stories, poems and excerpts from novels to illustrate the depiction of women in literature during the past two centuries.

Olsen, Tillie. Tell Me a Riddle. Dell, 1971. Grades 10 and up
Powerful short stories with important insights into women's role and the relationships between men and women.

Plath, Sylvia. The Bell Jar. Bantam Books, 1972. Grades 10 and up
Confused and frightened by her "woman's role," the young protagonist retreats into insanity.

Sargent, Pamela, Editor. Women of Wonder: Science Fiction by Women about Women. Vintage, 1975.
Collection of 12 science fiction stories by and about women with an introduction on sex roles in traditional science fiction.

Segnitz, Barbara and Carol Rainey, Editors. Psyche: The Feminine Poetic Consciousness. Dell, 1973. Grades 10 and up
An anthology which concentrates on ten major women poets--Emily Dickinson, Marianne Moore, Gwendolyn Brooks, Elinor Wylie, May Swenson, Denise Levertov, Anne Sexton, Adrienne Rich, Sylvia Plath and Margaret Atwood and includes ten lesser known ones.

Shulman, Alix Kates. Memoirs of an Ex-Prom Queen. Bantam Books, 1973. Grades 10 and up
A very readable book about the problems of a young woman going from adolescence to womanhood trying to please men and also develop her intellectual self.

Singer, Frieda, Editor. Daughters in High School: An Anthology of Their Work. Daughters, Inc., 1974. Grades 9 and up
An anthology by high school women solicited by brief notices in newspapers around the country stressing both literary excellence and their responses to growing up female today. Short fiction, non-fiction and poetry are included.

Smedley, Agnes. Daughter of the Earth. The Feminist Press, 1973. Grades 10 and up
The autobiographical novel of a woman growing up in Missouri and then in small mining towns in the West in the 1890's who was a saleswoman and radical journalist and worked in left-wing politics.

Spinner, Stephanie, Editor. Feminine Plural: Stories by Women about Growing Up. Macmillan, 1972. Grades 10 and up
Growing up female in a traditionally male-oriented world is the theme of these ten stories by women writers including Colette and Carson McCullers.

Sullivan, Victoria and James Hatch, Editors. Plays By and About Women: An Anthology. Random House, 1973. Grades 10 and up
Eight plays on women are presented. Some are traditional

and some experimental. They deal both positively and negatively with women in Western society. Among the plays included are Lillian Hellman's The Children's Hour and Claire Booth's The Women.

Professional Books

Ahlum, Carol and Jacqueline M. Fralley. Feminist Resources for Schools and Colleges: A Guide to Curriculum Materials. The Feminist Press, 1973, 16 p.

An annotated bibliography of women's materials for schools and colleges. Non-print as well as print materials are listed.

Dawson, Bonnie. Women's Films in Print: An Annotated Guide to Over 750 Films. Booklegger Press, 1975, 150 p.

Includes over 350 women filmmakers working in 16 mm plus distributor's index.

Gersoni-Stavn, Diane. Sexism and Youth. Bowker, 1974.

An anthology of articles on sexism in children's and young adult literature and in the schools as well as on socialization and the impact of media.

Harrison, Barbara Grizzuti. Unlearning the Lie: Sexism in School. William Morrow, 1974.

The work of a mother's committee to combat sexism in a private school is described.

Harrison, Cynthia Ellin. Women's Movement Media: A Source Guide. Bowker, 1975.

An annotated list of over 500 publishers, periodicals and organizations which provide print and non-print materials.

Key, Mary Ritchie. Male/Female Language. Scarecrow Press, 1974, 200 p. Illustrations.

A book for the layperson as well as the linguist on the use of language and its implications in writing and literature.

Little Miss Muffet Fights Back. Revised Edition. Feminist Book Mart, (162-11 Ninth Ave., Whitestone, N.Y. 11357), 1974.

Bibliography produced by Feminists on Children's Media which contains approximately 300 critical reviews of children's books.

MacLeod, Jennifer and Sandra T. Silverman. You Won't Do: What Text-Books on U.S. Government Teach High School Girls. Know, Inc.

A discussion of what a group of N.J. women found out about textbooks.

Positive Images, Films for Changing Sex Role Concepts. Positive Images.

Films for women ages 5-17.

Wheeler, Helen. Womanhood Media: Current Resources about Women. Scarecrow Press, 1972.
Resources for information on the women's movement--both print and non-print materials listed.

Women and Literature; An Annotated Bibliography of Women Writers. 2nd Edition Revised and Expanded. The Sense and Sensibility Collective, 1973.
A good starting point for developing a collection of the literature of 20th-century women writers. The bibliography is annotated.

Reference Books

Barrer, Myra, Editor. Women's Organizations and Leaders Directory. Today Publications, 1975.
Lists women's organizations, their state and local chapters, committees, task forces, and advisory boards, state and local officers, and other pertinent information. There is an alphabetical index, geographical index, subject index and periodical index. Accomplishments of individuals are also noted.

Engelbarts, Rudolf. Women in the United States Congress, 1917-1972. Libraries Unlimited, 1974.
A guide to the accomplishments and voting records of the 81 women who have served in Congress. Arrangement is by house and then chronological. An introduction discusses the early feminists and women's role in Congress.

Gager, Nancy, Editor. Women's Rights Almanac 1974. Elizabeth Cady Stanton Publishing Company, 1974, 620 p.
Information is in four sections-state by state, national, women's issues and women in time. Sex breakdown by state and county elected officials is given. Essays analyze controversial issues.

Ireland, Norma Olin. Index to Women of the World from Ancient to Modern Times. Faxon, 1970.
An index to biographies of women found in collective biographies throughout the ages. Portraits are included when available. Essays on women in religion, fine arts, history, etc. are also included.

James, Edward, Janet Wilson James and Paul S. Boyer, Editors. Notable American Women, 1607-1950: A Biographical Dictionary. Harvard University Press, 3 vols.
Biographical sketches of 1359 exceptional women with bibliographical references.

Rennie, Susan and Kirsten Grimstad. The New Woman's Survival Catalog: Total Information. Coward, McCann & Geoghegan, 1973, 223 p. Illustrations.
A directory of information for women on communications, art, health, children, education, self-defense, jobs, laws and women's organizations done in the Whole Earth Catalog format.

Social Studies

Cade, Toni, Editor. The Black Women: An Anthology. New American Library, 1974.
A collection of political, historical and critical essays by black women as well as fiction and poetry by Nikki Giovanni and others.

Carlson, Dale. Girls Are Equal Too; The Women's Movement for Teenagers. Atheneum, 1973. Grades 7-10
An introduction to feminism for high school women. There are three sections: "The Way It Is," "How We Got This Way" and "What You Can Do About It."

DeCrow, Karen. Sexist Justice: How Legal Sexism Affects You. Random House, 1974. Grades 10 and up
Citing court decisions and case histories, DeCrow discusses women's legal status including job discrimination, alimony, welfare, abortions and family economics.

DeCrow, Karen. The Young Woman's Guide to Liberation. Pegasus, 1971. Grades 7-12
Written for young women as an introduction to the alternatives offered by the women's movement, the second-class status of women in education, employment and marriage is well-documented.

Faber, Doris. Petticoat Politics: How American Women Won the Right to Vote. Lothrop, Lee & Shepard, 1967. Grades 7-10
The story of the women's struggle to get the vote from the abolition movement to the passage of the 19th Amendment.

Feldman, Sylvia. The Rights of Women. Hayden. Grades 10 and up
An up-to-date account of women's legal status.

Friedan, Betty. The Feminine Mystique. Dell. Grades 10 and up
The book that began the present woman's movement. It describes how women were lured back into their homes after World War II and kept there.

Garskof, Michele H., Editor. Roles Women Play: Readings toward Women's Liberation. Brooks/Cole, 1971.
A collection of essays on women.

Harris, Janet. A Single Standard. McGraw-Hill, 1971. Grades 10 and up
The author traces the work and philosophy of several reformers seeking a single standard for men and women including Mary Wollstonecraft, John Stuart Mill and the Grimkes.

Heyman, Abigail. Growing Up Female: A Personal Photo Journal. Holt, Rinehart and Winston, 1974, 120 p. Illustrations. Grades 10 and up

A photographic journal about the women's experience from a feminist point of view. A brief narrative accompanies the photographs of youth and age, birth and abortion, work and motherhood, and love and sex.

Ingraham, Claire R. and Leonard W. An Album of Women in American History. Franklin Watts, 1973, 88 p. Illustrations. Grades 4 and up

Brief sketches of prominent American women. This album concentrates on the contribution of women throughout United States history emphasizing their struggles for equality. The photographs are excellent.

Kahn, Kathy. Hillbilly Women. Doubleday, 1973. Grades 10 and up

Kahn spent two years in southern Appalachia and has recorded the lives of nineteen women--their attitudes, strength and poverty.

Komisar, Lucy. The New Feminism. Franklin Watts, 1971. Grades 7-12

An introduction to the women's movement written for high school students which includes information on the social and sexual revolution, women in history and the women's movement.

Kraditor, Aileen S., Editor. Up From the Pedestal: Selected Documents in the History of American Feminism. Quadrangle, 1968. Grades 10 and up

A volume which uses primary sources spanning 300 years to document the role of women in society.

Ladner, Joyce. Tomorrow's Tomorrow. Doubleday, 1972. Grades 10 and up

A study of black womanhood through excerpts from taped interviews with black women. Growing up black and womanhood are discussed.

McHugh, Mary. The Woman Thing. Praeger Publishers, 1973. Grades 7-12

A book aimed at high school students which discusses the attitudes of people towards the women's movement and the changes brought about in various areas such as the educational and job worlds.

Martin, Del and Phyllis Lynn. Lesbian-Woman. Bantam Books, 1972. Grades 10 and up

The founders of the Daughters of Bilitis tell what it's like to be a gay woman in the U.S. and why the oppression should stop.

Morgan, Robin, Editor. Sisterhood Is Powerful. Random House, 1970, 602 p. Grades 10 and up

An early anthology on the women's movement including articles from a wide variety of women--high school women, chicanas, blacks, secretaries, etc. Also included are historical documents of the women's movement, poetry, and early writings on marriage, orgasm, media and prostitution.

O'Neill, William, Editor. Women at Work, Including the Long Day, the Story of a New York Working Girl by Dorothy Richardson and Inside the New York Telephone Company by Elinor Langer. Quadrangle, 1972, 360 p. Grades 10 and up

An overview of employment conditions for women at the beginning and middle of the twentieth century. O'Neill contrasts the study of the New York Telephone Company in 1905 and pieces on the New York Telephone Company in the New York Review.

Parker, Gail, Editor. The Oven Birds: American Women on Womanhood. Doubleday, 1972. Grades 10 and up

Writings by American women on American womanhood written between 1820 and 1920. The collection includes both fiction and journalism.

Rowbotham, Sheila. Women, Resistance and Revolution: A History of Women and Revolution in the Modern World. Random House, 1973, 287 p. Grades 10 and up

An historical perspective from the 17th century to the present of the changes in the status of women. It explores the relationship between feminism and social revolution. Sources for the book include pamphlets, manifestos, folk songs, novels and labor histories.

NON-PRINT

Career Education

Community Helpers. Feminist Resources for Equal Education. Photographs (8 1/2" x 11" in black and white). Grades 2-5

A set of non-sexist photographs.

8 Photographs (P.O. Box 3158, Saxonville Station, Framingham, Mass. 01701) $2.50.

Professional Women. Feminist Resources for Equal Education. Photographs (8 1/2" x 11" in black and white). Grades 2-5

A set of good role models for women and girls.

8 Photographs, $2.50.

Women at Work. Change for Children. Photographs (8" x 10" in black and white). Grades 2-6

A set of photographs of women performing traditionally male jobs from TV producer to shoe repairer.

15 Photographs (2588 Mission Street, Rm. 226, San Francisco, Calif. 94110) $6.00.

Women in Athletics. J. Weston Walch. Posters. Grades 2-6

Posters of famous women in sports from Chris Evert to

Wilma Rudolph.
18 Posters, $4.00.

Women in Music. J. Weston Walch. Posters. Grades 2-6
A series of photographs of famous women in music from Clara Schuman to Joni Mitchell with short biographical notes.
18 Posters, $4.00.

Women in Sports. Photographs (8 1/2" x 11" in black and white). Grades 2-6
Photos of women in baseball, track, gymnastics, weightlifting and judo.
6 Photographs (2103 Emerson, Berkeley, Calif. 94705) $3.35.

Language Arts

Anne Sexton Reads Her Poetry. Caedmon. Disc or cassette. Grades 10-Adult
Sexton reads from several of her volumes of poetry--one of the excellent modern poets.
1 Disc, $6.98; 1 Cassette, $7.95.

A Doll's House. Caedmon. Discs or cassettes. Grades 10-Adult
Claire Bloom and Donald Madden star in this version of A Doll's House. This 19th century play has an ironically modern note.
3 Discs, $21.94; 3 Cassettes, $23.85.

Edith Sitwell Reading Her Poems. Caedmon. Disc or cassette. Grades 10-Adult
Sitwell reads from a wide variety of her poetry.
1 Disc, $6.98; 1 Cassette, $7.95.

Edna St. Vincent Millay Reading Her Poetry. Caedmon. Disc or cassette. Grades 10-Adult
This reading which includes some of Millay's political poetry, i.e., "Where Can the Heart Be Hidden in the Ground" (dedicated to Sacco and Vanzetti), was recorded in 1941 when she was 49.
1 Disc, $6.98; 1 Cassetts, $7.95.

Emily Dickinson--A Self Portrait. Caedmon. Disc or cassette. Grades 9-Adult
Poems and letters of Emily Dickinson read by Julie Harris. The letters provide a most interesting portrait of one of America's unconventional poets and an early feminist.
1 Disc, $6.98; 1 Cassette, $7.95.

Free to Be You and Me. Bell Record Co. Disc. Grades 3-Adult
Songs for and about children who challenge sex roles.
1 Disc, $5.98.

Gertrude Stein Reads From Her Works. Caedmon. Disc or cassette. Grades 10-Adult

Stein reads The Making of Americans, Parts 1 and 2 A Valentine To Sherwood Anderson, If I Told Him; (A Completed Portrait of Picasso), Matisse, Madame Recamier.

1 Disc, $6.98; 1 Cassette, $7.95.

Gwendolyn Brooks Reading Her Poetry. Caedmon. Disc or cassette. Grades 9-Adult

Gwendolyn Brooks reads from several volumes of her poetry including A Street in Bronxville and Annie Allen with an introductory poem by Don L. Lee.

1 Disc, $6.98; 1 Cassette, $7.95.

Marianne Moore Reading her Poems and Fables from La Fontaine. Caedmon. Disc or cassetts. Grades 10-Adult

Marianne Moore reads her poems and from her translation of The Fables of La Fontaine.

1 Disc, $6.98; 1 Cassette, $7.95.

Mary Cassatt: An American Impressionist. Educational Dimensions. Filmstrip with disc or cassette. Grades 10-Adult

Description of the life and the development of the work of Mary Cassatt, an American impressionist. The influence of Degas in her work is discussed. Her technique is described in detail.

1 Filmstrip, 1 Disc, Teacher's Guide, $20.50; 1 Filmstrip, 1 Cassette, Teacher's Guide, $22.50.

Mothers and Daughters. Pacifica. Cassette. Grades 10-Adult

An examination of the relationships between mothers and daughters drawn from the words of Sylvia Plath, George Sand, Colette, Harriet Beecher Stowe, Adrienne Rich and Sapho.

1 Cassette (BC 0860), $12.00.

The Negro Woman. Folkways. Disc with notes. Grades 9-Adult

Excerpts from black women including Sojourner Truth, Harriet Tubman, Phyllis Wheatley and Mary McLeod Bethune.

1 Disc, Descriptive Notes (FH 5523), $6.98.

Poems and Letters of Emily Dickinson. Caedmon. Disc or cassette. Grades 9-Adult

Emily Dickinson's poetry and letters to friends and relatives read by Julie Harris.

1 Disc, $6.98; 1 Cassette, $7.95.

Poetry Is Alive and Well and Living in America. Media Plus. Filmstrips with discs or cassettes, teacher's guide. Grades 7-Adult

Visual interpretations of May Swenson's poems "Still Turning" and "The Pregnant Dream" and G. C. Oden's "The Way It Is" and "Speculation."

6 Filmstrips, 6 Discs, Teacher's Guide, $90.00; 6 Filmstrips, 6 Cassettes, Teacher's Guide, $90.00.

Sadie & Maude. Pacifica. Cassette. Grades 10-Adult

Two young black women, Jeanette Henderson and Linda Taylor, read the poetry of black women, and discuss the black liberation movement and its relation to women's liberation.

1 Cassette (BB 5133), $12.00.

Songs of Suffragettes. Folkways. Disc with booklet. Grades 7-Adult

Songs of the 19th century suffrage movement including "The Suffrage Flag" and "Winning the Vote."

1 Disc, 1 Booklet (FH 5281), $6.98.

To Be Young, Gifted and Black with James Earl Jones, Barbara Baxley and Claudia McNeil. Caedmon. Discs or cassettes. Grades 10-Adult

The story of Lorraine Hansberry in her own words. The material for this album is drawn from A Raisin in the Sun, The Sign in Sidney Brustein's Window, To Be Young, Gifted and Black, Les Blances, The Movement and Posthumously: In Defense of Life.

3 Discs, $21.94; 3 Cassettes, $23.85.

To the Lighthouse. Mrs. Dalloway. Caedmon. Disc. Grades 10-Adult

Selections from two of Virginia Woolf's best known novels read by Celia Johnson. The Mrs. Dalloway selection includes Woolf's comments on relationships among women.

1 Disc, $6.95.

Virginia Hamilton Reads Zeeley. Caedmon. Disc or cassette. Grades 5-8

A very popular children's book reflecting the author's early years in Ohio. Zeeley is the story of a young girl's growing independence and maturity.

1 Disc, $6.98; 1 Cassette, $7.95.

Women in Literature Reading Their Own Works. Caedmon. Cassettes. Grades 10-Adult

Gwendolyn Brooks, Marianne Moore, Katherine Anne Porter, Edith Sitwell, Gertrude Stein and Eudora Welty read from their works.

6 Cassettes, $45.00.

Social Studies

America in Crisis: The Women's Movement. Audio Visual Narrative Arts, Inc. Filmstrips with discs or cassettes, guide. Grades 8-Adult

Part I: The Suffragettes describes the long struggle of woman to get the vote. Part II: The Women's Libbers (an unfortunate title) describes the birth of NOW, the need for the women's movement and the progress made by the women's movement.

2 Filmstrips, 2 Discs, Guide, $37.50; 2 Filmstrips, 2 Cassettes, Guide, $41.50.

<u>American Woman's Search for Equality</u>. Current Affairs. Filmstrip with disc or cassette, discussion sheet. Grades 9-12

The major issues in the women's movement are discussed. It touches on opposition to the movement as well as discussing the various levels of interest in the movement. The need for the end to job inequality is stressed.

1 Filmstrip, 1 Disc, Discussion Sheet, $20.00; 1 Filmstrip, 1 Cassette, Discussion Sheet, $22.00.

<u>American Women in History</u>. Pacifica. Cassette. Grades 10-Adult

Judy Chicago and Isabel Welsh talk about several noted American women and their struggle with the culture of their time.

1 Cassette (BC 0602), $14.00.

<u>Angela Davis Speaks</u>. Folkways. Disc with descriptive notes. Grades 10-Adult

In this interview by Joe Walker of "Muhammed Speaks" produced by WABC-TV "Like It Is" in 1971, Angela Davis discussed Communism and her imprisonment awaiting trial.

1 Disc, Descriptive Notes (FD 5401S), $6.98.

<u>Angelina and Sarah Grimke</u>. Pacifica. Cassette. Grades 10-Adult

These two sisters, born around 1800, were public speakers and writers, and were the only Southern white women in the abolitionist movement.

1 Cassette (BB 3802.03), $14.00.

<u>The Basis of Our Beliefs; the Cult of True Womanoood; Male and Especially Female, 1800-1860</u>. Multi-Media Productions, Inc. Filmstrips with disc or cassette, teacher's manual. Grades 9-Adult

An historical view of the development of the 19th century "cult of womanhood," when women were regarded as pure, as the salvation of man and as the keeper of the home. Cultural, social and economic factors that encouraged its development are explored.

2 Filmstrips, 1 Disc, Teacher's Manual, $16.95; 2 Filmstrips, 1 Cassette, Teacher's Manual, $16.95.

<u>But the Women Rose: Voices of Women in American History</u>. Folkways. Disc. Grades 10-Adult

Statements by women through American history from the 1700's to the present.

2 Discs (FD-5535, FD 5536), $6.98.

<u>Dorothea Dicks</u>. Pacifica. Cassette. Grades 10-Adult

Starting as a volunteer in the Cambridge jail, Ms. Dicks became the prime mover in reforming laws affecting the insane in prison. She also organized, much to the displeasure of the male doctors, nurses for the Civil War.

1 Cassette (BB 3802.04), $11.00.

Elizabeth Cady Stanton and Susan B. Anthony. Pacifica. Cassette. Grades 10-Adult

These two women, who struggled for women's voting rights, are explored not as suffragettes, but as people, and their women's way of solving women's problems.

1 Cassette (BB 3802.05), $11.00.

Feminism As A Radical Movement. Multi-Media Productions, Inc. Filmstrips with disc or cassette, teacher's manual. Grades 10-Adult

Development of the theme of radicalism on women's issues among American women even during earlier times when the emphasis was on women as mothers and as passive creatures who needed the guidance of men.

2 Filmstrips, 1 Disc, Teacher's Manual, $16.95; 2 Filmstrips, 1 Cassette, Teacher's Manual, $16.95.

Frances Willard. Pacifica. Cassette. Grades 10-Adult

Willard's temperance crusade, and her Political School for Women, were significant in that they were the first mass political movement for women in this country (mid-19th century), and they provided organizational training for women.

1 Cassette (BB 3802.06), $11.00.

Francis Wright. Pacifica. Cassette. Grades 10-Adult

Ms. Wright was the first woman traveler to write an account in the United States; the first woman playwright to have a play produced in New York; a campaigner for free public schools, divorce law reform, and birth control, all in the first half of the 19th century.

1 Cassette (BB 2802.01), $11.00.

Great American Women's Speeches. Caedmon. Discs or cassettes. Grades 9-Adult

Speeches of the early women's movement including Lucretia Mott, Sojourner Truth, Lucy Stone, Elizabeth Cady Stanton, Susan B. Anthony, Carrie Chapman Catt, Florence Kelley, Ernestine Potowski Rose and Anna Howard Shaw read by Eileen Heckart, Claudia McNeil and Mildred Natwick.

2 Discs, $13.96; 2 Cassettes, $15.90.

Here She Is! The Making of Miss America. Pacifica. Cassette. Grades 9-Adult

A probing look at the Miss America contest recording both the pros and cons.

1 Cassette (BB 4155), $12.00.

Interview with Dr. Margaret Mead, Anthropologist. Folkways. Disc with descriptive notes. Grades 10-Adult

Dr. Mead discusses social anthropology, the American character and primitive societies. Though done in 1959, it is amazingly current.

1 Disc, Descriptive Notes (FC 7354), $5.98.

Letters from a Woman Homesteader. Pacifica. Cassette. Grades 10-Adult

A dramatic production from the diary of Elinore Pruitt Stuart, a young widow who left her job in 1909 in Denver to go to Wyoming, filed on 320 acres, hired herself out as a housekeeper and married her employer with the provision that she work her own land and pay for it herself.

3 Cassettes (BC 0721.01, BC 0721.02, BC 0721.03), $28.00.

Male/Female: Changing Lifestyles. Educational Audio Visual Inc. Filmstrips with discs or cassettes, teacher's notes. Grades 10-Adult

The set begins by presenting facts about sexual development. There is a two-part history of sex roles including the development of the women's movement from the 19th century to today. The final part offers comments by grade school and high school students on issues such as the family, social pressures, work and relationship.

4 Filmstrips, 4 Discs, Teacher's Notes, $60.00; 4 Filmstrips, 4 Cassettes, Teacher's Notes, $68.00.

Sexism, Racism, Classism in the Schools. National Education Association. Cassette with discussion sheet. Professional

Florence Howe discusses changing relations between Third World women and the White feminist movement. She also discusses ways to utilize the women's movement in producing change.

1 Cassette, Discussion Sheet, $9.00.

The Silenced Majority. Media Plus, Inc. Filmstrips with discs or cassettes, multimedia guide, posters, stickers. Grades 8-Adult

A five-part media kit produced by feminists covering jobs, education, advertising and other women's issues. A recommended first purchase. Includes Liberation Now; Women, Jobs and the Law; Women and Education; This Ad Insults Women; Rapping with the Feminists.

5 Filmstrips, 5 Discs, 1 Multimedia Guide, 1 Poster, Stickers (#108-FR), $85.00; 5 Filmstrips, 5 Cassettes, 1 Multimedia Guide, 1 Poster, Stickers (#108-FA), $85.00.

Training the Woman to Know Her Place. Pacifica, 1971. Cassette. Grades 11-Adult

A fast-moving lecture by Darryl and Sandra Bem, on how sex role conditioning is responsible for the lack of motivation among women to pursue non-traditional careers.

1 Cassette (BC 0426), $14.00.

What Have Women Done. Pacifica, 1974. Cassette. Grades 10-Adult

A sound essay on the history of working women in the United States which also explores these myths: the housewife doesn't work, women can't be organized, women are docile, and women work for pin money. An informative look at the types of work and the social positions achieved by women in America since colonial times.

1 Cassette (BC 1992), $12.00.

A Woman's Place. Schloat Productions. Filmstrips with discs or cassettes, program guide. Grades 9-Adult

A look at the important issues in the women's movement. An extremely interesting presentation of biological facts and the myths about women and work. The progress of the Women's Movement since 1966 is also discussed. Includes: Images; Biology and Destiny; Myths; The Women's Movement.

4 Filmstrips, 4 Discs, Program Guide, $80.00; 4 Filmstrips 4 Cassettes, Program Guide, $95.00.

Women in Politics - Why Not? Pacifica. Cassette. Grades 10-Adult

Shirley Chisholm, New York congresswoman, speaks about the key role of women in forming a coalition of the powerless to gain power.

1 Cassette (BC 0622), $14.00.

Women in Revolt; the Fight for Emancipation. Grossman. Document facsimiles (Jackdaws). Grades 7-Adult

A collection of document facsimiles on the early women's rights movement as it began in Victorian England.

Document Facsimiles (No. 49), $3.95.

Women: Perspectives on a Movement. Thesis. Cassettes with study resources and leader's guide. Grades 11-Adult

A series of discussions on various aspects of the women's movement reflecting on its impact and the changes it is making. It discusses the views of the black woman, changing relationships, the role of women in the church, the way society views women and the changing views of women towards themselves. Titles include: Powerless Majority, Socialization, Church and Theology, Identity, Changing Lifestyles.

3 Cassettes, Study Resources, Leader's Guide, $14.95.

Women Today; Options, Obstacles, Opportunities. Mass Communications, Inc. Cassettes with discussion guide. Grades 9-Adult

Eleven women and one man discuss today's women and their drive for equality and individualization from their individual fields of expertise. Those taped are Margaret Mead, Jean Baker Miller, Ida Davidoff, Matina Horner, Gerda Lerner, Sheila Tobias, Mary Daly, Ashaki Taka, Ruth Bader Ginsburg, Caroline Bird, Elizabeth Janeway and Sanford Perlis.

6 Cassettes, Discussion Guide, $65.00.

Women's Movements in Our History. J. Weston Walch. Posters. Grades 6-Adult

Posters that trace the women's movement from the early 19th century to the present. Each poster has a photograph and a short commentary.

18 Posters, $4.00.

The Women's Role: America and England. Current Affairs Films. Filmstrip with cassettes. Grades 10-Adult

A review of women's role in the development of England and America.

1 Filmstrip, 2 Discs, $25.00; 1 Filmstrip, 2 Cassettes, $30.00.

Women's Role in Society. Educational Record Sale. Disc. Grades 10 and up

A discussion of the emerging debate over women's role in the modern world, including cultural expectations, stereotypic notions, access to school and job opportunities. Elizabeth Janeway, narrator.

Disc, $5.95.

Women's Work America: 1620-1920. Schloat Productions. Filmstrips with discs or cassettes, program guide. Grades 8-Adult

A historical survey of some of the diverse roles occupied by women. The filmstrip begins with the life of women in colonial America, then describes the beginnings of mechanized industry in America and the beginnings of legal protection for working women and the beginnings of education for women in America. The women's rights movement to get the vote is discussed beginning with their participation in the abolition movement until they obtained the vote. Includes: Part I: "... her place is to guide the house," Part II: "... against God and nature," Part III: "... like hens that crow," Part IV: "... mostly mannish women."

4 Filmstrips, 4 Discs, Program Guide, $80.00; 4 Filmstrips, 4 Cassettes, Program Guide, $95.00.

WOMEN IN HIGH SCHOOL ENGLISH LITERATURE*

By Merle Froschl and Phyllis Arlow

The literature which is taught in secondary schools is used not merely as a tool for improving reading, written expression and general information. To a great degree, literature defines values and reality. The effect of reading material on the beliefs of students is immediate. While all are not in agreement, at least one study using reading content as a means of changing attitudes has demonstrated that these attitudes change in a positive direction with positive character presentations, and in a negative direction with negative character presentations.[1] Considerable evidence supports the fact that not only are females portrayed differently from males in secondary school literature, they are portrayed as inferior, less capable or less significant beings. It is therefore important for educators to recognize the messages which secondary school literature is transmitting to adolescents.

While a number of studies have already clearly established the sex-bias of high school English texts, we decided to review these theses and as many of the most widely used books as possible, with the aim of writing our own report. We examined for evidence of sexism those anthologies now in use in the secondary school English curriculum,[2] and those textbooks which according to the National Council of Teachers of English were the most widely used in secondary school English classes in the United States.

Our main focus was on the portrayal of female character in these anthologies. We examined the number of male and female authors in the anthologies now in use, the overall focus of the books, the language and editorial comments describing them, and the inclusion of minority women in selections.[3] Finally, we correlated our findings with other surveys and studies which included both anthologies and other supplementary reading selections.[4] Our report is a compilation of the research that reflects the most recent thinking about the portrayal of women in literature presently in use in the secondary school English curriculum.

---

*Reprinted by permission of the authors and the publisher from High School Feminist Studies, compiled by Carol Ahlum and Jacqueline Fralley with Florence Howe, pp. xvii-xxviii.

The Maleness of Literature

As our study of secondary school literature progressed, it became clear that we could not begin to discuss the female image in literature without first noting the overall "maleness" which characterized every anthology we examined. Most of the literature taught in high school classrooms, whether in anthologies or in supplementary readings, is male-centered in imagery, theme and characterization. Literature which focuses around the endurance and courage of men is plentiful, while almost no literature presents women who are physically strong or courageous. Stories about male athletes are abundant; those about female athletes are rare. Similarly, men who are successful in their work outside the home are portrayed often in the literature examined, while almost no literature presents women who are engaged in work outside the home. The fact that one-half of the adult female population is presently in the labor force, and that many women are responsible for the support of their families is almost totally ignored.[5] Women are still portrayed as perennial cake-bakers, too fragile and dependent to do the important work of life. Even in their role as wife and mother, women are not portrayed in these books as people capable of intelligently caring for and guiding the lives of children.

Our study of secondary school literature corresponds with the findings of such researchers as Broverman, Reisman, Griffin, Maccoby and Horner, who have shown that the traits identified as feminine are valued less than those considered to be masculine.[6] According to these psychological studies, the masculine image is synonymous with that of the healthy adult person--independent, aggressive, competitive, task-oriented, assertive, innovative, active. The feminine image--passive, fragile, yielding, dependent, empathetic, nonaggressive, supportive and graceful--is antithetical to that of the healthy adult.[7]

The language used in anthologies is also male-centered. The editor assumes the reader is male, rather than both male and female. The allegedly generic "he" and "man" are used consistently in editorial comments, questions to students and in chapter divisions. For example, in the introduction to one eleventh-grade textbook, masculine imagery prevails:

> We begin by assuming that literature is controlled energy. The energy is man's need to express himself.... Control ... is a successful football player's use of his strength ... a painter communicating his feelings ... a Grand Prix driver winning his race, and a writer achieving his goal through the controlled use of his medium.[8]

Another anthology divides its contents into two sections, "This Man, This World" and "Man's Destiny, Man's Choice."[9] In another text, published in 1974, the editor refers to the author as "he" throughout, whether the particular author being discussed is male or female.[10]

A disproportionately small number of female authors appears in anthologies currently in use. This is true whether the content is limited to twentieth-century fiction, or expanded to include European and American literature from its beginnings to the present day, and whether the book was published in 1974 or earlier. The Oregon Curriculum, for example, includes sixty-nine male authors and three female authors in one volume; and sixty-two and nine in another. In Adventures in Appreciation, there are sixty-three male authors and four female authors. Other studies revealed similar findings. A NOW survey of 171 anthologized selections counted 147 male authors to twenty-four female authors.[11] The most comprehensive survey involved 400 selections: of these, 306 were written by males, ninety-four by females.[12]

It is not uncommon for textbooks to include the same popular women writers--for example, Emily Dickinson and Willa Cather--while more contemporary female writers like Doris Lessing or Mary McCarthy rarely, if ever, appear. Yet, many unknown or undistinguished male writers like Mickey Mantle, George Freitag or Clifford Simak comprise a large part of the majority of anthologies. Furthermore, no attempt is made to represent women writers in various historical eras. Adventures in Appreciation includes four women writers (out of sixty-seven authors) who lived at approximately the same time (1830-1933) despite the fact that this book includes European and American literature from its beginnings to the present day.

The woman writer herself is regarded as an aberration. She is often depicted as a recluse, a mad woman, childless and unfulfilled. In one anthology, a page devoted to Gertrude Stein sums up her career in the following manner: "Miss Stein's experiments make her unintelligible to the general public."[13] Her most important contribution to literature is described as the stimulus she gave to other writers, notably Ernest Hemingway and Sherwood Anderson. Despite the fact that this page bears a portrait of Stein upon it, and that a few sentences are initially about her, the real subject of praise is Hemingway, whose achievements are discussed in great detail. Of course, the selection that follows is by Hemingway only.

Characterization is also male-dominated. In many stories, there are no female characters at all, and in the majority of selections, there are no female main characters. Females may appear briefly, but they are not developed as whole persons, and they are not integral to the plot. Often, the categories which are chosen (sports, war, nature) are those which have traditionally excluded female participation. For example, out of the eight divisions of one book, five of them (Survival, Spaceways, Mystery, Decision, Battleground) contain no female characters at all.[14]

In order to determine whether this male-centered pattern is balanced by supplementary readings, we consulted Scarvia B. Anderson's comprehensive study of the major works most often assigned in high school.[15] According to this 1964 survey conducted in 691 high schools throughout the United States, the most frequently assigned books are Macbeth and Julius Caesar, followed by Silas Marner, Great Expectations, Tale of Two Cities, Pride and Prejudice, Return of the Native, Our Town, Red Badge of Courage, The Scarlet Letter and Huckleberry Finn. This rather extensive reading list is hardly representative from any point of view. Almost all of the main characters are male, all the authors but two (Jane Austen and George Eliot) are white males, and only one item was written in the twentieth century. With the exception of Our Town, this list could have appeared seventy years ago as well as today. Why, for more than a half century, these Shakespearean plays and nineteenth-century novels have been read consistently in high schools throughout the United States is a matter worthy of scrutiny by educators, (Silas Marner, for example, was a daring choice once when the Harvard-Yale reading list for the year 1887 required a modern novel.) Whatever the original reasons, much of the literature now being taught in our schools is not necessarily useful to adolescents today.

Portrayal of Female Character

Women are relegated to secondary status in the literary curriculum not so much because they are omitted, but because of the distasteful way they are included. Female characters are stereotyped either by the roles they fulfill or by the personality traits with which they are endowed. The majority of the stories in anthologies depict women in the traditional roles of wife and mother. Their roles are secondary ones--they are supportive of the male main characters. Often, they are the servers bringing in the tea or dinner. In "Alone at Sea" by Hannes Lindeman, for example, an adventure story of a man's struggle against the elements, the only female appears at the beginning in her role as server:

> Now Ruth is preparing breakfast for me. Fried eggs, sunny side up, on an ocean of butter, to give me more energy before taking off.[16]

In another story, "Astronaut Away" by Russell A. Apple, Lt. Walker mentally reviews telling his wife and daughter about his mission:

> His daughter Peggy would be home from play, dinner would be cooking: he could talk to both of them. And what seemed more important; he would like them to hear his voice at least once more.[17]

In this story, the wife, Beth, and the daughter, Peggy, receive virtually the same treatment, so that one must constantly check names to be certain if the author is referring to the wife, or to the little girl. For example, a statement like, "Beth had waved from the window as usual when he left home," could apply either to the adult female or the child.[18]

In "Leaves from a Surgeon's Journal," a story by Harvey Cushing, women appear only in the following sentence: "Red Cross nurses were serving them hot soup and other things, ending up with the inevitable cigarette."[19]

"Papa and the Bomb" by William Iverson tells the story of a father who is a mad genius constantly having "brainstorms." The contrast among the interests of father, son and mother is noteworthy--the son is telling the story:

> For instance, the other night I'm sitting in the kitchen doing my geometry homework, and my mother is also in the kitchen baking a honey cake, when he comes up from the cellar with this expression on his face, and I could see he had another brainstorm.[20]

Only one mother was encountered who was not a "server," but she was a cruel, twisted individual. Indeed, some of the most interesting women in the curriculum seem to bear out the "witch" stereotype which is well recognized in fairy tales. In "The Rocking-Horse Winner," D. H. Lawrence describes this atypical mother:

> Only she herself knew that in the center of her heart was a hard little place that could not feel love, no, not for anybody. Everybody else said of her: "She is such a good mother. She adores her children." Only she herself, and her children themselves, knew it was not so. They read it in each other's eyes.[21]

Although most women are not depicted as malevolent beings, many are seen as detrimental to progress. Over and over again, women's helplessness in the face of disaster is evident. They are unable to cope--they panic, they are anxious, worried, over-protective, maudlin. The men, on the other hand, generally know how to behave during disasters--they are calm, competent, in control.

In "Fire in the Wilderness" by Benedict and Nancy Freedman, the wife is concerned with her husband's safety during a fire, but quite unnecessarily:

> ... 'What about you? Mike--I'm so frightened you won't be careful!' ... 'I'm fine, you know that. You do just what I tell you Kathy. Don't be frightened, don't get panicky, and don't leave the river.'[22]

Unfortunately, despite Mike's advice, Kathy does suffer burns, and it is Mike who tells her about them, as if she could not feel her own wounds--"You got second degree burns on that pretty face of yours," Mike states.[23]

Even little children in these stories can see how silly the fears of the average adult woman are. In "Dawn of the Remembered Spring" by Jesse Stuart, the little boy declares: "I love to kill snakes. I'm not afraid of snakes. I laugh to think how afraid of snakes Mom was...."[24]

In only one of the stories surveyed did a woman actually know more about a natural disaster than a man. In Walter van Tilburg Clark's "Why Don't You Look Where You're Going?" a woman has an excellent knowledge of the water's depth and, therefore, the ability to save the lives of the passengers aboard a ship. However, she is no "normal" woman--she is cruel and unfeminine. In fact, she has no real name, but is simply called "the masculine lady" as in the following illustration: "The masculine young lady disagreed .... The other passengers rebuked her heartlessness with silence."[25]

A frequent theme in literature portraying female character is the search for a marriage partner. Here can be found a variety of unwholesome women, from nagging mothers to females who are status-seeking, pushing, interfering, sarcastic and jealous. Most of these characters appear in connection with "romantic" stories which are grouped either by theme ("Relationships") or by genre ("Short Story"). The anthology selection "Sunday Costs Five Pesos," a one-act "comedy" of Mexican village life, is filled with stereotypic man-trappers who compete with each other to achieve their ultimate goal--marriage. Berta is described as "very pretty, but unfortunately she has a very high temper, possibly the result of her red hair."[26] She is never described in terms of her aspirations, abilities or intellect. Salome is introduced to the reader even more distastefully: "She is twenty-eight, and so many years of hunting a husband have left her with an acid tongue."[27] These women are bitter, ugly, competitive. They tell adolescents that woman's central goal is to find a man and to get married: the process itself is ugly, but if not successfully achieved, unmarried women become empty, hateful creatures, unfulfilled in every way.

When women are not being manipulative in such love fiction, they are being manipulated. They are often viewed as sex-objects--vain, silly creatures who, nevertheless, become desirable fantasies for the smitten male. In "The Chaser" by John Collier, Alan has approached an old man in order to obtain a love potion. The old man described the benefits of his potion and, at the same time, a rather perverse definition of love evolves:

> 'For indifference,' said the old man, 'they substitute devotion. For scorn, adoration. Give one tiny measure of this to the young lady ... and however gay and giddy she is, she will change altogether. She will want nothing but solitude and you.'
>
> 'I can hardly believe it,' said Alan. 'She is so fond of parties.'
>
> 'She will not like them any more,' said the old man. 'She will be afraid of the pretty girls you may meet.'

> 'She will actually be jealous?' cried Alan in a rapture. 'Of me?'
>
> 'Yes, she will want to be everything to you. ... You will be her sole interest in life.'
>
> 'That is love!' cried Alan.[28]

In another selection, "Love is a Fallacy" by Max Shulman, a young law student, who had observed that lawyers married beautiful, gracious and intelligent women, finds that the object of his affection almost fits these specifications perfectly. Although his love-object was not yet of pin-up proportions, the young man is certain that time would supply the lack. His most serious problem, however, was that she was not intelligent, but even here, he believed she could be molded more suitably:

> 'Intelligent she was not. In fact, she veered in the opposite direction. But I believed that under my guidance, she would smarten up. At any rate, it was worth a try. It is, after all, easier to make a dumb girl smart than to make an ugly girl beautiful.'[29]

The only females who are occasionally successful in escaping from the stereotyped pattern are the noncomforming "tomboys" or the tough, proud grandmothers. This bears out the notion advanced in one study that interesting female characters are generally not within their childbearing years, but are either premenstrual or post-menopausal.[30] Such females are not needed in their role as "server" to the male, and are therefore not threatening, and more free to do as they wish. Sometimes, however, because of their nonconformity, such characters suffer emotionally--such as Scout in _To Kill a Mockingbird_, Frankie in _A Member of the Wedding_ or Emily in "Bad Characters." However, they are dynamic personalities, who have an identity separate from the family or the males in their lives. They have goals and interests of their own, and unquestionably, they represent the most wholesome females in the curriculum.

Implications

It is apparent from the study that the anthologies used in high school English classes depict life unrealistically. Women are not being supplied with admirable role models, and both males and females are learning harmful lessons which accentuate prejudices and preferences for a white, male-dominated culture.

Most of the literature surveyed depicts women in the traditional roles of housewife and mother, but even here, they are characterized as inferior people. Often, women are portrayed as cruel, competitive with each other, or as passive and childish creatures. Only "tomboys" or grandmothers reveal positive personality traits, and they are often considered to be outside of the "mainstream" of life.

One of the most serious implications of the study of secondary school literature is the contribution of such texts to the underachievement of the adolescent female. Most researchers are in agreement with Anne Grant West, who has stated that it is in the junior and senior high school that students idealize the sex roles prescribed by our culture, and it is, significantly, in these years that girls start to underachieve.[31] According to a study by Shaw and McCuen:

> There is evidence that girls who are underachievers in high school usually begin to be so about the onset of puberty, while for boys underachievement in high school usually has an earlier outset. This contrast is a further indication that the achievement drop-off among girls as they reach maturity is linked to the adult female sex role.[32]

A study conducted by Mary Beaven, which sought to discover which female characters students could positively identify with, revealed that there were few, if any, admirable role models present in the curriculum.[33] Girls wrote unfavorable comments which pointed to the dearth of favorable women characters in literature. They stated either that they could not recall reading anything at all about females, or that they were unimpressed with those they had read about. One male student commented: "We have read about so few women in English class that they are hardly worth mentioning. The few we have read about I wouldn't care to have for a wife or mother."[34]

It is highly significant that most girls could not recall reading about any women they could admire and those who did, did not wish to resemble any of the characters they had read about. When they did name admirable characters, highest on the list of characters girls could admire were Hester Prynne, Scarlett O'Hara and Juliet. Although all of these women were victims in one way or another, they were singled out because at least they were main characters. In the conclusion of her study, Mary Beaven remarks:

> For the most part, women in the literature read and discussed in high school English classes play minor, unpleasant roles. The few major feminine characters tend to be either passive and insipid or vicious. And the result of the survey indicated that boys and girls can relate to few of these feminine characters.[35]

It is clear that adolescents, especially, are very much in need of the feminine contributions to consciousness and women and men need to understand and value the nature of these contributions. We need to read about what is happening to us in the context of realistic life situations and to provide learning experiences which are meaningful to our lives. Since the present texts are overwhelmingly biased, we will have to provide, for the next decade or two, supplementary materials which express the experiences of our lives with greater accuracy.

Notes

1. Sarah Zimet, "Does Book Reading Influence Behavior?"
2. For a complete list of anthologies used in this study, see bibliography.
3. Most of the literature we surveyed was not only sexist, it was racist as well. The selections reinforce the American preference for a white, middle-class, male-dominated culture. Of the few female authors included in the anthologies in our survey, only four were black poets. When minority women are included as characters in literature, there is little awareness that strategies which may be appropriate for one group are wrong for another. There is an overemphasis on dialect, and a tendency to assume that all low-income families are the same. According to a NCTE Task Force on Racism and Bias in the Teaching of English, educational materials now suffer from the following deficiencies:
    a. The inadequate representation of literary works by members of nonwhite minorities in general anthologies which serve as basic texts, and in basal readers and other language arts kits, including audio-visual materials, in most elementary, secondary and college English courses.
    b. Representation of minority groups which is demeaning, insensitive or unflattering to the culture.
    c. The inclusion of only popular and proven works by a limited number of "acceptable" writers, resulting in a mispresentation of the actual range of the group's contributions to literature.
    d. Biased commentaries which gloss over or flatly ignore the oppression suffered by nonwhite minority persons.
    e. The inclusion of commentaries in anthologies which depict inadequately the influence of nonwhite persons on literary, cultural and historical developments in America.

    Although we have not here attempted to document racist attitudes found in the English high school curriculum, we acknowledge that sexism is intrinsically linked with racism. We are concerned not only with stereotypes assigned to white, middle- or upper-class women, but to those attributed to working-class women, as well as to all minority women.
4. For a complete list of studies used, see bibliography.
5. Francine Blau, "Women and Economics," pp. 48-50.
6. Eleanor Maccoby, ed., _The Development of Sex Differences_, p. 31.
7. Inge Broverman, et al., "Sex-Role Stereotypes and Clinical Judgments of Mental Health," pp. 1-7.
8. Albert R. Kitzhaber, ed., _Literature V_, p. 2.

9. Leo B. Kneer, ed., Compass.
10. Albert R. Kitzhaber, ed., Viewpoints in Literature.
11. Gayle Hurst, "Sex Bias in Junior High Literature Anthologies," passim.
12. Susan L. Wiik, "The Sexual Bias of Textbook Literature," p. 228.
13. Robert C. Pooley, ed., The United States in Literature, p. 246.
14. Leo B. Kneer, ed., Perspectives.
15. Scarvia B. Anderson, "Between the Grimms and 'The Group': Literature in American High Schools."
16. Kneer, Perspectives, p. 139.
17. Kneer, Perspectives, p. 210.
18. Kneer, Perspectives, p. 210.
19. Kneer, Perspectives, p. 376.
20. Kneer, Perspectives, p. 412.
21. Kneer, Exploring Life Through Literature, p. 93.
22. Kneer, Perspectives, p. 160.
23. Kneer, Perspectives, p. 164.
24. Kitzhaber, Viewpoints in Literature, p. 74.
25. Kitzhaber, Viewpoints in Literature, p. 158.
26. Kneer, Focus, p. 33.
27. Kneer, Focus, p. 34.
28. Kitzhaber, Viewpoints in Literature, p. 7.
29. Kitzhaber, Viewpoints in Literature, p. 166.
30. Hurst, p. 12.
31. Anne Grant West, "Women's Liberation or Exploding the Fairy Princess Myth," p. 6.
32. Maccoby, p. 31.
33. Mary H. Beaven, "Responses of Adolescents to Feminine Characters in Literature," pp. 48-68.
34. Beaven, p. 56.
35. Beaven, p. 55.

English Literature Anthologies Reviewed

Fuller, Edmund, and Kinneck, Jo. Adventures in American Literature. Vol. I. New York: Harcourt, Brace & World, 1963.

Kitzhaber, Albert R., ed. Viewpoints in Literature. New York: Holt, Rinehart and Winston, 1974.

______. Literature IV (The Oregon Curriculum). New York: Holt, Rinehart and Winston, 1974.

______. Literature IV Teacher's Guide. New York: Holt Rinehart and Winston, 1970.

______. Literature V (The Oregon Curriculum). New York: Holt, Rinehart and Winston, 1970.

Kneer, Leo B., ed. Perspectives. Glenview: Scott, Foresman and Company, 1963.

______. Compass. Glenview: Scott, Foresman and Company, 1971.

______. Accent: Each His Own. Glenview: Scott, Foresman and Company, 1972.

_______. Focus. Glenview: Scott, Foresman and Company, 1969.
_______. Exploring Life through Literature. Glenview: Scott, Foresman and Company, 1973.
Perrine, Laurence; Jameson, Robert; Silveri, Rita; Harrison, G. B.; Gurney, A. R., Jr.; Pritchett, V. S.; Loban, Walter; and Folds, Thomas. Adventures in Appreciation. Vol. I. New York: Harcourt, Brace & World, 1968.
Pooley, Robert C., ed. The United States in Literature. Glenview: Scott, Foresman and Company, 1963.

Bibliography

Anderson, Scarvia B. "Between the Grimms and 'The Group': Literature in American High Schools." Princeton: Cooperative Test Division, Education Testing Service, 1964.
Baumrind, Diana. "From Each According to Her Ability." School Review, February 1972.
Beaven, Mary H. "Responses of Adolescents to Feminine Characters in Literature." Research in the Teaching of English, Spring 1972.
Blau, Francine. "Women and Economics." In 51% Minority. Connecticut Conference on the Status of Women, 1972.
Broverman, Inge K.; Broverman, Donald M.; Clarkson, Frank E.; Rosenkrantz, Paul S.; and Vogel, Susan R. "Sex-Role Stereotypes and Clinical Judgments of Mental Health." Journal of Consulting and Clinical Psychology, February 1970.
Cornillon, Susan Koppelman, ed. Women's Liberation and Literature. Bowling Green: Bowling Green University Popular Press, 1972.
Ferguson, Mary Anne. Images of Women in Literature. Boston: Houghton Mifflin Company, 1973.
Fowler, Lois Josephs. "Women in Literature & the High School Curriculum." English Journal, November 1973.
Frazier, Nancy, and Sadker, Myra. Sexism in School and Society. New York: Harper & Row, 1973.
Hartman, Joan E. "Part II: Editing and Publishing Freshman Textbooks." College English, October 1972.
Howe, Florence. "Identity and Expression: A Writing Course for Women." College English, May, 1971.
_______. "Sexism, Racism, and the Education of Women." Today's Education, May 1973.
Hurst, Gayle. "Sex Bias in Junior High Literature Anthologies." St. Louis: St. Louis National Organization for Women, n.d.
Kagan, Jerome. "The Emergence of Sex-Differences." School Review, February 1972.
_______. "Check One: Male-Female." Psychology Today, July 1969.
Kelly, Ernece B., ed. Searching for America. Urbana: National Council of Teachers of English, 1972.
Lysne, Ruth, and Warner, Margo. "A Woman's Place: What's Cooking in Junior High School English Anthologies." Minnesota English Journal, Fall 1972.

Maccoby, Eleanor E., ed. The Development of Sex Differences. Stanford: Stanford University Press, 1966.

Maccoby, Eleanor E. "Women's Intellect." In The Potential of Woman, edited by Seymour M. Farber and Roger H. Wilson. New York: McGraw-Hill Book Company, 1963.

Minuchin, Patricia. "The Schooling of Tomorrow's Woman." School Review, February 1972.

Mullen, Jean S. "Freshmen Textbooks." College English, October 1972.

Oetzel, Roberta. "Annotated Bibliography." In The Development of Sex Differences. Stanford: Stanford University Press, 1966.

Scott, Foresman and Company. "Guidelines for Improving the Image of Women in Textbooks." Glenview: Scott, Foresman and Company, 1973.

Showalter, Elaine, ed. Women's Liberation and Literature. New York: Harcourt Brace Jovanovich, Inc., 1971.

Showalter, Elaine. "Women and the Literary Curriculum." College English, May 1971.

U'Ren, Marjorie B. "The Image of Woman in Textbooks." Woman in Sexist Society, edited by Vivian Gornick and Barbara K. Moran. New York: Basic Books, 1971.

Warren, Barbara. The Feminine Image in Literature. Rochelle Park: Hayden Book Company, 1973.

Wells, Nancy. "Women in American Literature." English Journal, November 1973.

West, Anne Grant. "Women's Liberation or Exploding the Fairy Princess Myth." Scholastic Magazine, November 1971.

Wiik, Susan L. "The Sexual Bias of Textbook Literature." English Journal, February 1973.

Zimet, Sarah. "Does Book Reading Influence Behavior?" Presentation to Colorado Library Association Annual Conference, December 1972.

THE YOUNG ADULT GAY NOVEL*

By David White

This article is a review of The Man Without a Face by Isabelle Holland (Lippincott, 1972) and Sticks and Stones by Lynn Hall (Follett, 1972).

When I was thirteen, I had my first crush on another boy. I was afraid to tell anyone, because I had never heard that there were people in the world who were attracted to their own sex. A couple of years later I ran across an obscure reference in a dusty old psychology textbook in the reference room of the Louisville (Ky.) Free Public Library, which said that "all male homosexuals secretly want to be women." I felt much relieved. I knew I didn't want to be a woman, so that must mean I am not a homosexual, even though some of the other things the article said about these strange people seemed to hit very close to home.

That was fifteen years ago. Today's it's not quite as bad as all that, but there is still an enormous conspiracy at work in our culture to keep gay young people from finding out who they are, or from getting any factual information about themselves. When writers of books for young people touch on this subject, which they occasionally do, they seem to be at considerable pains to avoid depicting gayness as worthwhile and valid, and to prefer instead to show it as a distortion or a flaw in what might have otherwise been a healthy personality.

Isabelle Holland has written a tender and moving story of Charles Norstadt, a lonely fourteen-year-old boy isolated in a summer resort with his indifferent mother and his impossible sister. Charles feels himself stifled by the women in his family, and sees his only hope as passing the entrance examination to St. Matthew's, a boys' boarding school, where he can be away from women and get the male influence he needs. But Charles is no scholar, and in order to pass, he must have help. Summoning remarkable courage, he approaches the Man Without a Face, Justin McLeod, a middle-aged recluse living in the community whose face is horribly scarred and disfigured as if by fire. McLeod is rumored to be a writer or

*Reprinted by permission of the author and publisher from SRRT Newsletter, No. 33, pp. 21-23.

an ex-teacher, and Charles senses that he can help him pass the exams. McLeod is reluctant at first, but consents if Charles agrees to follow his very strict regime. A friendship develops between the two, and the reader comes to see McLeod as a loving human being who is nursing his own personal tragedy. Charles improves scholastically, and the two become closer friends, until one night, following a family crisis--Charles's dog is killed by his sister's boy friend--Charles deserts his own home and stays with McLeod, and they have their one and only sexual experience. McLeod leaves the next day, and Charles never sees him again.

We are expected to come to love Justin McLeod and to feel a certain bewildered pity for him. After all, didn't he bring his troubles on himself? If one reads carefully enough between the lines, one gathers that McLeod, once a highly respected teacher in a boys' school, disgraced himself by having some sort of forbidden relationship with one of his students, which terminated in an automobile accident where the boy was killed and McLeod scarred for life, on his soul as well as his face. And then, after showing Charles what was probably the only affection he ever had from anyone, McLeod disappears, and we learn later that he has died of a heart attack. There is such an uncomfortable parallel between gayness and death that one is made to feel that the two go hand in hand.

Charles, besides inheriting all of McLeod's property, ends up with a brand new stepfather, who is perfectly straight, and who, we are assured, will show him the affection he needs, but along conventional lines. And of course, no need to worry that Charles will turn out gay. This one incident doesn't count. Everything works out perfectly in the end, which, of course, it couldn't have done if McLeod had lived. Because we now know that Charles and McLeod really did love each other, and that isn't healthy.

A teen-age boy who reads this story (and I'm not trying to slight women, but it's obvious that a boy would find more to identify with than a girl) will come away from it with the feeling that he has just glimpsed a forbidden world--and be relieved that it was only a glimpse. A boy who suspects that he has something in common with McLeod may possibly be frightened into suppressing his identity for a few more years until something else happens to jar it loose.

Somewhat of an improvement is Lynn Hall's Sticks and Stones. Sixteen-year-old Tom Naylor and his mother have come to live in Buck Creek, Iowa, after his mother and father are divorced. Unlike the other novel, this mother-and-son relationship is close, loving, and--one senses--marked by mutual respect. Charlotte Naylor keeps a store, and Tom helps her after school. But Tom's real interest is music. His sensitivity and urban background (they're from Chicago) set him apart from his classmates, and his one companion is Floyd Schleffe, a misfit in a different way, a dull, slow, overweight boy who attaches himself to Tom, not because they have anything in common, but because Floyd sees that Tom, like himself, is friendless. Then into Tom's life comes Ward Alexander, who is somewhat older, but who shares Tom's interest in music. The two young men become friends, and Floyd is left out.

Ward has just been discharged from the Air Force, he says, for asthma. Homosexuality, say the town gossips. And Floyd, hearing the rumor, decides to get even with Tom for deserting him, and starts a rumor that Tom is gay and that he and Ward are lovers. The rumor spreads, and Tom, who was chosen to go to Des Moines for the state music finals, is told by his music teacher that he won't be allowed to go because the parents of the other boys don't want their sons staying overnight with Tom in a hotel. Tom realizes for the first time why the other kids have been avoiding him, and when he shares his unhappiness with his best friend Ward, Ward confesses that he is the cause of Tom's being rejected. He admits that he is gay, and even admits that he loves Tom, but assures Tom that he had no intention of making any sexual advances and that he would like to forget the whole thing and be friends as before. Tom avoids Ward in an attempt to clear his reputation, makes a few abortive attempts at dating girls, and finally gives in to despair. The other kids leave for the music finals in Des Moines and Tom is left with Floyd, whom he dislikes, and who dislikes him, but is still willing to use him. While driving home from school, Tom has an accident with the car and Floyd is killed. Tom survives, Ward comes to see him in the hospital, and the book closes with the suggestion that Tom and Ward will be friends again.

Judy Blume, who reviewed this book for the New York Times Book Review, said "Some will say that this is a book about homosexuality. It isn't. What it is about is far more important: injustice through the power of gossip." I disagree. We're supposed to think there is an injustice because Tom was accused of being gay when he wasn't really gay. If he were, would it have been right to ostracize him from the group, to deny him the trip to Des Moines? I don't think Ms. Hall is trying to tell us Tom is a straight person unjustly accused of being a gay person. We never really know whether Tom is gay or not. He expresses his own confusion about his sexuality, and in the end, when he and Ward are together again, we don't know if they go on to become lovers in the sexual sense or not. Ms. Hall, in a very guarded way (after all, it can't be easy getting a gay novel published) is telling us it doesn't make any difference. The injustice was still an injustice, whether Tom is gay or straight, and the restoration of his friendship with Ward is good and satisfying as a conclusion, whether they are lovers or not. For my part, I like to imagine that they are, but for those who aren't ready for that in a novel for teen-agers, it isn't explicit.

As a librarian, I would have less hesitation recommending Sticks and Stones than I would The Man Without a Face. Isabelle Holland wasn't quite able to avoid presenting gayness as a weakness or tragic flaw; Lynn Hall, on the other hand, comes closer to presenting it as a simple fact of life that must be dealt with like all other facts of life. In Sticks and Stones, the conflict arises not out of *being gay*, but out of the reaction of straight people to the situation. The great American gay novel is still a long way from being written, but *Sticks and Stones* is worth reading in the meantime.

CAN YOUNG GAYS FIND HAPPINESS IN YA BOOKS?*

by Frances Hanckel and John Cunningham

As many young adult novels suggest, contemporary American society is a difficult place in which to come of age. Judging from the number of these novels that focus on problems encountered during adolescence, one might conclude that the person who struggles through to adulthood without considerable emotional or physical scarring is indeed the exception. Recent YASD "Best Books for Young Adults" booklists were the basis for a quick survey we did of junior novels with major adolescent characters--the survey confirmed this trend in YA fiction.

Librarians also are familiar with which novels are most requested by YAs. Here, too, the pattern holds: Novels that deal with themes of drug abuse, unplanned pregnancy, difficulties in family or peer-group relations, and individual identity struggles are always among the most popular.

Adolescence is, by definition, a period of transition. It is a time when individual experiences are marked by physical, emotional, and social changes. Such changes often evolve gradually, but may be sometimes precipitated by a crisis or conflict. Through meeting the challenges of adolescence, the individual will, ideally, establish a positive self-identity and develop standards and value systems to guide her or his life. Throughout adolescence the role that both fiction and nonfiction books can play in promoting a healthy discussion of problems is considerable. It is important, therefore, in book selection and recommendation that librarians examine YA books describing adolescent problems to assess their contribution in informing YAs and in aiding their development to responsible adulthood.

On what principles should any critical analysis of young adult literature rest? Honesty and realism in addressing any given circumstance should comprise the base standard in any appraisal. Pregnancies do not just disappear; drug addiction is not easily overcome; poor and minority youth encounter real problems in struggling

*Reprinted by permission of the authors and publisher from Wilson Library Bulletin (March 1976), 528-534. Copyright © 1976 by The H. W. Wilson Company.

for equality of opportunity. But librarians and others evaluating YA literature should demand more than a cold rendering of reality. Honesty must be combined with hope, a hope that is life-affirming and encourages the reader to consider and develop a workable moral philosophy.

Books and Social-Sexual Identity

A large portion of YA fiction is devoted to the broad topic of social-sexual identity, with the complacent assumption of heterosexual orientation. But what about adolescents who are gay? A major burden that they carry is the sense of being "different" and somehow outside the norms of ordinary adolescent activity. They are unsure of how to define themselves in their homes and peer groups. Where are the role models for young gays? How do non-gay people learn about members of their communities and families who are also gay?

Homosexuality and the lifestyles of gay people have recently entered the realm of YA literature. Since 1969 four novels have been published in which adolescent homosexual experiences are a major theme: John Donovan's *I'll Get There. It Better Be Worth the Trip*; Isabelle Holland's *The Man Without a Face*; Lynn Hall's *Sticks and Stones*; and Sandra Scoppettone's *Trying Hard to Hear You*. Before examining these novels individually and collectively, we should mention the importance of libraries, books, and in particular, novels during the adolescence of gay people.

A Revolution Without Communication

In spite of all the talk about the sexual revolution in American society, many adolescents find it difficult to discuss sex frankly with their parents. Sex remains, primarily, a matter of speculation and information sharing within the peer group, aided occasionally by a book or two. When most young people are reluctant to talk with their parents about socially acceptable sexual concerns, imagine the plight of those who suspect or know they are gay.

Can young gays talk openly with their friends? Most young people's ideas about gays come from the media. And in our sexist, homophobic society, the media treats gays as persons to ridicule and/or fear. All adolescents are sensitive about themselves, and thus gay youngsters fear to identify themselves to their friends, who probably will have accepted the stereotype.

In this way social attitudes often force young people with questions about their sexual orientation into personal isolation, into the "closet." Under these circumstances nonpersonal sources of information on sex, sexuality, gay lifestyles, and similar concerns become extremely important. Thus many gays head for the library.

If young gays are to understand and react positively to homosexual experiences, then supportive information written specifically for this audience must be available. Similarly if the misconceptions and societal prejudice toward this minority are to be changed, then accurate, positive information on the gay community must exist and be available to all straight readers.

During the last five years the range and availability of information about gay people has greatly changed. In offering readers advisory services, librarians need to be aware of this redirection in materials. Most libraries now do contain a nuclear collection of positive materials on gay lifestyles.

Two popularly written books which have received the Gay Book Award of the ALA/SRRT Task Force on Gay Liberation are Peter Fisher's The Gay Mystique and Del Martin and Phyllis Lyon's Lesbian Woman. Woman Plus Woman; Attitudes Towards Lesbianism by Dolores Klaich is another excellent contribution to such popular literature. Directed specifically to YA audiences is Eric Johnson's Love and Sex in Plain Language (1974 edition), which contains a fairly written chapter on the experience of being gay.

There remains, however, a large body of written material that is far from supportive. Such information is usually found in psychological studies of "abnormality" or sociological inquiries into "deviance" or "victimless crimes." A catalog search for materials on homosexuality will more than likely turn up a preponderance of these negative books. Librarians aware of this situation can direct patrons to additional literature with an alternative viewpoint.

Also, catalog searches invariably lead only to nonfiction works --works that often are scholarly and contain an abundance of statistical data. Such information can be valuable if it is indirectly supportive: Gay teenagers may find it reassuring to learn that rather than being unique, they are members of a minority numbering perhaps 20 million.

But rather than scholarly studies, gay adolescents are looking for "flesh and blood" characters. Few adolescents are raised in an environment that includes exposure to the gay community, and so, once interest is aroused in exploring this aspect of identity, young people wonder how others have handled similar experiences. What are gay people *really* like? How and when do they meet each other? Do they find *love* and lead happy lives? How do straight people react to lesbians and gay men?

Adolescents are looking for answers to their personal questions. They are open and anxious to encounter positive role models, and young adult fiction is a logical place to find some of these models. For most young people the identification and location of such YA fiction is possible only through the active intervention of a librarian. Assuming the availability of the books and the ability to identify them, what kind of information will a young person find?

In order to encourage critical discussion about the perspective of gay life which all adolescents encounter in YA fiction, plot summaries of the previously mentioned four novels follow. They are meant to provide a basis for a critique of the handling of the gay experience in YA fiction as a whole.

I'll Get There. It Better Be Worth the Trip

Davy Ross, age 13, had been raised by his grandmother for the eight years since his parents' divorce. They got along terrifically; she gave Davy his best friend--his dachshund Fred. After his grandmother's death Davy (and Fred) went to New York to live with his mother. Davy visited his father on weekends and gradually came to feel at home in the city. At his new, private day school, he became friends with Altschuler, a classmate who also had divorced parents. One weekend Davy and Altschuler spent a night together. Afterward they were so uncomfortable with each other that Davy's mother suspected something had happened between them and arranged for Davy's father to "talk" to him. While they talked Davy's dog was killed by a car outside the apartment house. Davy felt not only grief over Fred but also guilt, and he blamed himself and Altschuler. Finally the two had a fistfight that allowed them to become regular friends again. Davy came to realize that the accident was not caused by what they had done, and the important thing was not to do it again.

The Man Without a Face

Charles Norstadt spent the summer that he was 14 on the island. With him was his mother, who was looking for her fourth husband and with whom he had never been close; his older sister Gloria, with whom he fought constantly; and his younger sister Meg, who was his only real friend, except, of course, for his cat Moxie. Facing a difficult boarding school entrance exam in the fall, Charles was having a hard time studying, until he asked a neighbor, a man known to be a recluse, for tutoring and help.

Initially Charles was afraid of Justin MacLeod, "the man without a face." But gradually through their working together, he became the first adult Charles could communicate with and trust. Justin confided to him that the scars on his face were from a car accident in which he had been drunk while driving. In the accident the boy with him was killed.

At the end of the summer Charles had a terrible encounter during which Moxie was killed by Gloria's boyfriend, and she told him that his real father was an alcoholic who had died a bum. Charles fled to Justin. The next morning he was very upset by what happened between the two of them, and Charles went off to his boarding school without seeing Justin again. Two months later Charles tried to find Justin to apologize for treating him badly and learned that Justin had died of a heart attack.

Sticks and Stones

Ward Alexander returned after a year in the army to his small hometown in Iowa to try to write a novel. During the summer he met Tom Naylor, 16, a talented pianist who was also lonely; they often talked about books and music and became good friends. At the beginning of the school year, Tom's classmate Floyd, always envious of his abilities, heard a rumor about Ward, then told his classmates that Tom was queer and that his relationship with Ward proved it. The other students and even the teachers ostracized Tom who had no idea what was behind their actions.

The reason came into the open when Tom was not allowed to attend the state music competition because the other parents did not want their children staying with a "known" homosexual. Tom was appalled; when he protested that it was not true, he was told that there was no way to prove it or disprove it.

After this he cut himself off from Ward, did not study or play the piano, and by the end of the semester learned that he would have to repeat the year. In shock he started home, offering Floyd a ride. The car crashed--Floyd was killed and Tom critically injured. While in the hospital Tom realized that nothing was the matter with him until he allowed other people to make him doubt himself. At last Ward came to visit, and Tom said he was glad to see him.

Trying Hard to Hear You

Jeff, 18, and Phil, 19, met and became friends through a summer theater company for young people. Shortly afterward their friends began to wonder why they hardly saw them after rehearsals. At a party they did attend one friend, Sam, accused them of being fags and fairies. After much heckling Jeff faced the group and admitted that he and Phil loved each other. The rest, afraid of being considered queer too, at first gave them the silent treatment. Jeff's best friend tried to understand; however, she still could not accept their relationship.

Another group of kids heard about Jeff and Phil and actually attempted to tar and feather them, only to be stopped at the last minute by outsiders. Even after this their friends continued to give the two young men a hard time. Phil finally tried to change the situation by announcing that he had a choice, that he could be straight if he wished. On a subsequently arranged date, he wrecked the car, killing both himself and his date, Penny. Most of the group now admitted how badly they had acted and began to rebuild their friendships with Jeff.

Pioneering Efforts on a Controversial Theme

The preceding plot summaries are useful to establish the

major characteristics of each novel. In addition, taken collectively, they enable librarians to make tentative judgments on the validity of criticism leveled against the novels. However, there is no substitute for reading the books themselves. In fairness to the authors, it should be obvious that these short summaries fail to convey forcefully the positive and commendable aspects of each book: The ability of the author as storyteller, the depth of characterization and style, and the degree of the author's success in clarifying complex moral and social questions.

All four novels can be viewed as pioneering efforts in dealing with a controversial theme and, as such, merit inclusion in YA collections. The point of this article, however, is to examine those areas where these novels fail to speak clearly and realistically about the gay experience. The purpose of the following criticism is constructive: The goal is better, more accurate, and more inspiring books for all young adults.

Taken as a group, these novels have two salient characteristics: Being gay has no lasting significance and/or costs someone a terrible price. Not one plot has a happy ending in which the protagonists meet hostile pressures successfully and go on to find fulfillment and a supportive relationship based on love and respect. For gay adolescents the negative impact of these novels cannot be minimized.

The theme of no lasting significance is strongest in the novels by Donovan and Holland. Davy's father and Charles's tutor go to some lengths to tell them that their experience will have no effect on their futures, and that they can grow up straight as a ruler. This may be fine reassurance for insecure straight youths, but it cheats the ones who want to be gay by presenting such experiences as "phases" instead of the first step toward a valid choice. Everyone does, in fact, remember his or her initial sexual experiences and is in some way affected by them. Nor is any concrete support provided to gay adolescents reading Hall's Sticks and Stones; the ambigious ending permits a variety of alternative conclusions.

The theme of gayness exacting a terrible price is so pervasive in all these novels that it needs little further comment. In response to a letter on this point, Sandra Scoppettone wrote: "Phil's death is not because he is gay, but because he tries not to be. That is a very important difference. By trying to be something he is not (heterosexual), he gets drunk and drives his car into a tree. In other books the characters are punished because they are homosexual. Please don't confuse the death of Phil with punishment for homosexuality."

While Phil may not be punished for being gay, he is forced by peer pressure into a situation where he is killed all the same. Surely the exceptional persons of any race, sex, or persuasion transcend prejudice directed against their being or life-style, but in an open democratic society, why must minorities be expected to withstand extraordinary pressures?

Indeed external pressure has been applied to one YA writer to insure that the theme of punishment was incorporated into the plot. Lynn Hall wrote: "I had begun writing the book to show the destructive potential of gossip, but by the time I got well into it, I'm afraid I lost sight of that theme. I wanted Ward and Tom to love each other, to live happily ever after, and that was the way I ended it. But the publishers would not let me do it. In their words, this was showing a homosexual relationship as a possible happy ending and this might be dangerous to young people teetering on the brink. One editor wanted me to kill Tom in a car accident.[!] At least I held out for a friendship at the end, one which might or might not develop into something more, depending on the reader's imagination."

Holland's novel contains one of the most destructive and fallacious stereotypes--the homosexual as child molester. Justin, whose scarred face is noted by the title, is responsible for the death of a boy under unclarified circumstances. In light of such limited coverage of the gay experience in YA fiction, the possible identification of such a major character as a corrupter of children is grossly unfair.

Where Do Women Stand?

Finally, taken as a whole, these novels are generally anti-female. The first obvious point is that none of them is about a lesbian experience. Those women that are portrayed are often negative stereotypes and failures. They are also insensitive or hostile to the young, gay men: Charles's older sister in *Man Without a Face* practically drives him from home; in *I'll Get There...*, Davy's mother's negligence is responsible for his dog's death; in *Sticks and Stones*, Tom's mother is so caught up in her own romance that she fails to notice that things are falling apart for her son; in the Scoppettone novel, Phil's friend Penny volunteers herself as a quick test of his "real" masculinity.

As previously stated, each novel does have individual merit and certain aspects do ring true. It can also be said that the young adult genre as a whole tends toward melodrama. One wonders, however, whether any random selection of four YA novels could produce eight central characters with five sets of divorced parents (two of whom are alcoholic) and have plots with three natural deaths and one by violence--plus four car crashes resulting in one mutilation, one head injury, and five fatalities!

Where is there honesty and realism in approaching the gay experience? Where is there a life-affirming hope for a young person who knows or suspects he or she is homosexual? What is the impression left upon young straights who will encounter gays in their schools, families or communities?

Because the consequence of a homosexual experience in these

novels are either irrelevant or grim, not to mention incompatible with the truth of real gay people's lives, the accompanying guidelines were designed primarily to assist librarians in evaluating and selecting books with gay themes for children and young adults. The guidelines also contain suggestions of how to handle those books which do not contain the "ideal" treatment of a gay theme. Finally, the problems inherent in the existing novels (and, fearfully, others to follow) argue for an active, sensitive, and informed readers advisory service by YA librarians.

It is absolutely essential that all human beings be presented fairly. Gay people only expect to be treated with the awareness and sensitivity now shown to other groups.

Appearing with this article originally was a set of guidelines, "What to Do Until Utopia Arrives," drawn up by the ALA/Social Responsibilities Round Table's Task Force. This is reproduced in the Appendix (see p. 441).

PART VIII

SF, COMICS, SERIES

(in search of wonder ... or escape from nowhere ...)

EDITOR'S NOTE

Until recently, series books, fantastic or science fiction (frequently available only in paperback), and comics were no-no's in libraries and schools. Nevertheless, they were avidly consumed by generations of young readers who mostly managed to survive the pernicious mind-damaging effects ascribed to this kind of reading matter. The gradual acceptance of these suspect sub-literary forms by librarians and teachers is an interesting phenomenon, somewhat related to the new academic respectability of popular culture studies, and considerably affected by the reading crisis. In the desperate effort to get kids to read, anything goes.

The credit for Nancy Drew's welcome on library shelves is claimed by feminists, who pointed out that *here* was an active, independent, and accomplished heroine (of which there are shockingly few in juvenile literature). Karla Kuskin in her article and Bobbie Ann Mason in her excellent *The Girl Sleuth*[1] contend that that view is debatable. But meanwhile, circulation statistics are booming, and many libraries are no longer telling children that their favorite books are not worthy of shelf space.

While the series books are now read at a younger age than they once were, comics continue to appeal throughout the teen age. Despite Leslie Fiedler's elegiac tone, there still are comics which are "part of an adversary culture, colloquial, irreverant and unredeemably subversive"[2] and which therefore have a perennial appeal for young adults.

Even schools have turned to the comic book format for its built-in motivation. The teaching of Black history in junior and senior high schools has been enlivened by the Golden Legacy comics, for "the visual approach has more impact on the reader ... it takes the drudgery out of history and replaces it with excitement and adventure."[3]

For libraries, including comics (or series books) is an effective way to attract reluctant readers. As Laurel Goodgion puts it, "comics are a great way to begin to convince children that the library *does* have something to offer them. If the library can build a reputation as a reliable source, then the children will continue to return as they mature and their reading and informational needs change."[4]

Notes

1. Bobbie Ann Mason. The Girl Sleuth; a Feminist Guide. The Feminist Press, 1975.

2. See p. 343.

3. The New York Times, February 17, 1974, p. 20.

4. See p. 347.

WHY SCIENCE FICTION?*

By Janet Kafka

In his novel, God Bless You, Mr. Rosewater, Kurt Vonnegut, Jr. has his main character, Eliot Rosewater, address a convention of science fiction writers:

"I love you sons-of-bitches," he says. "You're all I read anymore. You're the only ones who'll talk about the *really* terrific changes going on. You're the only ones with guts enough to *really* care about the future, who *really* notice what machines do to us, what cities do to us.... *You're* the only ones zany enough to agonize over time and distance without limit, over mysteries that will never die...."

This statement from a writer who has frequently been accused of trying to divorce himself from the science fiction brotherhood, is for me the best possible answer to the question, "Why science fiction?" But it is not only the matter of relevance that makes good SF more and more suited to classroom use. I believe--and I know I'm not alone in this--that the best writing in current science fiction is as good as, if not better than, the best writing in any other genre. Much of it bears analysis according to the same criteria you apply to other works of fiction. And unlike many other things your students will have to read, SF provides a critical vantage point for commentary on people and societies as we find them today, as well as extrapolating from this to give us a view of some possible alternate futures. Historically a pariah, free from the conventions and demands of the mainstream, SF can deal with any socio-political, ethical, or technological problem that the human race might meet, from nearly any point of view. In the words of veteran writer and teacher Jack Williamson, it might also be seen as "an unending debate about the value of science and the nature of man." ("Teaching Science Fiction," pamphlet. Available for $1.00 from Jack Williamson, P.O. Box 761, Portales, N.M. 88130.)

And something more: It's fun.

What Is Science Fiction?

There are nearly as many definitions of SF as there are

*Reprinted by permission of the author and publisher from English Journal (May 1975), 46-53.

writers of it. Personally, I have no patience with what I call the "rationalizers"--those who would argue for the literary legitimacy of SF by trying to demonstrate that the genre includes Plato's *Republic*, Chaucer's *Canterbury Tales*, and Swift's *Gulliver's Travels*.

I believe it is fair to say that science fiction, as we know it, has its literary origins in the 19th century English romantic novel. Brian Aldiss, in his excellent history *Billion Year Spree: The True History of Science Fiction* (Doubleday, 1973) claims Mary Wollstonecraft Shelley's *Frankenstein* as the first science fiction novel. Feminists--a new and vocal element in the field--enthusiastically support Aldiss' claim. But whether you adhere to the Shelley faction, or agree with Rober Silverberg that H. G. Wells "is the true father of today's science fiction, for it was he who set the canon of subject and technique that most contemporary writers follow" (*The Mirror of Infinity: A Critics' Anthology of Science Fiction*, Harper & Row, Torchbooks, 1974), you'll have to concede that what we today label SF covers a wider range of subject matter, style, and literary quality than was ever imagined by the readers of Wells and his French contemporary, Jules Verne.

This diversity, for better or for worse, is largely due to the influence of the pulp magazines. In 1926 Hugo Gernsback introduced *Amazing Stories*. Gernsback, who also has been called the "father" of science fiction and is credited with inventing the name "scientifiction," later shortened to science fiction, was, in Aldiss' words, "utterly without any literary understanding." He put great emphasis on scientific accuracy, but even while this was in fact practically ignored, Gernsback's influence resulted in a kind of "deadening literalism" quite lacking in the finer things like characterization or atmosphere.

In the mid-thirties John Campbell introduced *Astounding* (which later became *Analog*) and took SF one step further. Campbell's writers were still encouraged to emphasize man-and-machine plots, but they tended to be superior craftsmen. *Astounding*, complete with garish illustrations, ushered in the "Golden Age" of the pulps, during which SF reached its adolescence. Right up through the fifties these magazines were in control; there was a large readership of fans (mostly young men); and the magazines gave them the kind of writing they demanded and had come to expect: action-oriented, sexless and simplistic. Most of the writers we recognize today as the "heavies"--Isaac Asimov, James Blish, Arthur C. Clarke, Robert Heinlein, Fritz Leiber, L. Sprague de Camp, Clifford Simak, Theodore Sturgeon, A. E. van Vogt--got their start writing for the pulps at one-cent or a half-cent (and even sometimes quarter-cent!) per word.

Drastic changes began taking place after World War II. Some say it was the dropping of the atom bomb and the resulting changes in scientific consciousness that forced SF to "grow up." But whatever effect all that may have had, it was the launching of the first Sputnik in 1957 that wrote an end to the accepted conventions of the Golden Age. Suddenly space travel was a reality. Faced with the fact that they were no longer the exclusive purveyors of rockets, space suits and low-gravity gadgets, and having to share their materials with NASA and Walter Cronkite, SF writers began reaching out into the rest of the stuff of our daily lives for subject matter and ideas.

The magazines' heyday is long past. From about three dozen in 1953, their number has dwindled to only a few: Galaxy, Analog, Vertex and Fantasy and Science Fiction have the field pretty much to themselves. The decline of the magazines has accompanied changes in subject matter and style, and perhaps has accelerated some of them. But at the same time, the rise of the book anthology, especially the original paperback, and the increasing strength of the SF novel, have given writers more freedom to experiment with both ideas and forms. Theodore Sturgeon, who now reviews SF for the New York Times Book Review, has suggested calling this "if-fiction" rather than science fiction, and it is clear that as SF becomes more and more concerned with ideas and with such un-alien entities as social forces, it is turning away from little green men with unpronounceable names to considerations of the question, "What if... ?"

So what is SF? I leave it to you to work out your own definitions--they will be as satisfactory as any others around. SF can be as brilliant and imaginative as Frank Herbert's Dune (Ace), in which he creates a totally believable alien world, complete with culture, philosophy, ecology, language; it can be as perceptive and (prematurely) feminist as Ursula K. LeGuin's The Left Hand of Darkness (Ace) which explores socio-sexual interaction on an alien planet where all the people are hermaphrodites; it can be a traditional space-adventure like Arthur C. Clarke's Rendezvous with Rama (Ballantine); it can be Kurt Vonnegut's sadly-comic explorations of human foibles or Michael Crichton's medical best-sellers; it can be as demanding as Stanislaw Lem's Solaris (Berkeley), or as straightforward and entertaining as Robert A. Heinlein's Starman Jones (Ballantine); it can be as despairing as J. G. Ballard's story "Terminal Beach" (Survival Printout, Vintage), or as optimistic as Clarke's Childhood's End (Ballantine).

Science Fiction in the Classroom

Like everything else, SF has its good and its bad; its real writers and its hacks. I'm not here to ask you to drop all your standards in the name of "relevance" and start teaching garbage because you can get the kids' attention with it. Nor am I going to tell you that Robert Heinlein is "as good as" Herman Melville. What I hope to do is encourage you to let down some of the prejudices you may have formed about SF and begin to consider it as a literary sub-genre rather than a sub-literary genre.

I'm going to tell you about some SF books I think are great, and some I think are not so great but interesting, and suggest some ways you might consider integrating them into your teaching. I am here on behalf of Vintage and Ballantine books, but I'm not going to confine myself to our titles; Vintage's list is small and new, Ballantine has always had terrific titles, but they haven't got everything. In fact, I'm not certain that every book I mention is even in print right now. But if you're interested, you'll find some of them. (A bibliography follows.)

If you haven't read much SF, I suggest giving yourself a brief survey course. Start with Aldiss' history--it has a real point of view and will give you plot summaries as well as critical discussion of the major works and a bibliography. Another good primer is Sam J. Lundwall's Science Fiction: What It's All About (Ace). A short and valuable overview comes attached to an anthology called A Spectrum of Worlds, edited by Thomas D. Clareson and published in hardcover by Doubleday. It surveys the history of SF from Ambrose Bierce (1893) through Robert Silverberg (1969). Another good survey anthology, which is in paperback, is Norman Spinrad's Modern Science Fiction (Anchor); it covers the period from the Golden Age of the pulps to the present. Spinrad's introduction is short, but there are extensive headnotes to each story.

A more scholarly view can be got from David Ketterer's The Apocalyptic Imagination: Science Fiction and American Literature (Anchor), and from H. Bruce Franklin's seminal anthology, Future Perfect: American Science Fiction of the 19th Century (Oxford). Franklin made history of a sort by teaching one of the earliest SF courses at the college level--at Stanford in the mid-sixties.

The Modern Language Association has a science fiction caucus, The Science Fiction Research Association, and publishes Extrapolation: A Journal of Science Fiction and Fantasy, edited by Thomas D. Clareson. The other scholarly journal is Science-Fiction Studies, which originates in the English department of Indiana State University and is edited by R. D. Mullen and Darko Suvin. An indispensable tool is Cliff's Notes' Science Fiction: An Introduction, by L. David Allen. It contains analyses of thirteen representative novels, as well as a reading list, critical bibliography, and suggestions for teaching SF as literature. Most of the works I will mention here--and many others, too--are listed and described briefly in "A Basic Science Fiction Collection," compiled several years ago by the Science Fiction Writers of America and published in the June 15, 1970 issue of Library Journal. If you are lucky enough to be able to find a copy of this list, you will discover that prices and publishers of the books mentioned have changed noticeably. Cross-reference with an up-to-date edition of Paperback Books in Print.[1]

One way to begin infiltrating SF into your classes is to substitute a couple of SF stories for the old chestnuts in your English texts. The Science Fiction Hall of Fame (in three volumes, from Avon), is a collection of the best SF stories and short novels of all time, chosen by the Science Fiction Writers of America. It contains some truly great stories, like Stanley G. Weinbaum's "A Martian Odyssey," which features a loveable ostrich-like creature named Tweel. Weinbaum is justifiably revered for his aliens; they are by far his best characters. His stories, more of which can be found in Ballantine's The Best of Stanley G. Weinbaum, belong to an earlier period; they are simple and well-constructed, and they might serve as models for an exercise in writing an SF short story.

Another good anthology is Terry Carr's annual Best SF of the Year (#3 is available from Ballantine). Carr--who also assembled the classic Science Fiction for People Who Hate Science Fiction (Funk & Wagnalls)--tends to pick idea-oriented stories with a strong humanist flavor, like Ursula K. LeGuin's "Those Who Walk Away from Omelas" and Vonda N. McIntyre's Nebula Award-winner, "Of Mist and Grass and Sand." There is some feeling among fans that this is not "true" science fiction, and in her Stellar series, Judy-Lynn del Rey is collecting what she called "good old-fashioned stories that are fun to read." Stellar 1 (Ballantine) contains a number of original, entertaining stories with no pretensions to art or literature. They might be especially suited to lower-level classes, reluctant readers, or people who have never read SF before (though some of these might be turned off by the very "good old-fashioned" simplicity).

Harlan Ellison, however, takes a lot of chances, with both subject matter and form; his Dangerous Visions anthologies (vol. 1 from Berkeley, vol. 2 from New American Library) reflect his very erratic and iconoclastic interests. Ellison's own work can be difficult, violent, shocking; he observes few of the standard taboos. Yet it is also sometimes brilliant. His "Deathbird" won this year's Hugo Award in the short story category. It can be found in Carr's Best #3. "A Boy and His Dog" (in The Beast That Should Love at the Heart of the World, Signet) has just been made into a movie. "I Have No Mouth and I Must Scream" (Survival Printout, Vintage) is probably the most anthologized short story in the history of SF.

I could go on for hours listing anthologies. There are literally hundreds of them and once you start looking you'll find some that suit your purposes. At Vintage I emphasize "theme" anthologies--stories are selected for the way they shed light on a particular problem. A whole teaching unit can be planned around just one of these books. The only trouble with them is that if you know what the theme is you can tell how the stories are going to come out, so there is less reader involvement and less plain suspense.

Vintage's Survival Printout is a theme anthology with a number of practical classroom applications. The editors selected factual articles by prominent scientists like Arthur C. Clarke and Loren Eiseley to be posed against SF stories that deal with the same subject matter, under the headings "evolution and identity," "earth probabilities," "ecosystems (cellular and solar)" and "time space travel." Conceived as one way to approach a unit in "future studies," perhaps along with Alvin Toffler's Future Shock (Bantam), it shows clearly how SF can be used to illuminate possible ways of dealing with currently recognizable problems like overpopulation, housing, travel.

Themes are an easy handle to hang a study unit on. Try examining current views of the man-woman relationship and then reading some SF stories or a short novel on that popular subject. Given what we know now, how might men and women relate to each other in a future society? What variations on the male-female relationship might be found among sympathetic aliens? What might catastrophe--like an atomic war--do to the conventional roles of men and women? Ursula K. LeGuin's masterful The Left Hand of Darkness places a human male in an alien world where the sexes are not differentiated--everyone can be both male and female at different times in their lives. Philip Jose Farmer's stories, collected in the Avon paperback Strange Relations, deal with this theme from a variety of different and amusing angles. The title story is about a man marooned on an alien world who finds himself falling in love with a giant, intelligent plant. Carol Emshwiller's "Sex and/or Mr. Morrison" is a hilarious treatment of the theme in Vintage's Women of Wonder. See also Chelsea Quinn Yarbor's apocalyptic "False Dawn" (Women of Wonder), and James Tiptree's "The Women Men Don't See" (Carr's Best #3).

One of my favorite subjects is "The Role of Women in SF." Women of Wonder, edited by Pamela Sargent, was born out of a debate about whether SF written by women was essentially different from that of their male counterparts. (See also Two Views of Wonder, by Chelsea Quinn Yarbro and Thomas N. Scortia, Ballantine.) Like life, SF has always been dominated by men, both as writers and as fans, and it dutifully reflects the values of the dominant society. Most stories, as Pam Sargent points out in her excellent introductory essay, feature women in certain stereotypical roles: the housewife who solves the problem through sheer inadvertence; the maiden who must be rescued from the alien menace (see Edgar Rice Burroughs' sexless wonders); the hero's girlfriend or the scientist's daughter who serves the author by having to have an essential piece of information carefully explained to her and, by extension, to the reader; and, perhaps most dangerous, the woman who is a competent scientist but at some point in the story must show herself to be subordinate to her male colleagues--like the doctor in Clarke's Rendezvous with Rama. There is also the woman-as-witch variation, in which it is assumed that women are dominating men by means of supernatural (or alien) powers. Fritz Leiber's Conjure Wife (Award Books) is a good example of this kind of story.

Get your classes to discuss the position of women in a number of different SF stories. This is an excellent opportunity to introduce the techniques of character analysis in literature, as well as the difficult question of the intrusion of the author's own ideas into his characters and situations.

One course I know of considers ways in which lifestyles and values we see operating in our society today (the Protestant work ethic, hippies, and communal groups, the church, zero-population-growth, paramilitary organizations like the Klan or Weatherpeople) might look in the future. Begin by reading some stories or novels that extrapolate from current social issues: Robert Silverberg's "A Happy Day in 2381" (*Survival Printout*) shows how a vertical community might operate; Ftitz Leiber's "The Secret Songs" (*Survival Printout*) is about the use of drugs; Silverberg's "Thomas the Proclaimer" (*Born with the Dead*, Vintage) examines a mass religious hysteria; his "Going" (*Born with the Dead*) shows what death might be like in a society that allows people to choose when they will "go"; Kurt Vonnegut's *Player Piano* (Dell) shows a fascist political order; John Brunner's *Stand on Zanzibar* (Ballantine) shows the possible effects of overpopulation and misuse of resources; Alan Dean Foster's story "A Miracle of Small Fishes" (*Stellar 1*) tells how a priest is able to intervene on behalf of one of his parishioners with the bureaucrats in charge of managing the food supply; in "Schwartz Between the Galaxies" (*Stellar 1*), Robert Silverberg shows what space-age commuting might be like; in "The Food Farm" (*Women of Wonder*), Kit Reed shows a future woman on a diet.

Ask students to discuss, or write their own stories about, a future world *they* would like to live in.

Some of the topics dealt with most frequently by SF writers are also well-suited to study units: What might the world be like after an atomic war? What might it be like to encounter aliens? What can we look forward to when we begin to explore space and colonize distant planets?

There is a whole sub-genre of after-the-holocaust SF, most of which, understandably enough, was written in the fifties. One of the most important novels in this group, and in fact a powerful work of fiction on its own terms, is Walter Miller, Jr.'s *A Canticle for Leibowitz* (Bantam). It is at the same time a terrifying vision of a devastated Earth, and a powerful reaffirmation of the knowledge that because man is what he is, he will never quite succeed in destroying himself. Miller brings to SF a deeply religious perspective that is unusual in the field.[2] This book is more demanding than most SF novels, but it is worth devoting considerable time to. If you don't have time for a novel, there is a short story version, with the same title, in *The Vintage Anthology of Science Fantasy*.

"First Contact" by Murray Leinster (*SF Hall of Fame*) is one of the earliest stories to explore the question of meeting aliens, and it remains one of the best in the "realistic" school: Here we are up in space and there they are, looking in on us. What do we do? Or, there is the friendly-but-confused alien visiting Earth: Robert A. Heinlein's *Stranger in a Strange Land* (Berkeley) introduces Valentine Michael Smith, who arrives on Earth with super-human abilities and a total ignorance of human sexual practices. Smith is not exactly an alien; he is an Earthman born on Mars. But his strangeness raises enough of the right problems and gives Heinlein an opportunity to make some pointed comments on contemporary Western society.

Zenna Henderson's stories about The People (People: No Different Flesh, Avon)--a group of gentle, human-like aliens who settle in an isolated area of Earth--deal sympathetically with the problems they have when they encounter humans. A TV series based on her work was produced a couple of years ago. And humans accommodating themselves to aliens is another variation. See Marion Zimmer Bradley's "The Wind People" and Vonda N. McIntyre's "Of Mist and Grass and Sand" in Women of Wonder.

Another change that can be hung on this question is the terrible alien, the unseen horror or malevolent force out to conquer mankind. John Wyndham is a master of this form in The Day of the Triffids (Fawcett) and The Midwich Cuckoos (Ballantine). But for sheer giggles and goose flesh, you can't beat H. P. Lovecraft's SF horror stories (several collections from Ballantine). Colin Wilson, in the only SF novel he has written to date, takes Lovecraft one step further: The Mind Parasites (Oneiric Press, Berkeley, Ca.) combines Lovecraft's technique and his own philosophy of evolutionary existentialism in a story about some archaeologist whose discoveries in an ancient tomb include the invisible and horrible "mind parasites."

Arthur C. Clarke is the acknowledged master of the exploration-colonization theme. Everyone is familiar with his epic 2001: A Space Odyssey. The story on which the movie was based, "The Sentinal," can be found in Ballantine's Expedition to Earth. Childhood's End (Ballantine) gives another view of Clarke's inspired and optimistic concept of the future of mankind. It could be read along with Olaf Stapledon's The Star Maker (Dover) as a unit, with discussion centering on the expansion of man's potential through contact with galaxies beyond the Earth. Another approach might be to compare either one or both of these books with some very pessimistic views of man's future, such as John Brunner's Stand on Zanzibar.

Another exploration-colonization novel is Alexei Panshin's Rite of Passage (Ace). It has proven to be very popular with teenagers and might be used successfully as an introduction to SF on the high school level. In it we see human survivors of a devastating Earth war living precariously in colony worlds. In order to assure that the fittest survive, all teenagers are cast out into the hostile environment to test their survival skills. Mia Havero is a teenager about to undergo her Trial.

As a composition exercise, you might ask students to create an alien world; people it; give it a culture, an ecology, a political system. Two of the best examples of this kind of SF are Frank Herbert's Dune and Larry Niven's Ringworld (Ballantine). Dune is a giant book in the epic tradition. The story concerns the political and personal development of Paul Atreides, ordered as a result of a political struggle to leave his home planet and take over the government of a hostile alien colony. In the novel, Herbert treats three extremely popular contemporary themes: the use and abuse of political power, the importance of maintaining a whole planet's ecological balance, and the spiritual development (based on consciousness of the functioning of mind and body) of the young hero. Few works of SF have ever achieved the depth and breadth of Dune.

Lary Niven's Ringworld is another brilliantly imaginative portrayal of an alien world, but it has never achieved the "cult" following of Dune.[3] Set some 1,000 years in the future, Ringworld brings together recognizable human characters and several varieties of intelligent alien life on an interstellar expedition. The rather spare plot is fleshed out with multifarious details of the explorers' societies and those they come into contact with. The book is classic SF at its best.

Interdisciplinary Possibilities

There is no need to confine SF to the English curriculum. Biology classes might find the whole subject more appealing if whatever they were studying could be illuminated by a science fiction story with a biological theme. Cloning is the subject of Ursula K. LeGuin's "Nine Lives" (Modern Science Fiction, Anchor). Ten cloned members of an exploring team are sent to an alien planet where nine are killed in an accident. The tenth has to learn to adjust to being alone. Every high school geometry class ought to begin by reading Edwin Abbott's Flatland (Dover). A painless introduction to the principles behind computers and information technology can be got from Stanislaw Lem's The Cyberiad: Fables for the Cybernetic Age (Seabury). This is brilliant intellectual slapstick, a series of stories relating the adventures of two robot "cosmic constructors" who constantly try to out-invent each other. Arthur C. Clarke's stories frequently extrapolate from pure science, as do Dr. Isaac Asimov's. Clarke's "Jupiter Five" (Reach for Tomorrow, Ballantine) is an exercise in applied mathematics. "Technical Error" (in the same collection) deals with a weapon that is just too good; the story is required reading at M.I.T.

Or what about history? L. Sprague de Camp's Lest Darkness Fall (Ballantine) is a classic time travel story about a modern archaeologist transported back to 6th-century Rome where he tries to stem the tide of barbarism by introducing modern technology. Fawcett has begun a series called Transformations, anthologies of SF stories illuminating American (vol. II) and world history (vol. I). Current events? Lester del Rey's Nerves (Ballantine) is about an explosion in a nuclear power plant.

You can do this as well as I can, if not better. The point is to get used to thinking about interdisciplinary possibilities. After your class has read some SF, get them to write a story based on something they are studying in another area: biology, or history, or math.

Some schools have started interdisciplinary programs under the label "future studies" or "futuristics." This is a rapidly-expanding area and one that makes considerable use of SF and related materials. A forthcoming Vintage book, Cultures Beyond the Earth brings together a number of prominent anthropologists to speculate on what extraterrestrial civilizations might be like and where and how they might be found. Is this science, or science fiction? Where do you draw the line? When we talk about cloning, or send men to walk on the moon, or give them artificial hearts, we have already integrated the stuff of science fiction into our lives. There is no longer any point in debating about its place there.

Good science fiction has as much of a place in your English classes as these fantastic events have in our daily papers. It is especially appealing to teenagers, both male and female, and you might find that with careful selection you can turn on even the most reluctant readers. Some high schools are offering special electives in SF and fantasy literature[4] and whole courses can be developed with a very specialized curriculum. There is an awful lot out there--both good and bad--and I urge you to sample it. And to enjoy.

Notes

1. The problem of books going in and out of print, often with different publishers, is one you are going to have to face. Plan your courses at least a year ahead of time to give you a chance to track down all the materials you will need. There is no guarantee you will get the books you order from the mass-market paperback houses. If demand for a title slips below a certain number, publishers will let it go out-of-print--either temporarily until enough back orders are built up to justify another printing, or permanently, in which case another publisher might pick it up. The so-called quality houses like Vintage print fewer copies of each title and can sometimes keep their book in print longer. But their prices will be slightly higher.

2. There has always been an "underground" religious current running through American SF, but it seldom surfaces to the point where major characters are priests or major themes ask religious questions. See also C. S. Lewis' Out of the Silent Planet, This Hideous Strength and Perelandra (Macmillan), and James Blish's excellent A Case of Conscience. Robert Silverberg's main character in "Schwartz Between the Galaxies" is the first Jewish main character I have come across, but there is an entire anthology of Jewish fantasy and SF called Wandering Stars, edited by Jack Dann and published by Harper & Row.

3. Both books have the unusual distinction, along with LeGuin's Left Hand of Darkness, of having won both Nebula and Hugo awards in the year they were published. Like all awards, the Nebula and the Hugo (named for Hugo Gernsback) are not necessarily indicative of the best writing around. But if you're new to SF, and don't know what to look for, the notice that a short story or a novel or a novella has won one of these is an indication that it is at least worth reading.

4. Some of you have probably noticed by now that I haven't said anything about fantasy. This is simply a function of my personal tastes: I don't read it, so I don't know anything about it, and I am not going to burden you with my ignorance. If your students have read J. R. R. Tolkein's Lord of the Rings, or this year's best-selling Watership Down, they might want to go on to some of Ballantine's extensive "adult fantasy" list: E. R. Eddison's The Worm Ouroboros, The Mezentian Gate, Mistress of Mistresses, A Fish Dinner in Memison: Mervyn Peake's Gormenghast Trilogy, or Anne McCaffrey's on-going SF-fantasy series, The Dragonriders of Pern. All are wildly imaginative, convoluted epics--the kind of book you can get lost in for days at a time.

A (Random?) Science Fiction Bibliography

NOVELS

God Bless You, Mr. Rosewater, Kurt Vonnegut, Jr. (Dell/Delta)
Dune, Frank Herbert (Ace)
Player Piano, Kurt Vonnegut, Jr. (Dell/Delta)
The Left Hand of Darkness, Ursula K. LeGuin (Ace)
Solaris, Stanislaw Lem (Berkeley)
Rendezvous with Rama, Arthur C. Clarke (Ballantine)
Starman Jones, Robert A. Heinlein (Ballantine)
Stand on Zanzibar, John Brunner (Ballantine)
Conjure Wife, Fritz Leiber (Award Books)
A Canticle for Leibowitz, Walter Miller, Jr. (Bantam)
Out of the Silent Planet, C. S. Lewis (Macmillan)
This Hideous Strength, C. S. Lewis (Macmillan)
Perelandra, C. S. Lewis (Macmillan)
A Case of Conscience, James Blish (out-of-print)
Stranger in a Strange Land, Robert A. Heinlein (Berkeley)
People: No Different Flesh, Zenna Henderson (Avon)
The Day of the Triffids, John Wyndham (Fawcett)
The Midwich Cuckoos, John Wyndham (Ballantine)
The Mind Parasites, Colin Wilson (Oneiric Press, Berkeley, Ca.)
2001: A Space Odyssey, Arthur C. Clarke (Ballantine)
Childhood's End, Arthur C. Clarke (Ballantine)
The Star Maker, Olaf Stapledon (Dover)
Rite of Passage, Alexei Panshin (Ace)
Ringworld, Larry Nivem (Ballantine)

Flatland, Edwin Abbott (Dover)
Lest Darkness Fall, L. Sprague deCamp (Ballantine)
Nerves, Lester del Rey (Ballantine)
Dragonflight, Anne McCaffrey (Ballantine)
Dragonquest, Anne McCaffrey (Ballantine)

ANTHOLOGIES

The Mirror of Infinity: A Critic's Anthology of Science Fiction, ed. Robert Silverberg (Harper Torchbooks)
A Spectrum of Worlds, ed. Thomas D. Clareson (Doubleday)
Modern Science Fiction, ed. Norman Spinrad (Anchor)
Future Perfect: American Science Fiction of the 19th Century, ed. H. Bruce Franklin (Oxford)
The Science Fiction Hall of Fame, vols. I, II A&B (Avon)
Best Science Fiction of the Year, ed. Terry Carr (#3 Ballantine)
Science Fiction for People Who Hate Science Fiction, ed. Terry Carr (Funk & Wagnalls)
Stellar, ed. Judy-Lynn del Rey (#1 Ballantine)
Dangerous Visions, ed. Harlan Ellison (vol. 1 Berkeley, vol. 2 NAL)
Survival Printout, ed. Total Effect (Vintage)
Women of Wonder, ed. Pamela Sargent (Vintage)
The Vintage Anthology of Science Fantasy, ed. Chris Cerf
The Vintage Bradbury, Ray Bradbury
Cyborg: The Man-Machine Symbiosis in Science Fiction, ed. Thomas N. Scortia and George Zebrowski (Vintage)
Two Views of Wonder, ed. Thomas N. Scortia and Chelsea Quinn Yarbro (Ballantine)
Born with the Dead: Three Novellas about the Spirit of Man, by Robert Silverberg (Vintage)
The Beast that Should Love at the Heart of the World, stories by Harlan Ellison (Signet)
Expedition to Earth, stories by Arthur C. Clarke (Ballantine)
Reach for Tomorrow, stories by Arthur C. Clarke (Ballantine)
The Best of Stanley G. Weinbaum, stories by Weinbaum (Ballantine)
Strange Relations, stories by Philip Jose Farmer (Avon Equinox)
H. P. Lovecraft--several anthologies available from Ballantine
The Cyberiad: Fables for a Cybernetic Age, by Stanislaw Lem (Seabury)
Transformations, edited by Daniel Roselle (Fawcett Premier)
    Vol. 1: Understanding World History Through Science Fiction
    Vol. 2: Understanding American History Through Science Fiction

SHORT STORIES

"Terminal Beach," J. G. Ballard (Survival Printout)
"Those Who Walk Away From Omelas," Ursula K. LeGuin (Best #3)
"Of Mist and Grass and Sand," Vonda N. McIntyre (Women of Wonder)

"Deathbird," Harlan Ellison (Best #3)
"A Boy and His Dog," Harlan Ellison (The Beast That Should Love...)
"I Have No Mouth and I Must Scream," Harlan Ellison (Survival Printout)
"Sex and/or Mr. Morrison," Carol Emshwiller (Women of Wonder)
"The Women Men Don't See," James Tiptree, Jr. (Best #3)
"A Happy Day in 2381," Robert Silverberg (Survival Printout)
"The Secret Songs," Fritz Leiber (Survival Printout)
"Thomas the Proclaimer," Robert Silverberg (Born with the Dead)
"Going," Robert Silverberg (Born with the Dead)
"A Miracle of Small Fishes," Alan Dean Foster (Stellar 1)
"Schwartz Between the Galaxies," Robert Silverberg (Stellar 1)
"The Food Farm," Kit Reed (Women of Wonder)
"A Martian Odyssey," Stanley G. Weinbaum (The Best of SGW)
"False Dawn," Chelsea Quinn Yarbro (Women of Wonder)
"A Canticle for Leibowitz," Walter Miller, Jr. (Vintage Anthology of Science Fantasy)
"First Contact," Murray Leinster (SF Hall of Fame)
"The Wind People," Marion Zimmer Bradley (Women of Wonder)
"The Sentinal," Arthur C. Clarke (Expedition to Earth)
"Jupiter Five," Arthur C. Clarke (Reach for Tomorrow)
"Nine Lives," Ursula K. LeGuin (Modern Science Fiction)
"Technical Error," Arthur C. Clarke (Reach for Tomorrow)

FANTASY

The Lord of the Rings, J. R. R. Tolkein (3 vols.) (Ballantine)
The Worm Ouroboros, E. R. Eddison (Ballantine)
The Mezentian Gate, E. R. Eddison (Ballantine)
Mistress of Mistresses, E. R. Eddison (Ballantine)
A Fish Dinner in Memison, E. R. Eddison (Ballantine)
Gormenghast Trilogy, Mervyn Peake (Ballantine)
Watership Down, Richard Adams (Avon)

CRITICAL STUDIES

Billion Year Spree: The History of Science Fiction, Brian Aldiss (Doubleday)
The Apocalyptic Imagination: Science Fiction and American Literature, David Ketterer (Anchor)
Science Fiction: What It's All About, Sam J. Lundwall (Ace)
Science Fiction: An Introduction, L. David Allen (Cliff's Notes)

JOURNALS

Extrapolation: A Journal of Science Fiction and Fantasy, ed. Thomas D. Clareson, The College of Wooster, Wooster, Ohio
Science-Fiction Studies, ed. Darko Suvin and R. D. Mullen, Indiana State University, Terre Haute, Indiana

THE MAGAZINES

Analog, ed. Ben Bova
Galaxy and If, ed. James Bean
Fantasy & Science Fiction, ed. Ed Fermen
Vertex, ed. Don Pfeil

OTHER

"Teaching Science Fiction," pamphlet. (Available from Jack Williamson, P.O. Box 761, Portales, N.M. 88130. $1.00)
"A Basic Science Fiction Collection," Library Journal, June 15, 1970.
Future Shock, Alvin Toffler (Bantam)
Cultures Beyond the Earth, ed. Magoroh Maruyama and Arthur Harkins with a Foreword by Alvin Toffler and an Afterword by Sol Tax (Vintage--forthcoming)

THAT GREAT CURRICULUM IN THE SKY*

By David F. Marshall

Why is science fiction read? The answer for other types of fiction seems easier to grasp. Espionage novels (James Bond, et al.) offer the hope of participating vicariously in adventures that can ease tensions between nations poised on the brink of thermonuclear destruction. The challenge of logical deduction and the desire for justice could account for an interest in detective novels. But what explains the enormous popularity of science fiction and fantasy?

The widely held idea that science fiction consists of the exploits of space heroes--Buck Rogers, Flash Gordon--is soon exploded by an examination of the richness and diversity of the field. There are, of course, space explorations, but added to these are the heroic fantasies of well-muscled adventurers who battle evil magicians and monsters in the distant and immemorially dim past--the _Conan_, _Thongor_, _Brak the Barbarian_ beef operas. There are also horror stories of the occult which range from the masterpieces of H. P. Lovecraft to the machinations of Fu Manchu. And then there are the "tomorrow's headlines" stories such as _The Andromeda Strain_, a runaway bestseller. Infinite variations on these classifications exist; for example, Tarzan is a modern beef-jungle opera; _Rosemary's Baby_ bemoans the occult on her way to the bank; and J. R. R. Tolkien's _The Lord of the Rings_ is so popular on campuses that the extended reading time necessary for its three thick volumes may alone have occupied students sufficiently to have prevented several campus riots.

Whatever the classification or type, there seem to be at least three persistent themes running throughout this corpus of fiction labeled "science" or "fantasy."

First, there is the search for order, a seeking for universal law which will aid man when something goes wrong. This something can be a prehistoric monster (Godzilla) run amok in a metropolis, or it can be as small as the Andromeda strain of microbes. But whatever its size, it disrupts the planned pattern of man's knowledge with deadly results. Somehow, before the story ends, the answer is found and some type of order is restored. Examples of this type of story are John Creasey's Dr. Palfrey series.

---

*Reprinted by permission of the publisher from _Colloquy_ (May 1971), 32-33.

The ultimate consequences of this type are excellently illustrated in Arthur C. Clarke's 2001: A Space Odyssey. After finding an unexplainably artificial black monolith on the moon, space explorers with their computer buddy Hal follow another monolith floating in space. Sighting these rectangular slabs as cross hairs on a target, one astronaut finally reaches a place where he communicates with the maker of the universe. In all stories of this type, the ultimate import is the assurance given by Robert Browning's "God's in his heaven, All's right with the world."

Besides the search for order, a theme in science and fantasy fiction is that of the quest. A great journey is necessary, and each traveller finds his own identity and meaning in life in the fulfillment of the quest. Isaac Asimov's novelization of the film Fantastic Voyage, in which people are miniaturized and travel in a submarine through a man's bloodstream, is a minor example, but the quest story par excellence is Tolkien's cycle of the rings. Frodo, the timid hero, must return an enchanted ring to the volcano where it was forged so as to break the power of chaos. Only then will the Middle Earth be saved from the forces of darkness and the rule of that which is without law except unto itself. The result of the quest story is a vicariously instilled understanding of individuality, of what it means to be a pilgrim in life. There is also in the best of these stories the added result of learning to live more creatively, including some means of learning to accommodate to injustice. Any returner from the quest, including the reader, will come back not only changed but also a little wiser in the ways of gods and men.

A third theme common to science and fantasy fiction emerges as a need for wholeness. There is a deep mistrust of what the mind alone creates, and this distrust can be manifested in the revolt of the robots or the invention or experiments of the mad scientist. Science without ethics is shown to be a dangerous thing. The prime example is Mary Shelley's Frankenstein, the story of a thing created by another man and not by God, a being without a soul. The mistrust of science inherent in our daily lives exists as a touchstone of science fiction. Anyone who suddenly realizes that he knows how to turn on the television but that he does not know why it works is on his way to becoming a science fiction reader. Implicit in this theme is the idea that it is necessary for man to know not only how but why; it is a cry for using all of man's potential; it is a demand that not just the thinking function be used, but also feeling. Man needs not only his scientific logic, the theme imparts, but also his religious emotions. Ultimately, it becomes a drive for the wholeness of this creature we find ourselves to be.

These three themes--the search for order in the universe even in the face of catastrophe, the quest for self-understanding and a rapprochement with injustice, and the pursuit of wholeness which balances man's scientific thinking with religious emotion--are repeated continually in science and fantasy fiction. One would be hard pressed to find more religiously oriented themes in any fiction. With careful reading, it is not hard to see that almost any novel written in this growing field is in its ultimate sense based on a deeply religious concern. Reading in the science fiction and fantasy field is a rapidly spreading habit, particularly within the ranks of the young. In an age which seems discontented with its religious institutions, it is not surprising that science fiction and fantasy are increasingly popular. In an age in which man is capable of annihilating himself, it is not astonishing at all that he continues to turn to fiction that stresses his accountability not only to himself but to the universe and to its maker.

Science fiction is a phenomenon that religious educators can build on with profit, given the necessary willingness and insight. What is needed now is an openness to utilize the themes of science fiction for religious education. It would not be far-fetched to imagine lesson plans written by religious educators based on common themes in the Bible and in science fiction. These lessons would be not only exciting but enlightening. They would have the added advantage of using materials with which the adolescent is familiar and with which he is fascinated. Science fiction and fantasy are not the longed-for panacea which will return the young to the churches; that panacea is a challenge for its own science fiction novel. However, wisely used, science fiction can be a valuable tool. Religious educators ignore it at a loss to their calling and perhaps to the church's future.

Sample Lesson Plan

I. Objective of the class: To raise and discuss value questions about the way man uses his knowledge in exploring the universe.

II. Preparation: Have each student read *The Andromeda Strain* by Michael Crichton (Dell). Paperback copies are available at newsstands and bookstores. Most libraries have hardbound editions. The novel can be read in one week by most high school students. Junior high school students may need two or three weeks to read it.

III. Teacher preparation: Besides reading the novel yourself, you might discuss it with several friends who have also read it. It should not be difficult to find others who have reflected on the meaning of this best-selling book. After talking with others about the novel, write down your own impressions of its meaning. Ask yourself these questions:

A. What is it in us that keeps us exploring, imaginatively and otherwise, the universe? Do we really hope to find something or someone out there? What do we hope to accomplish?

B. What caused the slaughter of so many innocent people by the unknown Andromeda Strain? Man's foolishness? Scientific inexpertise? Was it a natural tragedy? Is there a difference between this kind of tragedy and a flood or a hurricane? If so, what is that difference?

C. Scientists were able to tame the Andromeda Strain. Are there problems science cannot solve, no matter how hard scientists work at them?

IV. The class session: Have class members briefly outline the plot of the novel so that those who have not read the book can participate. This summary will break the ice and get the class involved in discussion. Now ask the questions under III. You will have your own written reflections to fall back upon but, instead of giving your own answers, help each class member arrive at his own conclusions. Class impressions will probably be as diverse and varied as those from the friends you talked with before class.

TREKKING SCIENCE FICTION'S STARS*

By YASD Media Selection and Usage Committee

Charting a Territory

What is meant when we speak of science fiction and science fantasy? One of the stranger than life facts is that there are as many definitions of these terms as there are readers of the kinds of works categorized by them. Many perceptive and concise definitions have been offered by leading critics of SF/Fantasy.

Professor L. David Allen, in his Science Fiction: An Introduction (Cliff, 1973), defines science fiction as "... a literary subgenre which postulates a change (for human beings) from conditions as we know them and follows the implications of these changes to a conclusion" (p. 121). It should be noted that Professor Allen regards science fantasy as a category of science fiction, a view which is widely accepted by other experts in the field. Another leading writer about SF/Fantasy, Sam Moskowitz, offers this definition: "Science fiction is a branch of fantasy identifiable by the fact that it eases the 'willing suspension of disbelief' on the part of its readers by utilizing an atmosphere of scientific credibility for its imaginative speculations in physical science, space, time, social science and philosophy." Definitions abound, even in a whimsical vein such as the comment by George Hay that "Science fiction is what you find on the shelves in the library marked science fiction," and the remark by Brian W. Aldiss that "Science fiction doesn't exist."

Searching the System

Getting around in outer space entails using selected bibliographies of works about SF/Fantasy. These include, in addition to Professor Allen's work cited above, Brian W. Aldiss' Billion Year Spree (Doubleday, 1973), Damon Knight's In Search of Wonder (Advent, 1967), Sam Lundwall's Science Fiction: What It's All About (Ace Books, 1971), Sam Moskowitz' Explorers of the Infinite (Hyperion Press, 1974), and Seekers of Tomorrow (Hyperion Press, 1974), as well as Donald Wollheim's The Universe Makers (Harper,

1971). Readers who would like to have a more extensive list of similar works are referred to the bibliographies included in the works just cited.

In the Beginning ...

What are the origins of SF/Fantasy as they are presently understood? Ben Bova, an eminent SF writer and the editor of Analog Science Fiction, Science Fact magazine, states that by the "... latter decades of the 19th century, English literature was rife with so-called scientific romances ... in which scientific discoveries or technological inventions were the key features of the plot" (School Library Journal, May 1973). Writing largely in that tradition, but presaging future developments in the genre in some of their works, were Jules Verne and H. G. Wells.

Any discussion of the origins of SF/Fantasy will elicit supporters for ancient prototypes, such as the myth of Icarus and Daedalus and, more recently, Voyage to the Moon (1656) and Voyage to the Sun (1661) by Cyrano de Bergerac. Whatever may be the merits of such propositions, many experts agree in giving major credit to Mary Shelley as being one of the earliest, if not the first, writer to create, in her 1818 novel Frankenstein (Dell), what is clearly a modern science fiction concept (i.e., irresponsible scientific experimentation unleashes forces that cannot be controlled). Of more recent vintage, but preceding the period of the scientific romances, some of Edgar Allan Poe's stories are frequently proposed as SF prototypes.

With the growth of literary respectability for the best works of Jules Verne and H. G. Wells, science fiction writing began a path of development which is still evolving.

A Galaxy of Stars

While accepting the vagueness of the term classic, Damon Knight claims one of the few genuine classic works is Karel Capek's War with the Newts (page 10, In Search of Wonder, cited above). This work is presently available in a paperback edition from Berkley Press (the first, in the original Czech, was published in 1936). Other classic works most would agree upon include Jules Verne's 20,000 Leagues under the Sea (Scholastic, 1972), H. G. Wells' The Time Machine (Bantam, 1965), and George Orwell's 1984 (Harcourt, 1971).

Working as librarians, we often have occasion to suggest specific titles to readers who want to become better acquainted with SF/Fantasy. Actually, anyone who reads has almost certainly come in contact with more SF/Fantasy than he or she may realize. For example, there are not many of us who haven't read one or more of the classic works mentioned above, or some of the more recently published popular SF novels, such as Ray Bradbury's *Fahrenheit 451* (Ballantine, 1972), Robert C. O'Brien's *Report from Group 17* (Atheneum, 1972), or Kurt Vonnegut, Jr.'s *Cat's Cradle* (Delacorte, 1971; Dell, 1970), or *Slaughterhouse Five* (Dell, 1971).

Anyone who would like to read more extensively in SF/Fantasy can hardly do better than to begin by reading from the list of works which have been winners of the Nebula and Hugo awards. The Nebula Award was founded in 1965 by the membership of the Science Fiction Writers of America. The annual awards are voted upon by the society's members; winners are authors who are considered to have written the best science fiction (or fantasy) published in the previous years, with separate categories for novel, novella, novelette, and short story. The Hugo awards were initiated at the eleventh World Science Fiction Convention in 1953 and are named for Hugo Gernsback, a pioneer in the publishing of science fiction magazines, who was given a special award in 1960 honoring him as "The Father of Magazine Science Fiction." Since 1953, and annually after 1955, these awards have been voted upon the World Science Fiction Convention members by mail ballot. In addition to the awards given in the novel, novella, novelette, and short story categories, awards are given for professional magazines, amateur publications, fact articles, new science fiction author or artist, feature writer, critic, dramatic presentation, professional artist, fan artist, and publisher; and occasionally for various special categories such as movies and television shows. Interested readers may wish to look at a copy of the June 1973 issue of *Amazing Stories* for an editorial by Ted White in which he wrote expressively about the phenomenon of fandom in the Hugo awards. The winners of these awards will be especially noted in the remainder of this essay.

For a complete listing of all award-winning works, including shorter prose works as well as plays, the reader is referred to *Literary and Library Prizes*, ed. by Jeanne Henderson (8th ed.; Bowker, 1973).

Constellations

It may come as a surprise to those who are not aficionados that SF/Fantasy may be divided into specific types or categories. There is an order in which these categories are usually listed, and the first, frequently called Hard SF, is SF in which the major explorations take place in one of the "hard" or physical sciences (e.g., chemistry, physics, biology). Until fairly recently Hard SF predominated and much of the SF that appeared prior to about 1950 was of this type; for example, Jules Verne's *20,000 Leagues under the Sea* (cited above) and *From the Earth to the Moon and Round the Moon* (both available from Airmont, 1968). Other more recent works of this type are George Stewart's *Earth Abides* (Fawcett, 1971), John Wyndham's *Day of the Triffids* (Fawcett, 1972), Clifford D. Simak's *Way Station* (Manor Books, 1973), Isaac Asimov's *I, Robot* (Fawcett, 1970), and the *Foundation* series (Avon, 1970), Hal

Clement's Mission of Gravity and Needle (both currently OP), Arthur C. Clarke's Rendezvous with Rama (Harcourt, 1973), Fred Hoyle's Black Cloud (NAL, 1973), and, with Geoffrey Hoyle, Inferno (Harper, 1973), and Larry Niven's Ringworld (Ballantine, 1972), of which the last cited won both the Hugo and Nebula awards.

There were many notable exceptions to the early predominance of Hard SF. These works are in the second category, called Soft SF. In Soft SF the emphasis is on human activities and the so-called soft sciences (e.g., sociology, psychology, political science), such as H. G. Wells' famous anti-utopian novel The Time Machine (cited above), which, though integrally bound to the hard science notion of a marvelous machine, is not about future prospects in the hard sciences but, rather, presents one disturbing extrapolation of our future development socially and politically. Everyone will recognize Aldous Huxley's Brave New World and George Orwell's 1984 (cited above) as examples of this category. Other, mostly recent, notable works in the Soft SF category include Alexei Panshin's Rite of Passage (Ace Books, 1973), Walter Miller, Jr.'s A Canticle for Leibowitz (Lippincott, 1969), C. S. Lewis' Perelandra (Macmillan, 1968), Out of the Silent Planet (Macmillan, 1965), and That Hideous Strength (Macmillan, 1965), Roger Zelazny's This Immortal (Ace Books, 1973), Poul Anderson's Brain Wave (currently OP), Harlan Ellison's Dangerous Visions (Berkley, 1972), and Again Dangerous Visions (NAL, 1973), Zenna Henderson's The Anything Box (currently OP), Lester del Rey's Pstalemate (Putnam, 1971; Berkley, 1973), Andre Norton's Witch World series (especially Witch World, Ace Books, 1974), Ray Bradbury's The Martian Chronicles (Doubleday, 1973; Bantam, 1974), Arthur C. Clarke's Childhood's End (Harcourt, 1972; Ballantine, 1972), Alfred Bester's Demolished Man (NAL, 1970), Samuel R. Delaney's Babel 17 (Ace Books, 1973), Ursula K. LeGuin's The Left Hand of Darkness (Ace Books, 1972), and Isaac Asimov's The Gods Themselves (Fawcett, 1973), the last two cited having both won the Hugo and Nebula awards.

The third category is Science Fantasy, which assumes an orderly universe with regular and discoverable laws that differ from the natural laws governing our sciences. In contrast, "straight" fantasy sometimes borders on SF, but its connection with any of the sciences as such is minimal. A representative selective of Science Fantasy titles should include Frank Herbert's Dune (Ace Books, 1965), which won both the Hugo and Nebula awards, James H. Schmitz' A Pride of Monsters (Macmillan, 1973), Anne McCaffrey's Dragonflight (Ballantine, 1973), Sterling Lanier's Hiero's Journey: A Romance of the Future (Chilton, 1973), and Fritz Leiber's Conjure Wife (Universal Pub. & Dist., 1970).

Since there is currently a resurgence of interest in the so-called sword-and-sorcery subcategory of Science Fantasy (often abbreviated S & S), one could choose to read Conan, by Robert E. Howard and others (Lancer, 1970), or any of the Conan stories (many are presently available in paperback editions); something by L. Sprague De Camp, such as The Incomplete Enchanter, with

Fletcher Pratt, if you can get hold of a copy (currently OP), or the Conan Grimoire, with Lin Carter (Mirage Press, 1972), or Flashing Swords 1 (Dell, 1973) and Flashing Swords 2 (Dell, 1974), edited by Lin Carter. Any of these will serve as excellent introductions to sword-and-sorcery.

Another type of SF, which may be thought of as a sort of hybrid of the scientific romance and the early Hard SF, is the naive but rousing space opera of late 1920s and early 1930s vintage. The leading contender among the writers of this kind of material, which is being revived and avidly read by teenagers especially, is E. E. "Doc" Smith, who had a prodigious output of what has been aptly referred to as space westerns (the six-shooter is plainly recognizable in its raygun incarnation and the male-female relationships are painfully decorous in the best Western tradition). Of Doc Smith's works, one should be familiar with his Lensman and Skylark series. Of the former, one title in particular, Spacehounds of IPC (Pyramid, 1974), is really a thrilling concoction of adventures and would be a good first choice for the reader who wants to become acquainted with vintage space opera.

For each of the foregoing categories there are other definable sub-categories. These finer distinctions can be better understood when one has read fairly extensively in the full spectrum of SF/Fantasy; but, for those who would like to refer to Professor Allen's Science Fiction: An Introduction (cited above), on pages 5 through 11 he gives definitions for the categories and subcategories with examples and analyses.

Prozines and Fanzines

Moving to periodical publications of and about SF/Fantasy, there are primarily two kinds: professional magazines (called "prozines" by SF/Fantasy fandom) and amateur publications ("fanzines"). Some difficulties arise in giving a list of these publications, and especially so in the cases of the amateur "fanzines," due to cessations, title changes, transfers of ownership, and so forth. However, the following list, if not exhaustive, does attempt to list the principal titles available at the time of this writing.

Professional SF/Fantasy magazines include Amazing Stories (bimonthly; ed. Ted White, Ultimate Publishing Company), Analog Science Fiction, Science Fact (monthly; ed. Ben Bova, Conde Nast Publications, Inc.), Galaxy (irregular, 12 issues per year; ed. Jim Baen, UPD Publishing Company), Magazine of Fantasy and Science Fiction (monthly; ed. Edward L. Ferman, Mercury Press, Inc.), Science Fiction Research Association Newsletter (monthly; ed. Fred Lerner, SFRA), Extrapolation; journal of the Modern Language Association Seminar on Science-Fiction (twice annually; ed. Thomas D. Clareson), Vertex (bimonthly; ed. Donald L. Pheil, Mankind Publishlishing Co.), and World of If (bimonthly; ed. Ejler Jakobsson, Universal Publishing and Distributing Corp.).

In the category of amateur SF/Fantasy magazines, there is such a vast number of fanzines published that it is not possible within the scope of this article to try to list all of them, or even an ample selection. Consequently, without doubt some readers will feel that one or more of the very best of the fanzines has been omitted. Fortunately, there is now available Dr. Frederic Wertham's The World of Fanzines: A Special Form of Communication (Southern Illinois Univ. Pr., 1973), which is, to date, the definitive work on the subject. In the following list of selected fanzines only addresses and some comments will be given due to the frequent changes in their publishing characteristics and prices: Alfol: A Magazine about SF (ed. and pub. by Andrew Porter, Box 4175, New York, NY 10028); Amra (Box 8243, Philadelphia, PA 19101), advertised as the leading Sword-and-Sorcery fanzine and winner of the Hugo Award for best fanzine in 1964 and 1968 under the editorship of George Scithers; ERB-Dom (ed. John Flint Roy, P.O. Box 550, Evergreen, CO 80439), devoted to the study of Edgar Rice Burroughs and his works, and one of the oldest fanzines at present; Kaballah: The Worlds of Fantasy (subscription inquiries to: Gerard Houarner, 25-33 48th St., Long Island City, NY 11103); Locus (Locus Publications, 2078 Anthony Ave., Bronx, NY 10457), winner of the Hugo Award for best fanzine in 1971 and 1972; Mythlore (Mythopoeic Society, Box 24150, Los Angeles, CA 90024), now incorporating the Tolkein Journal, which was, until recently, one of the leading SF/Fantasy fanzines; and Mythprint (Mythopoeic Society). Others are Outworlds (ed. William L. Bowers, P.O. Box 148, Wadsworth, OH 44281), which advertises itself as "something a little different" and as "the eclectic fanzine"; Phantasmicom 11 (Jeffrey D. Smith, 4102-301 Potter St., Baltimore, MD 21229); The Witch and the Chameleon (Amanda Bankier, Paisley Ave. S., Apt. 6, Hamilton, Ontario, Canada), advertised as a feminist-oriented SF/Fantasy magazine; and Yandro (Robert Coulson, Route 3, Hartford City, IN 47348), one of the longest running fanzines and winner of the Hugo Award for 1965.

Readers who want to inform themselves about SF/Fantasy in the cinema and on television will find available some very helpful source books. Foremost among these is a new reference guide which is at present the definitive one, the Reference Guide to Fantastic Films, Science Fiction, Fantasy and Horror, edited by Walt Lee and Bill Warren (3 vols., Chelsea-Lee Books, 1973). This excellent guide contains full information about some 20,000 films, including serials, short films, experimental films, and privately produced films. This work also includes an extensive bibliography of works about SF/Fantasy in the cinema, such as John Baxter's excellent Science Fiction in the Cinema (Paperback Library, 1970), Denis Gifford's Horror and Science Fiction Film (Dutton, 1971), and Don Willis' Horror and Science Fiction Films: A Checklist (Scarecrow, 1972). Two additional sources are Burt Goldblatt and Christ Steinbrunner's Cinema of the Fantastic (Saturday Review Press, 1972) and William Johnson's Focus on the Science Fiction Film (Prentice-Hall, 1972).

Acknowledgments

Following the appearance in a number of library publications of announcements asking for help in writing this SF/Fantasy mediagraphic essay, ideas for things to be included began coming in from all parts of the country. The committee is grateful for all suggestions and has incorporated many of them in the essay. From this very helpful and welcome response it became evident that there is a great diversity of opinion as to what and how much should be included.

This article is a joint effort of the members of the YASD Media Selection and Usage Committee: Elaine Adams, Robert Barron, Kathleen Gosz, Esther Helfand, Donald Reynolds, Ruth Smith, Rosemary Young, Barbara Duree, and Susan Uebelacker, chairperson.

The following contributed ideas, opinions, and comments: Janet Polacheck, Judy-Lynn del Ray, Raymond Barber, Elaine Simpson, Mary K. Chelton, Cathi Reed, Polly and Ben Timms, Terry Goldman, Dennis Livingston, and Christine Kirby.

Much credit goes to Craig Moore, who helped Susan Uebelacker, chairperson, on the final draft of this essay.

The raw file consisting of reports and ideas from members of the committee as well as from eleven other interested persons, booklists, photocopies of articles, numerous SF/Fantasy magazines, newspaper clippings, and comments on the rough draft used in preparing this essay is available for loan in exchange for round-trip postage. It can be obtained from Susan Uebelacker, Chairperson, ALA YASD Media Selection and Usage Committee, Hillcrest Heights Branch, 2342 Iverson St., Hillcrest Heights, MD 20031.

Recent Science Fiction/Fantasy Titles for Many Tastes, on Various Reading Levels

Aldiss, Brian. Galaxies Like Grains of Sand. New American Library, 1971.

Anderson, Poul, ed. by Roger Elwood. The Many Worlds of Poul Anderson. Chilton, 1974.

Asimov, Isaac, ed. Nebula Award Stories Eight. Harper, 1973.

Bova, Ben, ed. The Science Fiction Hall of Fame. Vols. 2A and 2B. Doubleday, 1973; pa., Avon.

Brunner, John. The Sheep Look Up. Ballantine, 1973.

Carr, Terry, ed. Universe 4. Random, 1974.

Colin, Kapp. The Wizard of Anharitte. University Pub. (Award), 1973.

Dann, Jack, ed. Wandering Stars: An Anthology of Jewish Fantasy & Science Fiction. Harper, 1974.

Dickson, Gordon R. Alien Art. Dutton, 1973.

Elwood, Roger, ed. The Far Side of Time. Dodd, 1973.

_______. The Learning Maze & Other Science Fiction. Messner, 1974.
Engdahl, Sylvia. Beyond the Tomorrow Mountains. Atheneum, 1973.
Fast, Howard. A Touch of Infinity. Morrow, 1973; Large Print Books, G. K. Hall.
Gerrold, David. When Harlie Was One. Ballantine, 1972.
Haldeman, Joe, comp. Cosmic Laughter: An Anthology of Humorous Science Fiction. Holt, 1974.
Harrison, Harry, ed. Nova 3. Walker, 1973.
_______. Nova 4. Walker, 1974.
Harrison, M. John. The Pastel City. Doubleday, 1973.
Herbert, Frank. The Book of Frank Herbert. Daw, 1973.
Herzog, Arthur. The Swarm. Simon and Schuster, 1974.
Hughes, Zach. The Legend of Mairee. Ballantine, 1974.
Jones, Adrienne. The Mural Master. Houghton, 1974.
Knight, Damon, ed. Orbit 14. Harper, 1974.
Laubenthal, Sanders A. Excalibur. Ballantine, 1973.
Laumer, Keith. The Glory Game. Popular Library, 1974.
LeGuin, Ursula K. The Dispossessed. Harper, 1974.
McKenna, Richard. Casey Agonistes & Other Science Fiction & Fantasy Stories. Harper, 1973.
Munn, H. Warner. Merlin's Ring. Ballantine, 1974.
Norton, Andre, and Donaldy, Earnestine, eds. Gates to Tomorrow: An Introduction to Science Fiction. Atheneum, 1973.
Page, Thomas. The Hephaestus Plague. Putnam, 1973.
Pope, Elizabeth Marie. The Perilous Gard. Houghton, 1974.
Priest, Christopher. The Inverted World. Harper, 1974.
Simak, Clifford D. Cemetery World. Berkley Pub. (Medallion), 1974.
Sleator, William. House of Stairs. Dutton, 1974.
Total Effect, ed. Survival Printout: Science Fact, Science Fiction. Random, 1973.
Weinbaum, Stanley G. The Best of Stanley G. Weinbaum. Ballantine, 1974.
Wul, Stefan. Temple of the Past. Seabury, 1973.
Zelazny, Roger. The Guns of Avalon. Doubleday, 1972; pa., Avon.
_______. To Die in Italbar. Doubleday, 1973.

UP, UP AND AWAY:
The Rise and Fall of Comic Books*

By Leslie A. Fiedler

I read my first comic book on a school playground in Newark, N.J., sometime in the late 1920s, with a sense of entering a world not only forbidden but magical, like the world of my most unconfessable dreams. It was an "eight-page Bible" slipped to me by the class Bad Boy: a pornographic burlesque of the comic strip "Tillie the Toiler" in which she and her usually impotent admirer, Mac, performed sexual acts beyond the scope of my unaided 12-year-old fantasy. That they had bodies at all under the conventional garb they never shucked in their daily adventures seemed to me wondrous enough, and that they had usable genitals as well at once blasphemous and miraculous.

I have, however, recently looked at a scholarly collection of such erotic travesties once bootlegged across the border from sunlit Tijuana, where all was permitted, to darkest Newark, where all was forbidden; and I have been appalled to discover how ill-drawn, perfunctorily plotted and anaphrodisiac they now seem. Yet neither the magic nor the threat of subversion has wholly departed from me, either from those Bibles themselves or indeed from the whole genre to which they introduced me.

True, comic books had to make a somewhat more respectable second start in the late 1930s before they were accepted as fit for children in whose innocence parents were still pretending to believe. Moreover, the children themselves demanded more than parody of the daily scripts in which sex was absent and violence trivialized; they yearned for a new mythology neither explicitly erotic, overtly terrifying nor frankly supernatural, yet essentially phallic, horrific and magical. Such a mythology was waiting to be released in pulp science fiction, a genre re-created in the United States in 1926 by Hugo Gernsback, who published the first magazine devoted entirely to the genre. He did not invent the name, however, until 1929, just one year before a pair of 16-year-olds, Jerry Siegel and Joe Schuster, reviewed Philip Wylie's _Gladiator_ in one of the earliest s.f. fanzines--journals dedicated to amateur criticism of fiction ignored by the critical establishment.

---

*Reprinted by permission from _The New York Times Book Review_ (September 5, 1976), 1, 9-11.

Out of that novel, at any rate, emerged the first and most long-lived of all comic book characters, Superman, whose adventures Siegel and Shuster were already trying to peddle in 1933, though not until 1938 did they persuade a publisher to buy the rights to Superman's name and legend for $130, thus launching the series with which the classic comic book began. Other mythological figures have moved through such publications in the four decades since ranging from Donald Duck to Dracula. But at its most authentic and popular, the form has belonged always to the avatars of Superman, beginning most notably with Captain Marvel, Batman and Wonder Woman and toward the end including the Fantastic Four of Stan Lee's Marvel Comics.

Yet it required the imminence of World War II before the super-goy dreamed up by a pair of Jewish teenagers from Cleveland in the Great Depression could reach an audience of hundreds of millions starved for wonder but too ill at ease with Gutenberg forms to respond even to science fiction. Only then did the paranoia that is their stock in trade become endemic--the special paranoia of men in cities anticipating in their shared nightmares the saturation bombing that lay just ahead and the consequent end of law and order perhaps of man himself. The suffering city, Metropolis, which under various names remains the setting for all subsequent Superheroes, is helpless before its external enemies because it is sapped by corruption and fear at its very heart.

But the old American promise of an end to paranoia is there too, the equivocal dream that had already created the Ku Klux Klan and the vigilantes and the lynch mob, as well as the cowboy hero and the private eye--the dream of a savior in some sense human still, but able to know, as the rest of us cannot, who the enemy really is and to destroy him as we no longer can--not with technology, which is in itself equivocal, but with his bare hands. Small wonder that those who went off to war and in most cases found only boredom, machine-tending, paper shuffling, meaningless drill and endless waiting made the comic books their favorite reading. To them, the dream of meaningful violence was a fantasy as dear and unreal as to any they had left at home.

My second exposure to the form came in 1942 as I too moved toward that war and discovered that the Indian boy who accompanied me on the first leg of my journey carried in his paper valise nothing but a spare suit of underwear and half a hundred comic books. Moreover, each time our train stopped, some concerned old lady would thrust into my hands a pack of cigarettes, a candy bar and the latest issue of *Superman* or *Captain Marvel*--tokens of condescension and good will, the last of which I must confess disconcerted me a little, since I was by then, despite my sailor suit, already a professor of literature. But I could not resist reading material pressed on me in much the same spirit as I had been pressing T. S. Eliot and Henry James on my equally reluctant students. I had actually not looked at any comic books since my days in the schoolyard, and this time around the appeal of the tabooed was gone

But I was determined to find out why such kid stuff satisfied large numbers of men moving perhaps toward death, as the high literature whose apostle I then was, did not.

And in fairly short order I was hooked, though I scarcely confessed the fact even to myself. What I discovered behind the seemingly artless style--more grunts and exclamations than words, more image than idea--was old-fashioned plot, right down to the O. Henry "hook" that I had taught my students was destroyed forever by Chekhov and Joyce, Gertrude Stein and Hemingway. But by virtue of that very fact, perhaps, there was also a sense of wonder able to compel even in me an ecstatic lifting up of the heart and a kind of shameful excitement in the gut, prompted this time not by sex, which I had grown enlightened enough to think desirable, but by unbridled violence, which I had learned to fear as my parents and teachers had once feared erotic porn.

But I found pathos as well in the double identity of the hero, that Siegel and Shuster invention, product of God knows what very Jewish irony undercutting what it seemed to celebrate. He was a man of steel in one guise, but in the other a short-sighted reporter, a crippled newsboy, an epicene playboy flirting with a teen-age male companion. Phallic but impotent, supermale but a eunuch, incapable of consummating love or begetting a successor; and, therefore, he was a last hero, doomed to lonely immortality and banned by an ultimately inexplicable taboo from revealing the secret that would make it possible at least to join the two halves of his sundered self and thus end his comic plight of being forever his own rival for the affection of his best beloved. Ultimately, therefore, the Siegel and Shuster Superman turns out to be not a hero who seems a shlemiel, but a hero who is a shlemiel. If this is not essentially funny (and none of the men who read comic books beside me throughout a long war could be persuaded it was so), it is because the joke was on all of us and there was no one left to laugh--not even when the war was over and it had become clear that what it had achieved was the end of heroism rather than of paranoia.

After all, that conflict was resolved not by hand-to-hand struggle but by the dropping (from an invisible machine) of a device contrived in laboratories by white-coated men indistinguishable from the hooked-nose eggheads against whom the Superheroes typically fight for the salvation of the city; and World War II was followed almost immediately by a contest between those forces, East and West, who for the duration were both labeled "good," not just for territory and power but for the exclusive right to that title.

Although the American comic book heroes continued to fight on behalf of the West as if nothing had really changed--substituting Commies for Nazis and, once the Korean War had begun, Chinks for Japs--somehow all conviction had departed. The images of bombed villages, raped and massacred civilians and especially the smashed-in, slant-eyed faces under the steel helmets satisfied for a while the hunger for apocalypse in those growing up at the moment when wartime ennui gave way to the boredom of back-to-school and work. But the world was no longer at war; only a handful of soldiers was engaged in a combat more dubious than mythological and heading toward inevitable stalemate. Besides, the notions of patriotism and heroism destroyed for intellectuals by World War I had begun to wear out for even the most naive by the end of World War II--especially for the young to whom the only uncompromised law seemed violence for its own sake and the real enemy, therefore, the forces of law and order who sought to make violence a monopoly of the state.

The old Supercomics had been too compromised by their espousal of official patriotism to satisfy the new hunger for unmediated violence and the new attempt to allay paranoia by identifying with the criminal rather than his victim or even the heroic crime fighter. What was needed was a new adversary literature, and once more the comic books proved resilient enough to respond. In the 1950s, E. C. Comics under the direction of William M. Gaines set the pattern by moving from priggish Superheroes at war to tales of war for violence's sake, to crime and finally to sadomasochistic fantasy. They found an audience particularly among the over-protected children of the white middle classes, for whom the crime in the street available to the poor and the black could be enjoyed only vicariously in a kind of unwitting dream rehearsal of the war against established society which their younger brothers and sisters would act out in the great demonstrations of the late 1960s, becoming the Commies and criminals threatening Metropolis as a new kind of paranoia overtook the adult world.

Embattled bourgeois parents, of the 1950s, convinced by their shrinks that even the unexpurgated Grimms' fairy tales, on which they themselves had been reared, bred anti-social violence in the young, were appalled to find their children reading in such comic books accounts of ball games played with the severed head of a victim whose entrails had been used to make the baselines. Finding it impossible to believe that such atrocities were produced in response to something within their children themselves--whether an impatience with the very notion of childhood innocence or a lust for naked aggression in a world that had outgrown its old social uses--parents were ready to believe almost any conspiracy theory that exculpated their kids at the expense of someone else; a conspiracy of the masters of media to profit by deliberately corrupting the young (as argued by Frederic Wertham in _Seduction of the Innocent_) or a cabal of homosexuals (a favorite theory in Gershon Legman's _Love & Death_) against the straight world they resented and envied.

These parents embraced a new kind of paranoia, not resolvable like the earlier ones by the comic books, since comic books themselves were the source of their illusive fears. Comics, therefore, had to learn to censor themselves or be suppressed by a new Puritanism disguised as an enlightened liberalism. What followed was the scandalous 1954 Comics Code, a "voluntary" set of restrictions that the publishers of comic books imposed on themselves as embattled parents, teachers and even Congressional committees closed in for the kill. No one was finally sent to jail, as Gershon Legman had continued to urge, but E. C. Comics, the most creative as well as the best drawn and plotted of the time, was driven out of business by the pious resolve of its less successful competitors to prove that the "medium ... having come of age on the American cultural scene" could "measure up to its responsibilities by banning all scenes of horror, excessive bloodshed ... depravity, lust, sadism, masochism" as well as discouraging the "excessive use" of slang and colloquialisms and promising to employ "good grammar" wherever possible.

It was at this point that I came out of the closet and defended the comics in public print. For this I was accused of being not only an enemy of high culture but also a crypto queer and a C.I.A. agent. The cultural cold war and the great repression that followed seemed to me at the time unmitigated disasters; but in retrospect it is clear that the comic books finally benefited by being thus reminded of their disreputable origins and their obligation to remain at all costs part of an adversary culture, colloquial, irreverent, and unredeemably subversive.

The kind of children who preserved behind the backs of their parents old copies of E. C. Horror Comics, identifying them with other forbidden pleasures like rock music, fairy tales, pornography and marijuana, later constituted an audience--unprepared ever to admit that they had grown too old for comic books, just as they had begun by refusing to grant that they were too young--for the new comics that emerged in the 1960s. These were, first the psychedelic fantasies of Stan Lee and Jack Kirby, which subverted the code from within, replacing the beautiful Superhero with a Superfreak, repulsive monsters with soap-opera hangups like the Hulk; then the autobiographical Head Comix of R. Crumb and Gilbert Shelton in which freaked-out characters, scarcely distinguishable from their dropout middle-class white authors, dedicate their life to pursuits, chiefly sex, sadism and dope, portrayable only by deliberately breaking every taboo of the Comics Code--which is to say bringing back porn "for adults only" more shamelessly than the "eight-page Bibles" ever dared and proffering models of violence more favorably than the ambivalent makers of E. C. Comics were willing to do.

But the 1960s are over and with them, it would seem, the heyday of the comic books that had served once as the scriptures of the cultural revolution at its height and have now become its most trustworthy record. Not that all such publications ceased--Marvel Comics continue to roll off the presses in New York and Head Comix off those in San Francisco and Berkeley where the cultural revolution has gone to die. Even Superman still appears, having survived a score of artists and writers as well as translation into a daily comic strip, radio, movies and TV.

But one does not have to consult the circulation figures, falling for Superman as for all comics characters, to know he will not survive the makers of anthologies, dictionaries, self-congratulatory retrospectives, encyclopedias and histories, which at the moment are piled so high on my desk I can scarcely see the shelves across the room that hold the handful of original comic books I have somehow managed to preserve. Why I agreed in the first place to review these great fat mortuary books I can no longer remember.

It is an absurd way to end a relationship that began in shame and passion, matured in the anguish of a great war and climaxed in an unfashionable defense of what the righteous had agreed to condemn in a time of repression. Yet I have been unable to resist becoming an accomplice in a process that threatens to turn what was once living myth into dead mythology. Perhaps I am writing in the hope of somehow mythicizing my own relationship to the form or even for one instant of magically transforming myself from a fat man with a gray beard who has just spilled a forgotten cup of coffee over his manuscript to the Superhero I have never ceased to be from the moment I realized he was also a Supershlemiel like me--as is only fitting for a fantasy bred by teenage paranoia and doomed to end in middle-aged scholarship.

"HOLY BOOKSHELVES!"
Comics in the Children's Room*

By Laurel F. Goodgion

Superman, Spiderman, and Batman and Robin have invaded the New Britain (Conn.) Public Library. Inspired by reports of libraries circulating comic books with success, the library's children's department started a comic book collection with the goal of attracting new borrowers to the library by providing this innovative service.

In the beginning, we took advantage of a new service being offered by a library jobber and purchased a package of 120 comics for $27.50. The comics, which included a variety of superhero, Disney, and Archie comics, were all checked out within a few days. We supplemented the collection with a few dozen more comics purchased from a local magazine distributor who agreed to sell to the library at a discount of 30 per cent. Most of the comics purchased recently were Marvel comics to meet the demand for more Batman, Spiderman, and Superman stories. These, too, were soon checked out and the staff began to feel that the library could never afford to keep up with the demand.

But then the donations began to pour in. Young children, teenagers, and adults, pleased to be able to contribute something that the library needed, donated hundreds of comics and felt more involved in the library as a result. An article in the local paper, listing the donors and reporting the success of the collection, resulted in more donations. The donations are quickly screened for acceptability, and most are included in the collection. The Comic Code Authority, 41 E. 42 St., New York City, provided criteria for acceptability.

Processing and Circulation

At first, we processed the comics by typing a card and pocket for each as we do for magazines. After we were deluged with donations, we simplified procedures to get the comics out on

*Reprinted by permission of the author and publisher from School Library Journal (January 1977), 37-39.

the shelves as soon as possible. Now all the comics are checked out by the same method we use for pamphlets. Large envelopes have been equipped with pockets and cards labeled "comics." Each envelope is numbered. The card is punched with the patron's number, and the due date on the Gaylord charging machine and the number of comic books is written on the card. No fines are charged and no overdues are sent. No record is kept of the comics acquired. Worn-out comics are thrown away. Some comics probably are ripped off but, because their cost is so minimal, we don't worry about it.

The comics are displayed on slanted shelves next to the children's magazine collection. The children have been delighted with the collection, and teenagers also come to the department to see what they can find. There are usually several kids busily reading comics in the library after school, either sitting in the reading pit or stretched out on the whistle seats. In order to share the wealth, the children are asked to limit themselves to borrowing only three comics at a time, but they often read many more than that before they leave the library.

To encourage children to make the transition from comics to these high-interest materials, we have shelved these materials next to the comics.

Publicity and Feedback

We knew that the comic book collection would be popular with children but we expected some complaints from adults. On the day the comic book service began, a news release was sent to the local media announcing the new collection. We carefully explained that the library's purpose was to attract new readers, especially reluctant readers, to the library. We hoped in this way to prevent some of the anticipated criticism. Instead of complaints, we have been overwhelmed with enthusiastic adults who want to know more about this service. We have yet to receive a complaint about the collection.

Unexpected publicity came from other sources. As a result of our press release, the local paper, The New Britain Herald, ran a front-page story on the comic book collection headlined, "Holy Bookshelves! Guess who's in the library now!" This story caught the attention of the United Press International (UPI) wire service, and the area reporter called the library for more information and then sent the story to the news wire service. Three radio stations in New York, and others located in Boston, St. Louis, and Salt Lake City, called for on-the-air interviews. The climax was when two local television stations came to the library and taped stories for the evening news broadcasts.

News stories ran in papers all over the country, and we heard from interested readers. A California comic book author wrote to express his appreciation of the library's acknowledgment of the fact that comics play a large part in children's reading. A New Britain city official, vacationing in Florida, read the story in a Miami paper and wrote a note to the library expressing both pride and pleasure.

Nothing the library had done before had so captured people's imagination and attention. The major reason for this reaction is that the public image of libraries is so negative and so out of date that the announcement of comic books as a part of a "scholarly" library completely amazed them and clashed with their own image of libraries. Most newscasters who called for interviews were amazed to hear that silence wasn't required in the children's library. All of this indicates that public libraries have a major public relations task ahead of them in showing the public what a modern public library can offer.

From Comics to Books

Comics are a great way to begin to convince children that the library *does* have something to offer them. If the library can build a reputation as a reliable source, then the children will continue to return as they mature and their reading and informational needs change. Not all the children drawn to the library by comics will be successfully led on to read other materials. But some will be, and we use several materials to encourage the transition from comics to more traditional reading materials.

In selecting transition material, we looked for the qualities that make comics so appealing to children. Format is the key--there must be strong visual appeal and limited text. Color also plays a part. The material must be short and look easy to master. Content is important, too. Humor and action are the key ingredients.

Magazines are a natural transition. *Spidey Man Super Stories* magazine already looks like a comic, but because the text is easier it may result in more actual reading. *Electric Company Magazine*, *Ebony Jr.*, and *Mad* are also successful. We keep multiple copies of each of these to meet the heavy demand.

Paperbacks and other books in cartoon formats such as *Peanuts*, *Ripley's Believe It or Not*, *Guiness Book of World Records*, joke and riddle books, and similar material easily digested in small portions get reluctant readers accustomed to a paperback format. From this type of book these patrons can be encouraged to go on to the paperbacks describing television personalities, movie plots and stars, and movie monsters. These paperbacks retain a strong visual appeal and an association with other mass media.

Hardbacks can be transitional materials as well. The new Creative Education series on famous personalities like Evel Knievel and the Osmonds, and the Putnam sports hero series, also have appeal. Other books in series, such as the Random House "Step-up books," Bowmar's racing books, and titles in the Nancy Drew, the Hardy Boys, Encyclopedia Brown, and the Alfred Hitchcock and the Three Investigators series, are also useful because they contain plenty of action.

Other Benefits

For years, comics have been thought of as harmful reading. It will be hard for many librarians to overcome these feelings, but opinion is changing. The armed services have known for years the usefulness of the comic book format in training classes, and educators are now beginning to capitalize on the appeal of comics. Sol Gordon, professor of Child and Family Studies at Syracuse University, New York, has successfully used the comic format to present facts about drugs, nutrition, and birth control to teenagers. The Electric Company, in a joint venture with Marvel Comics, is publishing *Spidey Man Super Stories*, a magazine in comic book format carefully designed for reluctant readers and children with reading difficulty. Because comics are visual, they compete successfully with television, which many people see as the biggest competitor for children's time.

The comic book venture has resulted in multiple benefits for The New Britain library. The children's circulation is up. Children are checking out more books--not just comic books. Not only has the comic book collection achieved its purpose of attracting a new group of children to the library, it has produced much positive publicity for the library.

Not all libraries need to circulate comic books, or should. But if your library is not drawing children in, if the majority of children in your area are reluctant or nonreaders or if you want to update your library's image in the community, then comics *do* have value. Why not start where the children are?

Related Reading

Comics Magazine Association of America, Inc. "Code of the Comics Magazine Association of America, Inc." *Unabashed Librarian*, Winter 1976. p. 4-6.

Eisner, Will. "Comic Books in the Library?" *School Library Journal*, October 15, 1974, p. 75-79.

Gauger, Lucia & Anne Arundel. "How I Use Comic Books Good At my Branch." *Unabashed Librarian.* Winter 1976, p. 3.

Gordon, Sol. *Ten Heavy Facts about Sex*; *VD Claptrap*; *Drug Use--a Survivor's Handbook*; *The Eater's Digest*; *Protect Yourself from Becoming an Unwanted Parent.* All pamphlets are available for 30¢ each from Ed-U Press, 760 Ostrom Ave., Syracuse, N.Y. 13210.

Gray, Kathleen. "Chronology of a Comic Book Collection." *Un-*

abashed Librarian, Spring 1975. p. 4.
Mazer, Norma Fox. "Comics, Cokes & Censorship." Top of the News, January 1976. p. 167-70.
Minick, Evelyn & Judy Kurman. "... and My Branch." Unabashed Librarian, Winter 1976. p. 3.
"Spidey." Unabashed Librarian, Spring 1975. Cover and p. 2.

Comic Book Jobber

Bookazine and Co., 303 West 10th St., New York, N.Y. 10014.

High Interest Materials

Trade Books in Series

Arthur, Robert. Alfred Hitchcock and the Three Investigators in the Mystery of the Green Ghost. Random House, 1965. Also other titles in this series.
Burchard, Sue & Marshall Burchard. Kareem Abdul Jabbar. Putnam, 1972. And other "Sports Hero" books by Burchard.
Cebulash, Mel. Baseball Players do Amazing Things. Random House, 1973. And other "Step-up Books."
Radlauer, Ed. Minibikes. Bowmar, 1971. And other Radlauer racing titles.
Sobol, Donald. Encyclopedia Brown: Boy Detective. Nelson, 1963. And other Encyclopedia Brown titles.
Zaleski, Rob. Evel Knievel. Creative Education, 1974. And other "Superstars" and "Rock'n Pop Star" titles by this publisher.

Magazines

Ebony Jr. $6 for ten issues. Johnson Publishing Co., 820 S. Michigan Ave., Chicago, Ill. 60605.
Electric Company Magazine. $4.50 for ten issues. Electric Company, North Road, Poughkeepsie, N.Y. 12601.
Mad. $10 for twenty issues. E. C. Publications, 485 Madison Ave., New York, N.Y. 10022.
Spidey Man Super Stories. $4.50 for 12 issues. Marvel Comics, 575 Madison Ave., New York, N.Y. 10022.

NANCY DREW AND FRIENDS*

By Karla Kuskin

That attractive strawberry blonde has been driving her blue convertible from clue to clue in the vicinity of River Heights since 1930. River Heights is just down the fictional road from Bayport, where the Hardys live. The area is a sort of all American Shangri-la. Forty-five years have passed. The convertible is still the newest, bluest model, while the boys and the blonde have aged just two years each. Otherwise Nancy Drew, heroine of 52 Nancy Drew Mystery stories and Frank and Joe of the 54 Hardy Boys Mystery books have hardly changed at all.

One group of readers isn't too happy about that. "They just aren't good literature" is a complaint of many librarians who have long fought to keep such series books off their shelves. In direct contrast is the policy of some bookstores to leave shelf space empty for the next shipment of Nancy Drews rather than fill it with slower moving merchandise.

Library attitudes are changing. "The first goal is reading," an executive of the children's services division of the American Library Association commented recently. Instead of saying "'No. we don't have a book because it's not a very good book.' They (librarians) feel you should provide that book." This past winter, for the first time, Grosset & Dunlap put all the Nancy Drew books into library bindings. They should have bound them in mink. The series has sold 60,000,000 since Nancy first stepped on the gas. The Hardy boys hover around 50,000,000.

To understand The Secret of Their Smashing Success one must begin at the beginning. Nancy and the boys are chips off the same writer's block. A block, it turns out, of pure gold. Rascals at Large (Doubleday) by Arthur Prager, tells their tale and others of early juvenile fiction. In the late 1880s a New Jersey stationer named Edward Stratemeyer jotted down a story for boys. He wrote fast. By 1908 his pseudonymous works were in such demand that he formed a syndicate. In other words, and heaven knows he had plenty of those, he would outline a story and contract it to a sub-

---

*Reprinted by permission from The New York Times Book Review (May 4, 1975), 20-21.

writer to fill in the spaces. When Stratemeyer died in 1930 his estate included 800 books written under 65 names. Among them are the Old Glory series, the Rover Boys (5,000,000 sold), the Tom Swift books (10,000,000), the Honey Bunch books, Bomba the Jungle Boy, the Bobbsey Twins (50,000,000) and more, much more. At present the syndicate is in excellent health in East Orange. Much of its yearly output is the personal work of Stratemeyer's daughter Mrs. Harriet Adams and her partner Andrew E. Svenson, who follow the formulas faithfully. Why not? Would Sara Lee stop making cheesecake?

Besides their age (late teens) and vocation (detecting) Nancy and the Hardy boys share other family resemblances. Nancy lives in ultra-comfort (housekeeper included) with her tall handsome father Carson Drew, "the outstanding attorney of River Heights." Since Mrs. Drew conveniently died when Nancy was three the two remaining Drews have "been very close." Frank and Joe live comfortably too. Their father Fenton Hardy, the well known detective, even looks a little Drewish: "Handsome, rugged ... confident." Mrs. Hardy, a shadowy figure, drops in every so often to put dinner on the table.

In the most recent Nancy Drew mystery, The Secret of the Forgotten City, by Carolyn Keene (Grosset & Dunlap), Nancy and the River Heights regulars (staff beau Ned Nickerson, boyish brave George [a girl] and girlish, nervous Bess [ditto] pursue a treasure of gold in the Nevada desert. Clues to its hiding place are cleverly deciphered by Nancy from ancient Indian petroglyphs. In the latest Hardy Boys adventure, The Mysterious Caravan by Franklin W. Dixon (Grosset & Dunlap), Frank and Joe and the Bayport troupe trace a treasure of gold from Jamaica to Morocco by cleverly deciphering clues etched into an ancient Arab death mask. The authors of both stories employ the same kind of bugging device, and there are other similarities that should delight some doctoral student researching "The Interconnective Overlappings of Hardyana and Drewism."

To quote Andrew Svenson, "The trick in writing children's books is to set up danger, mystery and excitement on page one." Unfailingly each new mystery is launched in the opening paragraphs. Plots are jerry-built, but there is always plenty of dialogue punctuated by travel. Even when nothing is really happening there is the constant appearance of action. Every chapter ends with a cliff hanger. "Look out! Look out! the elephants are stampeding!" is typical of the genre. As Svenson has succinctly put it, "Force the kid to turn the page."

And give the kid someone supremely easy to identify with, like Nancy Drew for instance, the perfect unimaginative fantasy figure living in a world where all the villains are out-of-towners and all the troubles are those she, personally, can cure. Nancy is not "different," a quality as highly prized as leprosy when you're young. There is no magic to her, no eccentricity, no humor. She is simply prettier (but not a raving beauty), brighter (but not a crazy genius) and nicer than most people.

She is a renaissance teen. Police chiefs are forever "astounded by her cleverness." When she tries ballet the professionals step back to applaud. Put a paint brush in her hand and watch the praise fly. As to her proficiency with foreign languages, Caramba!

John Donovan, president of the Children's Book Council, was a youthful Hardy devotee: "They were everything I was going to be in a few years: heroic, brave and ... rich."

My friend the mystery fan devoured Drews because they were not too mysterious to solve. "I was Nancy but I was smarter. I could stay a little ahead of her."

It is probable that nostalgia is another ingredient in the series' popularity. As Mrs. Adams has said, "Mothers love the Nancy Drew books and give them to their daughters." Those who feel there's no Drews like old Drews may be disappointed the books are continually updated. "Chums" have become friends, "frocks" are jeans and nobody gives "ritzy affairs" anymore. Also, fortunately, countless racially stereotyped servants and villains have been quietly rewritten or expunged.

Nancy remains all things to all persons. Ms. Magazine pronounced her "a role-model for young feminists ... active and brave. Active? It's true. She really gets around. But when she and Ned go driving he takes the wheel. And if there is car trouble she sits tight while a man checks under the hood. Brave? The girl has nerves of stainless steel. Unlike the Hardys, who carry weapons and throw punches, Nancy relies on quick wits and fancy footwork. But she's inclined to blush when Ned kisses her on the cheek. Unusual trait for a feminist role-model. It is also worth noting that Nancy has never accepted payment for sleuthing. Of course the Hardy Boy's skills have earned them numerous pretty pennies over the last 48 years. Totally protected from want, gainful employment, boredom and despair, Nancy would seem to be more of a suburban princess than a symbol of liberation, from anything except real life.

A common complaint is that "Nancy Drew books are the same books written over and over again." Perhaps that is also part of the charm they hold for their readers. A series combines the excitement of the unknown cushioned by the known. Add to that the fact that no one likes to come to The End when they're having a good time. "To be continued" beckons the crowd. It is the fuel of series writing and its counterparts: soap opera and situation TV. Dickens took advantage of its power when he wrote for periodicals. He made it an art. But he was Dickens. Such distinctions don't affect children. They don't read for style. Discrimination is acquired with time and exposure after one has picked up that wonderful habit of turning the page. The works of the Stratemeyer dynasty have no lasting literary value but they have helped lead many children past River Heights or Bayport further into the bewitched byways of reading for pleasure. It's a destination well worth the trip.

PART IX

NONFICTION

(all things bright and beautiful . . .)

EDITOR'S NOTE

Several of the articles in this section focus on informational books for children rather than young adults, but the points made apply equally well to the books marketed for the junior high to early high school level. Too many are produced "to order," in response to curriculum demands or in hopes of capitalizing on issues that are of current interest and therefore likely to become assignment topics. Few succeed in communicating complexities and subtleties without sacrificing clarity and readability.

On the other hand, young adults are hungry for information. As Jim Haskins says, an interest in a particular topic may be so intense that the reader will devour anything and everything on the subject which is within grasp. Problems arise when there is insufficient material at the reader's level, or when a potentially exciting topic is tediously presented. Good readers can usually be led directly to adult materials, but poorer readers who most desperately need really interesting books that will not defeat them are the ones who suffer. What do you do with a 16-year-old who has suddenly developed a fascination with aerodynamics, but reads at a fifth grade level? "Reluctantly Yours"[1] suggests some easy nonfiction, but there is never enough.

The problem is that writers and publishers have to respond to the demand that informational books for young people meet the criteria for good literature on the one hand and the need for easy material on the other. The rewards, at least in terms of the critical attention and prizes which help to sell books, shift the balance in favor of meeting the former demand.

For an overview of the standards by which children's nonfiction is measured, see Zena Sutherland's "Information Pleases--Sometimes" in Wilson Library Bulletin (October 1974), Margery Fisher's Matters of Fact (Crowell, 1972), and the bibliography following Robin Gottlieb's article in this section. The standards applied to children's nonfiction are generally also applied to nonfiction published for young adults. The following is representative of the criteria recommended:

> ... good format, clarity, accuracy, communication of the author's attitudes, adroit use of language, and concepts and vocabulary appropriate for the age of the intended audience: no jargon or writing down; no teleology or

> anthropomorphism; respect for the integrity and adaptability of the reader; humor where it is appropriate; logical structure or organization; a writing style that is distinctive for its originality in the use of words and word patterns ... for nonfiction, the ways in which the author demonstrates a scientific attitude, accuracy, currency, and sequential arrangement of material.[2]

The books that meet criteria such as the above are rare, of course. Moreover, many subjects which catch a teenager's attention are of the ephemeral or faddist sort which seldom receive serious, let alone literary treatment. As Harry Stubbs notes, young adult librarians tend to respond to readers' demands and will acquire materials that fall far short of Sutherland's criteria. They do so in the conviction that teenagers have as much right to read the latest successor to Chariots of the Gods as adults do to read the newest super-diet book. With reservations, Stubbs agrees that library collections should reflect user interests as well as professional expertise in selection, saying we should not "risk omitting books that many students will feel should be on hand ... student trust in and respect for the library as a source of information is very, very important."[3]

Notes

1. See p. 424.

2. Zena Sutherland, "Science as Literature," Library Trends, April 1974, p. 485.

3. See p. 372.

NON-FICTION BOOKS AND THE JUNIOR AND SENIOR HIGH-SCHOOLER: CHANGES IN SUPPLY TO MEET CHANGES IN DEMAND*

By Jim Haskins

Today's junior and senior high school students are the second, and in some instances, the third generation of television children. They have grown up seeing the world and national news in stark black and white or vivid color. World hunger, assassinations, wars are not abstract subjects to which they have heard veiled references when listening to adults converse--they are things they have seen first-hand. Childhood offered them no rose-colored view of the world--even the most conscientious parents could not screen their children's television viewing to this extent. Within their ranks is that same child who a few years ago was quoted as saying, "If I grow up," rather than "When I grow up." How can they not be deeply affected by what they have seen?

That they have been affected is axiomatic. How they have been affected is not as easy to perceive. Twenty-five junior and senior high schoolers from across the country and from various strata of our society would respond to this question with twenty-five different answers. This is not to say that they are unique in their variety, for the same would hold true if a sampling were done of their younger brothers and sisters or their parents. However, certain correlations can be made among the three groups, and one can see how the junior and senior high schoolers reflect traits of the other two groups, as might be expected of a group that is composed of people who are neither children nor adults. One such trait, and the one with which we in the writing-library-education field are most concerned, is the increased demand for non-fiction or informational literature. Television has given us all heightened exposure to the real world, and it follows that our tastes in literature have changed accordingly; and this is true for the entire age range of the reading public.

A couple of years ago a librarian wrote that her pre-schoolers were demanding true books along with their story books, that they wanted books that were "real." Junior and senior high school students have the same desires. They want their non-fiction to be

*Reprinted by permission of the author and publisher from Arizona English Bulletin (April 1976), 78-82.

very real and very true regardless of the subject. And the subjects vary as much as the adolescents do. One cannot predict what is going to spark the interest of a particular young adult. One might decide to read and absorb the information in all the books on flying and model airplanes. Another might undertake a study of black history. The subject interest might last a day, a month, or a lifetime; but the interest is there; and young adults require informational books to satisfy their interests. The days are gone when a librarian or teacher could feel safe with one book on a given subject. Several months ago I spoke at a Children's Literature conference about the fact that until this year, with the appearance of the Silversteins' Hamsters, there existed but one book for young people on the subject, Zim's Golden Hamsters (1951). With each new issue of Publishers Weekly come announcements of "new" cook books, interior decorating books, biographies, etc. for adults. One wonders how the "one book is sufficient for adolescents" theory could have been maintained as long as it was.

Fortunately for the pre-adult reader, this attitude is fast disappearing. In the publishing year 1973-1974 four or five books dealing with VD were published. Granted, some were better than others, and much of the material was repetitive, but could not the same be said of plant books or craft books? In May Delacorte published Fleming's Alcohol, and in October Lippincott will be issuing the Silversteins' Alcoholism; yet with the major problem alcoholism has become among today's youth, two books is not nearly enough. This is not to say that we need or want title after title on every current or important issue. History has shown that too often the result is one really good title and a number of mediocre or poor titles. Still the adolescent should be allowed the right of choice. Adolescent readers are very harsh judges and are no more accepting of trite or poorly written books than their adult counterparts.

The June 1975 issue of Top of the News carried under the broad heading of "Present Shock: Youth in the Seventies," a series of articles which originally were speeches presented at the 1974 ALA Conference in New York. While the articles deal primarily with adolescent fiction, there are some important and interesting points that help to reveal a clearer picture of adolescent reading patterns as a whole, and of the adolescent him/herself. Isabelle Holland has quite a bit to say about the adolescent:

> An adolescent is a human being on a journey in that great, amorphous sea called adolescence. That is, he or she is somewhere between age twelve and ages eighteen or nineteen. In this period almost anything can happen to a human being--and usually does. There are adolescents who do little but work. There are adolescents who do nothing but play. There are adolescents of nineteen (as indeed there are adolescents of fifty-nine), while some young people of thirteen or fourteen seem, emotionally anyway, to have achieved a maturity and a sense of responsibility usually associated with adulthood in the most complimentary

> sense of the word. An adolescent, therefore, is a human being who is journeying from childhood to adulthood. He or she is learning, whether for good or ill, to do without certain things that were important to him or to her during childhood. He is also learning how to acquire certain qualities, skills, defenses that will be important to him when he becomes an adult. But the adolescent is both a child AND an adult, and his tastes in reading, as in everything else, reflect this fact.

This dual identity is clearly revealed in adolescent reading habits. "An adolescent, depending on age, sex and taste, can read Beatrix Potter, Henry Miller, John Knowles, Leo Tolstoy, Louisa May Alcott, the Bobbsey Twins, ... --or all of them together within the same six months' period." We must, however, not forget that this same broad range of interests and types of literature consumed can hold true of the adult reader. Adolescents cannot be pigeonholed any more than adults or children, but we have created a basis for or a framework within which to discuss the adolescent and non-fiction books.

Non-fiction has been a part of literature since its advent, but the age of non-fiction for the child and the adolescent has really only come into its own in the 1960s and 1970s. Recently I did a study of non-fiction from 1950 to 1975 and was somewhat surprised to discover that instead of treating a brief span of twenty-five years in the whole history of adolescent non-fiction, I was basically doing a complete survey. Informational books for young people were written before 1950, but one would be hard-put to find more than a handful of such books available in any public or school library. If one had specific titles or subjects in mind, undoubtedly a librarian could offer an alternative book on the subject, but it would be of later date. Why are informational books so relatively young? One reason is the very nature of this area. A fiction title might become dated because of language or attitude but it is not likely to become totally inaccurate. Think how quickly the world has changed in the last twenty-five years. A space book written in 1956 would treat men walking on the moon as a possibility, not an accomplished fact. The attitude toward history has changed too. Books are no longer acceptable if they provide the history of white America with little or no reference to the contributions and problems of the nation's various minorities and there is a demand for books to fill traditional information gaps or to correct false accounts. The myths of the Civil War and Reconstruction are challenged in two books by William Katz--Album of the Civil War and Album of Reconstruction. He is also doing a multi-volume series on Minorities in America that does not paint a very proud picture of life for them in "the land of the free." S. Carl Hirsh's Riddle of Racism stirred much controversy when it appeared three years ago because it treated a subject considered too adult for adolescent and juvenile minds.

In 1966 the "New Journalism" came into being in adult literature, as reflected in the writings of Gay Talese and Jimmy Breslin, among others. The "New Journalism" involved a scene-by-scene reconstruction, a record of dialogue in full, and the first person point of view. Adolescents were introduced to this form with the publication of To Be a Slave by Julius Lester in 1968. Still considered a milestone today, it has ceased to be the only example. Franklin Watts Publishers has launched two new series in recent years--Focus Books and World Focus Books. In both series a particular historical event is presented in detail in a single book, averaging about sixty-five pages. Two recent additions to the series are The Purchase of Alaska by Peter Sgroi and The Berlin Olympics, 1936 by James P. Barry, which emphasizes how the outstanding performances of black athletes like Jesse Owens had an adverse effect on Hitler's racial superiority theory. In both series there is ample use of pictures, and there is always a bibliography of books and articles for further reading. These bibliographies or suggested readings are composed primarily or solely of adult material, though the books themselves are geared for 5th grade and up (World Focus) and 7th grade and up (Focus).

Including a bibliography or suggested readings list in the informational book for adolescents is a relatively recent development. It is one that this author has been part of since beginning to write for juveniles; but I am told that for a long time few adolescent book writers would list their sources because they were adult in nature. I have always felt this practice to be downgrading and unfair to the reader, who deserves the right and the opportunity to read further on any subject. Who am I to say that my biography of Adam Clayton Powell or Shirley Chisholm is the only book an adolescent needs to read on either personality? One of my aims as a writer is to spark interest and expand minds; it is impossible for me to remain faithful to that ideal if I refuse to share my sources.

The non-fiction explosion began in the 1960s with the advent of increased federal funding under various educational and library acts. It was also at this time that the United States became overconcerned about the scientific advances of the Russians and panicked over studies that focused on the low level of literacy in the United States. Up to that time, non-fiction served a purely functional role in any library collection and was not likely even to appear on book store shelves. There was a preponderance of series that were all packaged alike with little concern for outstanding illustrations or eye appeal. Why bother--after all they were solely geared for homework assignments, and if a person was really hooked on the subject the packaging would have no effect. Fiction was the be all and end all in nearly every library. More space, more attention, and more money was set aside for fiction titles.

Why the big switch? There is probably no clear cut answer. I asked a children's librarian in a large city branch when she first noticed the change. She said it was a gradual one that really did not have an impact on her until she faced the fact that she had many more non-fiction books than fiction books and thus had to do a massive re-shelving job. Working as she did for several years in areas where students read far below grade level, she soon discovered she was more likely to induce the slow- or non-reader to take a book out if she relied on the informational books, which seemed to have more appeal and did not have such a "babyish" format or appearance. There are other contributing factors like the advent of open classrooms where teachers are not as textbook oriented as in traditional classrooms. Students are expected to do more of their work with the assistance of trade books, magazines, and newspapers --not textbooks and not encyclopedias. This sort of independent study has caused many students to become interested on their own in a particular subject or to pursue other fields because the next book on the shelf caught their eye.

The paperback explosion is another important factor in the growth of non-fiction, or informational books. In some areas there is still some controversy over the value of paperback vs. hardcover; but for the most part, paperbacks are an accepted, and in many instances, a very welcome addition to the field of books. Book clubs like the one handled by Scholastic are instrumental in getting books directly into the homes of children on a permanent basis, because 60¢ or 75¢ is available each month for book purchases. Libraries have been sorely hit by the economic crisis in this country, and in response many of them have switched to the paperback book, especially in the areas where multi-copies are in demand (history, space, sports, science) or those specialized areas where the demand is minimal and there is not sufficient justification for buying the more expensive hardcover titles. Publishers, too, have seen the value of the paperback. Lippincott was the first to see the value of publishing books simultaneously in hardcover and paperback. The first year, about three years ago, they undertook this dual publishing with selected fiction and non-fiction titles, but after the first year limited it to non-fiction titles (an interesting and significant alteration in the normal patterns of publishing); fiscally, it was shown to be unprofitable to treat fiction titles in this manner because they were not selling. The titles they handle in this dual fashion remain selected, but the point is that the practice is maintained.

There is no doubt that the paperback is here to stay and that production and use will increase. One need only go into the local bookstore, drugstore or newsstand to see that the glossy-cover paper back is out there anxious to attract readers. My Shirley Chisholm biography had its paperback rights sold even before the book was published in May, and therefore before public or review media reaction could be known. More and more retailers of the adult paperback are beginning to stock material for the child or adolescent. Like their adult counterparts, this segment of our society likes the convenience and easy portability of the paperback. On every subway and bus in New York City people can be found reading, and most of them are holding paperbacks; paperbacks can be found on the beach, in lines at bank tellers' windows, sticking out of shoulder bags and back pockets. What is popular with the adult is equally as popular with the adolescent, with, currently, a heavy interest in the occult and astrology and a strong demand for more on the "Bermuda

Triangle." Monster books, especially ones involving the old movies, are also very popular. The new interest in ethnic heritage has resulted in special paperback collections on various ethnic groups being established and expanded in various libraries and even bookstores; and books for young people are substantially represented in these collections.

This discussion has treated only briefly the adolescent reader's demand for informational books and the efforts to supply that demand. The interests of these readers are as varied as they are, and non-fiction literature for them will continue to change and grow as quickly as they do. To quote Isabelle Holland again:

> ... adolescence is probably the only time of life when a large proportion of its membership inhales books--all kinds of books--in huge, indiscriminate drafts at all hours of the day and night and at the full peak of the reader's energy. The adolescent is not only encouraged to do this, he is pretty much forced to do it, if he wants to keep up with his required reading. So he balances his assignments for English Lit with his fancy from the nearest magazine stand, which could be *Popular Mechanics*, *Time* magazine ... or various erotica.

The adolescent is complex and so are his reading patterns, but the changes in juvenile reading patterns, and therefore in juvenile literature, are merely an indication of the changing attitudes in all strata of our population. The important considerations are truth, reality, the whole picture, and of course, portability, availability and attractive packaging. Hopefully, this means that soon it will not be only the adolescent who freely goes from children's books to adult books and back again. Perhaps someday there will simply be the category "informational books with no distinction as to suitability for child or adolescent or adult.

WHY NONFICTION BOOKS ARE SO DULL AND WHAT YOU CAN DO ABOUT IT*

By Sada Fretz

In the benighted past, school children were confronted each September with stacks of thick, drab, and boring textbooks, through which they would plod at a uniform and predetermined rate that was calculated to get them to the end in June. Today's teachers, in contrast, use a variety of hard and soft-covered sources, assign "outside" reports, and allow some choice of subjects--if only from a preassembled list. But too often the presumably vital and individualized reading material thus employed turns out to be as unstimulating as the demoted textbooks.

While the blame for this situation must be shared among many--including publishers, distributors and librarians--the condition is undeniable, and it will continue until teachers themselves go into the libraries to discover which books are inaccurate and useless, and which ones deserve to be read and used. But by and large, teachers are unaware of their influence, uncertain how to exert it, and far from a consistent force for change.

The Publisher's Role

The publishers' contribution is most clear. They produce books that continue to sell. They watch the classroom, looking out for those subjects not yet overexploited in children's trade books. So often it's not quality but predictable classroom utility that determines whether a book gets published. And there are those editors (fortunately a minority), knowing that their librarian customers can afford not to be choosy so long as the new title covers an area kids frequently have to report on, who hand out assignments to writers who may or may not have any knowledge of their subject, or any notion of the interests, background or cognitive capacity of their intended audience. Thus a book for young children can be written in such stiff academic language that it's clear the author never bothered to adapt his style to a child's level. More com-

*Reprinted, with some changes made by the author, and with permission of the author and publisher, from Learning: The Magazine for Creative Teaching (May/June 1976), 68-70.

monly the information is presented with so little imagination or evident interest on the author's part that it's bound to kill any curiosity a child might bring to it. And sometimes both these faults are mixed with factual errors so gross and shocking that any adult acquainted with the field would insist that the manuscript be revised or rejected. (One editor of a young-adult book on the Spanish Civil War confessed that she had never heard of the war when the author submitted the idea to her; she thought he must be talking about the Spanish-American War.) All too often books that this process produces are just quickie pastiches designed to fill in the blanks in homework assignments.

The overviews that abound on the various nations provide a typical example. One volume in a superior series, Mary L. Clifford's _The Land and People of Sierra Leone_, illustrates the weaknesses of the genre. Though the author had lived in Sierra Leone, she conveys no feeling for its people and culture, purveying instead a rundown of industries, political parties and personalities, and all administrative districts, subdistricts and towns. In the past, such soulless surveys were purchased almost automatically if they filled a geographical gap in the collection. Of late, however, librarians are reporting a growing demand for "daily life" material that the _Land and People_ approach cannot meet.

How responsive publishers will be to this shift depends partly on the fate of such recent breaks with series formula as Aylette Jenness' _Along the Niger River_ (T. Y. Crowell, 1974), a personal, richly informative introduction to the Nigerians which employs selected facts in the service of intelligent analysis and leaves readers with a firm impression of the "small profound world" the author learned to respect during her three years within its borders. If teachers will acquaint themselves with the diversity of geographic sources available, and will loosen up their assignments to make room for the Jenness approach, both students and collections will be the better for it.

The Librarian's Role

Librarians, caught in the middle between publishers' bottom-line decisions and teachers' constricting assignments, play a more passive role in the proliferation of shoddy juvenile non-fiction. The fact remains, however, that librarians are the primary buyers of children's trade books, far outstripping parents, grandparents, and of course children themselves. Yet these professionals who make the big-money buying decisions often fail to make teachers aware of the resources available to them. Many are content to hand out routine rehashes, complaining that more imaginative works sit on the shelves. When it comes time to order books, many librarians depend on distributors or jobbers who buy from publishers at a large discount and pass on part of the savings to their institutional customers. Jobbers exert a strong and unfortunate influence on the quality of the books that eventually end up in a reader's hands. They fill their stocks before the individual titles are reviewed and often cannot fill orders for the books which turn out to be most favored. Librarians know they're likely to lose money allotted for purchases if the books they order don't come and the money remains unspent, so they're in the habit of ordering 50 to 100 per cent above their budgets and taking whatever comes through.

But also librarians continue to order what circulates most, and what circulates most are usually titles that satisfy arbitrarily distributed report assignments from end-of-chapter suggestion lists; and neither the textbook editors who make the lists, nor the teachers who use them, have any idea what can be found between hard covers at this level.

The Teacher's Role

We're back with the teacher, who suffers her students to read insipid books, and must suffer greatly herself year after year through an unending parade of dull reports. It doesn't have to be that way. Often when the teacher of an African unit, for example, discovers such titles as Christine Price's *Made in West Africa* (Dutton), Adjai Robinson's *Singing Tales of Africa* (Scribner) and W. Moses Serwadda's *Songs and Stories from Uganda* (T. Y. Crowell)--all published in 1974--she can devise varied and stimulating programs and assignments based on those riches at hand. One fifth grade teacher, bored with colonial living projects, brought her class to life when a student called her attention to Leonard Everett Fisher's *Colonial Americans Series* (Watts), which had been on the library shelves for years. The end result was an open house demonstration, with the whole class participating, that rivaled a visit to Williamsburg.

Whatever the subject, imaginative library books can not only enrich but also determine the direction of classroom study. For example, teachers who, as an annual event, divide their classes into three groups to report on air, water and land pollution could at least offer a greater variety of more specific environmental topics by simply checking out the available titles. The Silversteins' *Chemicals We Eat and Drink* (Follett, 1973) and Laurence Pringle's *Pests and People: The Search for Sensible Pest Control* (Macmillan, 1972) are two fine books on specific problems. Pringle's *Estuaries: Where Rivers Meet the Sea* (Macmillan, 1973) and Patricia Lauber's *Everglades Country: A Question of Life or Death* (Viking Press, 1973) are among those on different ecosystems.

For a more general introductory overview that helps children understand the scientific basis of environmental interdependence, the whole class would do better with Helen Russell's *Earth, the Great Recycler* (Nelson, 1973) than with any of the many recycled pieties on dirty air and littered streets that find their way into textbooks. As for related experiments, a comparison of Harry Sootin's careful *Easy Experiments With Water Pollution* (School Book Service, 1974) with Seymour Simon's vague and perfunctory Science Projects in Pollution and Projects with Air shows how a choice between seemingly similar books can make the difference between learning by doing and haphazard time wasting. But without the guidance of a teacher who knows the books and knows the difference, students can't be expected to choose the more rewarding volume.

Librarians will listen to teachers, especially about the endless curriculum-oriented series that they have no way of testing directly. For example, the now numerous series especially aimed at beginning readers filled a huge gap when they first appeared, and both the silly line led by Dr. Seuss' Cat in the Hat (Beginner, 1957) and the beautiful Frog and Toad books of Arnold Lobel (Harper & Row, 1972) are still much in demand. But have their imitations multiplied beyond the point of no return? And does the genre as a whole really serve beginning readers any better than the stronger and often just as easy folktales that abound in picture-book format? How about the Young Math and the Let's-Read-and-Find-Out Science series published by T. Y. Crowell? Both series were hailed at birth as especially clear and elegant presentations of concepts previously considered too sophisticated for young children. Have subsequent titles been as relevant as the early ones, or is it time for selective ordering within the series? And how has the growing disenchantment with new math priorities affected the usefulness of the math series? How many of the dozen or more new introductions to the metric system can you use?

Do children really prefer to learn about animals via flatly fictionalized life cycles of Little Ant or Mother Caribou? And do junior high students really plow through all those deadly recapitulations of how "we" (from the Babylonians on) found out about black holes and stellar evolution--or would young adult readers too old for Franklyn Branley's exemplary presentations be better off with a popular, more readable adult writer such as Patrick Moore?

It should be clear that whatever the faults of others in this selection system, teachers have a central role. They can and should flex some muscle in favor of the publication of juvenile nonfiction with spark and sensibility. Certainly almost any children's librarian would welcome teachers' comments as a step toward reducing the guesswork in nonfiction book selection. But no matter what you tell the librarian, she or he will still look for the answers in circulation figures. The real decisions are made in the classroom.

Some Rules of Thumb for Judging Nonfiction Books

1) Does the book add significantly to what a student could find in an encyclopedia? Give the World Book credit where it's due, and ask from a trade book a little more than "just the facts."

2) Does the book deal with concepts and relationships, or is it simply an assemblage of facts, names and classifications?

3) Does the author encourage in his readers a sense of exploration, or is he too ready with labels, peremptory generalizations and answers that stifle curiosity?

4) Does the author have any special interest or background in his subject area? Or do his credits suggest a career of writing superficial children's books?

5) Does the author adapt his presentation to the intended readership? Specifically, does he avoid condescension while gearing his style and analogies to a child's experience and cognitive level?

6) Do the book's illustrations, format and general appearance indicate that the publishers took pride in its production? The truism about a book and its cover notwithstanding, shoddy production often reflects inferior content.

7) Above all, would reading this book put <u>you</u> to sleep?

THE STOCKPILE*

By Harry C. Stubbs

It is no news to a parent, teacher, or a librarian that the younger generation tends to react negatively to being told what to do, read, say, play, or like; and there seems little doubt that younger generations always have been this way. The result, or at least one result, is that the education and entertainment industries share a common problem--they want people to listen to them and be impressed--although the professionals in both groups might prefer not to put it that way.

I am aware of this from the viewpoint of both fields, having been a science teacher for more than a quarter of a century and a science fiction writer for even longer.[1] Both facts determine how much, and in what direction, the following article is slanted. I am certainly not a completely objective writer (if there is such a thing), so it seems only fair to provide some data on my more probable prejudices.

The teacher's most conscious aim is to indoctrinate his students with a reasonably large body of usable fact and a set of attitudes reasonably compatible with his culture. In the physical and biological sciences, the "facts" must include the fact that not everything is known yet, and that there are a few techniques available for learning more. The attitudes for learning these techniques should include strong curiosity, a certain dissatisfaction with any given state of knowledge or public affairs, and as complete an absence of personal arrogance as is consistent with an adequate supply of self-confidence. An imagination able to solve problems as they arise is needed, but not needed are any more of the types who feel justified in stopping everything else while the world implements their particular plan.

The science teacher and the librarian share the problem of deciding what parts of the really overwhelming supply of existing knowledge are important enough to demand student attention and consideration, or at least to be available to maturing (and to already mature) citizens. Both professions have their limits: the teacher

*Reprinted by permission of the author and publisher from Library Trends 22:4 (April 1974), 477-484. Copyright © 1973 by the University of Illinois Board of Trustees.

has only so much time to monopolize the pupil's attention, and the librarian only so much space for book storage and money for book acquisition. Both, therefore, tend to dip into the entertainer's budget of techniques, and compete for that part of the public wealth and student time usually budgeted for recreation and amusement. I do not criticize this at all; to the extent that acquiring useful knowledge and attitudes can be made fun, everyone is better off. Some may regret that one important criterion for any book is how much fun it is to read, but that must be accepted and lived with.

Another fact, of course, is that no one has time to read everything, even if there were nothing else to do. Far too many books are published to permit this. As a teacher I am required to form opinions on between three and four hundred books a year, and certainly cannot claim that every one of them is read from cover to cover in the process. A professional librarian must, I assume, make decisions on several times as many. We need not only criteria for final choice, but criteria for where to start looking.

One criterion heavily used by librarians, but not heavily tapped by teachers is customers' suggestions. Students do read, their bases of selection often being rather obscure to the over-thirty mind, and they sometimes like what they read. From the science teacher's viewpoint they may like some pretty silly stuff, since the human tendency to fall for fads and jump on bandwagons seems to develop rather early, but if they have read it and been impressed by it, the teacher has no choice but to know something about it. He may even find it advisable to have copies available so that more than one of his students may join in the debate. (Also, it is extremely unwise to risk giving the impression that you do not want people to read some item. The banned-in-Boston rating was eagerly sought by publishers in the days when things were still banned in Boston.)

Of course, reading the material may not be fun--although there is always a fair chance it will be. Nothing in this article is going to suggest an easy way to choose or advise on books. However, even the most irritating "science" books can be put to use (Velikovsky's Worlds in Collision,[2] which I had to put down every few pages to recover my temper, springs to mind). Specific claims or statements make good practice exercises in scientific reasoning, demanding both thought and further reading from the student. Therefore, while I would certainly not go out of my way to acquire every science book in which a student had expressed interest, I tend to jump at any chance to get a youngster into a thoughtful argument. There is astrology, most of the flying saucer material, pyramidology, the various health food fads--I grant that these should not take up too much of one's library shelf space, since there is far more valuable material to be housed, but neither the science teacher nor the librarian should permit himself to fossilize so thoroughly that nothing of the sort is available to his customers.

The students do not see everything, though, and often are not tempted by things we think they should study, so we cannot just wait for them to make suggestions. We have to do some picking of our own, and must therefore have some criteria determined by our own objectives and hopes--and not merely by asking "should they?" but also by asking "can they?" and "will they?" Difficulty is therefore a factor to consider.

The science teacher has some advantage in making this decision, but cannot claim the last word. Ideally, he wants a spectrum ranging from material pleasurable to his slowest students to things which will challenge his best. However, there are several factors which combine to make up the rather broad concept of "difficulty."

A subject itself may be inherently complex, abstract, or both, like quantum mechanics or psychology; but a book on these or any other subjects may still vary widely in difficulty because of the writing. Here, the librarian may actually be able to make a better judgment than the subject matter teacher.

One kind of difficulty which also stems from the writer rather than the subject, however, must be left to the subject matter specialist; and since the type of book in question is likely to be tempting both to student and librarian, the science teacher has a responsibility in helping with the selection. This is the sort of book which bears, usually, a give-away title of the general nature Golf (or Oil Painting, or Calculus, or Cooking) Made Easy. The writer of this type of book is claiming to supply shortcuts to achieving a difficult skill, or easier ways to express a difficult subject, or more familiar analogies for some abstraction. He may actually have accomplished this, and I say nothing against the attempt in any case although I am sufficiently middle-aged and corrupted by the Puritan work ethic to doubt that anything really can take the place of conscientious practice and careful thought.

The risk in the process is the loss of precision which accompanies simplification and the substitution of broad-meaning everyday words for the more specialized and precise scientific ones. My stock example is the child's (or amateur's) astronomy book which tries to explain orbital motion with the statement that "centrifugal force exactly balances gravity" so that the orbiting object neither falls nor escapes.

This statement is not exactly wrong, although many physicists would be bothered by the term "centrifugal force," which is merely one aspect of inertia, and the word "balance" is certainly ambiguous in this connection. Even though not wrong, however, the sentence has led to much misunderstanding because of its lack of precision. I have seen written expression, by literate adults, of the fear that sending spacecraft to the moon would upset this "exact" balance and send our satellite crashing to the earth or out into space. (If any of the present readers fall in this group, please read a work on astronomy which does not claim to be easy--e.g., a college freshman text.)

Simplifying or clarifying difficult scientific subjects is a tricky job, as is recognizing when the job has been well done. Even the best scientist or science teacher cannot spot all the possible ways in which a book, a paragraph, a sentence or even a word may be misunderstood. Simplification demands of the writer a good, clear understanding of the subject itself at the professional level, not just the level of the proposed reader. It demands a high degree of skill with language, or very close cooperation with an illustrator, or preferably both. The scientist who cannot write well and the writer who is not a scientist are both poor candidates for the job. It is quite common in present-day science books for children to put an impressive list of scientific consultants somewhere near the title page, but one sometimes wonders how much these people actually influence the final choice of words and illustrations. I tend to be somewhat more impressed when the scientist is listed as "coauthor," although this is not a really firm criterion.

I fear that a science book must be judged at least three ways: for accuracy by a scientist, for clarity by a nonscientist, and for effectiveness on the basis of ideas and understanding that it actually engenders in students. The last, I grant, does make things a little hard on author and publisher.

A widespread tendency exists to equate "simplified" with "nonmathematical." Indeed, I have seen the latter term used in textbook advertising as though it were a virtue. Using advanced mathematics in a science book intended for students untrained in the field is, of course, as pointless as employing any other language they have not yet studied. However, the physical sciences are essentially quantitative, and all students have had some mathematics. Mathematical notation is the clearest and most concise method of explaining any point which involves questions of "how much?" or "how many?" or "how big?"

The notation may merely involve written numbers for the child who has just learned to count, or numerical examples for the one just learning arithmetic, but it can and should also involve basic algebra, trigonometry, logarithms, or calculus if the intended reader can reasonably be expected to have any training in the use of these tools. I know about, and resent, the widespread antimathematical bias in the U.S. population, and feel strongly that something should be done to counter it. If the science writer makes it obvious that mathematical terminology is the easiest way to express and solve quantitative problems, we may hope that an occasional student will be stimulated to learn its use. I suggest that to the science teacher selecting books, the phrase "completely nonmathematical" on the jacket or in the sales literature is not a point in a book's favor.

The preceding criterion tended to overflow somewhat into the question of accuracy, which is also a point for independent consideration. I get the impression that librarians worry more about this aspect of a science book than do most science teachers, not because the latter care less, but because they feel more sure of themselves in judging the matter. I can offer the librarians some comfort.

Without belittling the importance of accuracy, please remember that no book has ever been written with *no* scientific mistakes--at least, there is no way to say that one has been, because we do not really know how many mistakes remain in our picture of the universe. Furthermore, if one ever is written it will be dated very quickly. As a science teacher I am not seriously bothered by an occasional misstatement of fact in a book, although I admit that some books go much too far in this direction.

There is, in fact, a variety of mistake, which rather pleases me, however much it embarrasses the author. This is the slip in internal consistency. I will name no names, but when a book says on one page that the year of Mars is more than twice as long as that of the Earth, and on another page that the year of Mars is 687 Earth days in length, I sit happily back and wait for my more alert students to spot the inconsistency and start finding out for themselves which of the statements (if either) is correct.

When two books intended for the same level of reader disagree on some point, I am equally happy. I regard it as extremely important that students learn, as early as possible, that scientific "knowledge" is constantly changing as new information comes in, and that unlike chess or baseball, there is no human authority in a position to state absolutely the rules of the universe we live in.

I realize and regret that this knowledge can lead to insecurity in some people. I consider this danger as much smaller than the one arising from *lack* of this bit of truth. A person who has grown up under the impression that everything he has learned (or even that *anything* he has learned) is unassailably correct is on thin ice. He *is likely* to suffer far more from his collision with a nonconforming fact than is his classmate from an inability to make decisions (I realize that this view is disputable). I feel that much of humanity's social and political troubles stem from people's misplaced confidence in the validity of their own beliefs and viewpoints.

Librarians should not be overly concerned about spotting all the scientific errors in a newly acquired book. If a young reader comes up indignantly to point a new one out to you, would you really want to deprive him of the pleasure? And science teachers should delight in the useful classroom situation where two students cannot agree on whether a certain book statement is correct. I am not proposing that a whole library, or even a whole shelf, should be devoted to horrible examples. But those too stuffy about accuracy and updating will not have a library.

I have not and will not mention any specific books; no such list could be very complete, and would date far too rapidly. The production of "recommended lists" is a specialty in itself. There are many sources of suggestion--the American Association for the Advancement of Science puts out evaluation lists every few months; there is Appraisal from the Harvard School of Education; there are reviews in Science, Scientific American, and The Horn Book Magazine.

There is, however, one other general criterion which should be mentioned--that of subject matter. I mentioned above that there should be a wide range of difficulty available to the student, which naturally demands shelf space. This demand is greatly increased by the enormous variety of subjects calling themselves sciences. Someone must decide on a balance between the traditional subjects on one hand and the borderline and bandwagon ones on the other. It might seem at first that this responsibility belongs chiefly to the science teacher, but there is a danger here. Some of my esteemed colleagues, including myself, have trouble controlling the urge to dismiss a book as nonsense when it does not fit the conventional pattern. This may be the conservatism of age, or a considered opinion that basics should come first. In either case, we risk omitting books that many students will feel should be on hand; and student trust in and respect for the library as a source of information is very, very important.

I happen to be on the basic side myself: I felt that Silent Spring was much too emotional, and still resent the instant ecologist who does not seem to realize that the first blow at the "balance of nature" was not the Flit gun but the garden.

Nevertheless, students become interested in such things, and professionally I have no choice but to qualify myself to discuss them. I cannot afford to exclude all this from the library, if only because I cannot afford to have students thinking that I am trying to censor their reading.

What I can do, and all I can do, with student food faddists is to have books on scientific nutrition available, backed up by basic chemistry and biology texts. For astrologers there are the astronomy texts, plus mathematical works on the analysis of observational errors and cause-and-effect criteria. For ecologists who disapprove of the Alaska pipeline there are books on ecology by professionals, again with chemistry, biology and meteorology backups.

I teach at the high school level, but make it a point to have at least a few college and graduate school books available in the library; I feel fortunate at being close enough to Boston to be able to use a number of local university libraries for backup. Teachers should attempt to make the library's scope as wide as possible, and think twice before rejecting a book because it is palpable nonsense.

I have emphasized chemistry, biology, and the like in the foregoing paragraphs, and have emphasized belief in the importance of basic studies in depth. I do not mean by that to discount the interdisciplinary fields which keep springing up. We need them, however negatively I may react to the bandwagon syndrome. We need people who can come as close as humanly possible to viewing the whole picture at once. We also need, however, people who are aware of the vast body of detailed fact which must be uncovered and the appalling amount of work which has to be done before we can _ever_ decently utter a sentence beginning with the words "I know."

There is the person who makes public pronouncements on ecological matters without knowing the difference between a microtome and a chromosome, or being able to balance a simple chemical equation. There is also the person who writes a tale of nautical adventure without knowing the difference between a sloop and a lugger, and believes that splicing the main brace is something done with rope.

The important difference between these two idiots is that the first is less likely to be found out (many readers of sea tales know something about ships) and more likely to do irreparable damage (we are irrevocably part of this planet's ecology ourselves) if he is a persuasive talker. Even if we do not produce an entire generation of scientists, it is up to us--writers, teachers, librarians, parents --at least to produce citizens competent to recognize the scientific faddist when he starts to talk. After all, it is now about two centuries since we committed ourselves to the technology-or-starve branch of history's roads. Maybe we should not have done it, but it is much too late to complain now.

Libraries have limited space and funds, and teachers have limited time, but both should do their best to provide reading collections of broad scope in both difficulty and subject matter. They must keep their ears, eyes, and minds open. They should remember that any book which can start debate has some potential use in communication bridges.

References

1. Science fiction fans know him as Hal Clement. --Ed.

2. Velikovsky, Immanuel. _Worlds in Collision._ New York, Macmillan, 1950.

MY STRUGGLE WITH FACTS*

By Olivia Coolidge

Facts are the bricks with which a biographer builds. The more facts I have to work with, the freer I am to design my own book. Biography, however, is not just a mass of facts, and the perfect biographer is not a tape-recorder. If this were so, and thus the more detailed a biography the better, there would be no place for young-adult biographies. Furthermore, an autobiography would be, potentially at least, a greater work than any biography. Who knows the facts of a life as well as the man who has lived it? Yet actually an autobiography can be as misleading as a poor book by somebody else. When I was writing the life of Edith Wharton, I read her autobiography and accepted without question a great many details which came from her personal knowledge. When I compared the book, however, with what Edith said in her letters, with what other people said about her, and even with what she put into her fiction, one conclusion was inescapable. Edith Wharton was a shy woman who led an intense and not always happy emotional life. Her autobiography was written as much to prevent the public's really knowing her as to give the basic facts of her career. The suggestion has even been made that her main purpose was to put off the evil hour when a biographer would try to understand her inner secrets.

Actually, a biographer has a different task from a man who is writing his memoirs. These last contain invaluable material, but a good biography is also concerned with the effect its hero has on other people, with environment and background, with the nature of the great man's achievements and their value. I find that I examine facts in all these and many other spheres before I form judgments and that it needs great care to do what sounds quite easy, namely to distinguish a fact from a judgment. For instance, a contemporary's opinion of my subject is a fact. Its reliability and importance are estimated by my judgment, which is shown by my decision to quote or not to quote it, and even by the tone in which I refer to it or the context in which I introduce it.

My struggle with facts starts, then, at the elementary stage

---

*Reprinted by permission of the author and publisher from Wilson Library Bulletin (October 1974), 146-151. Copyright © 1974 by The H. W. Wilson Company.

of recognizing what they are and why they are important. Let us look, for example, at a plain fact. Abraham Lincoln was born on February 12, 1809; anyone who denies this is wrong. By itself this fact seems one of those insignificant details which are hard to keep straight in the memory and about which accuracy does not matter very much. The 11th or 13th would presumably have made no difference to Lincoln's later career. Even a year or two one way or the other might not have mattered. Yet the date does have importance because it places Lincoln in history. If he had been born ten years earlier, for instance, he might have been too old to grow with the immense changes that were sweeping over the midwestern prairies in the Forties and Fifties. He might have become set in his ways and never risen to be presidential candidate in 1860, though he certainly would not have been considered too old for the job. Alternatively, he might have become President, but proved unable to cope with unfamiliar situations or to endure extraordinary emotional and physical strain. In other words, a good deal depends on this simple fact when we put it in combination with other facts of environment or background. Because it has this kind of importance, we must give some recognition to its shape. February 12, 1809, is the correct date. There is no other.

So far, so good. But what if the facts are in dispute? Joseph Conrad, escaping from effective supervision at seventeen, was in serious trouble in Marseilles at twenty. His uncle, summoned from the Polish Ukraine by an ominous telegram--CONRAD WOUNDED. SEND MONEY. COME--arrived to find his nephew recovering from a bullet wound in the chest. Conrad gives two accounts of his escapade, one in a book of reminiscences about his adventures at sea, which covers his smuggling arms into Spain on behalf of Don Carlos, pretender to the Spanish throne; the other in a novel written many years later about his affair with the mistress of Don Carlos and his wound in a duel fought on her behalf. Since Conrad assured his friends that the novel was true to life and told his wife that the scar on his chest was a wound from a duel, his own account of the incident is fairly plain. Unfortunately, Don Carlos had given up the fight and left Spain a year before Conrad--by his own account--was smuggling arms to him. One of Conrad's companions on the venture was, according to ship's records, at the time on a voyage to the East Indies. A boy who Conrad says was drowned turns up many years later as captain of a coasting vessel. Don Carlos' mistress did not speak French at this time, was almost certainly not in Marseilles, and would not yet have been capable of playing the role of chief conspirator which he assigned to her. Conrad's uncle in a letter to a friend says nothing of a duel and puts down Conrad's wound to attempted suicide. Must we conclude that Conrad was a big liar? This would contradict a great deal of what we know of him from other sources. Can the records which conflict with his story be explained? In detail they can, but it is at least remarkable that so many of them need an explanation. In some ways I found this an easy problem to tackle because it is so fundamental to the relationship between fact and fiction in Conrad's writings that we can consider our verdict in the light of other stories he wrote concerning adventures which paralleled events in his own life. Furthermore, what we conclude is so important to an understanding of the man that even in a short biography I can marshal the evidence and give the reader some chance to judge independently.

The Goose-Nest Prairie Dilemma

More difficult for me as a writer of short biographies are the contradictions which are not important enough to warrant discussion. In these cases, I often have to make up my mind, while yet the obligation to be right on matters of fact is just as binding on me as on those who have more space to argue about details. Let me take an admittedly small point by way of illustration because its simplicity makes it easy to see what is at issue. The most exhaustive book on Lincoln's pre-presidential years is the monumental work of Beveridge, published in 1928. In it he records that Lincoln's father died in 1851 at a place he describes as "Goose Nest Prairie." Nearly thirty years after Beveridge, Charles H. Coleman, professor at a state college only seven miles from the spot where Thomas Lincoln died, published a book on Lincoln's contacts with his relations in that area. In this he describes Thomas Lincoln's death at "Goose-nest Prairie." Both spellings are contradicted by a county history originally published in 1879 and recently revised, which calls the place "Goose-Nest Prairie." Which spelling shall I adopt? The spelling of the name today proves nothing about 1851. Lincoln's father was illiterate and had no version of his own. Legal documents may vary because spelling at the time was generally imperfect. Perhaps a biographer may be forgiven if he makes up his mind on this small matter on evidence which satisfies him but is not conclusive, like that for instance of a local paper. Nevertheless, it is just this kind of thing which represents one of the most serious difficulties which I face as a biographer for young-adults. I do not always have room to explain why I take the position I do. I try to be careful and even find myself asking questions to which I do not absolutely need to know the answer, since I do not plan to include the disputed detail in what I am going to write. It simply seems that I need to know everything possible--because knowledge may affect judgment or because I am not yet really certain what I shall use or omit. In other words, I find it necessary to have a habit of worrying about facts, small or large, because my buildings are made up of these bricks, stones, or even pebbles.

Can a Woman Judge Napoleon?

Perfect accuracy on simple facts may not seem important to those who deal in generalizations, but at least a date or a spelling is presumably right or wrong. Many facts, however, are not easy to disentangle from judgments. Everyone who studies the career of Napoleon with an understanding of military tactics seems to have come to the conclusion that he was a great master of artillery on the battlefield. May I then regard this as a fact? In some contexts it would be fair to do so. If, for instance, in writing a biography of Lee I wished to emphasize his skill in handling artillery, I might do so by comparing him with Napoleon, even though I had made no study of the latter's career. If, on the other hand, I were writing a biography of Napoleon himself, I would have to treat this statement as a judgment. I would not be doing Napoleon justice if I did not examine his battles in detail and come to this conclusion for myself. So important is the distinction between a fact and a judgment or opinion that I would not even like to embark on a life of Napoleon, simply because as a woman I have no experience of battle. I fear my conclusions about his tactics might not have enough basis to have any value.

Fact or Judgment?

It is clear that if the same statement may be used in one context as a fact and in another as an opinion, it will not always be easy to distinguish between judgment and fact. Most people are quite careless about doing so in ordinary life, just as their speech tends to be sloppier than their formal writing. Juvenile biographers often set a bad example also. The shorter and more elementary a biography is, the more likely its author will be to take other people's opinions and repeat them in positive tones as if they required no examination. To my mind this is exactly what people should never do if they are writing for those who have not finished their education. The distinction between a fact and a judgment is one of great importance, but we do not make it instinctively. We have to learn how. If we have not done so by the time our formal education ends, the chances are that we never shall. I cannot expect my readers to know what the difference is if I myself disregard it. In consequence, even where I think I know a good deal, I ought not to take opinions of others for granted.

Generally speaking, when I start a biography I already know something in a scrappy way about my subject. Both my parents, for instance, knew Bernard Shaw and the people who were closely associated with him in his political, as opposed to his dramatic, work. I had read most of his plays, had met him on a couple of occasions, and had seen several of his dramas on-stage, including the original production of *St. Joan.* Nevertheless, when I made up my mind to write about Shaw, I was careful to read his published works in the order in which they were written so that I might look at each in turn as the latest creation of his mind. In this way I formed opinions, though not at all unusual ones, about the development and decline of his talent. Only after this did I turn to what other people said about Shaw's writings, lest I adopt their ideas without realizing that Shaw's actual works were the facts and their value a matter of judgment.

I may in the last few paragraphs have sounded as though I were saying that a fifty-page biography for ten-year-olds requires as much research as a twelve-hundred one for adults. Clearly this is not the case, and I am ready to admit that my own biographies deliberately represent a certain class of effort. If, for instance, I had embarked on a life of Shaw or Gandhi for adults, I would have done so with the idea of adding somewhat to the total of general knowledge on my subject. Either I would have sought unpublished manuscripts or I would have expected to develop some new point of view by examining the known ones. Unless there seemed a fair prospect of doing one or the other, I would not have undertaken the task to begin with. But a young-adult biography is not necessarily trying to add to human knowledge. Only in the case of Edith Wharton does what I say rest on the examination of a good deal of hitherto-unused material. A young-adult biography is basically an attempt to present a life in broad outline for readers who have a great number of other books to study or who bog down in long volumes, but who are intelligent and like ideas.

The Shavian Letters

Unquestionably, it is necessary for me to know a great deal more than I can actually put into a book of this kind, but at the same time research has reasonable limits. Let us consider, for instance, the question of Bernard Shaw's letters. Shaw was a voluminous and delightful letter-writer. Indeed his correspondence with the actresses Ellen Terry and Stella Campbell (whom he called "Stella Stellarum"--the Star of Stars) are among the most readable of English letter-collections. People kept Shaw's letters not merely because he was famous, but because they enjoyed them. By the time I came around to writing about Shaw, a great many of them had found their way into print. It would have been possible for me to discover unpublished letters which have since been included in a "complete" edition. Considering, however, the large number and the variety of those already available, it was clear that I might well toil for years to unearth new ones without ever discovering any important enough to include in a book of young-adult length. If I had been writing an adult work, I would have had to make this effort--and several others also--such as studying Shaw's manuscripts in order to look at the corrections he made as a clue to his mind.

Gandhi from Afar

In similar fashion, Gandhi was a journalist of almost unbelievable output, writing with equal facility in English and several Indian languages. Essentially, however, he was not a man of letters, but was composing day-to-day articles for people who did not mind repetition of simple ideas. In fact, they welcomed it and, from Gandhi's point of view, even needed it because the re-education of a whole people had to take time. If I had gone to India to study Gandhi's papers in their original languages, I would undoubtedly have gained much. This being in practice impossible, I had to decide whether my upbringing in England during the period when Gandhi was at work in India had given me sufficient indirect contact with the man and the Indian problem to enable me to write something which would be of value for young-adults. I thought it would and am pleased with the book, but I could not possibly have undertaken a longer work on the subject. My heap of pebbles would not have been sufficient.

This, then, is another aspect of my struggle with facts. I have to decide in each case how much work is needed to amass them and how much may be dismissed as an unreasonable expenditure of effort. If I had set out to be a scholar, my solutions to this problem would have been quite different. I recognize this, but do not take my own research lightly.

What Caused the First World War?

Still another problem with facts which is especially important to the young-adult biographer is raised by his use of background material in broad outline. My books are intended for people who, by and large, have not finished their formal education. Their knowledge is consequently scrappy, and there is very little in the way of historical fact which I can assume that everybody who reads my book is bound to know. Thus in the late Fifties when I was working on a biography of Churchill, I had to face the prospect of explaining the causes of the Boer War, the British parliamentary system, the causes of the First World War, who fought in it on which side, and a number of similarly large subjects. Nobody likes to be lectured, so that I needed to introduce these explanations with great skill and to keep them short. Volumes have been written on the causes of the First World War, some blaming one set of circumstances or people, some another. I found it extremely difficult to outline such a subject, even though I could limit myself to some extent by showing events as they appeared to Churchill at the time. I may fairly say that such pieces of information dropped in with careful casualness or closely woven into my hero's life have nearly always represented a great deal of work. I have often been tempted to envy those who, writing for adults, can blithely assume that anyone interested enough to read their books will have a certain amount of background knowledge. A young-adult biography is designed for people who want to read straight through it, picking up all the background that they need along the way. They do not wish to be interrupted by footnotes or puzzled by the appearance of a character with an unpronounceable Indian name who may or may not have appeared fifty pages before. There is a smoothness required in the writing of such a biography which is extremely difficult to construct out of the hard shape of facts, especially if the author is trying not to impose his own opinions too forcefully.

Sotto Voce Views

This brings me to the real crux of my own struggle. Of course, I have opinions. Every biographer does, including those who labor to insert everything and pile up footnotes giving pros and cons on every question. Every such author has to arrange his or her material and will reveal himself by how he speaks of it. The young-adult writer, who is making decisions all the time about what to insert, what to explain, and how to compress, not only reveals himself in every line, but runs a very great risk of imposing his opinions on his reader as though they were not his judgments but absolute truth. It is fair to say that any biographer, whether he admits it or not, wants people to understand what he is thinking. He does not, however, wish readers to suppose that his is the only way of thought about his subject. We all know that our personalities limit our points of view and that other people in what we hope are less good books will be needed to give a rounded picture of our hero. We cannot regard our personal answers as final when dealing with another human being.

There is no one solution to this difficulty for the young-adult biographer. I need to impose my views upon the material because its handling requires special techniques. I have to find my solutions as particular ones at particular spots. In one place, I find it possible to debate an issue without actually telling the reader what is the answer. In another I may fling out a suggestion for an eager mind to grasp, but not develop it. Elsewhere I may leave a question hanging. The reception given my hero in his own time may be used to counterbalance what I am doing to him as author. By inserting the right phrase I can often indicate that these opinions of contemporaries are as important as the author's and are closer to my hero. In other words, I must constantly recognize in myself the desire to "tell people what" and try to counteract it. Where I do not succeed in being fair, it will be my own fault because my nature has an obstinate habit of breaking through. I build to my own design, but I do not try to plaster over the hard-core facts with my personal opinions. Facts should be left showing and not chipped away to conform with the shape of my building. I try to work with them in their original form in order to create a sound structure.

ON NONFICTION BOOKS FOR CHILDREN: TRADITION AND DISSENT*

By Robin Gottlieb

Certain musts and must-nots have been standard in nonfiction as well as in fiction books for American children over the years. Lately, of course, many of the walls traditionally surrounding children's fiction have crumbled. But are the walls crumbling in nonfiction also? A few authorities have recently approached nonfiction books for children in the areas of biography, science, and the social sciences. On some points they agree; on others they do not.

Concerning biography, they agree that when written for children it differs in several important respects from that written for adults. For one thing, biography for children is usually written about figures "whose lives are worthy of emulation."[1] Therefore, many reasonable subjects of adult biography are generally considered unsuitable subjects in books for children; for instance, people "whose sex lives were 'irregular,'" or "Those who have led violent lives outside the 'establishment.'"[2] A second difference is that children's biography does not always present the whole truth about a subject. If a life contains tragic or unsavory aspects, these are generally omitted. "Juvenile biographies should be true as far as they go, with no falsifications," say May Hill Arbuthnot and Zena Sutherland, "but the whole adult truth may not be within younger children's range of comprehension and judgment."[3] And another liberty often allowed in children's biography is the dramatization of actual events into scenes with invented dialogue to make the story more interesting to the child reader. The work then belongs to a genre called "fictionalized biography," or it may even pass out of the realm of nonfiction to become instead "biographical fiction."

A closer look at what some recent authorities have written about children's biography reveals some disagreements. While a consideration of any area of children's nonfiction might properly center on Margery Fisher's comprehensive book Matters of Fact, that work has already been mentioned in Ms. Sutherland's article in this issue. I shall therefore consider here some other recent publications--three textbooks and two journal articles.

Evaluating Children's Biographies

In a chapter of their textbook Children and Books, Arbuthnot and Sutherland first offer the student criteria for evaluating children's biography, then assess some biography series and a large number of individual works.[4] They point out that children's biographies, by omitting the tragedies and unsavory aspects of a subject's life, usually do not present "the whole man." But in their final paragraph they observe: "There is a growing trend toward presenting the subject of a biography without omitting important facts about unpleasant or unsavory incidents or traits, a trend that recognizes the right of young readers to know the whole truth and thus to understand more clearly the men and women about whom they are reading."[5] From these critics' thumbnail evaluations it is clear that they believe there are many outstanding children's biographies on the market today--so many, in fact, that they feel they cannot "include discussion of all the fine books that are available."[6]

A section of Charlotte S. Huck and Doris Young Kuhn's textbook, Children's Literature in the Elementary School, also presents guidelines for the evaluation of juvenile biography, followed by brief analyses of both series and individual works.[7] "There are some fine biographies that have been written for children," the student is told, and "there are many mediocre ones."[8] Huck and Kuhn acknowledge that often the tragic or unsavory is left out of children's biography, but they emphasize that a subject, even though he has been selected because of a commendable life, should be presented with his faults as well as his virtues. Good biography, they believe, is of value to children for two reasons. It "fulfills children's needs for identification with someone 'bigger' than they are," and it also serves to develop in children "an appreciation and understanding of our heritage that may not be obtained in any other manner."[9]

With their many brief appraisals, the chapters in both of these textbooks can be used as selection aids. Both are moderate in tone; neither is hypercritical. But very different from these, in structure as well as in viewpoint, is the biography chapter of William Anderson and Patrick Groff's A New Look at Children's Literature.[10] In a long, scholarly essay, the authors set children's biography against a background of adult biography. They first develop the history of adult biography and then proceed to analyze--unfavorably and at some length--only two children's biographies: George Washington, by Clara Ingram Judson; and Daniel Boone, by James Daugherty. (It is interesting to compare with their analyses the favorable opinions of these two biographies given by Arbuthnot and Sutherland and also by Huck and Kuhn.) Although only two specific titles are treated, Anderson and Groff believe "it is rather certain that little good biography for children is being written."[11] They discuss the taboos imposed by our society upon juvenile biography--taboos against writing about infamous people and against showing "the dark, unsavory, or undistinguished side" of a great person's life. And they present some speculations about the way in which children really read biographies of adult figures. They question, in short, the generally accepted idea that children take exemplary lives as moral models.

This last matter is pondered in greater detail in a provocative article by Groff entitled, "Biography: The Bad or The Bountiful?"[12] Groff questions whether children are really capable of understanding adult lives and therefore whether they are capable of identifying with the adult characters in their biographies. "Quite to the reverse of what is believed about children and biography," he writes, "a careful inquiry into the information about this relationship reveals that biography has little chance of exerting the extraordinary moral or psychological influences on children credited to it."[13] He challenges the accepted notion that biography has value for children, and he feels that this notion prevails because specialists, sincerely believing that children will be influenced for the good by reading about great lives, tend to see such a phenomenon occur.

In a paper given at the Seminar on Children's Literature of the Modern Language Association in 1971, Marilyn Jurich, a professor of English, addresses herself to the question of "What's Left Out of Biography for Children."[14] Jurich sees the need for more variety in the choice of subjects: for biographies of "great human beings who are not famous," of ordinary people, and also of anti-heroes. In addition, she would like to see the subjects given "a fuller treatment." Using specific examples, she shows how children's biography by its omissions often tends to oversimplify and distort. "The danger in the half truths of so many current biographies for children," she says in summing up, "is that when that child reads the total account of the life in an 'adult' book, he is understandably likely to distrust all adult information and instruction, and throw the good out along with the bad."[15]

Judging Information Books

Turning to science and the social sciences, one again finds some recent criticism of the status quo. As would be expected, the three textbooks discussed earlier follow approximately the same pattern in their chapters on "informational books" as they do in their chapters about biography.

Arbuthnot and Sutherland present basic criteria for the evaluation of information books and then apply those criteria to a large number of specific titles.[16] They examine books on religion and the arts as well as on science and the social sciences.

Huck and Kuhn offer a more extensive guide for the evaluation of information books, illustrating each point with specific titles.[17] In addition to listing obvious musts like accuracy, currency, originality, and interest, they raise such questions as: "Are differing viewpoints presented?" "Do science books indicate related social problems?" and "Does the book encourage curiosity and further study?" They close out their section with a documented description of the various types of information books (concept books, informational picture books, identification books, etc.).

Both of the above chapters can serve as selection aids, while Anderson and Groff again provide, in their "Information Books" chapter, a critical essay with few specific titles mentioned.[18] They offer criteria for judgment, they demonstrate why it is important that a science writer understand the mental development of the age group he is writing for, and they present some interesting ideas on taboos. Taking up the matter of accuracy, they point out that in addition to the more obvious requirements a science writer must "show the relationship of scientific facts to humanity, describing the social consequences they may have."[19] Noting that most information books for children fall into the science group, they explain: "This is partly because social studies perennially inflame people's passions and arouse their prejudices, while science is generally interpreted as a psychologically neutral subject which has few philosophical implications."[20] This interpretation is of course false, they are quick to add; scientists today are more likely than they were in the past to recognize the relationship between science and the social sciences.

These last two points--the social implications of scientific activity and the taboos riddling the social science field--form the basis of "The Changing World of Science and the Social Sciences," a strong paper delivered by Mary K. Eakin at the 12th Biennial Congress of the International Board on Books for Young People (IBBY) in 1970.[21] With eloquence, Professor Eakin expresses her concern over the all too frequent separation of these two interrelated disciplines. As protection against science writers without a social conscience, she makes the suggestion that publishers' science and social science editors "work as pairs to make certain that every science and technological publication of the future contains at least one section devoted to the social implications of the discovery or the new technique being described."[22] She deplores the traditional taboos in children's social science books and the perpetuation of the status quo, maintaining that in order to prepare children for the problems they will face as adults it is important to let them examine the world's controversies. "We applaud the inquiring mind of a child that causes him to take a piece of machinery apart and see what makes it run," she says, and "we should equally applaud and encourage the inquiring mind of a young person that takes a social institution, an account of history, a religious belief, or a human relationship apart and seeks to find out why they are as they are and if they need to always remain as they are now."[23]

These, then, are some of the voices that have been raised recently in favor of more realism and honesty in children's nonfiction books, paralleling the demand for more realistic children's fiction. But are such demands really new? Here is what one children's book editor wrote (with clear sarcasm) about juvenile biography a little more than forty-five years ago: "Let us preserve our nice outlook on life by protecting the children from unpleasant facts (which they get in the rawest form daily in the tabloid news). So the youth of the land needs to become a hard-boiled adult before he is to be allowed the pleasure of reading about real people."[24]

References

1. Charlotte S. Huck and Doris Young Kuhn, Children's Literature in the Elementary School, 2nd ed. New York: Holt, Rinehart and Winston, 1968, pp. 274-75.
2. Marilyn Jurich, "What's Left Out of Biography for Children," Children's Literature, 1 (1972), 145.
3. May Hill Arbuthnot and Zena Sutherland, Children and Books, 4th ed. Glenview, Ill.: Scott, Foresman, 1972, p. 537.
4. Ibid., pp. 534-85.
5. Ibid., p. 573.
6. Ibid., p. 572.
7. Huck and Kuhn, Children's Literature, pp. 274-95; 323-27.
8. Ibid., p. 274.
9. Ibid.
10. William Anderson and Patrick Groff, A New Look at Children's Literature. Belmont, Calif.: Wadsworth, 1972, pp. 176-99.
11. Ibid., p. 192.
12. Patrick Groff, " Biography: The Bad or The Bountiful?" Top of the News, 29 (April 1973), 210-17.
13. Ibid., p. 211.
14. Jurich, "What's Left Out," pp. 143-51.
15. Ibid., p. 150.
16. Arbuthnot and Sutherland, Children and Books, pp. 586-643.
17. Huck and Kuhn, Children's Literature, pp. 445-506.
18. Anderson and Groff, A New Look, pp. 200-15.
19. Ibid., p. 210.
20. Ibid., p. 212.
21. Mary K. Eakin, "The Changing World of Science and the Social Sciences," Top of the News, 27 (November 1970), 23-31.
22. Ibid., p. 28.
23. Ibid., p. 29.
24. Mary Frank, "Among the Children's Books: What There Is and What There Isn't," Publisher's Weekly, 115 (March 30, 1929), 1594.

PART X

SELECTION AND USE

(don't play dead before you have to ...)

EDITOR'S NOTE

Lillian Shapiro's provocative comments on the 1976 Best Books for Young Adults (American Library Association, Young Adult Services Division) raise a crucial issue in book selection for young adults. It is true that the potential popularity of a title is a significant factor in the decision of whether or not to include it in the list. It is not the only factor, however, as the introduction to the list makes clear:

> This list presents books published in the past year that are recommended for reading by thirteen- to eighteen-year-old young adults. Selection is based primarily on each book's proven or potential appeal and worth to young adult readers. Titles chosen must also meet the following standards: Fiction must have believable characterization and dialogue and plausible plot development; nonfiction must have an appealing format and a readable text. Although the list attempts to represent a variety of reading tastes and levels, no effort has been made to balance it according to subject or area of interest.[1]

Mary K. Chelton, in an article discussing the differences between children's and young adult librarianship, responds to another comment on the drift toward selection-by-demand evinced by the Young Adult Services Division lists:

> ... during a recent staff meeting here in Westchester our much-admired, really super children's consultant exclaimed to me, "You DO believe in book selection!" Most YA librarians think first, "Will the kids like this book, or can I promote it so they will? Because if they won't, it doesn't matter how good it is." I feel most CS [Children's Services] librarians think first and only, "Is it good??" Perhaps YA service is like the teenagers for whom it exists: a transition between the quality-oriented selection of children's services and the almost demand-only selection of adult services. Despite the all-information-is-neutral intellectual freedom posture of ALA, I join my children's services friends in the search for quality, humanistic titles to actively promote to kids. I just find myself less of a tastemaker than they seem to want to be, and more of a materials interpreter/facilitator for teenagers.... CS people have endless discussions of what

> topics are suitable (my most hated professional word) for children. YA librarians usually ignore suitability in its theoretical sense and buy whatever YA's need and they can get away with buying.[2]

In other words, selection for young adults has more to do with what YA librarians think YA's need than with what children's librarians think is good for children. How teachers select books for class and supplementary reading is a question with which I am less familiar, but the spate of articles urging teachers to pay attention to young adult reading interests suggests that many rely on old dictums that students should be exposed to the best literature, or on their personal stock of reading experience. Parents, on the other hand, have a nostalgic tendency to have their sons and daughters enjoy the books that they enjoyed in their youth, only to discover that their teenager much prefers to share the current best-seller.

To put the popularity-versus-quality question in perspective, Margaret Edwards' approach is helpful:

> While books ... must have definite appeal to young people, they should be selected because they contribute to the enrichment of the reader--not to enhance the popularity of the librarian or to prove he is IN. To include books in bad taste that advocate crime and anarchy or a manual on shoplifting--books with little or no positive value is to violate our aims and goals.... On the other hand, however liberal or frank a book is, it should be included if it has appeal for young people and its effect is to enlarge and enrich the reader....[3]

Paul Janeczko, while speaking of the classroom rather than the library, shares the attitude that appeal must be there before all else. This is reflected in his streamlined definition of literature as "vicarious life experience conveyed through language on the printed page," and insistence that "the life experience presented in the literature must be meaningful to its audience" and the language readily understood.[4]

Ross and Muller give some practical suggestions for getting books into schools and using them in the English curriculum, and Nilsen, Tyler and Kozrek present a sensible framework for choosing books for reluctant readers. Ideas on how to motivate young adults to read for pleasure are offered by Ross, and the Aaron, Miller and Smith study underscores the importance of reading guidance, providing dramatic evidence of the impact which teachers and librarians can have on the reading of teenagers.

One of the classic motivation techniques, booktalking, is an essential skill for young adult librarians. Chelton's "Booktalking: You Can Do It!" is an excellent primer. A videotape prepared by California young adult librarians, Easy YA Booktalking,[5] is another aid for developing this skill.

Notes

1. Best Books for Young Adults 1976. American Library Association, Young Adult Services Division, 1977.

2. Mary K. Chelton. "Surrogate Mothers vs. Surrogate Teenagers," Booklegger, Spring 1976, 40-41.

3. Margaret Edwards. "No Barefeet," prepared for ETN Series: Continuing Education for Public Librarians, 1971. Available as part of Survival Kit from the American Library Association, Young Adult Services Division.

4. See p. 397-398.

5. Available from CATVO Office, San Jose Public Library.

"BEST BOOKS" FOR WHOM, OR WHERE HAVE ALL THE GROWN-UPS GONE?*

By Lillian L. Shapiro

Is selection of materials a lost cause? When I visit my local public library, my reaction is that no professional has been assiduously searching through the floods of available titles, but rather that some kind of automatic shipment is the *modus operandi*. Only such a procedure could account for the hundreds of titles that appear in the "New Books" sections--ephemeral, superficial, inconsequential, and unrequested books, which remain on the shelves because they are not the titles being sought by the patrons using that particular branch.

On the other hand, where a title is arousing comment and will inevitably be in great demand because it has been widely reviewed, too few duplicates are purchased. Result--a discouragingly long wait for your reserve request to be filled. I recall asking for Kate Millett's *Sexual Politics* in August of the year it was published and receiving word in December that I could pick it up. Of course, by then I had already purchased the book.

Selection of materials for children and young adults should be shaped by even more stringent imperatives. Inherent in that responsibility, far more so than for adults, is the hope of opening new horizons for the youthful readers. As a practicing librarian in high schools and as a faculty member in library schools, I took rather seriously the criteria that were to be the guidelines by which we expended the never-quite-adequate budget. We all know them. Some bear repeating: Media should reflect problems, aspirations, attitudes, and ideals of a society; should be appropriate to the level of the user; should represent artistic and literary qualities; and (in these years) should be free of racism and sexism.

Because it has each year become more difficult, if not impossible, for librarians or media specialists to have first-hand knowledge of all the materials churned out by presses and producers, we look more and more to guidelines prepared by experts to steer us around the shoals to excellent collection building. These titles

---

*Reprinted by permission of the author and publisher from *Wilson Library Bulletin* (June 1977), 803-804, 862.

are familiar to the practitioner. We depend on such retrospective lists as the New York Public Library's Books for the Teenage, Wilson's Senior High School Library Catalog (and supplements), University Press Books for Secondary School Libraries, the National Association of Independent Schools' Books for Secondary School Libraries, and G. Robert Carlsen's Books and the Teen-age Reader.

For our current purchases we turn to School Library Journal, ALA's Booklist, and the fewer but often choice titles in the Wilson Library Bulletin, Media and Methods, and sometimes, the Young Adult Alternative Newsletter.

Especially valuable are those reviewing media whose annotations give us a clue as to the kind of reader for whom a specific title is best suited or hoist a warning signal where language or incident may possibly make the book a problem in a conservative community. The caveat is "Read before purchasing." This does not mean self-censorship, but rather becoming alert to the possibility of confrontation and learning how to gird oneself for it if one feels the book is worth acquiring.

Those of us who have worked with young adults know, or ought to, their main interests, and admittedly, sex is high on the list. However, to assume that this topic overrides the interest of all teenagers in biography, poetry, history, etc., is to be either patronizing toward adolescents or revealing of one's own adult insecurities and/or prurience.

In the past the Young Adult Services Division list, Best Books for Young Adults, was the sine qua non for my selection assistance. I used it in my own libraries and recommended it warmly as an excellent guide to the prospective librarians I taught. It is a sad disillusionment for me that, having observed the selection committee this year and last, I am no longer sanguine about the quality of that list.

As I listened to the discussion, I could not discern the criteria for selecting or eliminating a title other than the "popularity" of a theme or author. In this case it would seem that the list is improperly named "best" books, and high school libraries ought to be considering the purchase of The Happy Hooker, Joy of Sex, and Once is Not Enough. What evaluation is apparent in a committee member's remark, "It bored me," or "Blah, blah, blah," or "It was too deep for me"? One longed to hear whether the characters were drawn with credibility, whether the plot was well developed, whether the denouement showed integrity rather than easy solution, what the literary style was, how timely the theme was, etc., etc., etc.

Let us look at some of the specifics of the list for 1976. Although the recommended percentage of adult titles for the YA collection is 60-75 per cent, this list shows no such ratio. Out of a total of 15 nonfiction books (excluding the one poetry title), there are three books concerned with sex education, of which one--the best, Andrea Eagan's Why Am I So Miserable If These Are the Best Years of My Life?--would have been sufficient. One title, Ruby, contains so grotesque a portrayal of a New York City School teacher (with a slight odor of anti-Semitism) as to put to question the literary quality of the book.

Only one poetry title is offered; rejected as too dull or "not appealing to young people" was the excellent Alone Amid All This Noise, edited by Ann Reit, a collection of poetry written by women from Sappho to Marge Piercy--this at a time when women's studies are proliferating in the secondary schools. And no one on the evaluation committee mentioned Stevie Smith's Collected Poems. True, it is a fat book. But poetry books do not have to be read from cover to cover; they are meant to be dipped into--like sipping at a mountain spring.

I do not fault the entire list. It does, after all, include Judith Guest's Ordinary People, Mojtabai's The 400 Eels of Sigmund Freud, Sue Ellen Bridgers's Home Before Dark, Milton Meltzer's Never to Forget, and Joan Samson's The Auctioneer. What I seek is a little "truth in advertising." Let us call the list "popular" books--which students will probably find on their own. I would think that we, school and young adult librarians, have a more specific responsibility, and it is contained in this sentence from Bruno Bettelheim's The Uses of Enchantment: "The acquisition of skills, including the ability to read, becomes devalued when what one has learned to read adds nothing of importance to one's life."

I have been thinking lately how interesting it is that George Eliot's Silas Marner has long been a cliché, a kind of shorthand for "irrelevance" in the school curriculum, so described, one must add, by those whose own literary backgrounds are so meager that for them the only criterion for choice is trendiness. That book is part of very long ago time for me, and yet I have never forgotten the characters. Think of the ingredients: a dissolute son, an unsolved theft, a dour miser, an illegitimate child, and disappointed love--in a book written in the nineteenth century by a woman who dared to flout convention and live with the man she loved in what was termed "an irregular union" (not a "meaningful relationship"). I concede that the editions to which we were exposed were ugly, and the approach to the reading was similar to that explication de texte so revered by the French--and by most of the teachers of English in my youth. I would bet that if Silas Marner were to be a TV production, à la the other classics now available in that communications mode, there would be a run on the title in school and public libraries the very next day!

Given the young adult collection with popularity of title--"that's what the kids want"--as the prime criterion for selection, why could not a corps of volunteers run the library? Popular books need no selling. There would be no necessity for some adult, endowed with a good reading background, sensitivity, and a thought to the future, to be on hand--inspiring, encouraging, and gently but firmly pressing the young clientele to reach a little higher.

Is selection a lost cause, an obsolete accomplishment? If so, perhaps librarianship for young people is also an anachronism.

"THE PASSING OF HEROES"*

By Paul B. Janeczko

When I think back to my high school days and, in particular, the time I spent in English class, I recall not much more than a blank. A hostile blank. Oh, I can remember a teacher or two. Even a few of my classmates--the ones who made me laugh. But I can remember nothing of real significance. Except maybe for one Friday afternoon class. That was the day that we were discussing Paradise Lost. After searching the rows of desks for an innocent face, my English teacher settled for my face and asked, "How does the overall structure of the verse relate to the moral meaning of the poem?" (That was nothing. His first question had been, "According to Milton, of what substance are angels made?") As I stood there scanning the floor tiles for any possible help, I was saved by the proverbial bell. A fire drill emptied the entire school onto the parking lot.

Since I was a clock-watcher, I knew that by time the drill was over, it would be time for math. That meant more puzzles to solve, but at least I was off the hook on the structure-of-the-verse-related-to-the-moral-meaning-of-the-poem bit. Besides, I knew I could come up with some reasonable answer to that pressing problem when I asked around on the bus at 3 o'clock. I knew a couple of guys who would be able to give me some help. Some of them were real pros at answering English-class questions. One of the guys, in fact, even managed to hold his own during a discussion of King Lear when he was asked, "Is the Fool a fool indeed?" Whether or not I found help on the school bus, I figured I was still in pretty good shape because Friday-questions never seemed important enough to be pursued on Monday. We would be off on some other puzzle.

But that's about all I can remember from my high school English experience. A blank. A hostile blank. I call this blank hostile because what we did in English class meant nothing to me. Absolutely nothing. And to make matters worse, I actually did well in English! I actually received good grades for talking and writing about things that meant nothing to me!

---

*Reprinted, with some changes made by the author, and with permission of the author and publisher, from The Independent School Bulletin, 34:1 (October 1974), 58-61.

I was asked, and answered, questions like these: "How does Pip actually overcome his original snobbery?" and "Consider the storm, the lion in the forum, the soothsayer, and the ghost in Julius Caesar" and "Discuss the various ideas that the white whale has been interpreted to represent." What questions! (Hm. Pip to Brutus to Ahab? Sounds like a double play combination.)

Why did no one ever ask, "Did you like that book?" or "Do you think that Bo Jo and July did the right thing when they got married?" Why didn't anyone give me something that I could have enjoyed? Why couldn't they have given me a book that would have made me ask, "Do you have any more books like this one?" Instead, I said (to my friends, of course, never to the teacher), "There can't be any more books like this one!" Why couldn't they have given me books that would have allowed me to say in ten years, "I was led to a love of reading by my English teacher." Yes, I do love to read. Yes, my love of reading began about the time I was going to high school. But no, my love of reading had nothing to do with my English teacher or my English class, or my high school. No wonder my high school years are a hostile blank.

My love of reading and books began in a used book store that I had discovered while my parents were in a near-by store shopping. When I first entered the store I was awed by the floor-to-ceiling books. (In some spots the colorful spines were not unlike stained glass windows.) I wasn't sure what I wanted so I just sort of wandered around bumping into orange crates filled with books. Finally I came across a uniform row of brown books by a man who called himself Franklin W. Dixon. I pulled one down from the shelf and looked at the silhouette of two boys on the cover and the title: The Tower Treasure. I opened the book and saw 35¢ penciled in the upper right hand corner of the fly leaf. Not bad, I thought. Money from my paper route could cover that easily enough. As the owner of the shop took care of another customer, I began reading the first page. Not bad: two brothers who want to be detectives, out for a ride on a Sunday on their motorcycles. Okay, so far. I read on. What's this? Some idiot is trying to run them off the road! What was going to happen to them? I read through the final paragraphs of chapter one right there in the store:

> The road was narrow enough at any time, and this speeding car was taking up every inch of space. In a great cloud of dust it bore directly down on the two motorcyclists. It seemed to leap through the air. The front wheels left a rut, the rear of the car skidded violently about. By a twist of the wheel the driver pulled the car back into the roadway again just as it seemed about to plunge over the embankment. It shot over toward the cliff, swerved back again into the middle of the roadway, and then shot ahead at terrific speed.
>
> Frank and Joe edged their motorcycles as far to the right of the road as they dared. To their horror they saw that the car was skidding again.

> The driver made no attempt to slacken speed.
> The automobile came hurtling toward them!

I looked up and saw the smile of the shop owner beneath his walrus mustache. I guess he knew he'd made a sale. (I wonder if he knew he'd made a friend.) Anyway, after paying for the book I couldn't wait to get home and share my find with my brother, John. His reaction was the same as mine. John even talked my father into making a return trip to the bookstore so he could buy book two in the series. From that point we began trading with each other until we had devoured the entire series.

From the Hardy Boys series I went to paperbacks and read my way through several phases (gangster books being the most notable) as English 9 slowly evolved into English 12. My parents became alarmed that I could recite the rise and fall of "Dutch" Schultz but could not remember Samuel Johnson's "dates." But, as I progressed through my college career, their fears were laid to rest.

Now I'm an English teacher and whenever I face a class for the first time I ask myself, "How many of these kids already like to read? How many of these kids do you think you can turn on to reading? How many of them can you hook?" It's an awesome task. Society demands a reading skill of its members; otherwise those members are doomed. But more than the bare necessity, the skill, I would like to give kids a love of reading.

But where does one start exciting kids about reading and books? Surely the books that worked for me will not work for those space-age students. As much as I hate to admit it, my heroes are not their heroes. Frank and Joe Hardy and Nancy Drew still thrill hundreds of thousands of young readers each year, but today they belong to a younger audience. The heroes of my adolescent years have passed on to another, younger generation. The thrills and chills that I received from their mysteries at age twelve or thirteen are now being felt by ten-year-olds. And I'm glad of that. I'm glad that my heroes are really alive and still solving capers (although in revised editions at times). Younger readers must be allowed these ceremonies of innocence.

Today's older adolescents, on the other hand, are reading about subjects that were simply not openly discussed when I was in high school (and that was only ten years ago). One need only go to the books to see that what I am saying is accurate.

One of the heroes of the past was Tom Swift. Boy wonder, youthful inventor, taker-of-chances. At one point in his illustrious career he notes with exasperation:

> "I'm tired of inventing things. I just want to go off, and have some good fun, like getting shipwrecked on a desert island, or something like that. I want action. I

> want to get off in the jungle, and fight wild beasts, and escape from the savages!"

How many young boys thrilled as they read those words, sometime even by the light of a flashlight under blankets! Ah, the call for action! When it did involve members of the opposite s-e-x it was not uncommon to witness a scene like this one from one of the Rover Boys adventures:

> It was now growing late, and Dick took his departure, kissing Dora's hand a third time as they stood in the darkness of the porch.
>
> "You're terrible!" she murmured, but it was doubtful if she meant anything by it. Girls and boys are about the same the world over, and Dick's regard for Dora was of the manly sort that is creditable to anybody.

Go Ask Alice is a book that is currently enjoying a great deal of popularity with adolescents. It is written by a young drug-user in diary form. Her entry for January 24 reads:

> Oh, damn, damn, damn, it's happening again. I don't know whether to scream with glory or cover myself with ashes and sackclothes, whatever that means. Anyone who says pot and acid are not addicting is a mad, stupid, raving idiot, unenlightened fool!
>
> I've been on them since July 10 and when I've been off I've been scared to death to even think of anything that looks or seems like dope. All the time pretending to myself that I could take it or leave it!
>
> All the dumb, idiot kids who think they are only chipping are in reality just existing from one experience to the other. After you've had it, there isn't even life without drugs. It's a prodding, colorless, dissonant bare existence. It stinks. And I'm glad I'm back. Glad! Glad! Glad!

Not exactly the kind of thing you would find kids reading in an English class ten years ago, is it?

What to do? How does one go about getting today's young people interested in books and reading? Squire and Applebee's famous survey of high schools noted that literature occupies 52.2 per cent of curricular time. With so much time being spent on literature it is even more imperative to concentrate on exciting kids about books. Well, before you do anything else, you must have a good working definition of literature. My definition of literature is brief but, I think, good: Literature is a vicarious life experience conveyed through language on the printed page. I like my definition because it contains only two aspects that are essential: life experience and language. Once these aspects are understood, we can proceed.

First of all, "life experience." The life experience presented in the literature must be meaningful to its audience. I would think that the books you read relate life experiences that are meaningful to you. The same must hold true for the books I select for the students in my classes. In a 1967 study Sidney Shnayer discovered that high interests resulted in noticeably greater comprehension. In other words, when kids were keenly involved in what they were reading, they were able to read beyond their reading ability level. This is not to say that all my books must be about alienation, bad trips, and ignorant adults. What does it mean then? I think that in this age of the future-oriented now-generation there are three major areas that must be considered in our selection of reading matter for the young people who inhabit my classroom.

The first area that must be given my attention is the environment. It is no secret that we are involved in an environmental crisis from which we may not be able to extricate ourselves. Although the damage has been done by previous generations, it is up to the present generation of young people and generations that are yet to live on this planet to prevent disaster. Young people should be made aware of the seriousness of the crisis and at the same time they should be taught a reverence for plants, animals, and all the precious things of nature.

Science fiction and fantasy literature is another area that must have its share of books on our adolescent reading lists. The years since H. G. Wells told of the First Men on the Moon have passed more quickly than even he dreamed of. We are now exploring planets as well as allowing men prolonged periods in space. This area of literature could help students learn what the future holds for them. It will allow them an opportunity to speculate on the days yet to come.

The final area of concentration contains the largest number of titles. This category contains books that deal with the development of the individual. One of the battle cries of the younger generation has long been, "I don't want to be just a number on a computer punch card!" The adolescent wants to be an individual free of all the hassles of the nine-to-five rat-race. The teacher should take advantage of this need by providing books that show the development of individuals. The need is best met when the individual is a person their own age, someone who experiences some of the same problems that the adolescent is himself experiencing.

The second part of my definition that needs clarification is "language." Be careful to select a language that young people can understand with little difficulty. You may talk all you want about the beauty of Shakespeare's English, but, as an old comedian once said, "If you gotta explain 'em, they're no good." I'm not saying that the books must be written in a childish or simple manner. I am saying, however, that we must allow the students a chance to develop their language ability. The Bible says, "To everything there is a season" and I think the same holds true for language.

Meet the students where they are and guide and encourage their development.

What about the classics? If we don't give them Dickens and Shakespeare and Melville they may miss out on these greats. True, but I'm willing to gamble on the student's ability and desire to find these writers on his own *if* he's discovered the joy of reading. I work under the theory that once a student is hooked on reading, anything can happen. And that includes the classics.

But what attitude do parents and teachers project about reading? Do they believe what appeared in *McGuffey's Sixth Eclectic Reader*, that reading is "a most intellectual accomplishment?" This same school text of 1879 also said, "a man may possess a fine genius without being a perfect reader; but he cannot be a perfect reader without genius." Or do we believe, as Herbert Kohl does, that reading is a very natural human activity. Kohl further states:

> There is no reading problem. There are problem teachers and problem schools.... If walking and talking were taught in most schools we might end up with as many mutes and cripples as we now have non-readers. However, learning to read is no more difficult than learning to walk or talk.

Although Kohl oversimplifies a number of points in his book *Reading, How to*, I find his *attitude* toward reading commendable.

What is your attitude toward reading? Do we let our children and students *know* what we think of reading? Do we let them see us reading a *book*? Do we let them see us walking around with a paperback in our back pocket or purse? Let them know that you *enjoy* reading. Let them know that reading counts.

To do a satisfactory job of selecting books for young people you must become an expert in adolescent literature. That means you must *read*. In the September issue of *English Journal* Tom Barton of Washington State University stated what I consider an admirable goal for English teachers. Barton is looking for an English teacher "who reads a minimum of 52 books a year--two-thirds 'adult' literature and one-third 'adolescent' or 'children's literature' and exchanges views and opinions on those books with colleagues." And, I might add, with students as well.

However, you cannot be satisfied with merely reading books. You must read book reviews. You must read book ads. When was the last time you browsed in a book store? Do it! And by all means talk to kids. Find out some of the titles they've enjoyed. Talk to them about some of the titles that you've really enjoyed. Research indicates that students should be consulted about their interests more often than at present, and experts should be consulted less about grade level placement of reading material and reading interests. Experts like Stephen Dunning, Daniel Fader, and Robert

Carlsen can, however, be an excellent starting point. Also there are a number of professional organizations that are dedicated to encouraging good reading habits in young people. The National Council of Teachers of English, the American Library Association, and the International Reading Association are three such organizations that can serve as signposts to get us going in the right direction. A direction that will allow us to operate on our own.

Large city libraries can also give a great deal of help. The Young Adult section of the New York Public Library, for example, is responsible for helping teachers select books through its excellent bibliography _Books for the Teen Age_. Last year's bibliography included a study that was interesting because of the kinds of titles that were mentioned.

In observance of International Book Year, the Young Adult section of the New York Public Library wrote to member countries of the International Federation of Library Associations and asked them to send the library a short list of books in English or translated from English, which young people in their countries, aged 13 to 18, find important or enjoyable. Thirteen countries responded: Australia, Belgium, Canada, Denmark, England, Finland, France, Italy, Nigeria, Singapore, Taiwan, the U.S.S.R., and Yugoslavia. Ernest Hemingway's _The Old Man and the Sea_ was mentioned most often, by five countries. _The Catcher in the Rye_ and _Love Story_ were runners-up with four countries listing each title. The following titles were listed by two or more countries:

Jane Eyre
The Good Earth
The Adventures of Sherlock Holmes
The Deerslayer
The Citadel
Oliver Twist
The Endless Steppe
The Old Man and the Sea
The Outsiders
Martin Eden
Gone with the Wind
The Catcher in the Rye
Love Story
The Black Arrow

Authors for more than one book included:

Ray Bradbury for _Fahrenheit 451_ and _The Martian Chronicles_
Herman Hesse for _Siddhartha_ and _Steppenwolf_
Betty Smith for _Joy in the Morning_ and _A Tree Grows in Brooklyn_
Paul Zindel for _I Never Loved Your Mind_ and _My Darling, My Hamburger_

The most noteworthy thing about this list of books is not the number of classics, books that you would expect to be considered "important" in other countries, but rather the books that are currently popular with adolescents in our country. Books like _The Outsiders_, _My Darling, My Hamburger_, and _Siddhartha_. Although these books are considered by a great many teachers to be Number Two, they are trying harder to engage our students.

Last year I asked an eleventh-grade boy what kind of book he would like to read. He told me, "one with two covers and nothing in between." What an indictment of this boy's education and home environment! How crucial it is to give this boy books that he would enjoy, even though they may have pages between the covers.

Those of us who were brought up on a healthy diet of Tom Swift, Nancy Drew, and the Hardy Boys know what it's like to have a hero. We know that these heroes will never pass away. Just as our love of reading will never pass away. And who knows? If you encourage your children to read, if you give young people something to do besides watching television and hanging out on a street corner, you may become a hero to them.

THE PAPERBACK REVOLUTION*

By Frank Ross

It's a whole new ballgame.

When Dell's school imprint, Laurel-Leaf, pays $60,000 for Dinky Hocker Shoots Smack; when one of Avon's top ten sellers to schools is You Would If You Loved Me; when Media and Methods' Maxi Awards last May selected by thousands of teacher votes for most useful books went to Go Ask Alice and Pig Man; then you know that somebody has changed the rules. The old gray curriculum, she ain't what she used to be. The one who changed it, of course, is the student. Once the 1936 idea of Wilbur Hatfield finally took root--a student-centered curriculum--students routed out the sacred cows of nineteenth-century fiction, already milked dry, and replaced them with a more readily relevant list of books. Undoubtedly the penny pincher of Raveloe is being wedged down somebody's esophagus somewhere in the land at this moment, but you can bet there are a whole lot fewer force feedings.

As education historians in years to come look back for the culprits of change, they're going to have to beat a path to the doors of paperback publishers, paperback distributors, and imaginative teachers, as well as the assertive students.

Many pressures worked to bring about a new surge of interest in the lowly paperback, but the headlines from any autumn newspaper offer a key.

So what else is new! "Class Size Increased," "Non-contract Teachers Dismissed," "Millage Fails," "Budgets Cut," "Innovations Scrapped."

Good teachers have learned to breathe in with the traditional American belt-tightening rituals practiced every fall for the past 50 years. It wasn't always so. Only a short decade ago, Uncle Federal stood on the Potomac with his goody bag and passed out chits so that no American school child need be without a videotape recorder and an overhead projector. Now that the bag has snapped shut, panic permeates the land.

---

*Reprinted by permission of the author and publisher from Media & Methods, 10:3 (November 1973), 11-13, 38-43.

With budget cuts, the greatest loss to the education system is not the equipment order but the dismissal of the teachers with the least seniority and the stingy hiring of college graduates. The young new teacher has always been the force for change within a system. The vigorous, optimistic, irrepressible ones have moved their schools forward by their willingness to attempt new things, and especially their not knowing that something "cannot be done," so they try it and often manage to bring it off. It was just such teachers who first were willing to take the risks of field trips; who good naturedly lobbied for films; who brought into the classroom the compelling issues of the teen world: pre-marital sex, pregnancy, drug addiction, car culture, and introspective, Eastern philosophies. And it was these young teachers who snatched paperbacks off the drugstore racks and brought them, like Prometheus bringing fire, to their children.

Similar young teachers will not be around this year in the numbers they once were, but the innovative youths of twenty years ago, who peddled paperbacks when the books were generally considered wicked and certain to rot the mind, still remain true to their original intention: get students reading--anything, make books finger-tip accessible, part of the atmosphere, and move students up the ladder with ever increasing quality.

The school paperback has gone through four cycles, which is not to say it has been going in circles but only to indicate that it has been around a long time. For the first ten years the excitement lay with the fact that *Wuthering Heights* or *Hamlet* or *Moby Dick* were available at one-tenth the hardcover cost. Then came the thrill of being able to get inexpensive reprints of modern, popular adult books one year after their first "legitimate" appearance: O'Hara's *A Rage to Live* (Bantam); Walter Van Tilburg Clark's *The Track of the Cat* (Signet); John Updike's *Rabbit, Run* (Crest). The third stage was the special paper publishing of books for children and adolescence. Scholastic and Golden Books blazed an early path, but it was after they had awakened the market that other big houses sought such titles. *Hod Rod* (Bantam), *Johnny Tremain* (Riverside) and *Roosevelt Gray* (Tempo). Finally, a recent growing development is the original paperback publication: Scholastic's *Fakes, Frauds and Phonies* and *The Linebackers*; Dell's new series, "Sociology through Science Fiction," "Psychology through Science Fiction," and "Religion through Science Fiction."

Of course, all the cycles in the world won't help an impoverished school system, you say. There may be no budget for some teachers to order paperbacks through the normal channels. Then they can take a faster route. They can put away the Crackerjack Genie ring, and start a little friction with one of the following half dozen gambits:

1. *A lab fee.* Unless forbidden, the English and social studies teachers should have one, the same as the chemistry and biology teachers have.

2. The class gift. Seniors may leave to the school some hideous or useless memorial unless discreetly influenced. A gold-plated jock strap over the gym door is not really vital.

3. The P.T.A. donation. When the generous ear of a new president is reached, great projects have been known to evolve.

4. The local service club service. The Elks, the Lions, the Moose and all the rest of the jungle can be petted into outfitting one room--as kindly a lot as Kipling ever imagined.

5. The principal's contingency fund. It varied from $200 to $2000. Every coach knows about it from years of raiding it. Now it's the subject-matter teacher's turn.

6. The immortality bit. Each student donating a book from teacher's approved list (to reduce hard-core offerings) gets to write in it "Donated by __________ __________" and thereby be remembered long after he/she has passed on to another grade or school.

Probably readers of Media & Methods could flood the editor's mail with additional success stories of how they got 50 paperbacks in the face of adversity. The fact is, and a nod to Mr. McGuffey, where there's a will, there's a way. Probate or no, but if there's to be a will, there has to be a reason.

Whenever a teacher gets a paperback in circulation, he or she becomes an unpaid salesman for the industry. Who needs it? The industry is suffering along with the load of staggering profits. But whenever a teacher match-makes a student with a good book, the teacher raises the level of literacy in the country, promotes an intelligent citizenry, fosters contented students, and eases the burden of teaching all the disciplines that depend upon verbal skills. Now that should cause the halo to set comfortably at a rakish angle. But that halo can never be put in place if the student doesn't cooperate. What the teacher wants is not always what the students want.

Every teacher knows that paperbacks have built-in motivators --small size, appealing cover, selling blurbs, brief summary. But they won't do all the work; the teacher must make efforts to attract the student into a book. Here are my notes for getting my students into a Greek classic (ugh!):

> Did anyone watch Watergate hearings this summer? How is John Ehrlichmann connected to Daniel Ellsberg? Should Ellsberg have released the Pentagon Papers? Did he think he was doing the right thing? Dare we trust our own judgments? Should we not obey the government, right or wrong? What's to become of young men who shipped to Canada or Sweden to avoid Vietnam? Should one kill when his government so directs him? Are you familiar

> with the plea of most defendants in the Nuremberg trials? --'I was just gassing Jews because my superior ordered it.'
>
> Is not one of the great questions of our day: 'Should a citizen obey his government leaders when he believes they are morally wrong?' There is a short play in our Signet paperback that deals with this problem, a problem that has plagued people for at least 2500 years. That long ago Antigone was written by Sophocles. Please read it tonight and see what solutions he proposes, as, perhaps, a guide to us today.

Another way to motivate students to read paperbacks is even easier. Once begun, it functions without the teacher, kind of a perpetual motionivator. Two shoeboxes, without covers, and a couple of 3 x 5 cards are the supplies. Into one box students file, by title, the card they have filled out after reading or abandoning a book: title, author, reader's name, and one or two sentence comment on the book. The same information goes on another card into the second box, but filed by the reader's name. Students have free access to the boxes. When a student is considering investing time in a particular title, he can look it up to see what his peers have had to say about Gone with the Wind and The Guns of August, a recommendation far more valuable than any gushing a teacher might do. He can use the second box to see what books Ron Bright has been reading, a guy he loathes and would never ask for a recommendation, but a guy he secretly respects. What are the books that will do some of the motivating? Go ask experienced teachers. That's what M&M did last May.

The Media and Methods' Maxi Awards for paperbacks are revealing in several ways, all of them trendsetting. While Go Ask Alice and Pig Man were the winners, included are other notable titles:

The Outsiders (Dell)
That Was Then, This Is Now (Dell)
Bless the Beasts and Children (Pocketbooks)
Deliverance (Dell)
Grapes of Wrath (Bantam, Viking)
Johnny Got His Gun (Bantam)
To Kill a Mockingbird (Popular Library)
Two Blocks Apart (Avon)
When Legends Die (Bantam)

Five titles are established films (Bless, Deliverance, Grapes, Johnny, Mockingbird), and one (Alice) was a notable TV program last winter. It is possible that teachers find success with these titles because they are presold to the students through advertising reviews, gossip columns, and word of mouth. But there is little doubt that a well-talked up title helps motivate students to read.

The list also reveals that its users are concerned with the

pressing social issues of today: drug addiction, race, violence, pacificism, and economic and educational inequities. Whether the interests are primarily those of the students, which the teachers are merely feeding, or whether the interests are the teachers', which are being passed on to the students, one thing is certain: there are other ways to bring about a revolution besides marching, leafletting, and bombing. Teachers using books such as these are sensitizing large numbers of students to humane attitudes, which may, in another 10-20 years radically change television fare, education, politics in general, and the tax structure in particular. Any book by a socially conscious writer that is put into the hands of an able teacher becomes a time bomb, like Jonathan Livingston Seagull. Some, like Silent Spring and Unsafe at Any Speed, are hand grenades. Without the widespread distribution and the low price that paperbacks guarantee, this process would be much less incendiary.

Another curiosity is the shift from the May 1970 M&M report on the results of 1400 subscribers' preferences for "most effective works you have used in the last five years. Materials should be chosen that have elicited the best response from the students." In this list, clearly modern, the only classic in the first fifteen was Huckleberry Finn (#8), but nearly all titles were critically successful, bestselling adult fare.

1. A Separate Peace (Bantam)
2. Lord of the Flies (Capricorn)
3. Catcher in the Rye (Bantam)
4. To Kill a Mockingbird (Popular Library)
5. I Never Promised You a Rose Garden (Signet)
6. The Outsiders (Dell)
7. Flowers for Algernon (Bantam)
8. Huckleberry Finn (Pocketbooks)
9. Tell Me That You Love Me, Junie Moon (Popular Library)
10. 1984 (Signet)
11. Black Like Me (Signet)
12. Animal Farm (Signet)
13. The Pearl (Bantam)
14. The Chosen (Fawcett)
15. Siddhartha (Bantam)

In the first list only two titles are older than fifteen years (Grapes, Johnny), and no title on either list, except Huckleberry Finn, is older than 35 years. This is rather conclusive evidence that teachers who subscribe to M&M are keeping their reading lists modern. Despite the promotion of Mortimer Adler for his Great Books movement, classics are clearly not being taught to the degree that they once were. However, paperbacks have reduced considerably one of the biggest hangups. The librarian always had the books while the teacher always knew the students, but the college methods instructor had said, "Fit the right book to the right student at the right time." Now, when the time is right, the teacher can pick a book out of the classroom collection and press it into a hot little hand. Voilà! Happy student. Happy teacher. Less harried librarian.

When a paperback-clad teacher recognizes a student problem, if he is book wise, he can even practice a little bibliotherapy without the AMA or the ALA any the wiser.

Student problems range from the universal personal ones to the topical social ones. Whatever it may be, he always reacts the same way: he is sure it is hopeless, and he is certain no one else ever had to endure it. A carefully chosen book can dissuade him on both counts. Whether his problem is that he is too gangly, or too dumpy, too chunky, or too scrawny, or whether he is too freckled, or shy, or poorly coordinated, or a braggart, there is a book in the field of the junior novel which will help him see another person with a similar problem and how it was solved. If he has lost a parent, or gained a hated stepparent, if he has to live with a disfiguring injury, or he is worried that he will never be mature, there is a book for him. Lately, there have been an abundance of books that handle once taboo subjects yet problems of the real world that parents and teachers must now handle: drug use, pre-marital sex, pre-graduation marriage, homosexuality, and racial prejudice.

These books, with three or four exceptions, do not constitute the great literature that becomes petrified in college courses--Mary Stolz and Jane Austen are in different leagues--but they are well constructed young adult novels to be consumed purely for pleasure by junior high schoolers or poor readers of the senior high schools, or they may be used in the judiciously administered practice of bibliotherapy.

Adopted:
- Who Was Sylvia (Berkley)

Ashamed of Home:
- Pray Love, Remember (Tempo)

Can't Communicate:
- The Coach Nobody Liked (Dell)
- The Noonday Friends (Tempo)

Conceited:
- Hotshot (Dell)
- The Comeback Guy (Voyager)
- White Collar Girl (Nova)

Crippled:
- Room for One More (Dell)
- Johnny Tremain (Dell)
- The Kid Comes Back (Scholastic)

Divorce:
- The Divided Heart (Berkley)

Fears Abnormality:
- A Sense of Magic (Tempo)
- Sticks and Stones (Dell)

Lacks Self-confidence:
- Going on Sixteen (Berkley)
- Double Date (Berkley)
- Where Beauty Dwells (Bantam)
- The Shield Ring (Dell)
- Prom Trouble (Scholastic)
- A Chance to Belong (Dell)

Living Without Parent(s):
- Meet the Malones (Berkley)
- Double Feature (Berkley)
- A Long Time Coming (Dell)
- A Cup of Courage (Dell)

Lonely:
- The Ark (Voyager)
- Passport to Romance (Berkley)

Marry Early:
- Going Steady (Scholastic)

Perfectionist:
- Davey Logan, Interne (Berkley)

Prejudice:
- Mary Ellis, Student Nurse (Berkley)
- A Cap for Mary Ellis (Berkley)
- The Girl from Puerto Rico (Dell)
- Lions in the Way (Avon)
- Willow Hill (Scholastic)
- Portrait of Deborah (Tempo)
- Dinny Gordon, Junior (Berkley)

Stepmother:
- Dear Stepmother (Acorn)

One of the most engrossing young novels to appear in 1973 is Alexander Key's Escape to Witch Mountain (Archway--Pocket Books). The protagonists, a boy and girl (something for everyone) in early adolescence are hounded throughout the eastern seaboard as they struggle to locate relatives who can explain why their extra-sensory powers make them different from earthmen. A light touch of science fiction, a strong dose of mystery, some discrimination, and a lot of wise commentary on the relationship of adults to young people are strung along a picaresque structure. This is not a problem book really; it is intended to be pleasure reading and it is.

Students have an unnerving way of discovering paperbacks and creating such a stir about them that the titles find their way into the curriculum. This was the route taken by Catcher in the Rye, Lord of the Flies, and A Separate Peace. Right at this moment, some of the adult, mass-market interests are seeping into teen excitement, hence picking up support in school sales.

Prophecy and the supernatural are a normal outgrowth of teens' long time interest in science fiction, so books by Edgar Cayce, Ruth Montgomery, and Jeane Dixon are pushing into school sales, as are the numerous astrology books, and Sibil Leek and her coterie of witches. (The Black Mass, once Indexed and très hush, is now table talk over sticky, cold pizza in the school lunch-room.)

The idea that American and Russian astronauts were not the first to explore outer space, not by many thousands of years, has captivated young readers and older readers with young imaginations. Several of the following books were selling well earlier, but the NBC-TV program "In Search of Ancient Astronauts" last spring and again in September has caused a wild melee in the book racks. That the "God" and "Gods" referred to in the Hebraic-Christian Bible were actually visitors from a distant planet, who may have coupled with apes to provide the missing link, and that the pyramids of Egypt and the tikis of Easter Island and the Inca Temples are all better understood in connection with the new theory, are fascinating thoughts to general and advanced students, grades 9-12, and have been known to engross the underachiever, too.

Chariots of the Gods? (Bantam)
Gods from Outer Space (Bantam)
We Are Not the First (Bantam)
God Drives a Flying Saucer (Bantam)
Limbo of the Lost (Bantam)
Not of This World (Bantam)
Crash Go the Chariots (Lancer)
Gods and Devils from Outer Space (Lancer)
Mysteries from Forgotten Worlds (Dell)
Atlantis Rising (Dell)
The View Over Atlantis (Ballantine)
Those Gods Who Made Heaven & Earth (Berkley)
The Eternal Man (Avon)
Bibles and Flying Saucers (Avon)
Invisible Residents (Avon)

Film books are getting bigger. Students have always loved to dream together in a darkened theater or before a late-night TV, and burgeoning film courses in secondary schools have heightened their interest. Books on types of movies: gangster, comedies, etc., or on particular stars or directors; or scripts tied in with current releases; or even the criticism of a Pauline Kael or an Andrew Sarris all are free-choice books and sometimes class adoptions.

Creative Filmmaking, Kark Smallman. (Bantam)
The Disney Version, Richard Schickel (Avon)
Exploring the Film, William Kuhns and Robert Stanley (Pflaum)
Film: A Montage of Theories, R. D. McCann (Dutton)
Film Technique and Film Acting, Pudovkin (Grove)

Guide to Filmmaking, Edward Pincus (Signet)
The Liveliest Art, Arthur Knight (Bantam)
The Making of Feature Films, Ivan Butler (Pelican)
The Movies, Mr. Griffith and Me, Lillian Gish (Avon)
The Name Above the Title, Frank Capra (Bantam)
The Parade's Gone By, Kevin Brownlee (Ballantine)
A Short History of the Movies, Gerald Mast (Pegasus)
Young Filmmakers, Rodger Larson and Ellen Meade (Avon)

Teachers who may be struggling with a new film-course assignment will find Ralph Amelio's Films in the Classroom (Pflaum) a welcome assist over the hurdles. They may also want to use Film: The Creative Eye by David Sohn (Pflaum).

While the textbook publishers have always had charming hustlers presenting their wares to teachers, the school paperback industry would be nowhere if it were not for the conscientious teachers who take sometimes extreme measures to install a book in the school and in the minds of students.

Most school boards now permit paperbacks to be purchased, although they once believed the books too perishable to invest citizens' money.

Homeless waifs aren't the only things that need adoption. Probably, the most successful paperback adoption is McDougal, Littell's great Man series of anthologies designed specifically for today's students. Coming soon is a new series in the social studies area. But paperback adoptions are regrettably rare and require eager teacher advocates. The common route a teacher takes is through usual adoption procedures. Forms are filed and/or a simple request is made to the department head, principal, supervisor, or book selection committee, all bureaucratic steps necessary only in large systems. It is easier and quicker in those systems to take the secondary method: approval for the "supplemental list," (but also through the musical chairs). Often another way to get paperbacks into the school is just a word to the librarian, or several words at short intervals, to break down the traditional alarm at a book that will likely not be on the shelves ten years hence. Only the most forward-looking school libraries have paperbacks today, so there is much work to be done in that area. Still another way many teachers use is to run off and distribute short lists as suggestions for gift-giving at Christmas and birthdays, or vacation reading. Enthusiastic teachers are living testimonies to Henry Adams' idea that a teacher affects eternity, and they are often not satisfied with being an influence during class hours only.

The regularity of book clubs often encourages a new interest in the collection of books. It is vital for a teacher to stress the single most important element in building a personal library: do not collect only those books you have read, thus making your library a cemetery, but collect books that interest you and that you plan to read sometime in the near or even distant future. Scholastic Books has developed several clubs and a system whereby the teacher is never burdened with operational problems.

Books carefully selected, grouped by central theme, and accompanied by extensive teacher aids all packaged together in a "box" were first sold fifteen years ago by Scholastic, and wonderful things they were and still are. Now moving into the "box" field are Bantam's "Perspective" and "Venture" series, and American Book Co.'s "Individualized Literature Program 200." They do for the teacher what he could do for himself if he had more free time, more resources at his disposal, and the background of a doctoral specialist. In the absence of one or more of these elements, a teacher would do well to grab up a paperback "box."

There are several enlightened paperback distributors, and the lucky teachers who live within their service radius are blessed with prompt deliveries and gigantic warehouse stocks to choose from. Furthermore, although these distributors are in the business primarily for selling wholesale to city and campus bookstores and drugstores, many make strong overtures to teachers for the discount business. Gopher News Co., Minneapolis, engages able teachers to build study guides to be given away. Ludington News Co., Detroit, is underwriting a course at Wayne State University, "Creative Use of Paperbacks in Classroom Teaching," and the company each year sends out several hundred pre-packed book fairs. Milligan News Co., San Jose, encourages after school coffee-browsings. Inland Book Distributors, Chicago, sends representatives to schools and teachers' conferences for consultation. Suits News Company, Lansing, Michigan, offers their patented automated warehouse of one million copies (15,000 titles); their copyrighted Speedy Ship Paperback Book Service boasts instant order filling of 1,000 top school titles going out to 40 states. Magna, in Lynbrook, N.Y., and A&A in Boston offer speedy service for the most wanted school titles. These are some of the smiling, friendly distributors who understand teachers' problems, and help wherever they can. There are some 600 local paperback distributors, all of them of at least potential value to the schools in their areas. If the man nearest you is still dormant in the school market, perhaps _you_ can activate him. Why not look him up in the Yellow Pages and turn him on?

Once a man's wealth was determined by how many books he owned. Today a teacher's effectiveness may be ascertained by the paperbacks in his classroom. The writers have created the gold, but there are still countless teachers who have not discovered it. How enriched could be their students' study hours, and their own lives and lesson plans, if only those teachers realized what wealth was available to them.

Herein lies the weakness of the whole field. Many teachers in every state who are tucked away from great urban centers of supply have become discouraged with the poor mail contact of the paperback publishers and are going on generally oblivious to it all. Every now and then a publisher gets hot with a young man of vision and tries to create teaching materials and a house organ and tries to reach out to all the teachers everywhere. Pocketbooks began it with John Ware; Dell took over with Joe Mersand, Jerry Weiss and now Paul O'Donnell. Bantam pioneered with Dave Sohn and is sizzling at the moment with Gloria Steinberg. New American Library and Avon are ably represented by Marilyn Abel and Gillian Jolis. But what is needed is a concerted effort by the industry that would include but expand the good work of Dominic Salvatore's BiPad (Bureau of Independent Publishers and Distributors), and Harold Lashey's Combined Book Exhibit.

Why not a supra-public relations organization for the industry that would establish rapport with every potential teacher-user through a newsletter? Media and Methods sensed this need back in 1964 when it began a School Paperback Journal. Why not more and continuous paperback coverage in this now prestigious multimedia journal? Why not present at state and regional conferences a fair amount of space for each member publisher (with a limit so the giants don't swamp the little guys)?

A State Council on Paperbound Books could be organized in each state. The best coordinator probably would be someone with state-wide contacts, such as the supervisor of English or social studies in the state's largest city, or a well-known university instructor, or a leading county figure. That person, in turn, could find one person in each county who would agree to keep in touch with the public and private schools in his or her county. Some of the following goals might be among the two-fold purposes of such a network:

1. Inform teachers, administrators, and school boards
   a. what paperbacks are in print,
   b. what new paperbacks are coming out,
   c. where paperbacks may be purchased quickly.

2. Inform publishers, editors, and distributors
   a. what trends are being born,
   b. what problems can be overcome.

Until the industry comes around to this, it will only have realized a portion of its potential profit and influence, and teaching will continue to be marred by pools of instruction restrained by limited materials.

THE ADOLESCENT NOVEL IN THE CLASSROOM*

By Al Muller

In "Lipsyte's *Contender*: Another Look at the Junior Novel," John S. Simmons succinctly described the role of the adolescent or junior novel in the classroom. He promoted the use of the genre "in classroom instruction aimed at the promotion of interest in literature for early adolescents as well as the introduction to them of appropriate aspects of literary form." However, the incredible number of adolescent novels on the market makes the teacher's job of selecting novels for use in the classroom a difficult one. The following bibliography has been compiled as an aid to the teacher attempting to locate an adolescent novel for use in introducing students to specific aspects of literary art--aspects which may prove obstacles to successful reading when the students attempt to read sophisticated adult literature.

The titles listed have been selected according to the following criteria. (1) The novels are known to be popular with contemporary adolescents. (2) The novels demonstrate a distinctive aspect of literary art in a manner which may help the inexperienced reader learn to deal successfully with the aspect of literary art. For example, an adolescent novel in which flashbacks are printed in italics may help the inexperienced reader learn to deal with the literary device. (3) All of the novels are available in reasonably inexpensive paperback editions.

Flashbacks

Phoebe by Patricia Dizenzo (Bantam, 1970) is a sophisticated and candid novel dealing with the topic of premarital pregnancy. Flashbacks are used frequently; they are printed in italics.

You'll Like My Mother by Naomi A. Hintze (Fawcett, 1969) is a contemporary gothic novel dealing with a young widow's attempts to escape her diabolical mother-in-law. All flashbacks are printed in italics.

*Reprinted by permission of the author and publisher from *Media & Methods*, 10:8 (April 1974), 32-33.

Too Bad About the Haines Girl by Zoa Sherburne (American Education Publication, 1967) is an examination of the plight of a pregnant teenager. Flashbacks are not printed in italics, but Sherburne carefully supplies the inexperienced reader with ample context clues.

Interior Monologues

Durango Street by Frank Bonham (Dell, 1965) is a fast-moving story of a black youth's attempts to survive the violence of ghetto life. Interior monologues are used frequently, but the shifts from external to internal action are indicated through the use of italics.

Just Dial a Number by Edith Maxwell (Pocket Books, 1972) is a suspense novel which explores teenage guilt. The shifts from external to internal action are printed in italics.

The Peter Pan Bag by Lee Kingman (Dell, 1970) deals with a young girl's attempt to find herself in a "hippie" colony. Interior monologues are printed in italics.

You Would If You Loved Me by Nora Stirling (Avon/Camelot, 1970) is an examination of the sexual confusions of contemporary teens. Interior monologues are printed in italics.

In Medias Res

Bless the Beasts and Children by Glendon Swarthout (Pocket Books, 1970) is a funny novel about six young boys who set out to prove their personal worth. Past events are printed in italics.

The Longest Weekend by Honor Arundel (Grosset & Dunlap/Tempo, 1973) is a candid novel about a young, unmarried British girl attempting to raise her illegitimate daughter.

Run Softly, Go Fast by Barbara Wersba (Bantam, 1970) is about a young artist's battles with himself, his father, and his society.

Point Of View

Dave's Song by Robert McKay (Bantam, 1970) is about a young boy and a young girl who are trying to find themselves and each other. The novel is narrated from the first person point-of-view. The two characters narrate alternate chapters, but the narrator of each chapter is identified clearly.

The Pigman by Paul Zindel (Dell, 1968) is an extremely popular adolescent novel which deals with the initiation of two teenagers into the realities of adult life. The novel is narrated from the first person point of view, and, as in Dave's Song, the two characters narrate alternate chapters. The narrator of each chapter is identified in the context of each chapter.

In a Country of Ourselves by Nat Hentoff (Dell, 1971) is a novel which explores the problems and confusion of teenage "activists." The novel is narrated from the omniscient point of view and reveals the thoughts and actions of many characters.

I'm Really Dragged But Nothing Gets Me Down by Nat Hentoff (Dell, 1968) explores a young boy's attempts to rebel against the draft and the boy's father's attempts to understand his son. The novel is narrated from the third person limited point-of-view.

Symbolism

The Contender by Robert Lipsyte (Bantam, 1967) is a fast-paced novel about a young black who is attempting to play it straight in the ghetto. Light and dark imagery symbolize the alternatives from which the youth must choose. The well-lighted boxing ring, for example, symbolizes a willingness to face life, whereas the darkness of the movie theater or a secret, womb-like cave symbolizes escape from life.

Mr. and Mrs. BoJo Jones by Ann Head (Signet, 1967) explores the problems and conflicts facing teenagers who are forced into an early marriage. There are several key symbols developed in the novel.

My Darling, My Hamburger by Paul Zindel (Bantam, 1969) explores the problems, insecurities, and hazards of teenage romance. A single symbol carries the novel's theme, and Zindel carefully explains its meaning.

Irony

Is There a Life After Graduation, Henry Birnbaum? by Carolyn Balducci (Dell, 1971) is a funny adolescent novel dealing with a young boy's initiation into the world beyond high school. Much of the irony is based upon current events.

My Darling, My Hamburger by Paul Zindel is an excellent novel to use in introducing students to the use of irony. Zindel carefully provides the reader with the correct interpretations of scenes and situations which the adult characters, caught up in their own narrow concerns, misinterpret.

Phoebe by Patricia Dizenzo contains a great deal of irony. Dizenzo provides the reader with the necessary information to see the irony. For example, in one scene, Phoebe, who has just returned home from another interlude in her sexual affair with Paul, is accused by her mother of staying away from home to smoke cigarettes.

Integral Use of Literary Allusions

Mr. and Mrs. BoJo Jones by Ann Head contains many literary allusions which are used to reveal character and to describe situations.

A Girl Like Me by Jeannette Eyerly (Berkley Highland, 1966) is a novel about a young girl who is struggling to accept the fact that she is an adopted child. The literary allusions not only reveal character but also foreshadow emotional situations.

The Outsiders by S. E. Hinton (Dell, 1967) is a story about the problems and violence facing disadvantaged adolescents living in the inner city. The novel's theme is developed around Robert Frost's poem "Nothing Gold Can Stay," which is printed in the novel.

Red Sky At Morning by Richard Bradford (Pocket Books, 1968) is a sophisticated and candid initiation novel. Allusions to The Odyssey and to the "Hemingway Hero" are used and carefully developed in this narrative about a youth's struggle to reach manhood.

Integral Use of Setting

Durango Street by Frank Bonham is similar to the works of such naturalists as Stephen Crane and Theodore Dreiser. In this novel, the ghetto is not just a stage but is also a major force which acts upon the characters.

Bless the Beasts and Children by Glendon Swarthout is a good novel to use in introducing students to the artistic use of setting. The novel is set in the mountains of Arizona, and the setting incorporates the adventure of the six boys into the American myth of the "Old West" in which men prove themselves through dangerous missions. Swarthout carefully explains the role of the setting in the novel.

Subplots

That Was Then, This Is Now by S. E. Hinton (Dell, 1971) is a fast-moving novel about an alienated youth. The novel contains several carefully developed subplots which do not stand alone but are successfully integrated into the central plot.

The Witch of Blackbird Pond by Elizabeth George Speare (Dell, 1958) is a popular and frequently reprinted historical romance set in seventeenth-century America. The novel contains two fully developed subplots which are integrated into the central plot.

Journalistic Writing

Tuned-Out by Maia Wojciechowska (Dell, 1968) deals with the topics of growing up and drug abuse. The novel is presented as the central character's journal.

Extended Dramatic Monologue

Don't Play Dead Before You Have To by Maia Wojciechowska (Dell, 1970) is a sophisticated novel about a young boy trying to find his place in life.

Extended Metaphor

The Peter Pan Bag by Lee Kingman contains an extended metaphor developed from the allusion to James Barrie's "Peter Pan." Allusions to this work are used throughout the novel to describe the thoughts and feelings of the central adolescent character.

Parallelism

Sounder by William H. Armstrong (Scholastic Book Service, 1969) is the story about a black youth's attempt to improve himself and to accept the reality of change.

READING HABITS OF BEHAVIORALLY DISORDERED MALES: A Study*

By Robert L. Aaron, Lewis Miller & Elizabeth Smith

Numerous surveys are conducted each year, both formally and informally, to determine what adolescents are reading. However, the reading tastes of one segment of this age group, the behaviorally disordered adolescent male, have at this time not been adequately assessed. Attempts to measure the natural reading behaviors of this group often meet failure because most of these pupils simply do not read in the public school if they can avoid it. Nolte (1973) notes: "Studies of youth disorders and juvenile delinquency consistently show that children who get in trouble seldom read anything at all. One team of prominent researchers, for example, compiled a list of ninety factors that might promote or explain delinquent behavior. Reading was not one of them. Ignorance, after all, is perhaps the weakest of all defenses against evil."

Edwards (1969), in The Fair Garden and the Swarm of Beasts, has said, "It is essential, it seems to me, for the library to revise its middle class approach and devise new ways of making books a part of the lives of these people who desperately need the ideas found in books."

This study sought to evaluate some aspects of the reading interests and tastes of a group whose special relationships with books have previously been very poorly defined. The sample studied was chosen randomly from among 450 delinquent adolescents between thirteen and nineteen years of age who were confined in a Georgia youth offender center. The subjects were characterized by severe social, emotional, and learning problems. They represented the range of law violations from minor infractions to major crimes. They also exhibited a wide range of personal reactions to school and reading, dominated by a very low regard for both.

It has been generally agreed that people in confining situations usually do more reading than they would if there were less demanding, thus more attractive, activities on which to spend their time. Such was the case with this population. Because they were

*Reprinted by permission of the authors and publisher from Journal of Reading 19:1 (October 1975), 28-32. Copyright © 1975 by the International Reading Association.

confined and did considerable reading, some data were collected which can be useful in developing programs to stimulate changes in the reading behavior of similarly disordered pupils.

The center where these subjects were housed had a Georgia Association accredited high school. It also had a library that was sufficiently large and varied in its collection of books to meet most reading needs. It was staffed by a qualified librarian and a part-time clerical aide. During 1973, over 7000 books were checked out by a population of approximately 700 pupils who had regular access to the library and were free to check out books for a two-week period. Also, small collections from the main library were housed in each cottage for use by the pupils.

Circulation of books is not a good index of true reading behavior among these boys. Therefore, interviews were undertaken to define the extent of book completion for this population. Out of these interviews came the following information: 1) the relationship between method of book selection and percentage of books read; 2) the relationship between books selected and books completed by categories, based on the Dewey Decimal classification system; 3) the most popular fiction titles read, based on checkout records; and 4) the most popular biography read, based on checkout records.

When books were returned, the checkout cards were collected and a randomized assignment of subjects to be interviewed was made. During the interview each subject was asked if he had read the book. If he stated that he had, then he was asked to talk about the book. Based on this discussion, a determination was made as to whether or not the book had been read by using these criteria: 1) If the pupil could quote only limited facts or none at all, the book was classified as not having been read. 2) The ability to get the main idea or express an opinion about the book at the critical thinking level was classified as having been read. 3) Books checked out for reference purposes were counted as having been read if it was determined by evidence that the book had served the purpose for which it was checked out. Eighty-two individual interviews were held.

The study revealed that 44 per cent of the subjects interviewed completed the books they had checked out. This was considered a dramatic increase over this population's normal public school book reading behavior which, by adjudication of librarians and teachers, is normally at or near the zero per cent level. It was felt to be important to identify methods of selection as related to success/failure rate and classification of book as related to success/failure rate. Based on results from looking at the relationship of classification to success/failure rate, it was decided to look at the most popular titles in the two highest success categories.

Method of selection of books was determined during the pupil interview, and the results by percentage are shown in Table 1.

As might be expected, the overwhelming method of selection

Table 1

Percentage of Selection by Each Method

Method	Per cent
Shelf	74.4
Librarian	8.5
Teacher	7.3
Friend	7.3
Card catalog	1.2
Book citation	1.2

Table 2

Reading Success/Failure Rate by Method of Selection

Method of Selection	Per cent
Shelf	
Completed	44.3
Not completed	55.7
Librarian	
Completed	71.4
Not completed	28.6
Teacher	
Completed	66.7
Not completed	33.3

No books were completed in any of the other categories of selection.

---

was that pupils selected books directly from the shelf. These percentages generally hold true in most school libraries and for most populations because: 1) many adolescents prefer to do or find things for themselves; 2) the librarian or teacher may not be available 3) many adolescents are reluctant to ask for help; and 4) there is a lack of positive leadership in school libraries in which the librarian should, but does not, function as a remediator and motivator to the nonreading students.

Looking at the success/failure rate, Tables 2 and 3 reveal some very significant data. Table 2 compares success and failure within each selection method. It is significant that through helping them select books, librarians and teachers had a dramatic influence on students' rate of book completion. Therefore, providing reading guidance to these pupils can be very successful when implemented.

Although this is the age at which peer influence is greatest, this did not play a large role in book selection. Even more signifi-

Table 3

Reading Success/Failure Rate by Book Classification

Book Classification	Per cent
Fiction	
Completed	57
Not completed	43
Biography	
Completed	50
Not completed	50
Recreational and Performing Arts	
Completed	40
Not completed	60
Social Pathology and Services	
Completed	29
Not completed	71

cant is that this influence did not contribute at all to successful completion of a book. In looking at the reading success/failure rate according to book classification, four categories provided the major data from which conclusions might be drawn (Table 3).

Although books in recreational and performing arts were checked out almost as frequently as biography, they were not completed as often as the biography. Interest in several nonfiction areas was almost as high as in fiction and biography, but there was not as great an amount of material published in these nonfiction areas on a reading level suitable for this age group.

The two classifications with the highest success rates were fiction and biography. The titles listed in Tables 4 and 5 were those which were checked out most frequently by different subjects in these two classifications.

To Your Scattered Bodies Go was the most popular fiction title. The next four books listed were a close second. It is interesting to note that only one best seller was on the list. Three classics were included. Books about drugs were also well read by this group, as they are with most adolescents today.

The biography listing includes "books about a person" or lists particular titles. In this category, books about Dr. Martin Luther King Jr. were by far the most popular.

This study found a relatively high rate of book completion by behaviorally disordered adolescent males. It was also noted that the success rate could be very significantly affected by librarians and teachers through reading guidance.

Table 4

Fiction Titles

To Your Scattered Bodies Go, Philip Jose Farmer
Nitty Gritty, Frank Bonham
I Never Loved Your Mind, Paul Zindel
Werewolf, Bruce Lowery
Two Towers, J. R. R. Tolkien
Drop Out, Jeannette Eyerly
Huckleberry Finn, Mark Twain
Kidnapped, Robert Louis Stevenson
Airport, Arthur Hailey
Fellowship of the Ring, J. R. R. Tolkien
Queenie Peavy, Robert Burch
Dirty Dozen, E. M. Nathanson
Ghosts, William Mayne, editor
J.T., Jane Wagner
Stories to Stay Awake By, Alfred Hitchcock
Soul Brothers and Sister Lou, Kristin Hunter
Stories to Be Read with the Lights On, Alfred Hitchcock
Tuned Out, Maia Wojceichowska
Stories for the Not Nervous, Alfred Hitchcock
Hauntings: Tales of the Supernatural, Henry Mazzeo, editor
The Exploits of Sherlock Holmes, John D. Carr and Adrian C. Doyle

Table 5

Biography

Dr. Martin Luther King, Jr., Ormond DeKay, Jr.
John F. Kennedy, Patricia Miles Martin
Abraham Lincoln, Barbara Carey
Black and Free, Thomas Skinner
Daniel Boone, Patricia Miles Martin
Nat Turner, Judith Griffin
George Washington Carver, Rackham Holt
Elvis Presley, Jerry Hopkins
I Am a Man: Ode to Martin Luther King, Jr., Eve Merriam
Run Baby Run, Nicky Cruz
Come Out Smokin', Phillip Pepe
Unbought and Unbossed, Shirley Chisholm

Fiction and biography provided the best sources from which to draw in stimulating more reading among these youth. Hopefully, more stimulating and readable materials are becoming available in nonfiction which will lead to increased success in getting these pupils to read.

Title listings in fiction and biography reveal that their interests often paralleled the interests of all adolescents. This group also had a strong interest in ghost stories and their interest in drugs was probably stronger than usual. Many of their popular selections indicated an interest in how people face adversity, something to which they feel they can relate very well.

There is a great need for the library science community to develop a special competency in understanding, selecting books for, and motivating the reading performance of the behaviorally disordered adolescent male. A positive attitude and behavior toward book reading desperately needs to be extended to these students. The results of this study clearly indicate that the effort to guide the reading behavior of these students will pay dividends in an increased level of book completion.

References

Edwards, Margaret A. *The Fair Garden and the Swarm of Beasts: The Library and the Young Adult*. New York, New York: Hawthorn Books, 1969.

Nolte, Chester. "The Debate: Whether and How to Censor 'Objectionable' School Books," *The American School Board Journal*, 160 (May 1973), pp. 38-41.

RELUCTANTLY YOURS, BOOKS TO TEMPT THE HESITANT*

By Alleen Pace Nilsen, Karen B. Tyler and Linda Kozarek

EDITOR'S NOTE: It was in response to popular demand that we went looking for books that would tempt the reluctant reader. When we first started, the whole process reminded me of my teenage years when my mother used to try to convince me to wear clothes that I detested. First she would flatter me into agreeing that I had unusual taste--sort of a cut above the popular masses. Next she would take out the skirt or dress or whatever it was I couldn't stand, and when I expressed my dislike for the garment, she would remind me that my taste was unusual. Then would come the clincher; since I loathed it, that must mean that everyone else would love it!

The first similarity between this and our search for new books that reluctant readers would like is that deep down inside, book reviewers feel that their taste in books is a cut above that of the popular masses--especially above that of people who have read very few books. The second similarity is that as we started picking out books that we thought would be good for reluctant readers, the ones we reached for were the ones we disliked the most--cheap plastic books about motorcycle gangs and hot rods. We had subconsciously made the same leap in logic that my mother made with the clothing. Knowing that our own taste in books is somehow different from that of reluctant readers, we overgeneralized and assumed that whatever we didn't like, they would like.

Our next step was to find a few reluctant readers to serve as sample critics. That's when we came to our big realization. Reluctant readers come in all varieties. They aren't limited to the group referred to as "dirtheads." There are readers and there are non-readers in all high school social groups. And there are readers and non-readers with all levels of taste and all types of interests. We hope the titles discussed below will accommodate many of these differing interests.

---

*Reprinted by permission of the authors and the publisher from English Journal, 65:5 (May 1976), 90-93.

<u>The Academy Awards: A Pictorial History</u> by Paul Michael. Crown Publishers, Inc., 1975 (Third Revised Edition). 390 pgs.

<u>All About Motorcycles: Selection, Care, Repair, and Safety</u> by Max Alth. Hawthorn Books, 1975. 209 pgs.

<u>The Animal,</u> by Jack Jones. William Morrow and Company, 1975. 220 pgs.

<u>Be a Winner in Basketball</u> by Charles Coombs. William Morrow and Company, 1975. 126 pgs.

<u>Be a Winner in Tennis</u> by Charles Coombs. William Morrow and Company, 1975. 128 pgs.

<u>The Comic Spirit</u> by Joseph F. Littell (editor). Lothrop, Lee & Shepard, 1975. 155 pgs.

<u>The Complete Motorcycle Book</u> by Lyle Kenyon Engel. Four Winds Press, 1975. 195 pgs.

<u>Dictionary of American Slang</u> compiled by Harold Wentworth and Stuart Berg Flexner. Crowell, 1975. 766 pgs.

<u>Earthquakes</u> by Billye Walker Brown and Walter R. Brown. Addison-Wesley, 1974. 191 pgs.

<u>Fires</u> by Walter R. Brown and Norman D. Anderson. Addison-Wesley, 1976. 189 pgs.

<u>Floods</u> by Walter R. Brown and Billye W. Cutchen. Addison-Wesley, 1975. 175 pgs.

<u>Football Superstars of the 70's</u> by Bill Gutman. Julian Messner, 1975. 191 pgs.

<u>Guinness Book of Amazing Achievements</u> by Norris McWhirter and Ross McWhirter. Sterling, 1975. Also Bantam paperback, 1975. 96 pgs.

<u>If Beale Street Could Talk</u> by James Baldwin. The Dial Press, 1974. Also New American Library Signet paperback, 1975. 242 pgs.

<u>If You Could See What I Hear</u> by Tom Sullivan and Derek Gill. Harper and Row, 1975. 184 pgs.

<u>Literature of the Supernatural</u> by Robert E. Beck (editor). Lothrop, Lee & Shepard, 1975. 128 pgs.

<u>Movie Monsters</u> by Thomas G. Aylesworth. Lippincott, 1975. 79 pgs. (simultaneous paperback edition)

Rumble Fish by S. E. Hinton. Delacorte Press, 1975. 122 pgs.

Science Fiction edited by Sylvia Z. Brodkin and Elizabeth J. Pearson. Lothrop, 246 pgs.

Sunshine by Norma Klein. Holt, Rinehart, Winston, 1975. 218 pgs. Avon paperback, 1974.

Those Mysterious UFO's: The Story of Unidentified Flying Objects by David C. Knight. Parents' Magazine Press, 1975. 64 pgs.

UFO's and Other Worlds by Peter Ryan. Puffin Books, 1975. 48 pgs.

What reluctant readers have in common is that they've been disappointed with books. Perhaps it's just that their expectations are higher than those of book reviewers, or perhaps the effort required to read is so much greater that they don't feel properly rewarded. Many teachers euphemistically use the term "reluctant reader" to mean "poor reader." Although not always accurate, this is at least an understandable usage because poor readers have the greatest chance of becoming reluctant readers. They become reluctant because the effort they have to expend is so much greater than that required of a good reader. Even though both of them have the same book and stand to get the same rewards from reading it, the slow reader and the poor reader pay a higher price in time and effort. An obvious way to balance things out is to provide the poor reader with easier books and so we especially kept our eyes open for easy books.

But the thousands of limited vocabulary books that are never taken from library and reading clinic shelves prove that ease of reading is not enough to tempt the reluctant reader. What we found with those few reluctant readers who consented to help criticize our choices was that their prime consideration in choosing a book is the topic. If it is something they are interested in, then they are happy to tackle it. And contrary to having tastes just the opposite of ours, they want in their books the same things we want--only more so. Their preferences are heavily influenced by the purpose they have in mind when they pick up a book, hence we've organized our titles around some of the differing purposes that appear to be popular.

Books to Tell You What You Want to Know

If reluctant readers are looking for information then they want it to be clearly stated in a well organized manner so they can find what they need in the shortest possible time. And they want the information to be something they can use in their own lives right now. Of all the books we considered for this set, the one voted as the most likely to be ripped off from a library because it's so useful is The Complete Motorcycle Book. It has easy-to-find and easy-to-read directions for repairing motorcycles, plus some rather appealing and sensible talk which counteracts the stereotype of motorcyclists being "reckless speed-crazed" menaces to society. Following right behind this book in usefulness is All About Motorcycles: Selection, Care, Repair, and Safety. The reading style may be slightly easier, but the dust jacket is marred by a photograph of a couple who look as though they stepped right out of the fifties. The boy is wearing a plaid shirt which today is definitely "uncool."

Two other books that fit nicely into the category of useful books are Be a Winner in Basketball and Be a Winner in Tennis by Charles Coombs, who has done a series of this type. Although flawed by inadequate representations of women (one of fifty-nine photographs in Basketball; fourteen of fifty photographs with identifiable people in Tennis), the books are lucid explanations of the rules and procedures of each sport.

Books to Dabble In

Some teenagers are reluctant readers because they cannot find a block of time large enough to give to a book. But when books are around that invite dabbling, the time seems less important and the books get read in part, if not in whole. Three likely books, easy enough for very poor readers (third grade reading level) are Movie Monsters and the two mini-volumes, Guinness Illustrated Collection of World Records for Young People and Guinness Book of Amazing Achievements. Movie Monsters describes the cinematic creation of such favorites as King Kong, Wolfman, Dracula and The Fly. Well written and illustrated, the book is divided into short single monster chapters. The two Guinness books are just as interesting, but much less forbidding, than the standard Book of World Records. They are each about 100 pages long with cover art similar to the original book and a single illustrated page devoted to each event.

More sophisticated in content and presentation are the three anthologies: The Comic Spirit, Literature of the Supernatural, and Science Fiction. The Anthology format may seem textbookish at first, but the contents are not. All three books are reprinted from earlier paperback editions and include short selections from both well and lesser known authors and artists. In The Comic Spirit, for instance, such classic comedians as Thurber and Benchley, are next to nouveaus like Buchwald; and graffiti, cartoons, put-downs, and headlines. There is even a section called "Smashed Potatoes" which presents recipes in the hilarious words of young children. The genuine humor and sophistication, the variety and scope, and the relative brevity of the selections enhance the book's appeal to the reluctant. Photographic and artistic comedy is also included. The other two books are similarly organized. Literature of the Supernatural includes excerpts from The Book of the Dead, Dante,

O'Henry, Poe, Lovecraft, and contemporary writers. Blake, Munch, and Goya are among the artists whose work illustrates the book. Science Fiction includes examples of work by many authors popular with young people--Vonnegut and Clarke--for instance, and by artists whose styles complement the collection--Dali, Escher, Magritte, and others.

Two adult reference books with reluctant reader appeal are The Academy Awards and Dictionary of American Slang. The Academy Awards is useful for reference work on the movies (a list of losers and an index is appended to the year-by-year lists and photographs of winners). Some readers will also enjoy sitting down with this book and getting lost in the history of film.

As for The Dictionary of American Slang, its dust jacket acknowledges that its contents are vulgar, disreputable, bawdy, profane, and blasphemous: in other words, perfect for reluctant teenagers! If you can get away with having such a book in your room, you will find your students at least looking up the dirty words. They may have so much fun that they will get hooked on skimming other pages of the 766 page volume. A selected bibliography is appended for students seriously interested in pursuing the topic of slang.

Books with Hot Topics

All of us are reluctant to read certain things: advertisements for life insurance, district mandated curriculum guides, and directions for preparing income tax forms. We want to read about what's new and what everyone's talking about. It's the same with the reluctant reader. For many, Football Superstars of the 70's would be a good choice. Some fans will be baffled at first by Gutman's choices of superstars. Where is Namath? Where is Blanda? But, each player included joined the NFL in the late sixties or early seventies. Information on the twelve superstars (Simpson, Bradshaw, Harris, etc.) is up-to-date through the 1974-1975 season and should be appealing to sports fans.

Many readers, reluctant or enthusiastic, consider UFO's a hot topic. Two books, at different reading levels, will appeal to them. Written at an easy reading level is Those Mysterious UFO's. Background information on individual sightings of flying saucers since 1947 is covered with accompanying photographs. The stranger-than-fiction phenomena are reported factually, without attempts at explanation. UFO's and Other Worlds examines in greater detail the more mysterious flying saucer reports and suggests some possible explanations for their appearances. Since scientific evidence for the extraterrestrial visitations is insubstantial, the author dispels many of the myths that contribute to the credibility of UFO sightings. The author explores the possibility of life in other solar systems and the potential for interstellar communication. Scientific in approach, the vocabulary may present problems for the less able readers.

Three disaster books, Historical Catastrophies: Earthquakes, ... Fires, ... Floods, are more than slick commercial tales that teachers will want to use to capitalize on the current interest in disasters as seen in the movies. Each contains sound, scientific information on the causes of particular classes of catastrophies, documented historical facts, and eye-witness accounts that focus on individuals with whom readers can identify.

Books with an Emotional Wallop

If in their reading, reluctant readers are looking for an emotional experience, then they want the highs and the lows to be packed tight against each other. They haven't much patience with the long drawn out in-betweens. They want struggles where the odds are great and everything is super-sized.

One such struggle, with which most teenagers are now familiar, is the story of Jacquelyn M. Helton, the young mother who learns at eighteen that she has fatal bone cancer. Norma Klein's novel Sunshine is based on the television movie suggested by Helton's journals. Readers, reluctant and enthusiastic, who wept over the movie and watched the resulting TV special, will want to read this touching and unavoidably moving novel. The first person narrative is written in the honest and occasionally introspective style which permits identification with the brave young woman as she struggles to keep alive her hopes and dreams.

Tom Sullivan's story in If You Could See What I Hear is one of struggle and heartwarming success. Blind from birth, Tom is neither handicapped nor limited. He has seized every opportunity to live fully and develop his capabilities. He became a champion wrestler at school, a dean's list student, an avid sportsman, a composer of popular songs, and a loving father and husband. Some readers will be inspired by his testament to the striving and determination of youth.

A different kind of struggle is faced by Tish (nineteen and pregnant) and Fonny (wrongly jailed for the crime of rape) in James Baldwin's novel If Beale Street Could Talk. The bitter Baldwin of the sixties seems mellowed in this "love conquers all" story. There are many elements of soap opera clichês: unwed pregnancy, separated lovers, crime and wrongful accusation, evil parents and loving parents. The resulting story, though, is genuinely appealing. Baldwin writes from Tish's perspective convincingly and authentically. As with his other books, the flavor of city and ghetto life is evoked. Unlike some of his earlier books, however, family relationships, friendship, and the positive influence of love are emphasized. The story will capture romantics and optimists.

S. E. Hinton's new book Rumblefish, though set in an urban environment, has a much different focus. Fast paced and action packed, it will appeal to teenagers and younger readers who enjoyed

The Outsiders. Again, Hinton focuses on the loyal but competitive relationship between two brothers caught in the aftermath of the street gang world, now shattered by the upsurgence of drugs. Rusty James is indisputably tough, but he'll never be as "hard core" as his well known brother, the Motorcycle Boy. Can he match his brother's prowess as a street gang leader or will his own limitations save him from this misdirected life? Like the rumble fish in the pet store who must be kept isolated to prevent their killing each other, Rusty struggles in the loneliness of his hostile environment.

Jo Jo Jenkins, the central character in Jack Jones' novel The Animal, has a ticket out of a hostile environment. At 6'4" and 290 pounds, he is an "animal," and football (high school, college, and finally pro ball) is his ticket. But caged in his "jockstrapper" physique, is the sensitivity of an artist. Jo Jo loves to paint. Despite his physical strength and size, Jo Jo lacks the "killer instinct" to become a champion football player. He abhors the violence and racial tension so prevalent in pro-football, but he can't succeed financially as an artist. Torn between the two worlds, Jo Jo's fight for dignity and survival on and off the field makes this novel compelling reading for the sports-minded. With harsh language (adult reading level), The Animal tells the story of Jo Jo's frustrations and his ultimate ironic entrapment.

BOOKTALKING: YOU CAN DO IT*

By Mary K. Chelton

Skill in booktalking remains one of the most valuable promotional devices YA librarians can have at hand to interest teenagers in the library. Once acquired, this skill can be adapted to floor work with individual readers, radio spots, booklist annotations, and class visits in the library or in the classroom. It can be combined with slide-tape, film, or musical presentations, and with outreach skills. Its limitations are set by YA librarians who either refuse to learn the technique, have never learned it (and judge it valueless even after learning it), or who remain inflexible in chosen methods of doing it. The best young adult librarians I have known, whether they see their book selection role as one of expanding horizons and literary tastes or of just giving kids what they want (and most of us usually fall somewhere in between), have a "hidden agenda" for promoting the love of reading for pleasure, and have found booktalks a superb way of doing that.

It should be said here that booktalking skills do not preempt professional abilities in programming, information and referral, traditional reference work, audiovisual collection building, or community outreach, as is often unjustly assumed of the YA specialty. It is my contention, however, that the public still assumes that libraries deal in books and our nonbook related skills and materials will win us no friends or financial support for other information or enrichment media unless librarians do traditional reader's advisory work very well.

In my opinion, the two simplest definitions of booktalks are Amelia Munson's: "The booktalk falls into place between storytelling and book reviewing, partakes of both and is unlike either," taken from _An Ample Field_ (American Library Assn., 1950); the other is my own: "A booktalk is a formal or informal presentation about a book or group of books designed to entice the listener into reading them."

Elaine Simpson, in her YA course at Rutgers, describes a

---

*Reprinted by permission of the author and publisher from _School Library Journal_ (April 1976), 39-43. Copyright © 1976 by the R. R. Bowker Co., a Xerox Corporation.

booktalk as "That part of a librarian's visit to a classroom or during a class visit to the library devoted to presenting two or more books to the group. It is an art and a device by which the librarian tries to interest young people in all books in general and in some books in particular through a talk so carefully prepared as to seem spontaneous, in which he or she gives the subject, the flavor, and the appeal of each book presented." Simpson adds. "Indirectly through book talks we are able to show the teenager that he or she is welcome in the school of public library, and that he or she has a place there. We are also able to identify ourselves as friends...."

One of the axiomatic things about booktalking is that the talk is not to reveal everything about the book. This is a common beginner's mistake. Doris M. Cole's suggestion in "The Book Talk" in _Junior Plots_ (Bowker, 1967) is that booktalks should give only an "enticing sample of the book's contents." In the same article, Margaret Edwards calls the sample "a little piece of pie so good that it tempts one to consume the whole concoction." Learning how to find and then how to present just the right sample is the essence of learning to booktalk. In her book, _The Fair Garden and the Swarm of Beasts_ (Hawthorn, 1974), Edwards states that the objectives of booktalks are "to sell the idea of reading for pleasure; to introduce new ideas and new fields of reading; to develop an appreciation of style and character protrayal; lift the level of reading by introducing the best books the audience can read with pleasure; to humanize books, the library and the librarian."

To all of these objectives, I would add that booktalks keep librarians from becoming hypocrites who despair of their patrons' reading tastes while never reading for themselves or for their patrons.

There are probably as many types of booktalks as there are librarians doing them, but roughly they fall into long or short talks with interesting combinations of the two. A short talk, and the one which should be mastered first, usually presents only one title and lasts from 30 seconds to one minute. In it, the librarian tells listeners about something happening to someone in the book, without either divulging the entire plot or stringing along a variety of superlatives. Examples:

> When BoJo was 17 and July was 16 and they'd been going steady all through high school, July got pregnant and they ran away and got married, even though both sets of parents were disgusted; July had to drop out of school; and BoJo gave up his college football scholarship. _Mr. and Mrs. Bo Jo Jones_ will tell you how they made a go of a teenage marriage with three strikes against them.
>
> Even though Harold Krents went totally blind as a child, his parents refused to send him to special schools, and in _To Race The Wind_, he tells his true life story about how he played football, became a lawyer, got drafted into

> the army, and inspired the writing of Butterflies Are Free.
>
> As a baby, she had been fried alive by alcoholic parents. By the time Laura was twelve and Dr. D'Ambrosio discovered her in an institution, she had been diagnosed as schizophrenic (the severest form of mental illness), had a long list of physical problems, and had never spoken a word. No Language But a Cry is about how he helped her.

It is obvious in these examples how easily short talks can be adapted to floor work, when a teen asks what the book's about, to annotated booklists, and to prerecorded radio spots. Depending on the use or situation, the booktalks can be shortened further or lengthened. "Booktalk" is probably too formal a word, but these short talks do demand that YA librarians discipline themselves to think constantly about the books they've read in terms of plot and the teen audience rather than literary quality or a strictly personal reaction. Kids want to know what happens in a book, what is so exciting about it that they should want to read it. Keeping out your own adjectives lets them feel that they make the decision to read the book, despite your predilection, rather than that the librarian is just pushing either personal favorites or some sort of "literary spinach" down their throats. In other words, let the book sell itself.

A long booktalk lasts ten to 15 minutes and usually emphasizes one particular section of one particular title, whether memorized or told in your own words but not read aloud. Some examples of good sections of books to use are the dead horse scene in Red Sky at Morning, the first day on the tubercular ward in I'm Done Crying, Albert Scully meeting Mrs. Woodfin for the first time and getting drunk in The Dreamwatcher, being fitted for braces and shoes in Easy Walking, the race at Riverside with no clutch in Parnelli, discovering that Madek has left him naked to die in the desert in Death Watch, or Capt. Lebrun's escape in Escape from Colditz. Long talks are more formal than short talks and are best used to follow up several short ones on the same theme or as a break in the middle of a variety of unrelated shorts.

Typing out a long talk, double-spaced, helps both with editing it and learning it, because no matter how closely you follow the author's words, there's usually a sentence or two which can be eliminated for an oral presentation. It also helps you incorporate an introduction, ending, and transitions from short talks into one coherent, packaged talk, rather than relying on your own memory. Typed talks can also be kept on file and used repeatedly by the same person or for training new talkers. It is possible to get stale or become dependent on out-of-date talks or, worse still, to forget all other sections of the book except the typed talk, but I have found that because a much-used talk is new to the audience it also remains fresh for the librarian, unless the subject matter is no longer relevant.

The major disagreement among the YA service experts is whether to memorize the long talk or not. Some feel the preparation is too hard, that it is too easy to forget a memorized talk in public, or that such talks are not adaptable enough for all types of audience situations. Some feel the kids will not be interested in so formal an approach or that the librarian will get stale and sound wooden if the same talk is given repeatedly. Others feel that memorization, at least once during a training session, is the only way new booktalkers can learn delivery and talk-cutting techniques against which to evolve their own individual styles later. Having been trained and having trained people by the memorization method, I find the latter to be true, for myself and for most beginners. I do believe, however, that there is no *one* way to do booktalks and and that you should do what is comfortable for you--within the guidelines of experience outlined here--and what gets kids to read the books you talk about. It does seem illogical to reject a method just because it is difficult without trying it to see the results or how you might improve upon it.

The combination booktalk presentation can mean a combination of types of talks, librarians, books, genres, or media, and should generally not run more than 25 to 30 minutes. It is the most common type of presentation done for a teenage audience and is usually prearranged with the teacher or group leader to allow time for browsing, card registration, a film, discussion, questions, or just relaxing afterward. Examples would be interspersing poetry, cassette folk-rock lyrics, and short talks on a loneliness theme, or using themes like overcoming handicaps, teenagers in trouble, the future, love, etc.

Short talks could alternate with related slides of the books or the situations described, or of the library itself. Talks can be woven into a creative dramatic presentation or improvisation. If the theme is related to a particular curriculum unit, the combination of readable fun books with magazines, pamphlets, and reference works is valuable. With a little imagination, short talks can even be combined with a lesson on using the catalog. The combinations are limited only by your time, talent, ingenuity, and the audience response. It is always important to remember that your ultimate object in booktalking is to get the kids interested in reading the books you talk about. So if you get so AV-oriented that you are no longer connected with books or so entertaining that only your dramatic ability dazzles your audience, you may be missing the point.

Elaine Simpson further differentiates booktalks into the resource talk done by school librarians, which "is a supplement to a particular unit of work being done in a class, and its purpose is to show the useful, interesting, unusual materials available in the library on the subject"--done at the request of the teacher concerned--and the public library booktalk, which "is to show the great variety of materials and services available for all library users" and is not directed toward a specific subject. This distinction seems arbitrary to me with some of the popular curriculum topics now taught. It does seem unfair to ask public YA librarians to do only curriculum-related resource talks (which are extremely popular with teachers when they discover them) when a school librarian is available, but priorities must be decided by school and public YA librarians based on local circumstances, time, and talent, and should always be a fully cooperative, courteous, joint effort. The teenagers are the ultimate losers in territorial feuds between school and public librarians.

Titles Mentioned

Bradford, Richard. Red Sky at Morning. Lippincott, 1968.
Carr, John D. Death Watch. Macmillan, 1963.
D'Ambrosio, Richard. No Language But a Cry. Doubleday, 1970.
Ferris, Louanne. Edited by Beth Day. I'm Done Crying. M. Evans, 1969.
Gershe, Leonard. Butterflies Are Free. Random, 1970.
Head, Ann. Mr. and Mrs. Bo Jo Jones. Putnam, 1967.
Krents, Harold. To Race the Wind: An Autobiography. Putnam, 1972.
Libby, Bill. Parnelli: A Story of Auto-Racing. Dutton, 1969.
Lord, Walter. Night to Remember. Holt, 1955.
Nasaw, Jonathan. Easy Walking. Lippincott, 1975.
Reid, P. R. Escape from Colditz. Lippincott, 1973.
Tolstoy, Leo. War and Peace. Modern Lib.
Tyler, Anne. Slipping Down Life. Knopf, 1970.

To prepare for booktalks and the accompanying reader's advisory floor work, YA librarians should read widely all types of books and subjects of interest to their teen patrons and keep track of what they have read. Writing a short talk on every title read on a 3" x 5" card is a good way to discipline yourself to think of books in terms of how you would present a particular title to a particular teenager. This also helps you keep the names of the characters straight--an eternal problem with teen novels--and the cards can be filed according to themes, which then helps train you in associating similar titles for talks, lists, and reader's advisory service.

The next step is to master talk delivery techniques in private, preferably in a formal training session where the rest of the group is as nervous as you are, and where videotape playback and group criticism are encouraged. The horrible shock of seeing your unconscious mannerisms on a television monitor corrects them faster than any other method I know, and addressing any audience will give you practice in pitching your voice properly.

If you are in a small, isolated library, have no one more experienced to work with you, and have not learned the technique in library school--an all too common problem among YA librarians--practice on your family or clerical staff and use a full-length mirror and a tape recorder if you have no access to video taping. A tape recorder can help you memorize a talk in addition to correcting mistakes, but there is a danger that learning your booktalk this way will make you bored with it before you ever give it for the first time. Since a formal group training workshop is so valuable in learning to booktalk, I feel isolated YA librarians should pressure local library schools to provide this as continuing education in extension programs and pressure library associations to give regional workshops and create videotapes of different booktalks which can be borrowed.

Once you feel you have mastered the cutting and delivery of a talk in the abstract and have read widely enough so that you won't be undone because a kid has already read one of the books you're prepared to talk about and you can't suggest another one, announce your availability to do this (with a prior agreement with your supervisors as to how often you'll be available) by letters and/or visits to teachers, curriculum supervisors and department heads, school librarians, principals, reading specialists, and youth workers. Be sure to state in the letter what you will and will not do, and I suggest that you always insist that the teacher or leader remain with the class or group. You are a guest, not a substitute, and it is extremely hard to be an entertaining booktalker as well as an authority figure at the same time. Classes are notorious for going berserk when they think an inexperienced substitute is on the scene, and teachers who have never had booktalkers before are equally notorious for disappearing the whole period.

Be sure to state how long you will talk, usually 25 to 30 minutes and what you will do in any leftover time. If you will not do curriculum related talks, this is the place to say so, or to list which subjects or books you are prepared to talk about so they can be chosen in advance. English teachers will sometimes want you to discuss the literary merits of the books you talk about to reinforce their classroom objectives, and since it usually is disastrous to do this with booktalks, you can state this in your letter or in person as arrangements are finalized.

Another way to advertise yourself is to demonstrate the technique at faculty and department meetings and to invite teachers of other classes to observe you while you talk to a particular class.

Some schools assume that once you talk there you will never return and they will hit you with double classes and assemblies. So it is wise to state whether you will stay all day and talk to single classes successively or return at another convenient time. While I feel that assemblies are an awkward way to booktalk because of projection problems and the lack of personal eye contact, the Free Library of Philadelphia has perfected "On Your Own," a thirty minute multimedia assembly program featuring short films, slides, a tape of music and narration, and three librarians who present five short one-minute bookspots in person.

Ideally, the school librarian is the contact for the public YA librarian in neighboring schools and booktalk efforts should be coordinated through the school librarian.

A day or two before you are to appear, call to remind the person who invited you and check to see if circumstances have remained the same, and, if you're depending on school AV equipment, to make sure that the equipment is working and will be there when you need it. One piece of equipment you may need is some sort of podium if you're tall, and you can improvise with a dictionary stand or a pile of encyclopedias if necessary, on the spot, or carry a portable one with you. It's a useful crutch, and I suspect short people or those with photographic memories may scorn the use of such props.

You will find, as you booktalk more often, that the sheer public relations value of being so visible in the adolescent community makes rapport with them much easier because they remember you. "Hey, Miss, didn't I see you in my school the other day?" "Hey, what're you doing here?" Other youth service professionals will remember you also as a friendly helpful ally and often reciprocate with help at programs and recommend you as a resource person to others. Your own self-confidence grows immeasurably and you soon find that you're really not scared to talk to anybody anymore.

Best of all, though, is the immediate and immensely gratifying feedback from the kids who truly appreciate your presentation and will charge back to the library to get "the book about the guy who drank the blood" or say, in wonder, "Have you *really* read *all these books*?" or as one teen recently said, "that was a nice thing *you did for* us the other day."

There is almost no better way to let them know you're on their side than good booktalking, and I can only agree with Doris Cole who said, "Young people are the best, the most responsive audience in the world."

A Guide for Booktalkers

Don't wait until the eleventh hour to prepare, nor be unduly concerned by preliminary nervousness.

Make sure you know how to get where you're going to speak, unless the audience is coming to you. If the latter is true, make sure the room is reserved and set up in advance. If you are a librarian going to a school, always check in at the main office first to introduce yourself and announce the purpose of your visit.

Organize your books and equipment. Set them up in the order in which you'll talk about them and have chosen passages marked with a clip at the bottom of the page. Hold your notes up if you have to, use a podium, or clip them to the inside or back of the book.

Do not begin to speak until the audience is ready to listen, and wait for attention with good humor, unobtrusively. Introduce yourself or allow your host to introduce you and any other team members at the beginning of the period and be sure everyone in the room can hear all that is said and understands why you are there.

State clearly the author and title of each book you talk about. Sometimes it is wise to have a list of your talk titles prepared in advance you can distribute and let the audience keep and check off as you speak. This is especially good if your charging system or the circumstances don't allow you to circulate the books on the spot at the end of the period or visit.

Speak slowly and clearly, trying not to think too far ahead so you don't forget what you're saying. Talk to the back of the room and don't be afraid to smile occasionally or to laugh with the kids at a funny spot. Avoid any gestures or tones which do not enhance the story and call attention to yourself, and don't try to be hip or you'll be very embarrassing to the audience. On the other hand, don't talk down to them using phrases like "boys and girls" or "you young people," or you'll alienate them.

Try not to be monotonal, a quality which can be discovered and corrected if you have practiced with a tape recorder prior to your appearance and change the pace of your speaking as well as your loudness occasionally. Don't be dramatic unless it comes naturally or you've been coached by more experienced people.

Stand firmly without rocking and try not to lean, or play with rubber bands or paper clips. It looks terrible and distracts the audience. If you hold a book up so they can see it or show illustrations, hold it firmly and consciously and pan slowly so everyone can see it. A book held at an unconsciously lopsided, impossible viewing angle is an all too common fault among beginning booktalkers trying to remember everything at once, and it is very annoying to an audience.

Don't illustrate a book with an example or incident applicable to a class member. I once introduced Slipping Down Life to a class saying, "Evie Decker was the second fattest kid in her whole high school," only to see the entire class, to my horror, turn in unison to stare at an overweight member. It was awful, and I never used it again. Try to learn from your own mistakes.

Try to know the characters' names, especially in teen novels, or they all sound alike out loud, and don't frustrate the audience by making every talk a cliff-hanger or they'll tune you out as the tease you are in such a case. Don't get nervous and tell the whole story or no one will read the books. This is avoided by careful preparation and discipline on the spot if the kids beg you to tell them the ending.

Be flexible enough to wind up quickly and go on to another title or activity if the group seems restless or bored, and whatever you do, don't scold the audience for not being fascinated with you. It backfires every time.

Try not to use difficult words they may not understand. Don't be nonplussed if they say, "Hey, what's that mean?" Beware of rhetorical questions. Someone may answer them. Don't use dialect unless it's natural to you or you'll be ridiculed or will unwittingly insult the kids by making them feel you're making fun of them. And avoid profanity and *double entendres* because the kids usually either think it's hilarious from you and go into phony gales of shocked laughter or are actually shocked and forget what else you're saying. There are some exceptions to the *double entendres* like *Night to Remember* which always got asked about without fail by an unwitting teen who thought it was a torrid love story. One of those is usually enough because tricking the unknowing audience is hardly the point.

Don't oversell average books. There's no bigger bore than a librarian who gushes over every teen or sports story as if each is equal to *War and Peace*. The kids will peg you as a phony each time and you are guaranteed to bore them to death. Be sure of your terms and facts in technical and sports books and do not use explicit factual books on physical or sexual development unless you're sure of both community reactions and your own ability to speak without embarrassment.

Set up the books or give out the lists and, if you've gained enough experience, let the audience call out titles they want to hear about or ask them to tell you any they've already read so that you can match them with a similar story. On the other hand, always be honest and admit when they've stumped you, and never pretend to have read a book you haven't. You'll need to have a talk prepared in case you meet only stolid indifference despite your most artful efforts to stimulate comment.

Be prepared for interruptions by the kids saying "Oooo!" at scary spots and laughing at funny ones. The school PA system usually broadcasts daily announcements once or twice each day and finding out just when can save you much grief so you're not in the middle of a talk when these come on. There is no way to avoid the more dramatic interruptions, but knowing that they do happen will keep you reasonably calm in all circumstances.

Try never to read to the audience unless in the material you are presenting "the author's style is the important thing and can be communicated in no other way: poetry, some essays, fine writing in general. Even then you would do well to quote rather than to read or know the book so well that you are not bound to it--your eyes can still rove over the group and take cognizance of their enjoyment. Be watchful for signs of disinterest."

Go on to pre-arranged announcements of upcoming library events after you have finished talking. Tell how to get a card or check out a book, invite questions or browsing, distribute additional lists, etc.

Keep track of every class or group you've spoken to for periodic statistical reports which may help justify more staff assistance for your service specialty. Write a brief narrative report so there is a record of what you have done, both for your supervisor and for any possible successors.

Evaluate your success as a booktalker primarily by noting how many people read the books you discussed or come to the library asking for them or to get a card for the first time. You are often successful even when the audience seems indifferent, asleep, or incredibly itchy, although continual responses like these should make you alter your technique. Perhaps the selection wasn't right, or you spoke too long, or over the heads of your audience, or were too monotonal or too dramatic.

Appendix

WHAT TO DO UNTIL UTOPIA ARRIVES

The following guidelines were drawn up by the ALA/Social Responsibilities Round Table's Gay Task Force in order to help librarians evaluate the treatment of gay themes in children's and YA literature.

Central Characters

Young gay women and men can and should be portrayed as heroes as simply as their nongay counterparts, with no special emphasis on the sexual component of their identities. If, however, "gayness" itself is a major part of the plot, several points must be considered.

What is the result of a child's discovery that an important person in his or her life is gay? The positive acceptance of a parent, teacher, or best friend should be shown happening without destructive repercussions. If the book does contain stereotypic responses, the librarian can point out to the reader that positive acceptance often occurs, too.

The orientation of gay characters need not be "explained" by grotesque family situations or by the pseudo-medical observations of an adult in the story. If one of these "explanations" exists, the librarian can point out that no such effort is ever deemed necessary to account for straight characters.

Does the book serve primarily to reassure insecure nongay kids that one can have a gay experience and still turn out "normal?" If so, this may be a legitimate subject, but it is certainly not relevant to young lesbians and gay men. Librarians should be aware of the need for portrayals of growth and development of gay identity as a valid life choice.

Gay adolescents will, realistically, encounter social pressures, but they should be shown as coping adequately with them. A wide framework of support is, in fact, available to such young people in 1976. If it is not described, librarians can make readers aware of the positive nonfiction books and periodicals now in many libraries. They can also mention that gay communities are now quite visible, with such resources as counseling services, coffee hours, and churches and synagogues available.

Minor Roles

In many types of stories, there can be incidental characters --friends, relatives, or neighbors--who are gay. They should be included as a natural part of all kinds of situations, not themselves being the "situation." A few novels of this sort exist today with no explicit identification of the gay character. Librarians should be aware of this kind of book and be able to refer readers to such stories.

Illustrations

Certainly it is impossible to draw a gay person. Yet it is very easy to picture same-sex couples. In books for children there should be illustrations of gay couples as parents, as older sisters and brothers dating kids of the same sex, and as just ordinary people. No books like this are currently available. In this area, as in all areas covered by these guidelines, librarians have a clear obligation to their readers to make publishers aware that such books are desperately needed and will be used when available.

Degree of Explicitness

Librarians know that in contemporary YA fiction, nongay relationships are hardly shrouded in a veil of mystery. Comparably there ought to be more gay relationships in such novels, with more realistic portrayals of affection and falling in love. It is important to show, with an appropriate amount of physical detail, how gay women and men find each other and how they allow the expression of their emotions to develop.

Impact on Readers

In terms of orientation, there are three kinds of young readers--the straight, the gay, and the famous "in-between, teetering-on-the-fence." Before selecting any book with a gay theme, librarians should evaluate each book's effect on all three: Does it give an accurate, sympathetic picture of gays for nongays, so that they can learn to appreciate and not fear differences in sexual and affectional preference; does it give young gays a clear view of the decisions facing them and show that these can be made successfully?

The entire culture rather frantically reinforces the choice of a heterosexual lifestyle. Surely if those on-the-fence adolescents exist, they have the right to also see an up-front picture of gay life, not just the old caricatures.

Author's Attitudes

In our homophobic society any work dealing with a gay theme

is prone to include clichés and preconceptions of "gay character." It would be excellent to have a reviewer who is proudly self-identified as gay examine relevant books to point out negative stereotypic attitudes when they occur and to make suggestions as to how the librarian can best counteract such stereotypes.

BIBLIOGRAPHY

Background for Materials Selection

American Library Association. Young Adult Services Division. Research Committee. Media and the Young Adult: A Selected Bibliography, 1950-1972. ALA, 1977.

Broderick, Dorothy. Image of the Black in Children's Fiction. Bowker, 1973.

Carlsen, G. Robert. Books and the Teenage Reader. Harper, 1971.

Donelson, Ken. "Current Reading: A Scholarly and Pedagogical Bibliography of Articles and Books, Recent and Old, about Adolescent Literature, Adolescent Reading, and the English Class," Arizona English Bulletin, April 1972, 136-156, and April 1976, 231-248.

Edwards, Margaret A. The Fair Garden and the Swarm of Beasts: The Library and the Young Adult. Rev. ed. Hawthorn, 1974.

Fader, Daniel. The New Hooked on Books. Putnam, 1977.

Gersoni-Stavn, Diane. Sexism and Youth. Bowker, 1974.

Human (and Anti-Human) Values in Children's Books: A Content Rating Instrument for Educators and Concerned Parents. Council on Interracial Books for Children, 1976.

Issues in Children's Book Selection. Bowker, 1973.

Macmillan. Guidelines for Creating Positive Sexual and Racial Images in Educational Materials. Macmillan, 1975.

Mason, Bobbie Ann. The Girl Sleuth: A Feminist Guide. The Feminist Press, 1975.

Meade, Richard A. and Small, Robert C., eds. Literature for Adolescents: Selection and Use. Merrill, 1973.

Norvell, George W. The Reading Interests of Young People. Michigan State University Press, 1973.

Tanyzer, Harold and Karl, Jean, eds. Reading, Children's Books, and Our Pluralistic Society. International Reading Association, 1972.

Retrospective Selection Aids

Alameda County Library. Basic Young Adult Book List. Alameda County (California) Library, 1976(?)

Donelson, Kenneth, ed. Books for You: A Booklist for Senior High Students. National Council of Teachers of English, 1976.

Junior High School Library Catalog, 3d ed. (including four annual supplements, 1976-1979). H. W. Wilson, 1975.

Senior High School Library Catalog, 11th ed. (including four annual supplements, 1978-1981). H. W. Wilson, 1977.

Still Alive: The Best of the Best, 1960-1974. American Library Association. Young Adult Services Division, 1976.

Walker, Jerry L., ed. Your Reading: A Booklist for Junior High Students. National Council of Teachers of English, 1975.

Withrow, Dorothy W. Gateways to Readable Books: An Annotated Graded List of Books in Many Fields for Adolescents Who Are Reluctant to Read or Find Reading Difficult. H. W. Wilson, 1975.

Annual Lists

Best Books for Young Adults. American Library Association. Young Adult Services Division.

Books for the Teen Age. The New York Public Library. Office of Young Adult Services.

Books for Young Adults. Books for Young Adults, University of Iowa.

"Best Books of the Spring" and "Best Books of the Year," in School Library Journal, May and December.

Wisconsin Library Winners, Runners-Up and Rejects. Wisconsin Division of Library Services.

Young Adult Reviewers of Southern California Annual. California Library Association.

Regular Review Sources

Booklist (ALA)

Kirkus

Kliatt

News from ALAN

School Library Journal

Science Books and Films (AAAS)

Wilson Library Bulletin

YACBRG Book Reviews

Regular Reading

English Journal (NCTE)

Interracial Books for Children Bulletin

Media & Methods

News from ALAN

School Library Journal

Top of the News (ALA)

Young Adult Alternative Newsletter

Addresses

Alameda County Library
224 West Winton Avenue
Hayward, CA 94544

American Association for the Advancement of Science (AAAS)
1515 Massachusetts Avenue, N.W.
Washington, D.C. 20005

American Library Association (ALA)
50 East Huron Street
Chicago, Illinois 60611

Arizona English Bulletin
Department of English
Arizona State University
Tempe, Arizona 85281

Assembly on Literature for Adolescents, NCTE (ALAN)
c/o Mary Sucher
Dundalk Senior High School
1901 Delvale Avenue
Baltimore, Maryland 21222

California Library Association
717 K Street, Suite 300
Sacramento, California 95814

Council on Interracial Books for Children
1841 Broadway
New York, New York 10023

International Reading Association
800 Barksdale Road
Newark, Delaware 19711

Kirkus Reviews
200 Park Avenue South
New York, New York 10003

Kliatt Paperback Book Guide
6 Crocker Circle
West Newton, Massachusetts 02165

Media & Methods
North American Publishing Co.
401 North Broad Street
Philadelphia, PA 19108

National Council of Teachers of English (NCTE)
1111 Kenyon Road
Urbana, Illinois 61801

New York Public Library
Office of Young Adult Services
8 East 40 Street
New York, New York 10016

School Library Journal
R. R. Bowker Co.
1180 Avenue of the Americas
New York, New York 10036

University of Iowa
Books for Young Adults
W312 East Hall
Iowa City, Iowa 52242

Wilson Library Bulletin
950 University Avenue
Bronx, New York 10452

Wisconsin Department of Public Instruction
Division for Library Services
DPI Publications Sales Office, Room 113
126 Langdon
Madison, Wisconsin 53702

Young Adult Alternative Newsletter
c/o Carol Starr
37167 Mission Boulevard
Eremont, California 94536

Young Adult Cooperative Book Review Group of Massachusetts (YACBRG)
c/o Margaret L. Patti
Winchester Public Library
80 Washington Street
Winchester, Massachusetts 01890

CONTRIBUTORS*

ROBERT L. AARON is an assistant professor at the University of Georgia, Athens.

JULIE N. ALM is associate professor of Education at the University of Hawaii.

JANE AMELINE is Young People's Librarian at the George H. Locke Branch of the Toronto Public Library.

PHYLLIS ARLOW is with The Feminist Press, Old Westbury, N.Y.

NATALIE BABBITT is an author of children's books.

DOROTHY BRODERICK, formerly on the faculty of Dalhousie University School of Library Service, is now a freelance writer.

PATTY CAMPBELL is assistant coordinator of Young Adult Services at the Los Angeles Public Library.

PHYLLIS CANTOR is director of media sources for the Greenwich (Conn.) High School.

G. ROBERT CARLSEN is head of the Books for Young Adults program at the University of Iowa and author of _Books and the Teenage Reader_.

KAY CASSELL is Adult Services Consultant for the Westchester (N.Y.) Library System.

MARY K. CHELTON is Young Adult Services Consultant, Westchester (N.Y.) Library System.

OLIVIA COOLIDGE is the author of more than twenty books for teenagers, including both biography and historical fiction.

JOHN CUNNINGHAM is the YA librarian at the Girard Avenue Branch of the Free Library of Philadelphia.

PAT DAVIS is a Young Adult librarian at the Los Angeles Public Library.

---

*Unless obviously later information has been added, authors are identified as they were at the time of writing their articles.

KENNETH DONELSON is Professor of English at Arizona State University, Tempe.

CAREN DYBEK is the reading specialist at Comstock Middle School, Comstock, Michigan.

SYLVIA ENGDAHL is the author of science fiction novels for young people.

RENEE FEINBERG is reference librarian at the Brooklyn College Library.

LESLIE FIEDLER is Samuel L. Clemons Professor of English at the State University of New York at Buffalo, and the author of Love and Death in the American Novel, among other books.

SADA FRETZ is Juvenile Books Editor of the Kirkus Review.

MERLE FROSCHL is an editor at The Feminist Press, Old Westbury, N.Y.

LAUREL F. GOODGION is Children's Librarian, New Britain Public Library, Connecticut.

ROBIN GOTTLIEB is a writer and the librarian of the Children's Book Council.

BEVERLY A. HALEY is an English teacher at the Fort Morgan (Colorado) High School.

FRANCES HANCKEL is the administrator and technical coordinator for a university hospital cardiology unit in Philadelphia, and is active in ALA's Social Responsibilities Round Table's Gay Task Force.

JIM HASKINS is an author of nonfiction books for young adults.

NAT HENTOFF is a frequent contributor to The Village Voice and Commonweal and the author of Jazz Country, among other books for teenagers.

MARGARET HUTCHINSON is librarian of the Venable School, Charlottesville, Virginia.

PAUL B. JANECZKO is an English teacher at Masconomet Regional High School, Topsfield, Massachusetts.

JUNE JORDAN is a poet and the author of His Own Where, among other books.

JANET KAFKA was the Science Fiction Editor for Vintage Books.

LINDA KOZAREK is a graduate assistant in the Department of

Educational Technology and Library Science at Arizona State University.

W. KEITH KRAUS is on the faculty of Shippensburg State College, Pennsylvania.

KARLA KUSKIN is a writer and illustrator of children's books.

LINDA F. LAPIDES is a young adult field worker at the Enoch Pratt Free Library, Baltimore.

DAVID F. MARSHALL is director of book publication, Pilgrim Press.

JOAN MARSHALL is chief of the Catalog Division at the Brooklyn College Library.

DOROTHY MATTHEWS is on the faculty at the University of Illinois.

NORMA FOX MAZER is the author of _I, Trissy_ and _A Figure of Speech_.

JOAN BODGER MERCER has worked in librarianship, publishing, children's literature and education and is now setting up children's day-care centers in Toronto.

LEWIS MILLER is a media specialist at Gainesville High School, Georgia.

R. KATHLEEN MOLZ, former chairperson of ALA's Intellectual Freedom Committee, is a professor at the School of Library Service, Columbia University.

AL MULLER teaches at the Development Research School, Florida State University, Tallahassee.

ALLEEN PACE NILSEN is on the faculty of the Department of Educational Technology and Library Science, Arizona State University, Tempe.

ENID OLSON is the former director of publications and public relations, National Council of Teachers of English, Urbana, Illinois.

RICHARD PECK is the author of _Dreamland Hotel_, among other novels for teenagers.

CORRINE POLLAN is a student at the Graduate School of Education, C. W. Post Center, Long Island University, Greenvale, N.Y.

JERRI QUINN is a young adult librarian at the Los Angeles Public Library.

FRANK ROSS could not be identified by the compiler.

ANNE G. SCHARF is an English teacher at Watseka Community High School, Illinois.

PETER SCHARF is assistant professor, Program in Social Ecology, University of California at Irvine.

PATRICIA GLASS SCHUMAN is president of Neal-Schuman Publishers, Inc., New York.

BETTY-CAROL SELLEN is chief of the Circulation Department at the Brooklyn College Library.

LILLIAN SHAPIRO, a former school librarian and teacher of library science, is a school library consultant.

ELAINE SIMPSON, formerly associate professor at the School of Library Service, Rutgers University, recently retired.

ELIZABETH SMITH is librarian of the Social Circle High School, Georgia.

LOU WILLETT STANEK is vice-president of Meredith Associates, Westport, Connecticut.

HARRY C. STUBBS is a science teacher at Milton Academy, Massachusetts.

KAREN P. TYLER is an instructor in the Department of Educational Technology and Library Service at Arizona State University.

ROBERT UNSWORTH is a library media specialist at Scarsdale Junior High School, New York.

JANA VARLEJS is a consultant with the Massachusetts Board of Library Commissioners and the film columnist for Wilson Library Bulletin.

SUSAN VAUGHN is a reference librarian at Brooklyn College Library.

JOAN TALMAGE WEISS is Professor of English at Orange Coast Community College, California.

DAVID WHITE is a young adult librarian at the Queens Borough Public Library, New York.

JAN MILLER YODER is with the Books for Young Adults program at the University of Iowa.